Communications in Computer and Information Science   2804

Series Editors

Gang Li, *School of Information Technology, Deakin University, Burwood, VIC, Australia*
Joaquim Filipe, *Polytechnic Institute of Setúbal, Setúbal, Portugal*
Zhiwei Xu, *Chinese Academy of Sciences, Beijing, China*

Rationale

The CCIS series is devoted to the publication of proceedings of computer science conferences. Its aim is to efficiently disseminate original research results in informatics in printed and electronic form. While the focus is on publication of peer-reviewed full papers presenting mature work, inclusion of reviewed short papers reporting on work in progress is welcome, too. Besides globally relevant meetings with internationally representative program committees guaranteeing a strict peer-reviewing and paper selection process, conferences run by societies or of high regional or national relevance are also considered for publication.

Topics

The topical scope of CCIS spans the entire spectrum of informatics ranging from foundational topics in the theory of computing to information and communications science and technology and a broad variety of interdisciplinary application fields.

Information for Volume Editors and Authors

Publication in CCIS is free of charge. No royalties are paid, however, we offer registered conference participants temporary free access to the online version of the conference proceedings on SpringerLink (http://link.springer.com) by means of an http referrer from the conference website and/or a number of complimentary printed copies, as specified in the official acceptance email of the event.

CCIS proceedings can be published in time for distribution at conferences or as post-proceedings, and delivered in the form of printed books and/or electronically as USBs and/or e-content licenses for accessing proceedings at SpringerLink. Furthermore, CCIS proceedings are included in the CCIS electronic book series hosted in the SpringerLink digital library at http://link.springer.com/bookseries/7899. Conferences publishing in CCIS are allowed to use our online conference service (Meteor) for managing the whole proceedings lifecycle (from submission and reviewing to preparing for publication) free of charge.

Publication process

The language of publication is exclusively English. Authors publishing in CCIS have to sign the Springer CCIS copyright transfer form, however, they are free to use their material published in CCIS for substantially changed, more elaborate subsequent publications elsewhere. For the preparation of the camera-ready papers/files, authors have to strictly adhere to the Springer CCIS Authors' Instructions and are strongly encouraged to use the CCIS LaTeX style files or templates.

Abstracting/Indexing

CCIS is abstracted/indexed in DBLP, Google Scholar, EI-Compendex, Mathematical Reviews, SCImago, Scopus. CCIS volumes are also submitted for the inclusion in ISI Proceedings.

How to start

To start the evaluation of your proposal for inclusion in the CCIS series, please send an e-mail to ccis@springer.com

Preface

Welcome to the proceedings of the 5th International Conference on Artificial Intelligence and Knowledge Processing (AIKP 2025). It is a great honor and pleasure to present this collection of research contributions, innovative ideas, and forward-looking perspectives that capture the remarkable progress being made across the diverse fields of Artificial Intelligence (AI) and Knowledge Processing. As AI continues to shape nearly every aspect of modern life, its influence has grown from being a technological enabler to becoming a transformative force redefining how we learn, work, communicate, and solve problems. AIKP 2025 served as a platform for scholars, practitioners, and industry experts to share insights, exchange ideas, and collectively envision the future of intelligent systems.

The discussions and discoveries emerging from this conference reflect our collective commitment to advancing AI responsibly and creatively for the betterment of society. This year, AIKP 2025 was proudly organized by the AI Research Centre, Woxsen University, Hyderabad, India, in collaboration with Woxsen University (India), ENAE International Business School (Spain), University of St. Thomas (USA), University of Johannesburg (South Africa), University of Fujairah (UAE), and Dar Al-Hekma University (Saudi Arabia). This international collaboration symbolizes the spirit of unity and diversity that defines the AIKP community, bridging continents and disciplines to advance shared goals in research and innovation. AIKP 2025 brought together thought leaders, researchers, and professionals from around the world to explore a broad spectrum of themes including machine learning, natural language processing, computer vision, robotics, data science, quantum AI, cognitive computing, and ethical AI. The interdisciplinary nature of these contributions highlights the growing synergy between artificial intelligence and knowledge processing, fostering a deeper understanding of how data, cognition, and automation intersect to create meaningful impact.

This year's conference received 111 manuscripts, out of which 22 were selected for publication in these proceedings after a rigorous double-blind review process conducted by domain experts in which each submission received three reviews on average. Each accepted paper represents the high standards of scholarship, originality, and scientific rigor that define AIKP. We sincerely thank all the authors for their dedication, the reviewers for their careful and constructive evaluations, and the session chairs and keynote speakers for their invaluable contributions to the success of this event. AIKP 2025 continued the legacy of promoting open dialogue, collaboration, and innovation in the field of AI and knowledge processing. We hope that the research presented in these proceedings will inspire further exploration, foster new partnerships, and contribute meaningfully to the global discourse on the responsible and transformative use of artificial intelligence.

With warm regards,
The Editors
Proceedings of AIKP 2025

Hemachandran Kannan
Raul Villamarin Rodriguez
Manjeet Rege
Abejide Ade-Ibijola
Miguel López González de León
Vincenzo Piuri
Ben Dhaou

Organization

Patrons

Raul V. Rodriguez	Woxsen University, India
Manjeet Rege	University of St. Thomas, USA
Miguel López González de León	ENAE International Business School, Spain
Alvaro David Orjuela Cañón	Universidad del Rosario, Colombia
Abejide Ade-Ibijola	Johannesburg Business School, South Africa

Chairs

Hemachandran K.	Woxsen University, India
Raul V. Rodriguez	Woxsen University, India
Vincenzo Piuri	University of Milan, Italy

Co-chairs

Muhammad E. H. Chowdhury	Qatar University, Qatar
Ganesh Naik	Torrens University Australia, Australia
Murugappan M.	Kuwait College of Science and Technology, Kuwait
Sivarama Krishnan Rajaraman	National Institutes of Health, USA
Rajesh Kumar	Woxsen University, India

Conveners

Amar Kumar Verma	Woxsen University, India
Shyam Krishan Joshi	Woxsen University, India
Chhavi Sharma	Woxsen University, India

Co-conveners

Pranjali Gajbhiye	Woxsen University, India
Amit Swamy	Woxsen University, India

Publication Chairs

Chhavi Sharma   Woxsen University, India
Shyam Krishan Joshi   Woxsen University, India
Amar Kumar Verma   Woxsen University, India

Publicity Chairs

Pranjali Gajbhiye   Woxsen University, India
Amar Kumar Verma   Woxsen University, India

Technical Program Chairs

Shyam Krishan Joshi   Woxsen University, India
Pranjali Gajbhiye   Woxsen University, India
Anto Lourdu Xavier Raj Arockia   Grand Valley State University, USA
  Selvarathinam
Amar Kumar Verma   Woxsen University, India
Dinesh Kumar   Woxsen University, India
Sameek Ghosh   Woxsen University, India
Amit Swamy   Woxsen University, India

Publicity and Operations Committee

Pankaj Kumar Singh   Woxsen University, India
Sai Adarsh Maddu   Woxsen University, India
Praveen Rajarathinam   Woxsen University, India

International Advisory Board Members

Umashankar Subramaniam   Prince Sultan University, Saudi Arabia
Xiao-Zhi Gao   University of Eastern Finland, Finland
Llorenc Valverde   Universitat de les Illes Balears, Spain
Gabriel Kabanda   Zimbabwe Academy of Sciences, Zimbabwe
Ezendu Ariwa   University of Warwick, UK
Petia Radeva   University of Barcelona, Spain
Anto Lourdu Xavier Raj Arockia   Grand Valley State University, USA
  Selvarathinam

Vasos Pavlika	University College London, UK
Thinagaran Perumal	University Putra Malaysia, Malaysia
Linda Mary Simon	Christ University, India
Imed Ben Dhaou	Dar Al-Hekma University, Saudi Arabia
Juan R. Jaramillo	Adelphi University, USA
Sivarama Krishnan Rajaraman	NLM, National Institutes of Health, USA
Ravi Dadsena	DZNE, Germany
Ephias Ruhode	University of the Witwatersrand, South Africa
Ganeshsree Selvachandran	UCSI University, Malaysia
Anil Pise	University of the Witwatersrand, South Africa
Rana E. Jisr	Lebanese University, Lebanon
Cynthia Jabbour Sfeir	Notre Dame University-Louaize, Lebanon
Manas Ranjan Pradhan	Skyline University College, UAE
Ashok Chopra	Amity University, Dubai Campus, UAE
Ram Kumar Nimmakayala	Western Governors University, USA
Nawaz Ahmad	Shaheed Benazir Bhutto Women University, Pakistan
Mohammed Abdul Matheen	King Saud University, Saudi Arabia
Neyara Radwan	King Abdulaziz University, Saudi Arabia

National Advisory Board Members

Santanu Kumar Behera	NIT Rourkela, India
Ramesh Gardas	IIT Madras, India
Saravanan Chandran	NIT Durgapur, India
David Samuel Azariya S.	Sona College of Technology, India
Sivarama Krishnan	IIT Madras, India
Thiruvikraman Kandhadai	BITS Pilani, Hyderabad Campus, India
Debashis Guha	SP Jain School of Global Management, India
Pavan Kumar Damaraju V. R. S.	Tata Consultancy Services, India
Justus Rabi	Christian College of Engineering and Technology, India
Sujayandra Vaddagiri	Laminaar Aviation Infotech (India) Pvt. Ltd., India
Kannan A.	Dr. MGR Educational & Research Institute, India
Deepika	Bennett University, India
Sandip Vijay	Tula's Institute, India
Reeba Korah	Alliance University, India
Clement King	Mount Carmel College, India
Kiran Pandey	Technocrats Institute of Technology, India

Technical Program Committee

Murugappan M.	Kuwait College of Science and Technology, Kuwait
Jude Hemanth	Karunya University, India
Alexiei Dingli	University of Malta, Malta
Patrick Glauner	Deggendorf Institute of Technology, Germany
Thomas Heinrich Musiolik	University of Europe for Applied Sciences, Germany
Djamel Mostefa	Shory, UAE
Philipp Plugmann	SRH Hochschule fur Gesundheit Gera, Germany
Jordan Bird	Nottingham Trent University, UK
Channabasava Chola	Kyung Hee University, South Korea
Anil Audumbar Pise	University of the Witswatersrand, South Africa
Waseem Rawat	Toyota, South Africa
Joel Ugborogho	CenHealth, London
Jens Stapelfeldt	AMD, Germany
Johan Steyn	Stellenbosch University, South Africa
Saidani Begum	University of Saudia at Ministry of Higher Education, Saudi Arabia
Rejwan Bin Sulaiman	Northumbria University, UK
Annappa B.	NIT Surathkal, India
Lavanya Ramapantulu	AlphaICs Corporation, India
Akila Muthuramalingam	KPRIET, India
Shubam Tayal	SR University, India
D. Vetrithangam	Chandigarh University, India
S. Deepajothi	Nagarjuna College of Engineering and Technology, India
Jaspal Kumar	Mahaveer Institute of Science and Technology, India
Balaji Ganesh	Vellammal Engineering College, India
Prasant	SVCET, India
Sheila Mahapatra	Alliance University, India
Javeed M. D.	SDIES, India
Sanjay Vishwakarma	PsiQuantum, USA
Srinjoy Ganguly	University College London, UK
Arvind Kumar Bhardwaj	Capgemini, USA
Pradeep Chintale	New World Foundation, USA

Contents

Optimization of Routes for Hospitalary Subnetworks in Bogota Through Genetic Algorithms

Mateo Alejandro Lopez Garcia[1,2]($\boxtimes$), Camilo Eduardo Sotelo Galeano[1,2], and Alvaro D. Orjuela-Cañón[2] (iD)

[1] Escuela Colombiana de Ingeniería Julio Garavito, Bogota D.C., Colombia
mateoal.lopez@urosario.edu.co
[2] School of Medicine and Health Sciences, Universidad del Rosario, Bogota D.C., Colombia

Abstract. The objective of this project is to optimize the routes of the different healthcare subnetworks in the city of Bogotá, aiming to provide support to the city's residents, ambulances, patients, or hospitals for their transportation needs. Additionally, we aim to propose changes in the distribution of the subnetworks, if necessary, to enhance and optimize travel times between medical centers. To achieve this, we will employ the technique of genetic algorithms, which involves crossbreeding individuals (solutions) from a pool of potential solutions to find the most optimal route in terms of time for traversing the northern, southwestern, central-eastern, and south subnetworks. This approach provides us with a tool to deliver hospital services in the most efficient manner possible, thus mitigating potential tragedies and ensuring the well-being of the citizens

Keywords: Genetic Algorithms · Hospitalary Subnetworks · Optimization · Public Health

1 Introduction

Bogota is one of the largest cities in Latin America, with around 10 million people and different and complex problems. The accelerated and disorganized population growth during recent decades has placed important challenges related to the supply of public services, including health services, and more with the additional issues from current migration in Latin American countries [1, 2]. The extension of the city with 1636 km^2 is covered by a hospitalary network, which became highly saturated and centralized by a few downtown locations. In addition, different consequences of complicated traffic, severe inequities in access, and emergency levels, among other causes, make promoting good practices for attending patients a hard problem to solve [3].

In 2017, the city adopted a regionalized hospitalary subnetwork structure, establishing four big zones: north, center-east, south, and southwest. Each subnetwork holds a set of hospitals, health centers, and emergency care units to serve the specific localities in their geographical area. This redistribution of infrastructure and decentralization of

H. Kannan et al. (Eds.): AIKP 2025, CCIS 2804, pp. 1–12, 2026.
https://doi.org/10.1007/978-3-032-14706-6_1

management has helped to enhance service coverage, reducing inequities in access to medical care and better tailoring processes to specific needs.

Nonetheless, logistical challenges associated with the traffic difficulties in the route of the patient's transportation continue to impact the operation of emergency medical services across these subnetworks [4, 5]. The ambulance routing problem (ARP) is one of the analyses of this type of vehicles related to the mobilization and routing for attending to urgent calls and transportation of patients [6–9]. Difficulties arise due to traffic congestion in a dense urban area, the need to cover very large geographical zones with limited vehicle resources, and unforeseen events such as road works or accidents that may block paths. Developing optimization solutions for ambulance routing would maximize response capacity and minimize life-threatening delays.

For the ARP different solutions have been proposed. Stochastic algorithms and heuristical methods were employed for the problem in Iranian cities [9, 10]. Other proposals are based on metaheuristic strategies, for example, multi-objective bees algorithm and genetic algorithms [6, 11–15]. Genetic algorithms (GA) are an adaptive metaheuristic optimization technique inspired by the process of natural selection in biological evolution. They initiate with a population of candidate solutions to a problem, each with defined characteristics. Through iterative processes of selection, crossover, and mutation, solutions evolve exchanging parts with the fittest characteristics, approximating gradually to optimal variable ranges [16]. These techniques have allowed for exploring very complex search spaces effectively. Besides finding optimum mathematical values, they can optimize multiple objectives, model dynamic constraints, adapt to new information, and discover less intuitive solutions. They also leverage large historical databases to analyze statistical relationships among variables. These capabilities make them highly suitable for solving real-life routing optimization problems.

For the present case, the application of custom GA tailored to each hospitalary subnetwork allowed the discovery of ambulance routing and relocation possibilities that minimize total response time to critical events inside of a chaotic city. The algorithms can assign ambulances to optimal bases and stand by dynamically while coordinating real-time dispatch to emergency calls considering changing factors: accident locations, evolving traffic conditions, ambulance availability, patients' priority level, and road connectivity across different geographical sectors. As Bogotá's population and road infrastructure continue expanding, an adaptive system based on GA keeps routes constantly optimized. It also helps manage resources efficiently despite limitations in vehicles and staff. The objective of this study is to provide an approach as a viable solution to overcome current logistical barriers and improve emergency medical services for the city.

2   Methodology

2.1   Data Collection

The local government from Bogota holds the health secretariat where are the four subnetworks are managed. This information is public and available, then, searching in the website, data from health centers and institutions associated to the health city system was collected. The information includes location, hours for opening and closing, neighborhood, and complexity level. Later, employing the geocoding it was possible to get the longitude and latitude from the address for each institution.

2.2 Metric Map Generation

Employing the routing API based on the GraphHopper library allowed to obtain timeoptimal routes between a node (health center) and the rest (remaining health centers) using their longitude and latitude coordinates [17]. For this, for each node was built a matrix of possible routes, taking into account real data form the streets from Bogota city. This offers a difference compared to other approaches due to the real information about routes, crosses, traffic lights and other components that are part of the transportation system.

2.3 Implementation of Genetic Algorithms

GA are iterative optimization techniques that emulate the process of natural selection to solve complex problems [16]. The process begins with the codification of a population comprising potential solutions represented as chromosomes or genes, often encoded as binary strings or numerical vectors. Figure 1 shows how the representation of the solutions was coded for converting the phenotype to genotype in the GA technique.

Each population is evaluated using a predefined fitness function, which quantifies its effectiveness in solving the optimization problem. For the present case, this function was based on minimization of the time for each route, according to an emergency scenario. During the selection phase, individuals are chosen from the current population based on their fitness, the best individuals were selected as parents for reproduction.

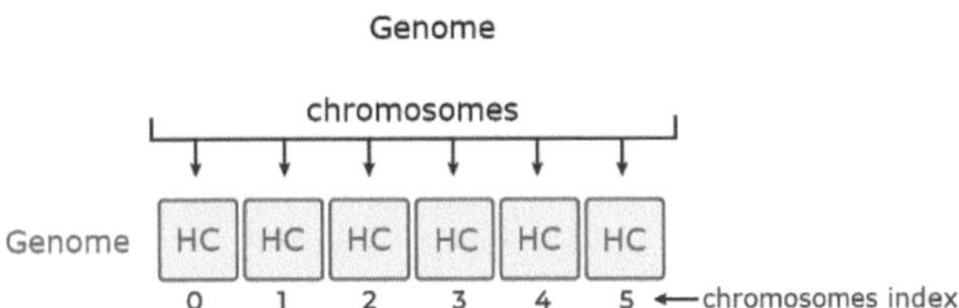

Fig. 1. Genome of Genetic Algorithms.

The selection process was accomplished through the roulette wheel method, guiding the evolutionary process towards promising regions of the search space. However, this selection process was calculated after a random initialization of the population. Genetic operators such as crossover and mutation were applied to the best individuals in each population, searching the evolution that improve the solutions over several generations. Crossover involves combining genetic information from selected parents to create new solutions, mimicking the genetic recombination process in nature. Mutation introduces random changes to offspring chromosomes, ensuring exploration of new solution space and preventing premature convergence to suboptimal solutions [16]. The offspring, along with some or all of the parent population, form the next generation. This replacement process, whether through generational or steady-state replacement strategies, ensures the population's continual evolution. The algorithm iterates through these steps until a termination condition is achieved.

For evaluation the hyperparameters of the technique, it was performed different iterations for two parameters the number of individuals in the population and the number of generations. For the number of generations, values were set in 100, 200 and 300, and for the number of individuals, the values were 2000, 5000, 7000, 7666, and 10000 individuals. These values were employed for finding the best route in terms of time for each from the four subnetworks, and a specific case with all subnetworks together (entire city), where a population with 20000 individuals was evaluated.

3   Results

Results can be displayed with the points and the best route in terms of time minimization for the northern (see Fig. 2), southwestern (see Fig. 3), central-east (see Fig. 4), and south (Fig. 5) subnetworks. There it is possible to visualize the points with the localization of health institutions, and the best route.

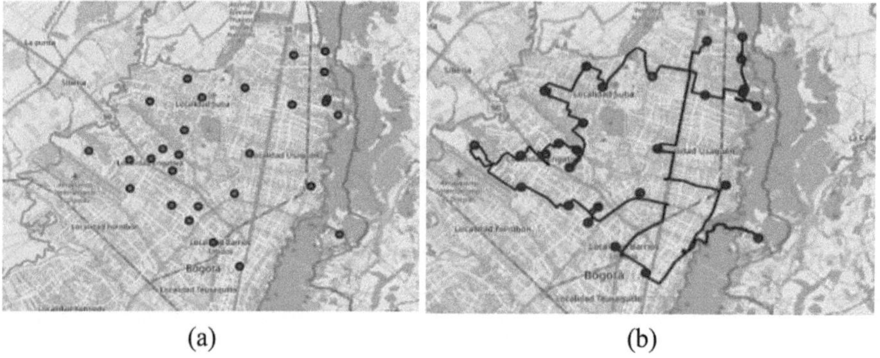

(a)   (b)

Fig. 2. Healthcare center points (a) for the northern subnetwork and the optimal route (b) given by the time minimization through the points.

Figure 6 exhibits the behavior of the fitness function through the generations for each subnetwork. It is possible to see the differences for the convergence in every subnetwork. However, the population was not the same for the cases, the north subnetwork found the best result in the generation 120 approximately, and a population of 5000 individuals. For southwestern (generation 160, approx.), central-east (generation 60, approx..), and south (generation 120, approx.) subnetworks, the population with best results was the same with 7666 individuals.

(a)   (b)

Fig. 3. Healthcare center points (a) for the southwestern subnetwork and the optimal route (b) given by the time minimization through the points.

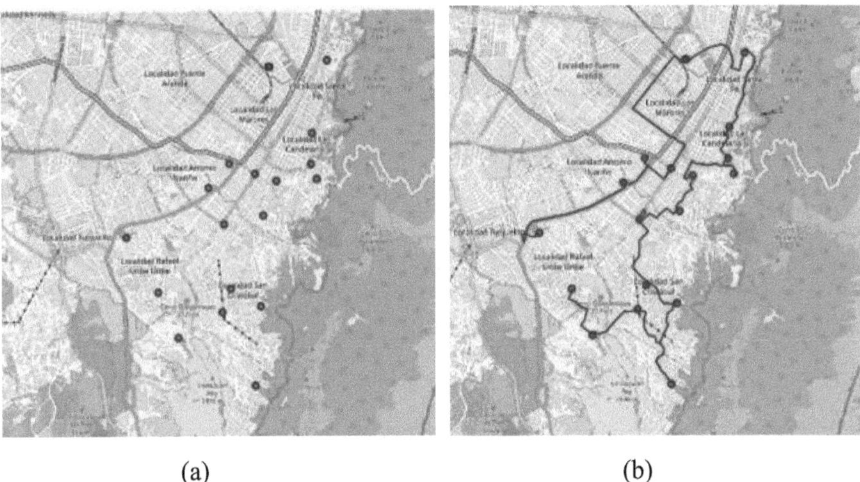

(a)   (b)

Fig. 4. Healthcare center points (a) for the central-east subnetwork and the optimal route (b) given by the time minimization through the points.

Finally, the visualization for the entire city approach can be seen in Fig. 7. There is located each subnetwork with blue (north), green (southwestern), red (central-east) and yellow (south) colors to distinguish the areas for each subnetwork. In this case, all points were analyzed as just one huge network, and the result is considered as the route was in the health institutions of Bogota city. Figure 8 shows the fitness function through the generations for a population of 2500 individuals, which presented the best route in terms of time minimization.

In addition, the Fig. 9 exhibits a comparison of the number of generations employed to find the solution. There, values of 100, 200 and 300 generations were tested, and the number of populations was analyzed in the interval 2500 to 20000 individuals.

As observed, the south subnetwork holds an institution almost out of the urban area, which is considered by the local government as part of the country around the city, but under the city administration. Figure 10 displays the entire city the colors mentioned previously, excepting the distant rural point to appreciate better the routes.

Table 1 resumes the time found for each subnetwork and the entire city approach. Measures were computed in hours, showing that according to the area of each subnetwork the time increases due to the area for covering.

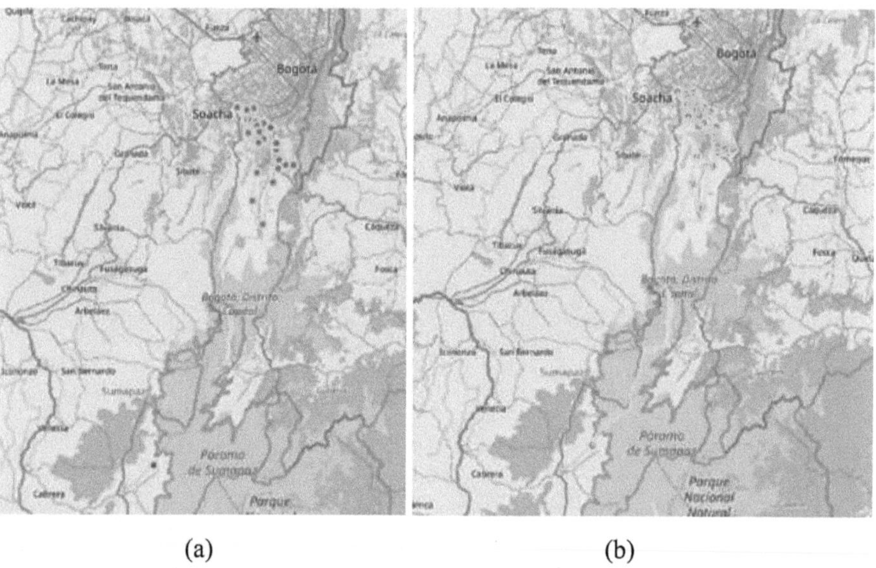

(a)   (b)

Fig. 5. Healthcare center points (a) for the south subnetwork and the optimal route (b) given by the time minimization through the points.

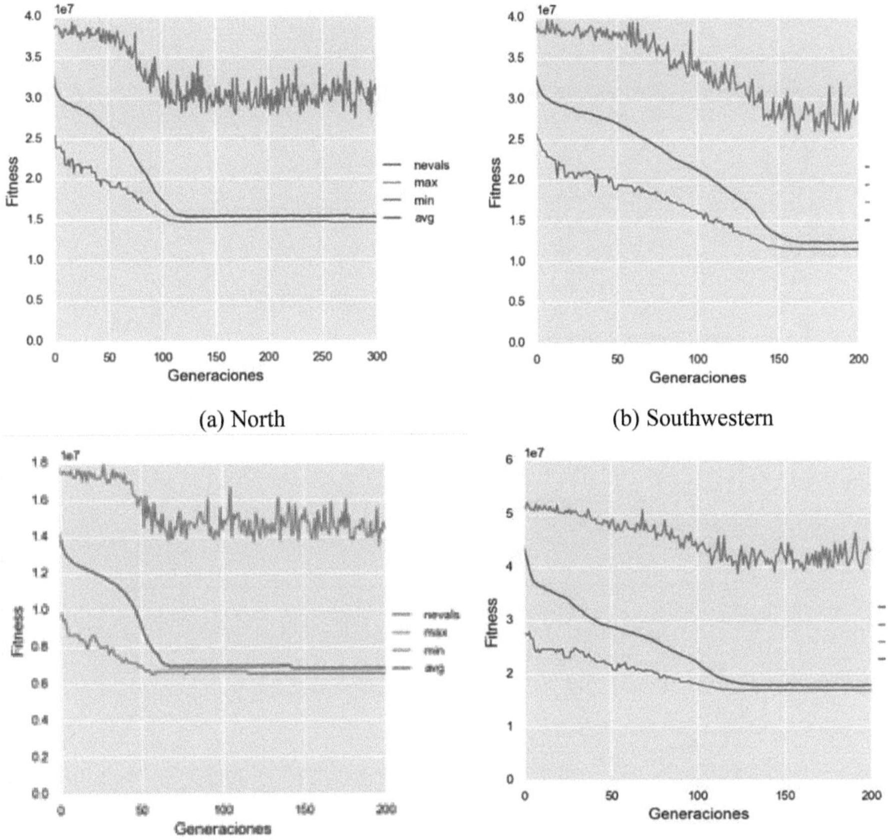

(a) North

(b) Southwestern

(c) Central-East

(d) South

Fig. 6. Fitness function behavior for all considered subnetworks.

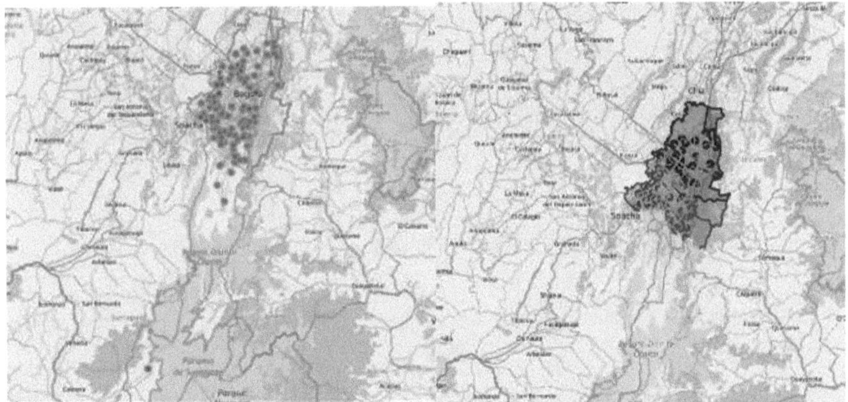

Fig. 7. Healthcare center points for Bogota D.C. and the optimal route in time to traverse all points.

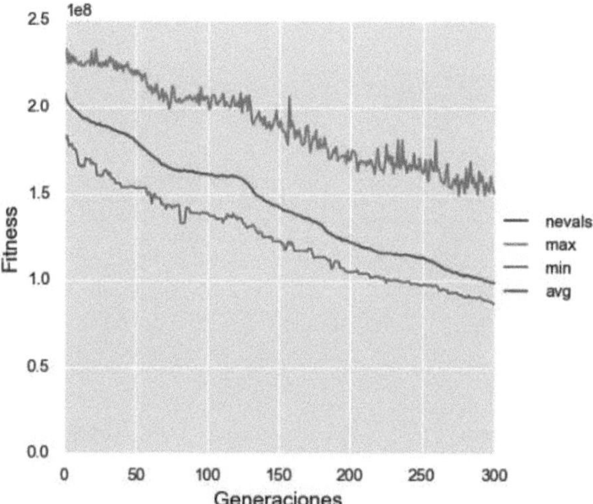

Fig. 8. Fitness function value over generations for a population of 2500 (all subnetworks together).

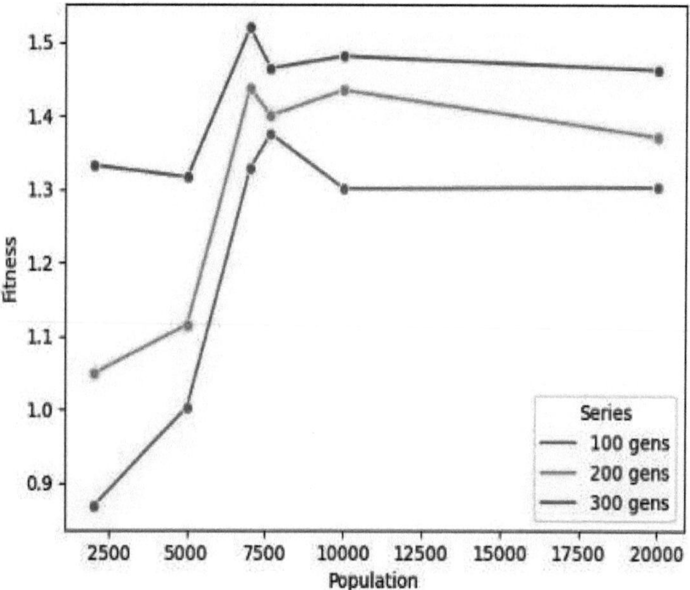

Fig. 9. Fitness functions for different numbers of generations and population.

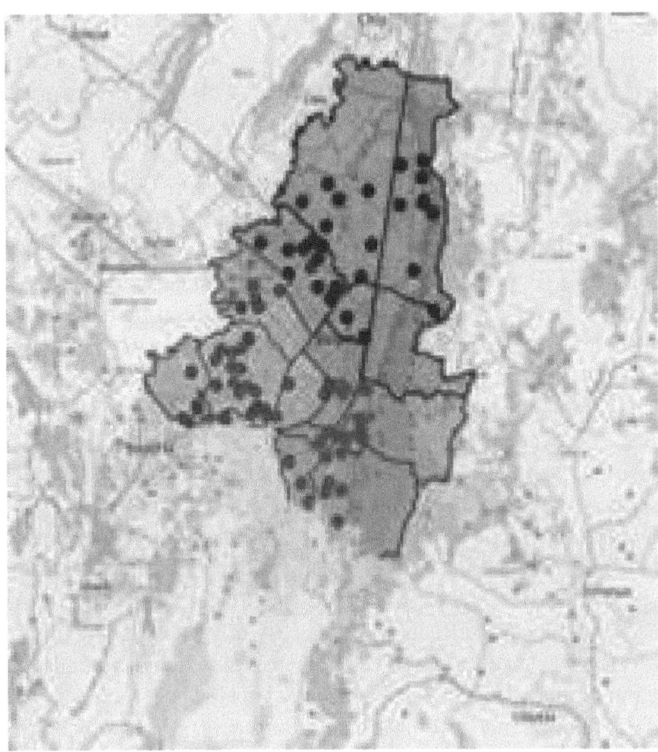

Fig. 10. Map of Bogotá divided by sub-networks and their healthcare centers.

Table 1. Minimum time found for subnetworks.

Subnetwork	Minimum time found (hours)
South	4.659
Central east	1.812
Southwestern	3.190
Northern	4.057
Entire city	24.108

4 Discussion

For the northern subnetwork, a time route of approximately 4.057 h to change the position through the healthcare centers was computed. This optimization was achieved with a population of 5000 individuals over 200 generations (Fig. 6a). Although the trajectory is not closed, it could be considered so since its starting and ending points are close. Additionally, this subnetwork does not have hospitals or healthcare centers far apart from each other, resulting in significant time savings.

In the case of the southwestern subnetwork obtained the optimal route for this pointto-point journey in approximately 3.19 h, which was achieved with a population of 7,666 individuals over 300 generations (Fig. 6b). The area of this subnetwork is the special interest due to holds the highest number of healthcare centers and residents, making this time optimization crucial, for example in public health as air quality [18].

For the subnetwork center-east, with fewer healthcare centers of interest for the study, achieved a time route with the littlest value, close to 1.812 h. This result was achieved with an optimization process that employed a population of 5000 individuals over 100 generations (Fig. 6c). Finally, the southern subnetwork, has an optimal time route considerably longer than its counterparts, with a duration close to 4.057 h which was accomplished with a population of 7,666 individuals over 200 generations. The increased travel time is due to a point located on the outskirts of the urban area of Bogotá, which significantly increases the time to traverse the points of this subnetwork and, in general, to cover all healthcare centers in the city. Due to this, this area that includes rural zones like the Sumapaz, has been analyzed from the public health point of view, given by its needs and health access services [19, 20].

Lastly, for comprehension of the entire city, all four subnetworks (north, centraleast, southwest, and south) were combined. This aimed to propose a route through whole of them and to assess the effectiveness of dividing healthcare centers according to the geographical area. This can cause effects in the successfully of providing timely patient care and health services. The route also showed how to explore the different subnetworks and how could be interconnected. The results revealed that the best route was achieved with a population of 2500 individuals over 300 generations (Fig. 10), taking approximately one day to complete the journey (see Table 1). This time does not consider stops at medical centers, only the time spent on the route.

5 Conclusions

In general, it could be observed that four subnetworks have travel times ranging from 1 to 5 h for each. However, there is possibilities for the improvement of the results. This was notice by some healthcare centers which are located at distances far from others within of the same subnetwork area, but closer to another subnetworks. This is evident in the case of the north and southwest subnetworks, where an institution inside of the north one is closer to other institutions of the southwest subnetwork. Even, if this healthcare center were moved to the north, it could further optimize travel times and provide more efficient assistance to patients.

In addition, it could be considered redistributing healthcare centers from the north and southwest subnetworks to the central-east one, aiming to reduce the travel time in the first two subnetworks, and maintaining a potential balance among these three subnetworks.

Similarly, the remote point in the southern subnetwork, located away from the city itself, presents not an optimization issue but a service challenge. During this journey, there are no facilities to provide necessary assistance to residents, making travel to a healthcare center more complicated.

Finally, it is important to emphasize that these times are estimates and do not consider the current city traffic. This aspect could be considered for an application that operates in real-time to assist with travel between different centers. This analysis can be modified according to user requirements, adjusting points of interest, such as specialized hospitals, public or private partners, and hospitals equipped with facilities that are not found in others. This would streamline healthcare services for the population, not only in Bogota but for the global population at large.

Acknowledgment. Authors acknowledge the support of the Universidad del Rosario for funding this project. In addition, the contribution of research incubator team *Semillero en Inteligencia Artificial en Salud:* Semill-IAS.

References

1. Vélez, L.D.J., García-Juan, L.: Retos actuales de la atención sanitaria de la población inmigrante irregular en Colombia. BARATARIA. Revista CastellanoManchega de Ciencias Sociales. 15–31 (2019)
2. Parra-Henao, G., Henao, E., Escobar, J.P.: Environmental health and infectious diseases: challenges and perspectives in Latin America. Ther Adv Infect Dis. **10**, 20499361231217812 (2023)
3. Okinedo, P.: Promoting a better public health quality with urban green space in an informal settlement, Bogota, Colombia (2022)
4. Sánchez González, S., Bedoya-Maya, F., Calatayud, A.: Understanding the effect of traffic congestion on accidents using big data. Sustainability. **13**, 7500 (2021)
5. Babajide, O., et al.: Others: Improving decision-making for population health in nonhealth sectors in urban environments: the example of the transportation sector in three megacities— the 3-D Commission. J. Urban Health **98**, 60–68 (2021)
6. Tikani, H., Setak, M.: Ambulance routing in disaster response scenario considering different types of ambulances and semi soft time windows. J. Indust. Syst. Eng. **12**, 95–128 (2019)
7. Cabral, E.L. dos S., et al.: Response time in the emergency services. Syst. Rev. Acta Cir Bras. **33**, 1110–1121 (2018).
8. Tassone, J., Choudhury, S.: A comprehensive survey on the ambulance routing and location problems. arXiv preprint arXiv:2001.05288. (2020)
9. Shetab-Boushehri, S.-N., Rajabi, P., Mahmoudi, R.: Modeling location–allocation of emergency medical service stations and ambulance routing problems considering the variability of events and recurrent traffic congestion: a real case study. Healthcare Anal. **2**, 100048 (2022)
10. Khoshgehbari, F., Al-e, S.M.J.M.: Others: Ambulance location routing problem considering all sources of uncertainty: progressive estimating algorithm. Comput. Oper. Res. **160**, 106400 (2023)
11. Talebi, E., Shaabani, M., Rabbani, M.: Bi-objective model for ambulance routing for disaster response by considering priority of patients. Int. J. Supply Oper. Manage. **9**, 80–94 (2022)
12. Rabbani, M., Oladzad-Abbasabady, N., Akbarian-Saravi, N.: Ambulance routing in disaster response considering variable patient condition: NSGA-II and MOPSO algorithms. J. Indust. Manage. Opt. **18** (2022)
13. Nahavandi, B., Homayounfar, M., Daneshvar, A., Shokouhifar, M.: Hierarchical structure modelling in uncertain emergency location-routing problem using combined genetic algorithm and simulated annealing. Int. J. Comput. Appl. Technol. **68**, 150–163 (2022)
14. Kaur, B.: Maximum geographical coverage deployment of ambulances using genetic algorithm. In: 2021 Third International Conference on Intelligent Communication Technologies and Virtual Mobile Networks (ICICV), pp. 1493–1499 (2021)

15. Schjølberg, M.E., Bekkevold, N.P., Sánchez-Díaz, X., Mengshoel, O.J.: Comparing Meta-heuristic Optimization Algorithms for Ambulance Allocation: An Experimental Simulation Study. In: Proceedings of the Genetic and Evolutionary Computation Conference. pp. 1454–1463 (2023)

16. Katoch, S., Chauhan, S.S., Kumar, V.: A review on genetic algorithm: past, present, and future. Multimed Tools Appl. **80**, 8091–8126 (2021)

17. Choudhary, R., Ratra, S., Agarwal, A.: Multimodal routing framework for urban environments considering real-time air quality and congestion. Atmos. Pollut. Res. **13**, 101525 (2022)

18. Molina-Gómez, N.I., Calderón-Rivera, D.S., Sierra-Parada, R., Díaz-Arévalo, J.L., López-Jiménez, P.A.: Analysis of incidence of air quality on human health: a case study on the relationship between pollutant concentrations and respiratory diseases in Kennedy. Bogotá. Int J Biometeorol. **65**, 119–132 (2021)

19. Alejandro, H.R.E., Milena, L.C.A., Alejandra, T.M., Mayler, B., Enrique, D.J., others: Hipertensión enfermedad silenciosa que está afectando en los estados de salud a la población de la localidad 20 de Sumapaz de la ciudad de Bogotá. (2022)

20. Bautista-Gómez, M.M., van Niekerk, L.: A social innovation model for equitable access to quality health services for rural populations: a case from Sumapaz, a rural district of Bogota. Colombia. Int J Equity Health. **21**, 23 (2022)

Enhancing Tuberculosis Diagnosis Through AI-Powered Chest Radiograph Classification

Sanjana Singam[✉] and Jayaprakash Vemuri

Mahindra University, Hyderabad, Telangana, India
`{se22uari153,jayaprakash.vemuri}@mahindrauniversity.edu.in`

Abstract. Tuberculosis (TB) remains one of the most fatal infectious diseases, particularly in developing countries where healthcare accessibility is inadequate. Although conventional diagnosis methods like sputum smear microscopy and chest radiographs are still prevalent, they lack sensitivity, are subjective, and remain difficult to access in rural communities. Medical imaging based on deep learning has also been a strong remedy to automate TB diagnosis with enhanced accuracy and efficiency. Yet, image variation and class imbalance are still significant issues. In this paper, we introduce a thorough framework consisting of data augmentation and supervised ML models to classify the chest X-ray images into Normal and TB-positive categories. With a curated and enriched dataset of 7,000 images, these models were tested for accuracy and generalization, with fine KNN and Naïve Bayes producing the best accuracy of 94.44%. These findings indicate that traditional machine learning models, when appropriately tuned and balanced, can be used as lightweight yet dependable tools for TB detection, especially in low-resource settings.

Keywords: Tuberculosis · Machine Learning · Chest X-rays · Classification · KNN · Naïve Bayes · Logistic Regression

1 Introduction

Tuberculosis (TB) is a contagious infectious disease caused by the bacterium *Mycobacterium tuberculosis*, which mainly infects the lungs but can spread to other organs like the brain, spinal cord, or kidneys [1]. As per the World Health Organization (WHO), an estimated 10.6 million new cases and more than 1.6 million deaths were reported worldwide in 2021, demonstrating its ongoing burden on public health services [2]. It affects low- and middle-income countries more disproportionately, specifically those with low healthcare access, poor living standards, and underdeveloped public health infrastructure [3]. It is often transmitted through airborne droplets when patients with active pulmonary TB cough, sneeze, or talk [4]. After inhalation, the bacteria can be latent (latent TB) or progress to active disease, particularly in persons with impaired immunity, e.g., those with HIV, diabetes, malnutrition, or in elderly persons [5]. Active TB symptoms are incessant cough, fever, night sweats, weakness, and substantial loss of weight. If not treated, it can cause serious complications or death. Children, health care providers, and individuals in crowded living conditions are particularly at risk because of chronic exposure or compromised immunity [6].

© The Author(s), under exclusive license to Springer Nature Switzerland AG 2026
H. Kannan et al. (Eds.): AIKP 2025, CCIS 2804, pp. 13–28, 2026.
https://doi.org/10.1007/978-3-032-14706-6_2

Conventional TB screening methods like sputum smear microscopy, chest X-ray, and molecular assays like GeneXpert are all very common, but they are usually plagued by limitations such as sensitivity variability, reliance on skilled personnel, and restricted access in rural areas [7]. In response, worldwide health programs like the WHO's *End TB Strategy* prioritize early detection, timely treatment, and preventive treatment to manage transmission. Despite this, significant challenges persist, such as delayed diagnosis, stigma, increasing drug resistance, and the interruption of TB services during the COVID-19 pandemic [8]. The recent developments in medical imaging and artificial intelligence hold promising solutions to facilitate quicker, more precise TB diagnosis and enhance disease surveillance, particularly in limited-resource settings [9].

2 Data Description

The TB Chest Radiography dataset employed in this research was obtained from a public Kaggle. The dataset initially comprised a total of 4,200 grayscale chest X-ray images that were classified as Normal: 3,500 images and Tuberculosis positive: 700 images. All the images are of.png format, 512×512 pixels resolution, and have been sourced from the publicly available collection of medical imaging repositories like the NIAID TB Portal, the RSNA Pneumonia Detection Challenge, and the National Library of Medicine (NLM). The dataset has been prepared with the cooperation of different researchers based in Qatar University, the University of Dhaka, and the associated hospitals. It was published to help AI-based tuberculosis detection research and as a benchmark dataset [10].

Figure 1 is a bar graph of class distribution, which verifies the 5:1 class skewness between Normal and TB cases. This class skewness directly affects training classification models and highlights the necessity of sampling strategies and performance metrics, taking into account class imbalance. Figure 2 also emphasizes this contrast: histograms of control cases (Fig. 2a) have a more evenly distributed x-axis (Pixel Intensity) with mid-level contrast across lung regions, while the y-axis (Frequency) values show a smoother spread, reflecting uniform tissue density. In contrast, TB-infected films (Fig. 2b) show higher variability in the x-axis (Pixel Intensity) range and sharp peaks on the y-axis (Frequency), indicating compact pixel clusters that are characteristic of opacities and shadow areas produced by disease-specific abnormalities. These results are consistent with earlier studies indicating that intensity differences at the upper lobes are good indicators of TB infection [10].

To balance the unequal distribution, a data augmentation-based oversampling method—similar in principle to SMOTE (Synthetic Minority Over-sampling Technique)—was applied to the minority TB class. Unlike the default SMOTE method of synthesizing tabular feature vectors, our method generated additional images of TB by executing visual manipulations such as rotation, scaling, and horizontal reflection. This enhancement produced 2,800 artificial TB images, increasing the size of TB class from 700 to 3,500 and thus balancing both classes in effect. The resultant class distribution due to augmentation is presented in Fig. 3, where an equal number of Normal and TB samples (3,500 each) is quite clear.

The database was developed from a number of publicly available repositories in the research done here, hence introducing some variation of imaging conditions and sources.

This is not necessarily capturing demographic heterogeneity, differences in imaging equipment, or regional ones. Also, no external validation was done on an independent dataset, something that would potentially limit generalizability to real-world clinical populations.

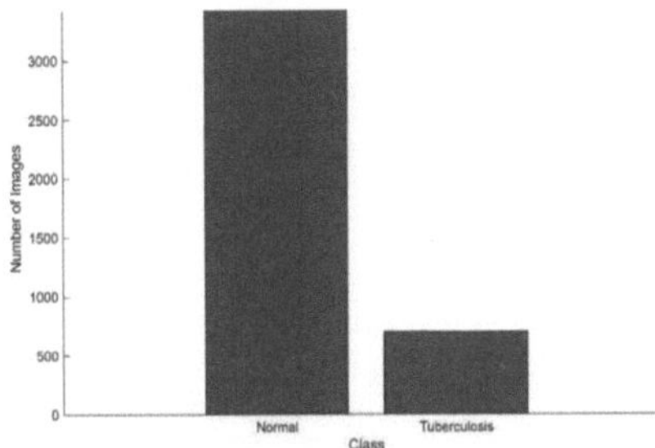

Fig. 1. Bar Graph Class distribution of the dataset.

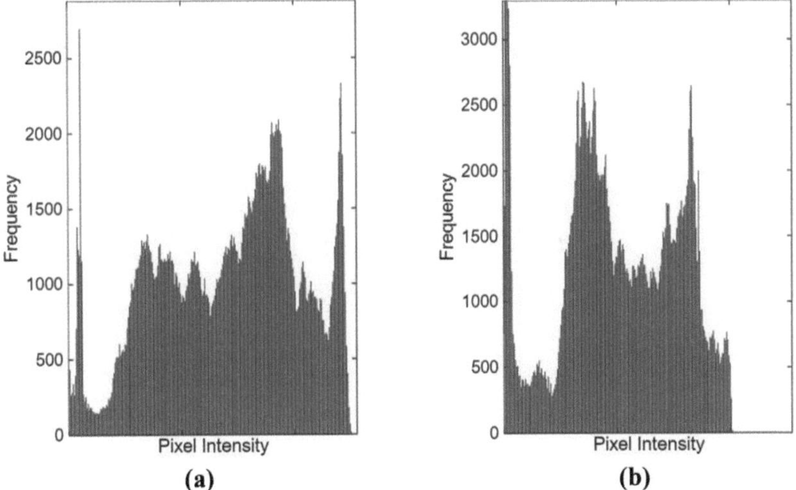

Fig. 2. **(a).** Histogram of input image intensity in normal image, **(b).** Histogram of input image intensity in Tuberculosis image

A representative sample from the dataset is depicted in Fig. 4. A Normal image (Fig. 4(a)) illustrates well-defined lung fields with no abnormalities, whereas an original TB image (Fig. 4(b)) indicates infection-associated alterations in the form of opacities or cavitations. The synthetic TB image (Fig. 4(c)), created by rotation and reflection, effectively replicates the pathogenic features of the original TB image while injecting variability to enhance model generalizability. The respective histograms of the images are depicted in Fig. 5. The histogram of the Normal image (Fig. 5(a)) is a relatively flat distribution along the x-axis (Pixel Intensity), with the y-axis (Frequency) spread more

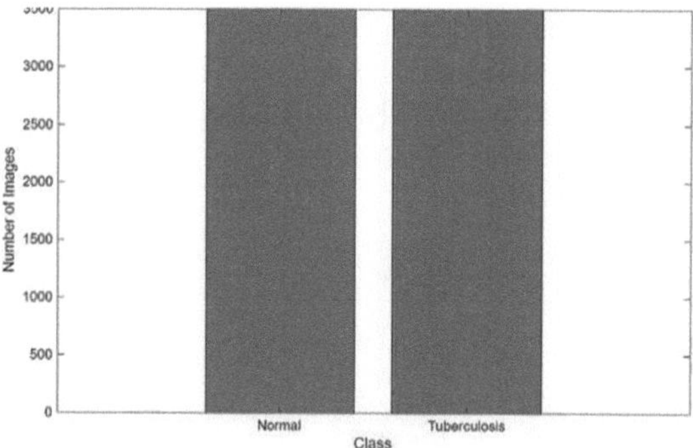

Fig. 3. Class distribution after augmentation

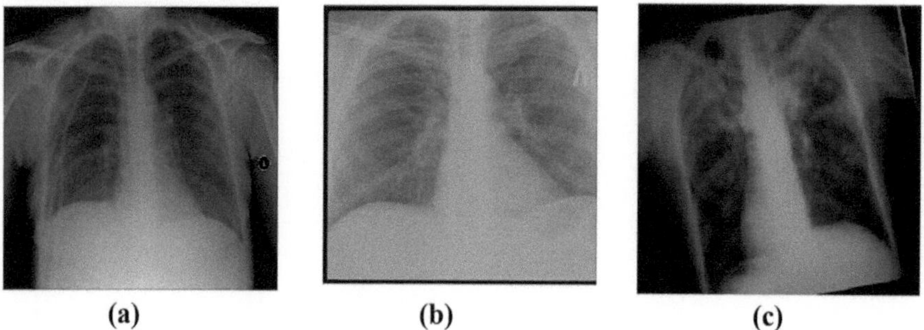

Fig. 4. (a) Normal chest X-ray image,(b) Original TB-affected chest X-ray image,(c) Synthetic (augmented) TB chest X-ray image.

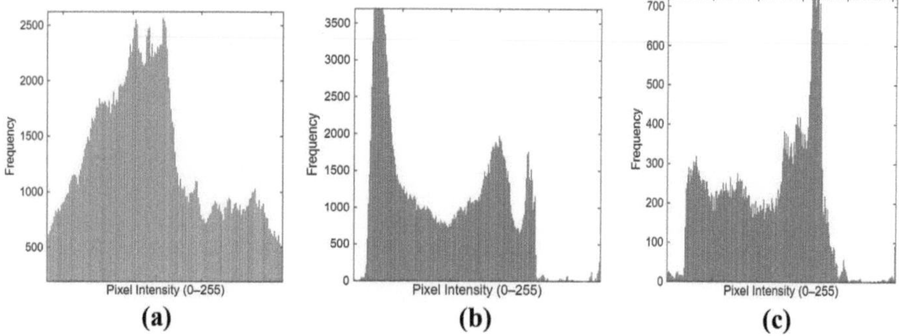

Fig. 5. (a) Histogram of the Normal chest X-ray image,(b)Histogram of the original TB chest X-ray image,(c)Histogram of the augmented TB chest X-ray image.

evenly, indicating uniform tissue density. The original TB image histogram (Fig. 5(b)) shows greater variance on the x-axis (Pixel Intensity) with sharp rises in the y-axis (Frequency), reflecting pathological features such as lesion shadows and focal opacities.

The augmented TB histogram (Fig. 5(c)) retains this variability across the x-axis (Pixel Intensity) while redistributing y-axis (Frequency) counts, thereby introducing diversity without compromising disease-pertinent features.

Although deep learning methods such as CNNs (AlexNet, ResNet, VGG) have excellent accuracy and AUC (up to 0.99) for TB detection, they need large tagged datasets, high computational power, and long training time. In this research, traditional ML models were utilized, offering a lightweight and explainable solution. With SMOTE-based augmentation, these models registered competitive accuracy (94.4%) when trained on an ordinary laptop (Intel i5, 8 GB RAM, no GPU) in a few minutes. This proves that such methods are feasible for deployment in environments with limited resources where deep learning infrastructure is not an option.

3   Methodology

The process used in this research for the diagnosis of TB from chest X-rays adopted a systematic pipeline and involved five major steps:

Step 1: Dataset Collection

The chest X-ray dataset utilized in this research was gathered from various publicly accessible repositories, such as the NIAID TB Portal, RSNA Pneumonia Detection Challenge, and National Library of Medicine (NLM) [11]. The dataset originally had 3,500 Normal images and 700 Tuberculosis-positive images. In order to rectify the imbalance, data augmentation was performed and created a final dataset of 7,000 images (3,500 Normal and 3,500 Tuberculosis).

Step 2: Preprocessing and Augmentation

All images were grayscale with the original resolution of 512×512 pixels and were resized to 227×227 pixels for consistency with the input size requirement of the models. Augmentation methods like rotation, flipping, and scaling were specifically applied only to the Tuberculosis class to randomly oversample the class to balance the dataset, simulating the Synthetic Minority Oversampling Technique (SMOTE) principle for image data.

Step 3: Feature Extraction

Because the models used (KNN, Logistic Regression, Naïve Bayes) are standard machine learning classifiers, features were extracted from the preprocessed image pixel intensity distributions directly. Histogram-based evaluation and pixel value distribution contributed the numerical representation needed for model input.

Step 4: Model Training and Hyperparameter Tuning

The data was split into training and validation sets. The three classifiers (KNN, Logistic Regression, and Naïve Bayes) were trained with default parameters, then hyperparameter tuning was performed to enhance classification accuracy. Grid search and cross-validation were utilized to find the best number of neighbors (for KNN), regularization strength (for Logistic Regression), and kernel types (for Naïve Bayes).

Step 5: Evaluation

The performance of the models was measured with various metrics such as accuracy, precision, recall, F1-score, and area under the receiver operating characteristic (AUCROC) curves. Confusion matrices were also used to plot the classification results for both the classes. Precision-recall curves were also plotted to compare the models' performance based on class imbalance.

4 Machine Learning Models for Classification

Over the past few years, machine learning (ML) models have demonstrated remarkable performance in the area of medical image analysis, especially in identifying pulmonary diseases, such as tuberculosis. ML algorithms can identify intricate patterns in labeled image data and perform quick and precise classification of chest radiographs. Here, three established supervised learning models—Logistic Regression, Naïve Bayes, and K-Nearest Neighbors (KNN)—were used to classify chest X-ray images into either normal or TB-positive. These models have been selected based on their simplicity, interpretability, and successful implementation in earlier medical use cases. Conventional machine learning models, when used with suitable preprocessing and balancing of the dataset, can be used as cost-effective alternatives to tuberculosis detection with comparable accuracy and lower computational cost [12].

4.1 K-Nearest Neighbours (KNN)

The K-Nearest Neighbours (KNN) algorithm is a non-parametric, instance-based learning technique that has been extensively used for classification purposes in medical image analysis. KNN operates on the intuitive principle that instances with similar features tend to belong to the same class.

$$d(x, y) = \sqrt{\left\{ sum_{\{i=1\}}^{\{n\}(x_i - y_i)^2} \right\}} \tag{1}$$

The boundary of the decision in KNN is defined implicitly from the neighborhood distribution of the training data, which enables the classifier to respond adaptively to intricate data patterns without the need for explicit model training. Choosing an appropriate value of k is important: low values of k will pick up noise and cause overfitting, while high values will produce smoother boundaries and perhaps underfitting. KNN was applied in this work to classify chest X-ray images into Normal or Tuberculosis classes, from pixel-derived features. The model benefits from local data geometry; hence, it is highly interpretable and efficient for datasets with separable clusters. KNN performed competitively in TB detection when adequately tuned and applied to balanced datasets, and is still a robust baseline procedure in medical image classification workflows [13].

Although simple, the performance of KNN heavily relies on considerations of metrics used in measuring distances, the choice of the value of k, and the scaling of data.

Feature normalization guarantees that all attributes have an equal influence on the calculation of the distance. For example, on high-dimensional clinical data like radiographs, feature standardization by z-score normalization avoids large-scale features from dominating the computation of the distance:

$$z = \frac{x - \mu}{\sigma} \tag{2}$$

To further improve classification performance, weighted KNN can be employed, where neighbors that are closer to a point contribute more significantly to the decision than those farther away. Inverse-distance weighting is typically used for this, and the formula for it is provided as:

$$wi = \frac{1}{d(x, xi)^2} \tag{3}$$

KNN's lack of parametric form implies that it does not have any assumption regarding the underlying data distribution, thus making it adaptable to various kinds of datasets. Its only major weakness is in high computational cost at prediction time, as it involves computation of distances to all training samples. This can be alleviated using efficient data structures such as KDTrees or Ball Trees, particularly for big datasets. In practice, KNN is still widely used in medical imaging tasks because it has the advantage of being transparent, easy to apply and having robust baseline performances. Its naturally flexible decision boundaries readily accommodate complex data distributions, and hence it is especially suited where prior knowledge of the data structure is scarce.

4.2 Logistic Regression

Logistic regression is a statistical tool used for binary classification, where it is aimed to classify something into one of two possible values, for example, "yes/no," "0/1," or "true/false." It allows for an estimate of the probability of an event by studying how the input variable aligns with the group it is most likely to belong to. It is therefore suitable for forecasting a binary outcome. Logistic regression was run with different settings in order to generate independent and dependent variables forming relationships, thus improving the capability of achieving predictability in the output based on features in the input. The Logistic function $\sigma(x)$ is

$$\sigma(x) = \frac{1}{1 + e^{-x}} \tag{4}$$

In logistic regression, the decision boundary is determined by a linear combination of input features. Each feature is multiplied by its corresponding coefficient and then processed through a logistic function. The model would then be:

$$\hat{y}_i = \sigma\left(w^T x + b\right) = \frac{1}{1 + e^{-(w^T x + b)}} \tag{5}$$

$\hat{y}_i$ is the predicted probability of the positive class, x is the vector of attributes, w is the vector of weights, and b is the bias term. For logistic regression, the parameters to be fitted (w and b), are primarily used for the maximum likelihood estimation (MLE) technique. A likelihood function is the probability of the occurrence under a certain set of parameter values. Then, we maximize the likelihood by estimating the parameters.

Binary cross-entropy loss, which can be expressed as:

$$L(w, b) = -\frac{1}{N} \sum_{i=1}^{N} [y_i \log(\hat{y}_i) + (1 - y_i) \log(1 - \hat{y}_i)] \tag{6}$$

N is given as the number of observations, y_i is the actual label for observation iii (either 0 or 1), $\hat{y}_i$ is the estimated probability for the positive class. Simplicity, interpretability, and its ability to handle binary classification problems efficiently have made logistic regression one of the widely used methodologies in medicine, finance, and social sciences [14].

4.3 Naïve Bayes

Naive Bayes is a family of probabilistic classifiers derived from Bayes' theorem with robust independence propositions amongst every pair of features. The key principle of the Naive Bayes algorithm is to classify based on the class label C, which has the highest posterior probability P(C|X), where X denotes the input features. Naive Bayes models, both Gaussian and Kernel-based, rely on feature distributions to estimate probabilities of membership in certain classes, thus framing the classification as a probabilistic task. By Bayes' theorem:

$$P(C|X) = \frac{P(X|C)P(C)}{P(X)} \tag{7}$$

Since classification is based on the maximization of the numerator, P(X|C) P(C), because P(X) is uniform for every class. Here, P(C) denotes the prior probability of class C, and P(X|C) denotes the likelihood of observing the feature vector X given the class C. The Naive Bayes classifier assumes that each feature, x_i, is conditionally independent of every other feature x_j, Given the class C. Thus, the likelihood P(X|C) can be written as the product of likelihoods:

$$P(X|C) = \prod_{i=1}^{n} P(x_i|C) \tag{8}$$

Consequently, Naive Bayes classifiers can deal with high-dimensional data efficiently through the exploitation of feature conditional independence. They classify instances on the basis of posterior probability of a class, computed through Bayes' theorem, and is widely used due to their applied simplicity and effectiveness despite the strict independence assumptions [15].

Supervised ML methods are found to work effectively in medical image classification, especially in the case of tuberculosis diagnosis. All these models learn patterns from labeled data to aid in diagnostic decision-making. They are simple, interpretable, and effective in exposing important features, which are important in clinical practice. Ongoing improvements to these techniques might increase diagnostic precision further and facilitate personalized medicine, further validating the expanding role of machine learning in medicine.

5 Results

This section demonstrates various machine learning models on the dataset and reviews the results of the feature importance based on their impact on model performance, identifying which attributes result in the most significant impacts on model performance.

Hyperparameter tuning and feature ranking were used to optimize and evaluate the developed models.

5.1 Model Evaluation Metrics

The effectiveness of each model in classifying thyroid problems was tested using classification metrics shown in Table 1. Evaluation metrics have a crucial role in estimating the classification model's effectiveness through their accuracy and effectiveness. They explain how well a model can classify the different classes.

Table 1. Description of Evaluation Metrics

Classification metrics	$Accuracy = \dfrac{TP + TN}{TP + TN + FP + FN}$ Accuracy: Overall correctness measure
	Precision: Positive Prediction accuracy $Precision = \dfrac{TP}{TP + FP}$
	Recall: Identifying actual positives $Recall = \dfrac{TP}{TP + FN}$
	F1 Score: Balance between Precision and Recall $F1\ Score = 2 * \dfrac{Precision * Recall}{Precision + Recall}$
	AUC -ROC : Discrimination ability evaluation

5.2 Accuracy Comparison

Accuracy is an important measure that gives the proportion of correct classifications predicted by a model and, therefore, acts as a reference for the overall effectiveness of the model. The accuracy % enables us to know how well a model does in predicting the correct outcome for all instances within a dataset (Table 2).

Table 2. Accuracy of Different Machine Learning Models

Model Type	Accuracy % (Validation)
Tree (Fine)	84.56
Tree (Medium)	85.11
Tree (Coarse)	83.50
Binary GLM Logistic Regression	85.50
Efficient Logistic Regression	85.31
Efficient Linear SVM	80.92
Naïve Bayes (Gaussian)	94.10
Naïve Bayes (Kernal)	94.10
SVM (Linear)	80.15
SVM (Quadratic)	83.53
SVM (Cubic)	84.87
SVM (Fine Gaussian)	80.11
SVM (Medium Gaussian)	81.52
SVM (Coarse Gaussian)	80.54
KNN (Fine KNN)	94.44
KNN (Medium KNN)	94.32
KNN (Coarse KNN)	94.38
KNN (Weighted KNN)	94.27
Ensemble (Boosted Trees)	85.50
Ensemble (Bagged)	85.12
Ensemble (Subspace KNN)	94.44
Ensemble (RUSBoosted)	85.38
Neural Network (Narrow)	83.14
Neural Network (Medium)	83.32
Neural network (Wide)	83.38
Neural Network (Bilayered)	83.27
Neural Network (Trilayered)	83.19

In the final table of results, for each of the classification models, the highest accuracy— either from the original imbalanced data or the SMOTE-enlarged data—was used. In other words, if a model was better after using SMOTE, the enlarged accuracy was used; otherwise, the original accuracy was used. This is done so that the reported results show the best performance found for each model for both cases.

Out of them, Naïve Bayes (Gaussian and Kernel) models and KNN-based models like Fine KNN, Coarse KNN, and Ensemble (Subspace KNN) performed with the highest accuracy of 94.44%, reflecting their good performance in separating between Normal and Tuberculosis cases. On the other hand, some models like SVM and Decision Trees performed comparatively moderate (usually in the range of 80–85%), reflecting the superiority of ensemble and instance-based approaches for this classification task. These results highlight the necessity of model tuning and algorithm selection in medical image classification.

5.3 Hyperparameter Selection and Tuning

Hyperparameter tuning is the readjustment of the parameters in ML models to improve their performance. This is done by selecting the right value for some parameters like the number of learners, the number of splits, and the learning rate. We improve model accuracy and generalization by systematically searching all the hyperparameter combinations. Table 3 shows the hyperparameters for each model. Hyperparameter tuning ensures that models perform well on a training dataset as well as unseen data, enhancing its ability to predict.

Table 3. Hyperparameters for different ML models

Model name	Hyperparameters used
Naïve Bayes (Gaussian)	uses VMN naming for categorical predictors
Naïve Bayes (Kernal)	uses VMN naming for categorical predictors
KNN (Fine KNN)	employs 1 neighbor, equal distance weighting, and no data standardization
KNN (Medium KNN)	uses 10 neighbors, Hamming distance metric, equal weighting, and no standardization;
Ensemble (Subspace KNN)	-uses nearest-neighbor learners, 30 learners, and subspace dimension

5.4 Confusion Matrix Analysis

The confusion matrix also in Fig. 6 provide a breakdown of exactly how the model performs: it outlines how frequently true positives and true negatives are detected versus when it fails to do so through false positives and false negatives. This helps point out exactly where the model is getting its predictions wrong. Helps in finding the positives and negatives of a model for improvements.

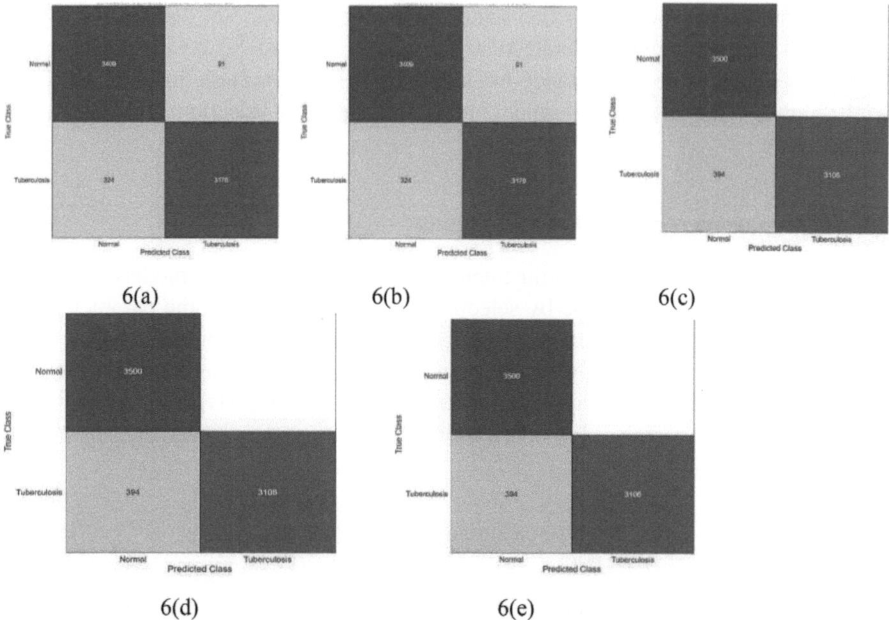

6(a)　　　　　　6(b)　　　　　　6(c)

6(d)　　　　　　6(e)

Fig. 6. Confusion matrices of the top 5 models (a) Naïve Bayes (Gaussian) ,(b) Naïve Bayes (Kernel),(c) KNN (Fine), (d) KNN (Medium),(e) Ensemble (Subspace KNN).

Figure 6(a) shows the results from the Naïve Bayes (Gaussian). The model accurately predicted 3,409 Normal and 3,176 TB instances and incorrectly classified 91 Normal and 324 TB instances. This shows a low rate of false positives and false negatives, reflecting excellent performance across both classes. Figure 6(b) shows the results from the Naïve Bayes (Kernel), and the confusion matrix is the same as 6(a), with the same values. This indicates that both Naïve Bayes implementations (Gaussian and Kernel) produced the same classification results on the data. Figure 6(c) shows results from KNN (Fine), and the model classified all 3,500 Normal cases accurately, with no false positives. However, it also misclassified 394 TB cases as Normal, indicating that it had a greater false negative rate than Naïve Bayes. Figure 6(d) shows results from the KNN (Medium), and similar to the Fine KNN model, the medium KNN model accurately identified 3,500 Normal and 3,106 TB cases, with 394 TB cases being misclassified. While having high true positives for Normal cases, its performance is low in classifying TB cases. Finally, Fig. 6(e) shows the confusion matrices for Ensemble (Subspace KNN), where the performance is the same as models 6(c) and 6(d), with 3,500 correct Normal and 3,106 correct TB labels. This indicates that ensemble learning in this case did not perform much better than standalone KNN models.

5.5 Precision- Recall Curve

The Precision-Recall (PR) curve is a useful metric in judging classification models, especially for imbalanced datasets like tuberculosis detection where false negatives are of critical importance. It measures precision (positive predictive value) against recall (true positive rate), giving an insight into the trade-off between sensitivity and positive prediction accuracy. A larger area under the PR curve (PR-AUC) indicates improved performance for the detection of true positives with reduced false positives.

Figure 7 shows the PR curves of the top five models. Figure 7(a) (Naïve Bayes Gaussian) had a PR-AUC of 0.9933 and presents a balanced curve with some moderate precision-recall trade-off, reflecting consistent performance in both normal and tuberculosis classes. Figure 7(b) (Naïve Bayes Kernel) had a PR-AUC of 0.99331, with lower recall at higher levels of precision than 7(a), showing performance that is similar to the Gaussian version. Figure 7(c) (KNN Fine) had a moderate drop in PR-AUC (0.89882 in Normal, 0.97186 in Tuberculosis) and indicates a sharp drop in precision for every increase in recall, reflecting less balance between precision and recall. Figure 7(d) (KNN Medium) had comparable PR-AUC to KNN Fine but indicates a smoother decline, reflecting an improvement over 7(c). Lastly, Fig. 7(e) (Ensemble Subspace KNN) has PRAUC values similar to the KNN models but the worst recall at all precision levels, indicating difficulty in appropriately labeling the positive class.

Overall, these findings indicate that the Naïve Bayes models, especially the Gaussian one, offer the best stable and consistent trade-off between precision and recall for both classes in this data.

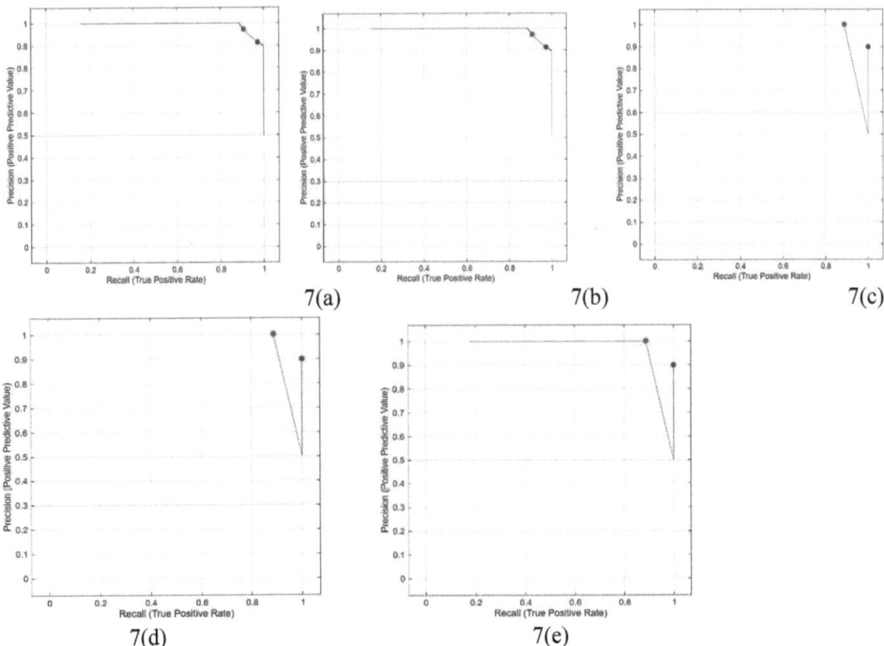

Fig. 7. Precision-Recall Curve of top 5 models **(a)** Naïve Bayes (Gaussian) **(b)** Naïve Bayes (Kernel) **(c)** KNN (Fine) **(d)** KNN (Medium) **(e)** Ensemble (Subspace KNN).

5.6 AUC-ROC Curve Analysis

The AUC-ROC curve plots the discrimination ability of the model between positive and negative classes at different values of thresholds. The higher the value of AUC, the more accurate the discrimination ability of the model.

Figure 8 presents the ROC curves for the top four models. The models are all well discriminated from tuberculosis and normal cases, and the ROC curves show the tradeoff between sensitivity and specificity. These results confirm goodness of top models in correctly classifying instances and managing false positives.

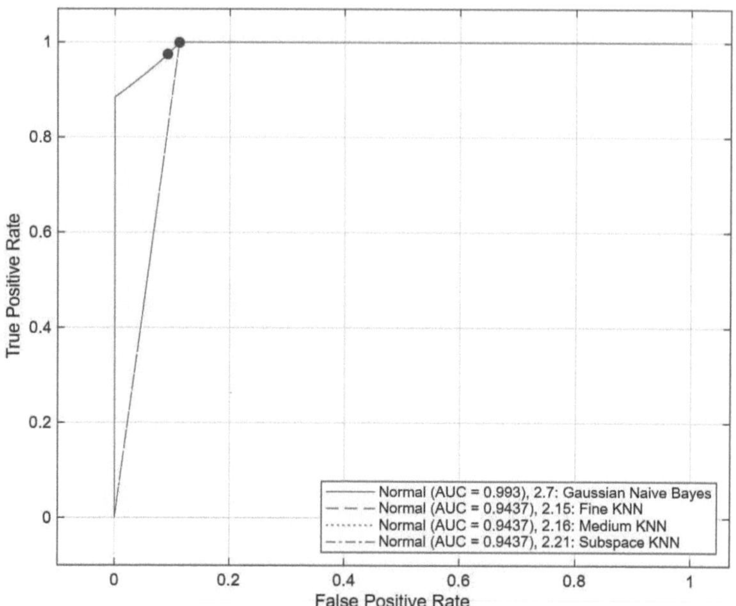

Fig. 8. AUC-ROC curves for top 4 models

6 Conclusion

This research investigates the feasibility for detecting tuberculosis automatically from chest X-ray images. The algorithms were trained on a dataset of 7,000 grayscale images divided equally into Normal and Tuberculosis classes, which initially corrected class imbalance by applying data augmentation techniques.

- The K-Nearest Neighbors classifier had the highest classification accuracy, reflecting its strength in using local feature patterns to separate TB-positive from Normal cases. Its ease of use and robust performance make KNN an appealing option for medical image classification.
- Hyperparameter adjustment and preprocessing—resizing, normalization, and class rebalancing by augmentation—were essential in fine-tuning the model performance. This equilibrium between complexity and interpretability made the classifiers generalize well on new data.

- Histogram and intensity distribution analysis showed distinguishable patterns between the pixel distributions of TB and Normal classes, which were well leveraged by the models for proper classification.
- One of the significant drawbacks of the current research, is the limited dataset size derived from a comparatively less heterogeneous population and also the existence of class imbalance. Moreover, the low resolution of the input images may potentially result in misclassification of subtle lesions. The study has the limitation of a lack of external validation, as the dataset—although drawn from many repositories—can still contain demographic biases and equipment-specific artifacts. Until independently tested on hospital datasets, however, the clinical robustness and generalizability of the models cannot be conclusively determined. As for future directions for this field, it is seen that the findings of this study may be corroborated with real-life clinical trials on a diverse population of patients. Furthermore, the most highly performing ML models may be implemented on imaging devices to be utilized in real-world applications. As for future directions for this field, it is seen that the findings of this study may be corroborated with real-life clinical trials on a diverse population of patients. Furthermore, the most highly performing ML models may be implemented on imaging devices to be utilized in real-world applications.

This research reiterates that traditional supervised models, when accompanied by appropriate preprocessing and a wellbalanced dataset, can provide strong support for the detection of tuberculosis. Particularly in resource-poor environments, such light models will facilitate quick, affordable, and intelligible diagnostic services, potentially enhancing early detection and public health outcomes.

References

1. World Health Organization (WHO): Tuberculosis (2025). https://www.who.int/newsroom/fact-sheets/detail/tuberculosis
2. World Health Organization: Global tuberculosis report 2022 (2022). https://www.who.int/publications/i/item/9789240061729
3. Lönnroth, K., et al.: Drivers of tuberculosis epidemics: the role of risk factors and social determinants. Soc. Sci. Med. **68**(12), 2240–2246 (2010). https://doi.org/10.1016/j.socscimed.2009.03.041
4. Sharma, S.K., Mohan, A.: Extrapulmonary tuberculosis. Indian J. Med. Res. **120**(4), 316–353 (2004). https://www.ijmr.org.in/article.asp?issn=09715916;year=2004;volume=120;issue=4;spage=316;epage=353;aulast=Sharma
5. Pai, M., et al.: Tuberculosis. Nat. Rev. Dis. Primers **2**, 16076 (2016). https://doi.org/10.1038/nrdp.2016.76
6. Tiwari, S., et al.: Artificial intelligence-based approaches in diagnosis of tuberculosis: a review. Tuberculosis **122**, 101923 (2020). https://doi.org/10.1016/j.tube.2020.101923
7. Lakhani, P., Sundaram, B.: Deep learning at chest radiography: automated classification of pulmonary tuberculosis by using convolutional neural networks. Radiology **284**(2), 574–582 (2017). https://doi.org/10.1148/radiol.2017162326
8. Pasa, F., et al.: Efficient deep network architectures for fast chest X-ray tuberculosis screening and visualization. Sci. Rep. **9**(1), 6268 (2019). https://doi.org/10.1038/s41598-019-42557-4

9. Hwang, S., et al.: A novel approach for tuberculosis screening based on deep convolutional neural networks. In: Proceedings of the SPIE Medical Imaging, vol. 9785, 97852W (2016). https://doi.org/10.1117/12.2216198
10. Rahman, T.: Tuberculosis (TB) Chest X-Ray Dataset. Kaggle (2019). https://www.kaggle.com/datasets/tawsifurrahman/tuberculosis-tb-chest-xraydataset
11. Lopes, F.M., Valiati, J.F.: Exploring deep learning for tuberculosis screening in chest X-rays. Pattern Recognit. Lett. **125**, 78–84 (2019)
12. Rahman, T., Khandakar, A., Kadir, M.A., et al.: Reliable tuberculosis detection using chest X-ray with deep learning, segmentation and visualization. IEEE Access (2020). https://doi.org/10.1109/ACCESS.2020.3031384
13. Tiwari, D., et al.: An improved KNN approach for classification of tuberculosis chest X-ray images. J. Med. Syst. (2021)
14. Ranjan, R., Sinha, A.: Application of logistic regression in TB detection using radiographic features. Biomed. Res. (2020)
15. Verma, P., Bhardwaj, S.: Bayesian classification models in pulmonary disease diagnosis: a case study on tuberculosis. Int. J. Med. Inform. (2019)

Comparative Analysis of Decision Tree and Random Forest Models for Prostate Cancer Classification

Priya Mittal[1(✉)] ⓘ, Bhisham Sharma[2] ⓘ, D. P. Yadav[3] ⓘ, Tapas Sharma[4] ⓘ, and Imed Ben Dhaou[5] ⓘ

[1] Chitkara University Institute of Engineering and Technology, Chitkara University, Rajpura, Punjab, India
`mittal.priya@chitkara.edu.in`
[2] Centre of Research Impact and Outcome, Chitkara University, Rajpura, Punjab, India
`bhisham.pec@gmail.com`
[3] Department of Computer Engineering and Applications, G. L. A. University, Mathura, India
`dhirendra.yadav@gla.ac.in`
[4] Chitkara University School of Engineering and Technology, Chitkara University, Himachal Pradesh, India
`tapas.sharma@chitkarauniversity.edu.in`
[5] Department of Computer Science, School of Engineering, Computing and Design, Dar Al-Hekma University, Jeddah, Saudi Arabia
`Imed.bendhaou@utu.fi`

Abstract. This study compares the performance of Decision Tree and Random Forest Classifier models on a binary classification medical data set that includes images of prostate cancer. The two models are evaluated through metrics like accuracy, precision, recall, F1 score, ROC curve, etc. After the testing, the random Forest classifier showed better performance than decision tree classifier. The random forest showed an accuracy of 85%, whereas the decision tree could only record an accuracy of 80%. The results mentioned that Random forest gives better performance than Decision tree.

Keywords: Decision Tree · Random Forest · Prostate Cancer · Classification

1 Introduction

Affecting millions of people and imposing major social and financial loads, cancer remains one of the most important global health issues. Among the several forms of cancer, prostate cancer is one of the most common cancers that affect men globally and requires an early and correct diagnosis for proper therapy and control. Traditional diagnostic techniques, often based on biopsies and imaging, can be invasive, time-consuming, and limited by subjective interpretation.

H. Kannan et al. (Eds.): AIKP 2025, CCIS 2804, pp. 29–41, 2026.
https://doi.org/10.1007/978-3-032-14706-6_3

Consequently, machine learning and artificial intelligence (AI) have emerged as promising approaches to enhance diagnostic accuracy and streamline the disease detection process, particularly for cancers such as prostate cancer, where early identification is critical.

In recent years, machine learning algorithms have shown remarkable potential in processing and analyzing large datasets, uncovering complex patterns, and achieving robust classifications, especially in medical diagnostics. It also reduces human error, improves clinical workflow efficiency, and offers decision support to clinicians [14]. Studies have shown that machine learning models can effectively aid in cancer diagnosis by learning from data that represent key biomarkers, thereby improving both accuracy and reproducibility over traditional methods. This work classifies prostate cancer according to relevant feature retrieved from a publicly available dataset using multiple machine learning classifiers: logistic regression, support vector machine (SVM), naive bayes, decision trees, random forest, artificial neural networks (ANN). Furthermore used was a recurrent neural network (RNN) to improve classification accuracy even more and investigate the possibilities of deep learning for cancer diagnosis.

Using these several classification approaches is motivated by the search for the most accurate and effective method for the diagnosis of prostate cancer. By means of comparison of various algorithms, we hope to clarify the advantages and drawbacks of every approach, so leading next studies and useful applications in the field. Previous studies have shown that, in tasks that involve cancer classification, neural networks, especially deep learning models, can achieve great precision. Our results confirm this even more as advanced deep learning models such as RNN can beat other conventional machine learning methods, therefore highlighting the possibilities of neural networks in improving cancer diagnosis.

The study uses a data set that includes several clinical criteria associated with prostate cancer, such as radius, texture, perimeter, area, smoothness, compactness, symmetry, and fractal dimension. We guarantee that the dataset is preprocessed to maximize the efficiency and accuracy of machine learning models by translating categorical diagnosis results into binary classes and standardizing the feature set. By using measures like classification accuracy and confusion matrices, the accuracy of every model is assessed, thus facilitating an all-encompassing study of the performance of every approach. In the end, this work emphasizes how well deep learning techniques, including RNN, achieve better classification results, therefore supporting the potential of neural networks to improve cancer diagnosis.

2   Related Work

This section discussed the various works of the authors in the area of glaucoma detection using different technologies. Litwin et al. [9] review the diagnosis and treatment of prostate cancer, focusing on screening, risk stratification, and management approaches. They report that prostate-specific antigen (PSA) screening reduces mortality by approximately 20%. Active surveillance, surgery, and radiation therapy show different success rates, with radical prostatectomy reducing mortality by 38% in localized cases. Rawla et al. [13] highlights prostate cancer as the second most common cancer in men, with a global incidence of 1.3 million cases annually. Mortality rates vary, with early detection improving survival. Five-year survival rates exceed 98% in localized cases but drop below 30% in metastatic stages.

Pernar et al. [11] discuss risk factors such as age, genetics, and lifestyle. Prostate cancer screening reduces mortality by 20%, while African American men have a higher incidence rate of 60%. Advances in diagnostic biomarkers improve early detection, reducing overtreatment, and improving patient outcomes. Crawford et al. [2] reviews incidence trends, noting that PSA screening has led to a 30% reduction in advanced-stage diagnosis. However, mortality remains high in metastatic cases. Lifestyle modifications and targeted therapies show promise in reducing risks, but disparities persist in different populations.

Ilic et al. [8] review analyzing randomized trials found that PSA screening reduces prostate cancer-specific mortality by 21% but does not significantly affect overall survival. The study emphasizes the need to balance early detection benefits with potential harms such as overtreatment and false positives. Dunn et al. [4] outlines prostate cancer risk factors, diagnosis, and treatment. Early detection through PSA screening improves results, with five-year survival reaching 99% for localized cases. However, side effects related to treatment, including incontinence and erectile dysfunction, affect 30 to 50% of patients.

Pienta et al. [12] identifies genetic predisposition, diet, and hormonal factors as key risks. A family history increases the risk 2.5 times, while high-fat diets correlate with a higher incidence 30%. Androgen levels influence tumor progression, highlighting the need for targeted preventive strategies. Gann et al. [5] discusses modifiable and non-modifiable risk factors. Regular screening detects cancer early, reducing mortality by 25%. The study finds that high calcium intake increases the risk by 30%, while diets rich in lycopene lower the risk by 25%.

Abate-Shen et al. [1] explores genetic alterations in prostate cancer, identifying the fusion of PTEN, p53, and TMPRSS2-ERG as key drivers. Genetic screening improves early detection, reducing mortality rates by 20%. Targeted gene therapies show potential to improve survival in aggressive cases. Hoffman et al. [7] evaluates PSA screening effectiveness, reporting a 20% reduction in mortality but a high false positive rate leading to unnecessary biopsies (over 30%). The study calls for better biomarkers to refine screening accuracy and minimize overdiagnosis.

Heidenreich et al. [6] emphasize early detection and multimodal treatment. Radical prostatectomy improves 10-year survival by 60%, while androgen deprivation therapy (ADT) improves outcomes in metastatic cases. The study advocates personalized treatment based on risk stratification. Mottet et al. [10] updated guidelines that recommend PSA-based screening for high-risk individuals. It highlights that active surveillance reduces overtreatment while maintaining a survival rate of 98% for low-risk cases. Combination therapies in advanced stages improve survival by up to 40%. DeMarzo et al. [3] examine the tumor microenvironment and molecular changes. Inflammation contributes to 40% of cases, while genetic mutations drive progression. Targeted therapies based on molecular profiling improve response to treatment and reduce recurrence rates by 25%.

3   Detailed Architecture

3.1   Decision Tree Classifier

A decision tree classifier is a supervised learning method in which data are divided into subsets depending on feature values, thus producing a tree structure with nodes (features) and branches (decision rules). At each node, it selects the feature that maximizes *Information Gain* or minimizes *Impurity*. Impurity measures include *Entropy*:

$$\text{Entropy}(S) = -\sum_{i=1}^{c} p_i \log_2(p_i) \tag{1}$$

and *Gini Index*:

$$\text{Gini}(S) = 1 - \sum_{i=1}^{c} p_i^2 \tag{2}$$

where p_i is the proportion of the class in a node. The algorithm continues until it reaches the leaf nodes with class labels. Though simple and interpretable, Decision Trees can overfit, especially with deep trees. *Pruning* is used to reduce the overfitting by trimming branches, improving generalization. Decision trees are valued for their flexibility and ease of implementation, but may lack accuracy and robustness compared to ensemble methods.

3.2   Random Forest Classifier

Random Forest is an ensemble method that enhances Decision Tree accuracy and robustness by building multiple trees on varied data subsets. Each tree is trained on a *bootstrap sample* (random subset with replacement) and considers a random subset of features at each split, introducing diversity among trees. For classification, Random Forest uses majority voting among trees:

$$\text{Prediction}(X) = \text{mode}(\text{Tree}_1(X), \text{Tree}_2(X), \ldots, \text{Tree}_T(X)) \tag{3}$$

where T is the number of trees. This approach reduces variance and overfitting, making Random Forests robust against noise and outliers. Although computationally expensive and less interpretable, they achieve high accuracy and are widely used across domains for their robustness and versatility.

4 Performance Comparison

4.1 Dataset

The prostate cancer data set is a publicly available data set that contains records of 100 patients and ten variables to implement machine learning algorithms. Of which eight variables have numerical values and one categorical variable along with a unique ID. Radius (mean distance from center to perimeter points), texture (variation in grayscale values), perimeter (boundary length), area (region size), smoothness (local radius variation), compactness (shape compactness), symmetry (shape symmetry) and fractal dimension (boundary roughness) comprise the numerical features. The diagnosis result is found in the Diagnostic_Result variable. This feature rich collection facilitates thorough investigation and evaluation of diagnostic model performance. The choice of this dataset was motivated by its availability, balanced distribution of classes, and its prior use in related studies, making it a reasonable benchmark for comparing machine learning models.

4.2 Data Pre-processing

Ensuring that the dataset is best structured for training the Decision Tree and Random Forest classifiers, the dataset undergoes various stages of pre-processing. The various pre-processing stages are discussed below:

- **Data Cleaning**: Missing values were found and handled to preserve data integrity. Whereas categorical values were handled using mode imputation, missing values for numerical variables were either imputed using the mean or median depending on the data distribution.
- **Feature Scaling**: Numerical features including Radius, Texture, Perimeter, Area, Smoothness, Compactness, Symmetry, and Fractal Dimension were scaled to standardize the data set and reduce the influence of different feature scales. These features were converted to a common scale between 0 and 1 using min-max normalization, therefore ensuring consistency in input for both classifiers.
- **Encoding Categorical Variables**: The Diagnosis_Result variable, a categorical feature, was encoded into binary values (e.g., 0 and 1) to make it suitable for the classifiers, since both algorithms require numeric input.
- **Data Splitting**: The dataset was evaluated using 5-fold cross-validation, where the data were divided into five equal subsets. In each iteration, four subsets were used for training and one for testing, ensuring that every sample was used for both training and validation in different iterations. This approach provided a robust assessment of the generalizability of the model while mitigating the bias of a single train-test split.
- **Feature Selection**: The most pertinent predictors were found by an investigation of significance of the characteristics. Through feature elimination, dimensionality reduction, and model performance optimization, this stage helped increase computational efficiency.

The preprocessed images of the Decision Tree Classifier and the Random Forest Classifier are shown in Fig. 1 and Fig. 2.

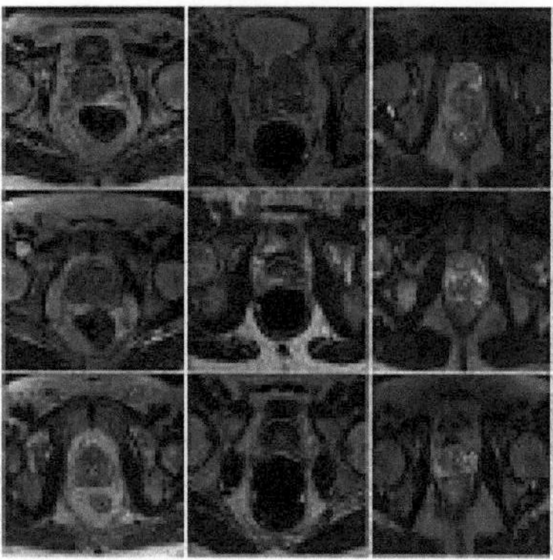

Fig. 1. Pre-processed image using Decision Tree Classifier.

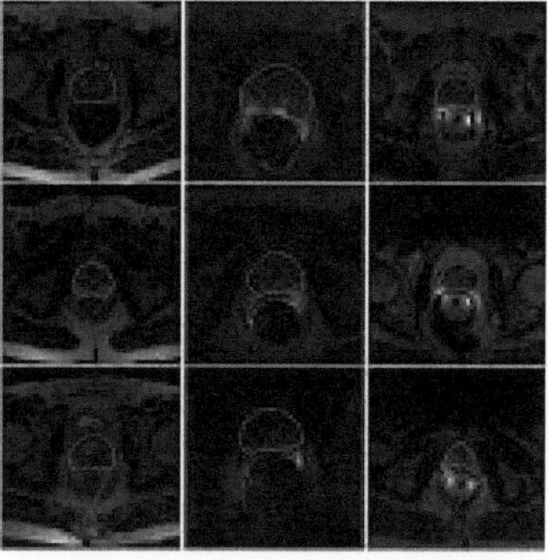

Fig. 2. Pre-processed Image using Random Forest Classifier.

4.3   Training

Training on the prostate cancer dataset employed binary cross-entropy loss, as the task is a binary classification problem with output values of 0 and 1. The Adam optimizer, with a learning rate of 0.001, was used to train the dataset for 100 epochs. The batch size was set to 32.

Hyperparameters play a crucial role in controlling the performance, complexity, and generalization ability of tree-based models. For the Decision Tree classifier, the quality of splits was determined using Gini and entropy criteria, while for the Random Forest classifier, the number of trees was controlled using n_estimators. To avoid overfitting, values of 10, 20, and 30 were tested for max_depth. For max_features, options such as $\sqrt{\cdot}$ and $\log_2 \cdot$ were used to define the number of features considered at each split.

4.4   Performance Metrics

A confusion matrix is a tabular representation of the performance of a classification model. Shows the number of correct and incorrect classifications, thus summarizing the predictions. The confusion matrices for the Decision Tree classifier and the Random Forest classifier are presented in Fig. 3 and Fig. 4.

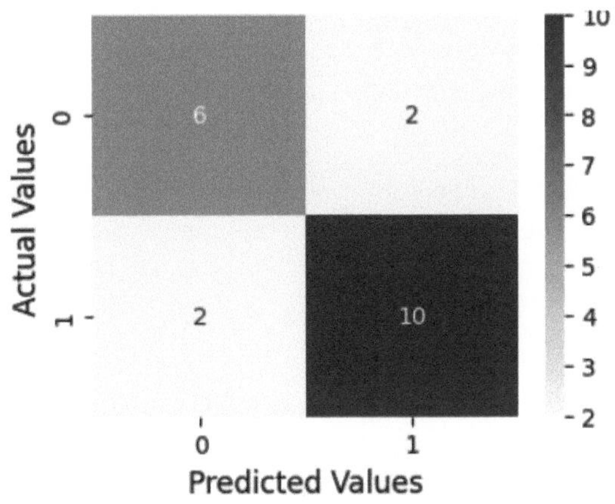

Fig. 3. Confusion Matrix using Decision Tree Classifier.

From the confusion matrices above, parameters such as accuracy, precision, recall, and F1 score are calculated. The calculated results are presented in Table 1.

Table 1. Comparison between Decision Tree and Random Forest

Parameters	Decision Tree	Random Forest
Accuracy(%)	80	85
Precision(%)	83	84.6
Recall(%)	83	91.7
F1 Score(%)	83	88.80

From Table 1, it can be determined that the Random Forest Classifier showed better results compared to the Decision Tree Classifier. The random forest surpasses the later showing accuracy of 85%. The random forest also showed a

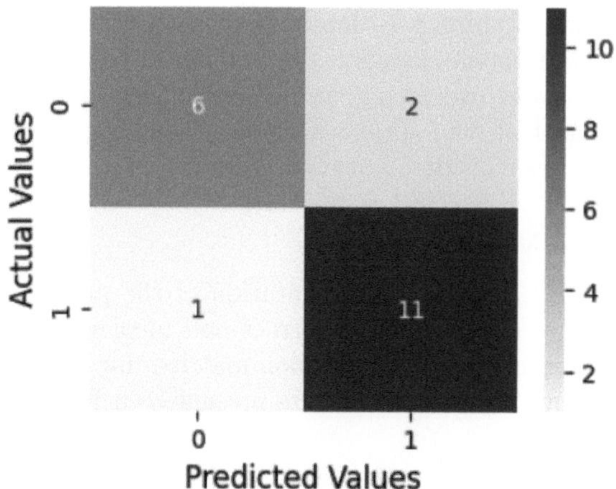

Fig. 4. Confusion Matrix using Random Forest Classifier.

recall of 91. 7%, while the decision tree only recalls 83% of the results. This clearly showed that the Random Forest classifier is a better option to predict performances.

4.5   Training and Validation Loss

Figures 5 and 6 present the training and validation log-loss curves for the Random Forest and Decision Tree classifiers in five cross-validation folds. For Random Forest, the training loss remains relatively stable and low across the folds, indicating a consistent model fitting. The validation loss starts higher in the first fold but decreases sharply in the second and third folds, reaching its lowest point in the third fold. In later folds, it increases slightly but stays well below the initial value, suggesting good generalization with minor variations across the folds.

In contrast, for the Decision Tree, the training loss is extremely low and consistent across all folds, reflecting that the Decision Tree is likely overfitting the training data. In contrast, the validation loss is significantly higher and fluctuates across the folds, with peaks and drops indicating instability and poor generalization to unseen data.

4.6   Training and Validation Accuracy

The learning curves in Figs. 7 and 8 illustrate the training and validation performance of the Random Forest (RF) and Decision Tree (DT) models, which vary between different combinations of hyperparameters, measured using the ROC AUC score.

For the Random Forest, the training accuracy remains consistently high (0.98-1.0) across all hyperparameter combinations, indicating that each ensemble of trees is able to fit the training data very well. The validation accuracy

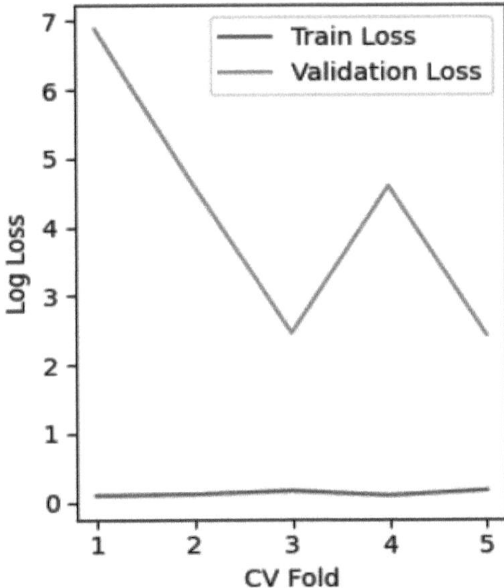

Fig. 5. Training and Validation Loss Plot using Decison Tree.

fluctuates between approximately 0.90 and 0.94, which is slightly lower than the training accuracy. This gap suggests some degree of overfitting, but the model maintains robust performance on unseen data due to the ensemble averaging effect of Random Forests. The general stability of the validation curve demonstrates the generalizability of the model and its resistance to noise in hyperparameter settings.

For the Decision Tree, the training accuracy is slightly lower (0.95-1.0) compared to Random Forest, but still high, indicating the model's strong ability to fit training data. However, the validation accuracy is substantially lower (0.700.80), and exhibits more pronounced fluctuations. This indicates that Decision Trees are more prone to overfitting, as a single tree can capture noise in the training data without the regularization provided by ensemble methods. The large gap between training and validation accuracy highlights the reduced generalization ability of single trees compared to Random Forests.

4.7 ROC Plot

The Receiver Operating Characteristic (ROC) curve is a graphical representation of the performance of a classification model by plotting the True Positive Rate (sensitivity) against the False Positive Rate at various threshold settings. The Area Under the Curve (AUC) provides a summary measure of the model's overall ability to distinguish between classes. A higher AUC indicates better model performance, as it reflects a better trade-off between sensitivity and specificity across different thresholds. Figure 9 shows the ROC curves for the Decision Tree

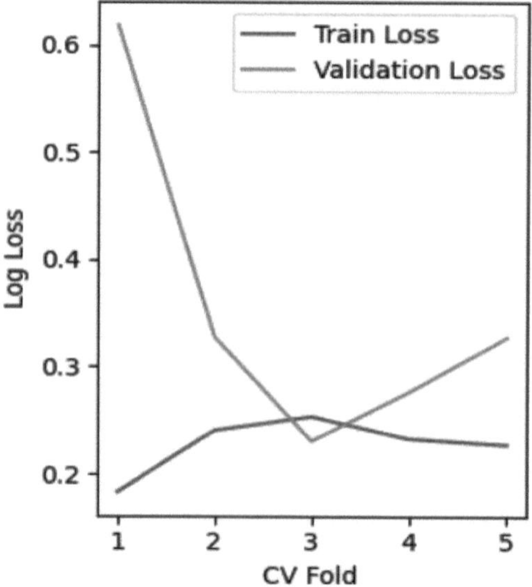

Fig. 6. Training and Validation Loss Plot using Random Forest.

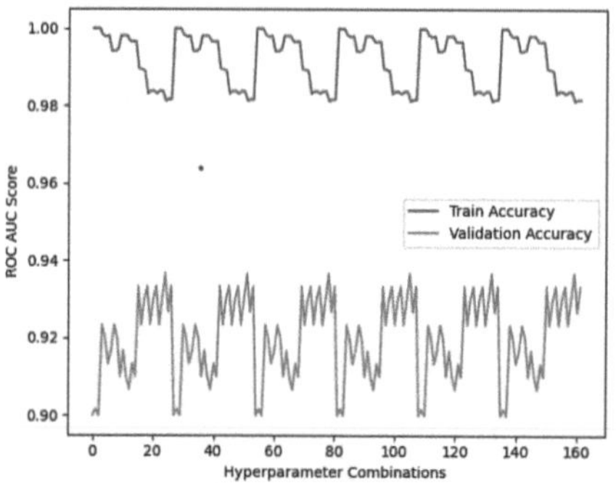

Fig. 7. Training and Validation Accuracy plot of Random Forest.

and Random Forest classifier models. The Random Forest classifier achieves a higher AUC of 0.90, indicating superior performance compared to the Decision Tree classifier, which has an AUC of 0.82.

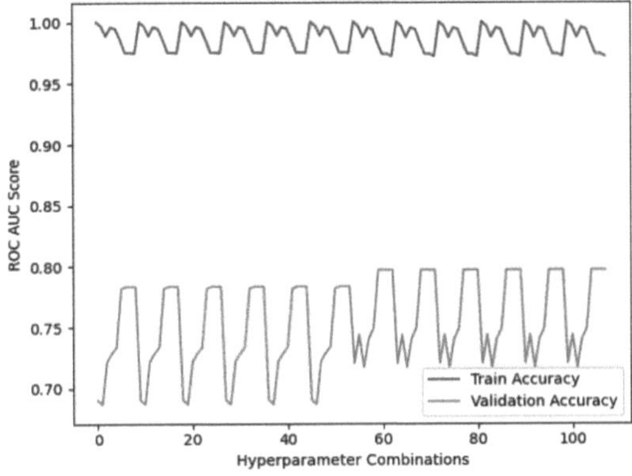

Fig. 8. Training and Validation Accuracy plot of Decision Tree.

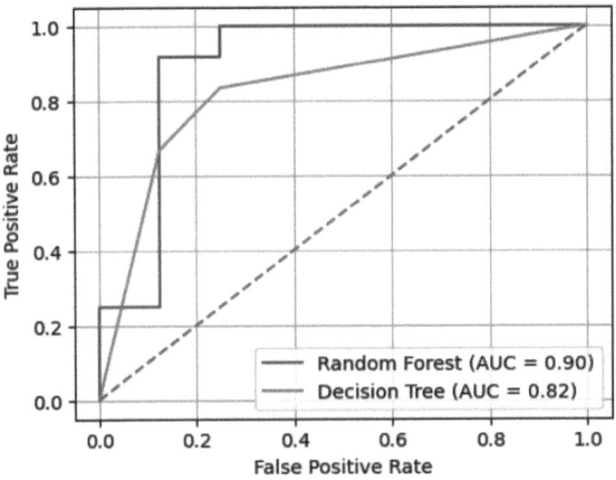

Fig. 9. ROC Plot for Decision Tree and random Forest.

5   Conclusion

In this study, we compared the performance of two widely used classification algorithms Random Forest and Decision Tree for the prostate cancer detection task. The Random Forest classifier demonstrated superior performance, achieving an accuracy of 85%, precision of 84.6%, recall of 91.7%, and an F1 score of 88.3%. These metrics highlight its effectiveness in correctly identifying positive cases while maintaining a strong balance between precision and recall. In contrast, the Decision Tree classifier achieved an accuracy of 80%, with precision, recall, and F1 score each at 83%. Although the Decision Tree model showed reasonably good performance, it was outperformed by the Random Forest model across all metrics.

From a clinical perspective, these findings suggest that ensemble-based methods such as Random Forest are preferable in diagnostic scenarios where sensitivity (recall) is critical, such as prostate cancer detection, since they minimize the risk of false negatives and improve early case identification. However, Decision Trees may still hold value in settings where interpretability and ease of use are prioritized, for instance in preliminary screenings or resource constrained clinical environments. Clinicians and researchers should therefore balance the trade-off between diagnostic accuracy and model transparency depending on the clinical context.

Future work could explore the integration of additional features, hyperparameter tuning, and the use of more advanced algorithms to further enhance model performance. Additionally, validation on larger and more diverse datasets would provide deeper insights into the generalizability and robustness of these models in real world clinical settings.

Ethical Considerations. This research was conducted using publicly available datasets, ensuring that no personally identifiable or sensitive patient data were compromised. The study adhered to responsible AI practices, with emphasis on fairness, transparency, and reproducibility. As with all applications of machine learning in healthcare, it is crucial to recognize that predictive models are intended to support, not replace, clinical decision making. Ethical use requires that clinicians remain accountable for patient outcomes, and that AI systems are integrated cautiously, with appropriate oversight and consideration of potential biases and limitations.

References

1. Abate-Shen, C., Shen, M.M.: Molecular genetics of prostate cancer. Genes Developm. **14**(19), 2410–2434 (2000)
2. Crawford, E.D.: Epidemiology of prostate cancer. Urology **62**(6), 3–12 (2003)
3. DeMarzo, A.M., Nelson, W.G., Isaacs, W.B., Epstein, J.I.: Pathological and molecular aspects of prostate cancer. The Lancet **361**(9361), 955–964 (2003)
4. Dunn, M.W., Kazer, M.W.: Prostate cancer overview. In: Seminars Oncol. Nursing, vol. 27, pp. 241–250. Elsevier (2011)
5. Gann, P.H.: Risk factors for prostate cancer. Rev. Urol. **4**(Suppl 5), S3 (2002)
6. Heidenreich, A., et al.: Eau guidelines on prostate cancer. Eur. Urol. **53**(1), 68–80 (2008)
7. Hoffman, R.M.: Screening for prostate cancer. N. Engl. J. Med. **365**(21), 2013–2019 (2011)
8. Ilic, D., Neuberger, M.M., Djulbegovic, M., Dahm, P.: Screening for prostate cancer. Cochrane Database Systematic Rev. (1) (2013)
9. Litwin, M.S., Tan, H.J.: The diagnosis and treatment of prostate cancer: a review. JAMA **317**(24), 2532–2542 (2017)
10. Mottet, N., et al.: Guidelines on prostate cancer. European Associat. Urol. **56**, e137 (2015)
11. Pernar, C.H., Ebot, E.M., Wilson, K.M., Mucci, L.A.: The epidemiology of prostate cancer. Cold Spring Harb. Perspect. Med. **8**(12), a030361 (2018)

12. Pienta, K.J., Esper, P.S.: Risk factors for prostate cancer. Ann. Intern. Med. **118**(10), 793–803 (1993)
13. Rawla, P.: Epidemiology of prostate cancer. World J. Oncol. **10**(2), 63 (2019)
14. Vidiyala, N., et al.: Artificial intelligence: a new era in prostate cancer diagnosis and treatment. Inter. J. Pharmaceut., 126024 (2025)

XAI-Driven Fine-Tuned EfficientNetV2 Model for White Blood Cell Classification

Channabasava Chola[1,2(✉)] ⓘ, M. Pramodha[1,3] ⓘ, J. Hanumanthappa[1] ⓘ,
B. Anjali[4] ⓘ, Abdullah Y. Muaad[1,5] ⓘ, and Atul Tiwari[6] ⓘ

[1] Department of Studies in Computer Science, University of Mysore, Mysore, India
channabasavac7@gmail.com
[2] School of International Education, Huanghuai University, Zhumadian, Henan, China
[3] Department of Artificial Intelligence and Data Science, Mysore University School of
Engineering (MUSE), University of Mysore, Manasagangothri, Mysore, India
[4] Department of Computer Science, Maharani Science College Women, Maharani Cluster
University, Bangalore, Karnataka, India
[5] AI Department, Sana'a Community College, Sana'a, Yemen
[6] Department of Pathology, Government Medical College, Chittorgarh, Rajasthan, India

Abstract. Automated recognition of white blood cells (WBCs) is essential for rapid and reliable hematological diagnosis. This study presents a deep learning approach using the EfficientNetV2L architecture with a customized classification head for multiclass WBC classification. The model was trained in two stages: an initial phase where the classifier head was optimized with the backbone frozen, followed by fine-tuning of the deeper layers. To improve generalization, dropout, L2 regularization, and label smoothing were incorporated. The proposed framework achieved an overall accuracy of 99%, with class-wise F1-scores ranging between 0.95 and 0.99. Confusion matrix analysis confirmed minimal misclassification, and the ROC curves yielded near-perfect AUC values across all five classes. These findings demonstrate that the proposed EfficientNetV2L-based model is highly effective for robust and reliable WBC classification, indicating its potential application in clinical decision support systems.

Keywords: Medical Imaging · Explainable AI · White Blood Cells · Classification

1 Introduction

White blood cells (WBCs), crucial components of our immune system often referred to as leukocytes or WBCs [1], are essential for defending infections and coordinating bodily responses. Changes in WBC's quantity or subtype mix, especially when considering cell appearance under a microscope, frequently provide the earliest signs for doctors while trying to diagnose serious conditions like Acute Myeloid Leukemia (AML), Acute Lymphoblastic Leukemia (ALL), and other hematological disorders [2–4]. Automating WBC's analysis is an important because small but meaningful differences in shape or

© The Author(s), under exclusive license to Springer Nature Switzerland AG 2026
H. Kannan et al. (Eds.): AIKP 2025, CCIS 2804, pp. 42–52, 2026.
https://doi.org/10.1007/978-3-032-14706-6_4

detail can be critical clues even experienced pathologists rely on cell morphology [5–7]. Yet, while WBC classification remains a core routine task for clinicians who need reliable results from blood tests, automated systems are still largely manual in many places due to the practical limitations.

Experienced pathologists deliver accurate diagnoses via microscopy but the process is slow and labor intensive, it also requires significant time and resources [8–10] Furthermore, interpretation can vary between different observers (inter observer variability), suffer from human fatigue affecting consistency over long periods [8], or become unreliable when faced with slight variations in blood samples are preparation across different labs (staining) or imaging (microscopes and camera) devices issues like inconsistent staining or equipment differences complicate the diagnostic picture. These constraints have fueled research into automated image based diagnosis systems, promising towards scalable screening (handle more tests), speed up results (reduce turnaround time), and provide reliable measurements for clinical guidance [8, 9].

Initial automation efforts adopted specialized classical classifiers or powerful pre-trained computer vision models from other domains via transfer learning. This proved highly effective at adapting strong visual capabilities quickly, offering a big advantage over traditional methods needing lots of manual feature engineering [8, 9]. Combining different CNN architectures (i.e. ensemble) technique enhanced diagnostic confidence by pooling diverse information sources together [11]. More recent developments focus on making models faster and lighter for wider use (e.g., edge deployment), capturing long-range context better, and developing attention mechanisms without sacrificing performance. For instance, lightweight networks combined with "attention" modules allow doctors to trust the diagnosis even when computational power is limited ("lightweight, explainable point-of-care") [12]. Architecture incorporating Attention with long-range context via combining pixel correlation blocks or embedding attention recalibration, aim specifically for finding subtle clues in noisy images. Transformer-based approaches and hybrid designs are also being explored to capture broader context missed by earlier CNNs [13, 14].

In Table 1 addressing the issue of limited data ("EfficientNet variants") allows reliable models to be trained even when expert-annotated samples with few-shot learning [16]. And work continues on improving sample preparation techniques, stain normalization, and segmentation methods to ensure consistent results across different labs or equipment types a major hurdle for widespread tool adoption due to acquisition artifacts like staining differences ("biomimetic perspectives," e.g., insights from redblood cell principles) are also being considered [4, 9, 17].

Taken together, these developments have significantly advanced automated WBC analysis. Yet, significant challenges remain: models often fail across labs or stains (dataset shift), ambiguity between closely related cell types persists (subtype confusion), and reliable generalization to all clinical settings requires a path towards lightweight, explainable AI that hasn't been fully found yet [4, 9, 10]. The pressing need is therefore for systems delivering robust feature modeling of global/local context and data-efficient learning strategies while ensuring clinical interpretability. This triple focus on robustness and data efficiency are essential for realizing practical automated WBC diagnostic

Table 1. Discussion of existing approaches for WBC detection.

Author	Method/Model	Dataset/Diagnosis	Result/Performance
Aryal et al.,2025 [15]	AFMNet with ARM & DFAB	PBC, Raabin (WBC classification)	99.57% (PBC), 98.89% (Raabin)
Li et al., 2025 [12]	Lightweight network + Bottleneck Attention Module	Private 5-class WBC dataset	High accuracy, precision, recall, F1
Yin et al., 2025 [4]	Dual-branch CNN with hyperspectral imaging	120 bone marrow smears (Normal, AML, ALL)	91.57% (external validation), 100% subset
Asghar et al., 2024 [8]	Transfer learning with pre-trained CNNs (VGG16, ResNet, MobileNet, DenseNet)	PBC, Kaggle, LISC (10 blood cell types)	98.79–99.91%
Wang et al., 2025 [16]	Few-shot learning with FRNE + Improved EfficientNetV2	LDWBC, Rabbin datasets	+3.67%, +1.27% accuracy improvement
Davamani et al., 2025 [9]	Deep transfer learning (VGG16, MobileNet, ResNet50, AlexNet, GoogLeNet, EfficientNetB0)	Kaggle WBC images (4 classes)	99.35–100% per class
Dong et al., 2024 [11]	Ensemble CNN (VGG16, ResNet50, InceptionV3)	WBC images	Improved reliability & accuracy (exact not specified)
Elghandour, 2025 [13]	ViT + PCA + NCA + Bayesian-optimized FC	Raabin-WBC (5 classes)	99.03%
Üzen & Firat, 2024 [14]	Hybrid SC-MP-Mixer (ConvMixer + Swin Transformer)	BCCD (4), PBC (8), Raabin (5)	95.66–99.65%
Luo et al., 2024 [10]	ResNeXt-CC(cross layer feature fusion + ECANet attention)	C-NMC 2019	5.5–20.43% accuracy improvement vs baselines

systems that can reliably assist doctors across different healthcare settings. In next we address the methods and results of proposed XAI based WBC classification model.

2   Methods and Materials

The proposed AI based WBC classification model is addressed in following subsections as input data of Fig. 1. Followed by overview of proposed model in Fig. 2 EfficientNetV2L [18] adopted as backbone for classification.

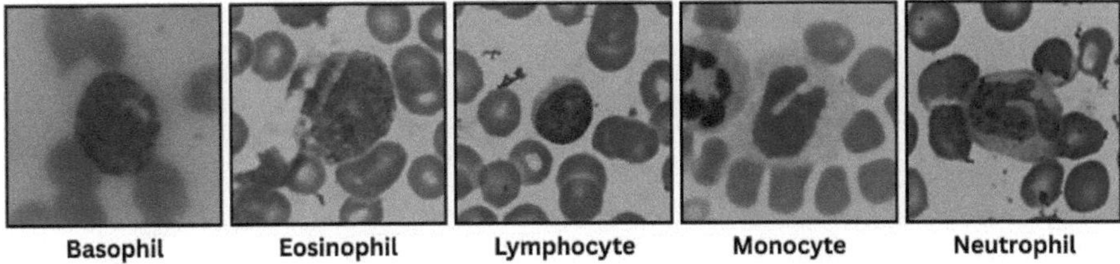

Fig. 1. Visualization of samples from WBC dataset.

2.1 Dataset

In proposed XAI based WBC classification model is developed on Rabbin-WBC[1] dataset. Data-imbalance present in dataset and captured with microscopes with 100x zoom on Zeiss and Olympus Cx18 setup with Geimsa staining. Then images were captured on Mobile phones for data digitization with Samsung galaxy S5 and LG G3, Later labelled with 2 experts [19]. The dataset consisted of images of five types of white blood cells (WBCs): basophils, eosinophils, lymphocytes, monocytes, and neutrophils [1]. Each image was paired with its corresponding class label, and the dataset was divided into training, validation, and test sets using a stratified split to preserve class distribution. Given the natural imbalance in WBC types, with neutrophils being the majority class, augmentation and label smoothing were employed to minimize bias.

2.2 Preprocessing

All images were resized to 224^2 pixels 3 channels to match the input size from the baseline size of 512^2 pixels 3 channels of EfficientNetV2L. Standard normalization based on ImageNet statistics was applied. To improve generalization and account for variations in microscopic imaging conditions, an online augmentation pipeline was used, including randomized rotation, flip, zoom and transformation. In addition this gaussian blur, brightness and contrast adjustment adopted overall the balance of classes which results in reduced overfitting of model.

2.3 WBC Classification Model

The Proposed Fig. 2. WBC classification model adopted was EfficientNetV2L, a state-of-the-art convolutional neural network pretrained on ImageNet. The network was loaded without the final classification layer, and a global pooling layer was used to reduce the feature maps. As addressed in Table 2.

The backbone of the model was the EfficientNetV2L convolutional neural network, set up with global max pooling to turn spatial feature maps into a fixed-length feature vector. Initially, we froze the backbone layers to avoid updates during the first phase of training. This approach allowed the added classifier head to learn representations specific to the dataset. The classifier head included two fully connected layers with 128

---

[1] https://raabindata.com/.

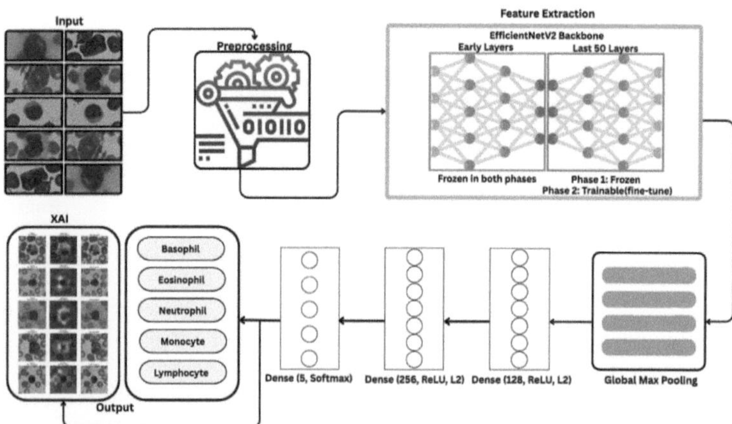

Fig. 2. Proposed WBC classification model with XAI integration.

Table 2. Proposed model parameters for WBC classification

Layer/ Block	Output Shape	Parameters (trainable in fine-tuning)	Context
Input Layer	$(224^2, 3)$	–	Input image
Efficient-NetV2L Backbone	(None, 1280)	~117M (frozen initially in Phase 1, last 50 layers unfrozen in Phase 2)	Pretrained on ImageNet
Dense Layer 1	(None, 128)	163,968	ReLU + L2 regularization
Dropout (0.45)	(None, 128)	–	Prevents overfitting
Dense Layer 2	(None, 256)	33,024	ReLU + L2 regularization
Dropout (0.45)	(None, 256)	–	Prevents overfitting
Dense (Softmax)	(None, 5)	1,285	Multiclass classification

and 256 neurons, respectively. Each was followed by a dropout layer with a rate of 0.45 to reduce overfitting. We applied L2 regularization (1e−4) to both dense layers to stabilize training. The final output layer had five neurons with a softmax activation function, corresponding to the five target classes.

2.4 Training Strategy

Phase 1: Feature Extraction

In the first phase, we only trained the classifier head while keeping the backbone frozen. We compiled the model using the Adam optimizer with a learning rate of 1e−4. We used categorical cross-entropy loss with label smoothing (0.1) to enhance generalization. Early stopping, model checkpointing, and validation monitoring helped prevent overfitting and ensured we kept the best-performing model. This phase lasted for 15 epochs.

Phase 2: Fine-Tuning

In the second phase, we unfroze the last 50 layers of the EfficientNetV2L backbone to allow fine-tuning of high-level features. We reduced the learning rate to 1e−5 to prevent large weight updates that could destabilize the pretrained features. We applied the same loss function and callbacks as in the first phase, continuing training for an additional 30 epochs. This two-stage approach ensured that low-level features remained stable while high-level representations adjusted to the specific dataset.

2.5 Evaluation Metrics

To evaluate the performance of ML models, we considered several evaluation methods including accuracy, precision, recall, F-1 score, and AUC (Area Under the Curve). These performances were assessed using the confusion matrix, which comprises true positive (TP), true negative (TN), false positive (FP), and false negative (FN) elements.

$$\text{Sensitivity (Recall)} = \frac{\text{(TP)}}{\text{(TP)} + \text{(FN)}} \tag{i}$$

$$\text{Specificity} = \frac{\text{(TN)}}{\text{(TN)} + \text{(FP)}} \tag{ii}$$

$$\text{Accuracy} = \frac{\text{(TP)} + \text{(TN)}}{\text{(TP + FP + FN + TN)}} \tag{iii}$$

$$\text{F1 Score} = \frac{2\text{(TP)}}{2\text{(TP)} + \text{(FP)} + \text{(FN)}} \tag{iv}$$

2.6 Explainable AI Approaches

To interpret the model's predictions and build trust, Grad-CAM and LIME were used. Grad-CAM visualizations pointed out which parts of the cells influenced the classification decisions, showing that the model focused on important structural features. Likewise, LIME provided explanations for individual predictions, confirming that the model's choices aligned with relevant biological features. These XAI analyses confirm that the model not only achieves high accuracy but also bases its decisions on significant cellular patterns.

3 Results

The experimental results show that the proposed EfficientNetV2L-based model effectively classifies five types of white blood cells (WBCs): basophils, eosinophils, lymphocytes, monocytes, and neutrophils.

Classification Performance: Table 1 summarizes the classification metrics. Fine-tuning the EfficientNet-V2 architecture leads to a significant improvement in classification performance compared to the baseline model trained without domain adaptation. The overall accuracy rises from 88% to an impressive 99%. This improvement reflects a substantial decrease in misclassifications across all five blood cell categories. Macro-averaged recall, which gives equal weight to each class, jumps by 28 percentage points, from 69% to 97%. This indicates that the fine-tuned network is now highly sensitive to minority classes like eosinophils and monocytes. Similarly, the macro-averaged F1 score increases by 25 percentage points, from 73% to 98%. This shows balanced improvements in both precision and recall. The most notable gains occur in the eosinophil class, where recall rises from a low 21% to almost perfect 97%, allowing for reliable detection of what was previously a challenging category. Monocyte recall also improves significantly, from 49% to 93%. Precision increases slightly across all classes, resulting in near-perfect per-class F1 scores for the fine-tuned model.

These results confirm the effectiveness of targeted fine-tuning strategies, likely involving class-balanced sampling and loss weighting, in addressing dataset imbalance and improving diagnostic accuracy. In a clinical context where accurately identifying rare hematological cell types is crucial, these performance gains make the fine-tuned EfficientNet-V2 more suitable for automated blood smear analysis than its untuned version (Table 3).

Table 3. Comparison of classification metrics between fine-tuned and non-fine-tuned Efficient-NetV2L model for WBC types

Classes	Fine-tuned			Without Fine-tuning		
	Precision	Recall	F-Measure	Precision	Recall	F-Measure
Basophil	1.00	0.99	0.99	0.95	0.88	0.92
Eosinophil	0.98	0.95	0.96	0.91	0.21	0.34
Lymphocyte	0.98	0.99	0.99	0.86	0.91	0.88
Monocyte	0.99	0.92	0.95	0.77	0.49	0.6
Neutrophil	0.99	1.00	0.99	0.89	0.97	0.93

The confusion matrix (Fig. 1) supports these findings. Most misclassifications occurred between monocytes and lymphocytes, while basophils and neutrophils were rarely confused. This suggests that the model effectively identified distinct morphological features. However, overlapping characteristics in certain subtypes still pose challenges (Fig. 3).

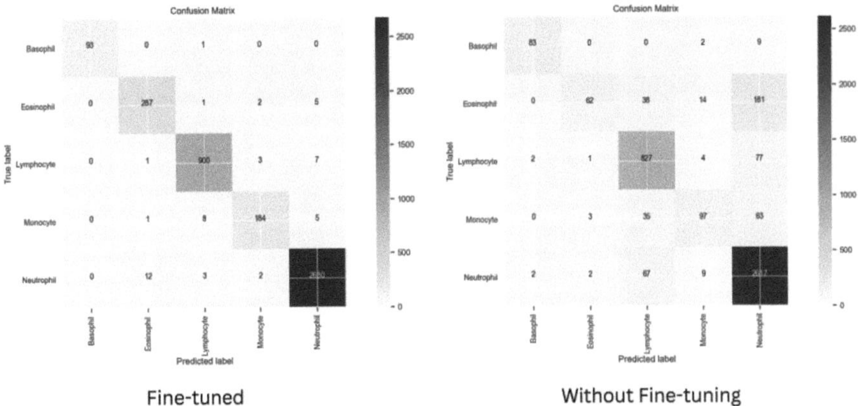

Fine-tuned   Without Fine-tuning

Fig. 3. Confusion Matrix of proposed WBC classification model

Robustness and Generalization: Despite the class imbalance in the dataset, particularly with neutrophils being the majority class, the model maintained consistent performance. This robustness comes from several regularization strategies, such as label smoothing, dropout (0.45), and L2 weight penalties. The ROC curves (Fig. 2) demonstrate the model's ability to distinguish between classes, with all classes achieving AUC values close to 1.0, indicating excellent separation (Fig. 4).

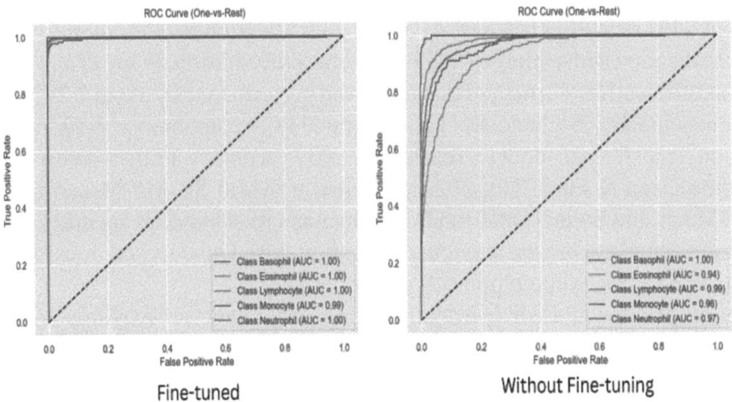

Fine-tuned   Without Fine-tuning

Fig. 4. ROC curve of proposed WBC classification model

Comparison and Training Strategy: Compared to traditional CNN-based approaches, EfficientNetV2L showed better performance and generalization. The two-phase training strategy, which involved freezing the backbone in the first phase and fine-tuning the last 50 layers in the second phase, was vital in preventing overfitting while adapting the model to specific features of the domain. The adaptive learning rate scheduler also helped ensure smooth and steady convergence (Fig. 5).

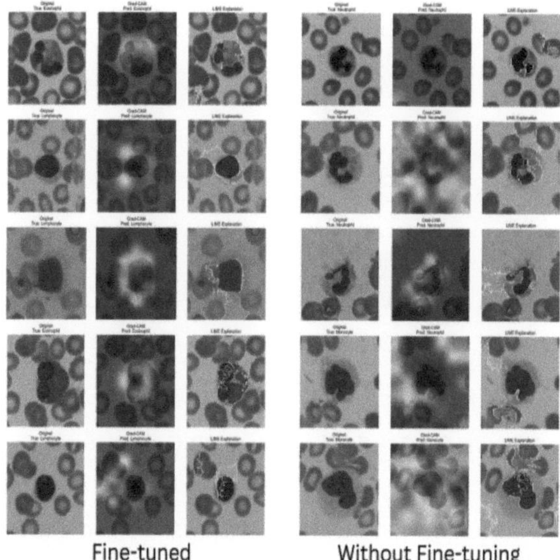

Fine-tuned   Without Fine-tuning

Fig. 5. Proposed WBC classification models XAI demonstration

4 Discussion

Recent research on white blood cell (WBC) classification shows impressive results. Aryal et al. [15] recently proposed AFMNet with attention recalibration for automated WBC classification and achieved 98.89% accuracy. In addition, Wang et al. [16] adopted a few-shot EfficientNetV2 method that improved performance by about 1.27% compared to earlier benchmarks. Elghandour [13], integrated PCA combined with NCA techniques into Vision Transformer models, reaching 99.03% accuracy in their latest study from 2025, while Üzen & Firat [14], 2024 presented a hybrid SC-MP-Mixer model merging ConvMixer and Swin Transformer architectures to achieve an accuracy of 98.68%. These findings underscore the strength of attention-based models and transformer-based methods in analyzing white blood cell morphology.

However, these studies share a common drawback: they lack explainable AI, or XAI techniques. Although these models perform well, their operation is opaque functioning like "black boxes" making them challenging to interpret, which limits clinical trust during validation for medical applications (Table 4).

Our work stands apart by using fine-tuned EfficientNetV2 and XAI integration in a five-class WBC classification setup, reaching 98.78% accuracy while addressing the need for explainability through visual explanations. This combination offers both high performance and transparency, making it suitable for clinical use with improved trust and reliability.

Table 4. Result comparative of proposed work with existing studies.

Author(s) & Year	Method	Classes	Accuracy/Result	Diagnosis	XAI
Aryal et al., 2025 [15]	AFMNet (Adaptive Feature Modulation Network with ARM & DFAB)	5 WBC classes	98.89% (Raabin dataset)	WBC classification for leukemia and blood disorders	No
Elghandour, 2025 [13]	Vision Transformer (ViT) + PCA + NCA + Bayesian-optimized FC	5 WBC classes	99.03%	WBC classification, improved feature separability	No
Üzen & Firat, 2024 [14]	SC-MP-Mixer (ConvMixer + Swin Transformer multipath)	5 WBC classes	98.68%	WBC classification for clinical diagnosis	No
Present study	Finetuned EfficientNetV2	5 WBC classes	98.78%	WBC classification for clinical diagnosis	Yes

5 Conclusions

This study demonstrates that EfficientNetV2L, when combined with appropriate regularization and a two-stage training protocol, can achieve state-of-the-art performance in WBC classification. The proposed model obtained 99% accuracy with high precision and recall across all five classes, confirming its reliability. Minor misclassifications between morphologically similar classes such as monocytes and lymphocytes suggest avenues for improvement, potentially through attention mechanisms or hybrid models. Given its robustness and interpretability, this frame-work can be integrated into clinical diagnostic pipelines as a supportive tool for hematologists.

References

1. Tavakoli, S., Ghaffari, A., Kouzehkanan, Z.M., Hosseini, R.: New segmentation and feature extraction algorithm for classification of white blood cells in peripheral smear images. Sci. Rep. **11**(1), 19428 (2021). https://doi.org/10.1038/s41598-021-98599-0
2. Devi, T.G., Patil, N., Rai, S., Philipose, C.S.: Gaussian blurring technique for detecting and classifying acute lymphoblastic leukemia cancer cells from microscopic biopsy images. Life **13**(2) (2023). https://doi.org/10.3390/life13020348
3. Devi, T.G., Patil, N., Rai, S., Sarah, C.P.: Segmentation and classification of white blood cancer cells from bone marrow microscopic images using duplet-convolutional neural network design. Multimed. Tools Appl. **82**(23), 35277–35299 (2023). https://doi.org/10.1007/s11042-023-14899-9

4. Yin, H., et al.: Classification of normal, AML, and ALL bone marrow smears based on deep learning and hyperspectral microscopic imaging. Sens. Actuators B Chem. **438** (2025). https://doi.org/10.1016/j.snb.2025.137800

5. Rastogi, P., Khanna, K., Singh, V.: LeuFeatx: deep learning–based feature extractor for the diagnosis of acute leukemia from microscopic images of peripheral blood smear. Comput. Biol. Med. **142**, 105236 (2022). https://doi.org/10.1016/j.compbiomed.2022.105236

6. Pramodha, M., et al.: A deep learning model for human blood cells classification. In: Saeed, F., Mohammed, F., Mohammed, E., Al-Hadhrami, T., Al-Sarem, M. (eds.) ICACIn 2022. LNDECT, vol. 179, pp. 410–418. Springer, Cham (2023). https://doi.org/10.1007/978-3-031-36258-3_36

7. Chola, C., et al.: BCNet: a deep learning computer-aided diagnosis framework for human peripheral blood cell identification. Diagnostics **12**(11), 2815 (2022). https://doi.org/10.3390/diagnostics12112815

8. Asghar, R., Kumar, S., Hynds, P.: Automatic classification of 10 blood cell subtypes using transfer learning via pre-trained convolutional neural networks. Inform. Med. Unlocked **49**, 101542 (2024). https://doi.org/10.1016/J.IMU.2024.101542

9. Davamani, K.A., Jawahar, M., Anbarasi, L.J., Ravi, V., Al Mazroa, A., Robin, C.R.R.: Deep transfer learning technique to detect white blood cell classification in regular clinical practice using histopathological images. Multimed. Tools Appl. **84**(9), 5699–5723 (2025). https://doi.org/10.1007/s11042-024-19133-8

10. Luo, Y., Xu, Y., Wang, C., Li, Q., Fu, C., Jiang, H.: ResNeXt-CC: a novel network based on cross-layer deep-feature fusion for white blood cell classification. Sci. Rep. **14**(1), 1–15 (2024). https://doi.org/10.1038/s41598-024-69076-1

11. Dong, N., Feng, Q., Chang, J., Mai, X.: White blood cell classification based on a novel ensemble convolutional neural network framework. J. Supercomput. **80**(1), 249–270 (2024). https://doi.org/10.1007/s11227-023-05490-y

12. Li, H., et al.: A high-performance and lightweight five-class white blood cell classification network optimized by attention mechanisms. Neurocomputing **653**, 131246 (2025). https://doi.org/10.1016/j.neucom.2025.131246

13. Elghandour, M.: PCA-NCA based VIT features for classification of white blood cell images **81**(13) (2025). https://doi.org/10.1007/s11227-025-07753-2

14. Üzen, H., Fırat, H.: A hybrid approach based on multipath Swin transformer and ConvMixer for white blood cells classification. Heal. Inf. Sci. Syst. **12**(1), 1–19 (2024). https://doi.org/10.1007/s13755-024-00291-w

15. Aryal, S., Kumar Naik, S., Madarapu, S., Ari, S.: AFMNet: adaptive feature modulation network for classification of white blood cells. Biocybern. Biomed. Eng. **45**(3), 539–548 (2025). https://doi.org/10.1016/J.BBE.2025.07.006

16. Wang, X., Ou, C., Pan, G., Hu, Z., Cao, K.: Few-shot leukocyte classification algorithm based on feature reconstruction network with improved EfficientNetV2. Appl. Sci. **15**(17), 1–21 (2025). https://doi.org/10.3390/app15179377

17. Waeterschoot, J., Gosselé, W., Lemež, Š., Casadevall i Solvas, X.: Artificial cells for in vivo biomedical applications through red blood cell biomimicry. Nat. Commun. **15**(1) (2024). https://doi.org/10.1038/s41467-024-46732-8

18. Tan, M., Le, Q.V.: EfficientNetV2: smaller models and faster training. Proc. Mach. Learn. Res. **139**, 10096–10106 (2021)

19. Kouzehkanan, Z.M., et al.: A large dataset of white blood cells containing cell locations and types, along with segmented nuclei and cytoplasm. Sci. Rep. **12**(1), 1–14 (2022). https://doi.org/10.1038/s41598-021-04426-x

RAG System Application for Supporting Drug Discovery and Docking Molecular Processes

Julián David Forero[1,2], Alexander Rodriguez-Lopez[2],
and Alvaro D. Orjuela-Cañón[2(✉)] (iD)

[1] Escuela Colombiana de Ingeniería Julio Garavito, Bogota D.C., Colombia
`julianda.forero@urosario.edu.co`
[2] School of Medicine and Health Sciences, Universidad del Rosario, Bogota D.C., Colombia
`alvaro.orjuela@urosario.edu.co`

Abstract. This work presents the design and validation of a semantic retrieval and natural language generation pipeline aimed at supporting molecular docking studies through compound recommendation and scientific literature contextualization. The pipeline integrates biomedical data processing, semantic indexing with FAISS, and language modeling using BioBERT and TinyLlama-1.1B-Chat to generate concise and informative responses. A curated scientific corpus was built from sources such as PubMed, and embeddings were generated to enable semantic similarity searches. The system was tested using ellagic acid as a query compound, successfully retrieving relevant literature and presenting detailed chemical information from the COCONUT database. In parallel, this research aligns with ongoing efforts from the Semill-IAS research group at Universidad del Rosario, which focuses on inclusive health technologies, particularly the use of artificial intelligence for different health contexts. The proposed solution demonstrates the potential of combining machine learning models with biomedical informatics for accessible, data-driven decision support in health and drug discovery domains.

Keywords: Molecular Docking; Semantic Retrieval · Natural Language Generation · Biomedical Informatics · Artificial Intelligence in Healthcare

1 Introduction

Retrieval Augmented Generation (RAG) is a set of artificial intelligence (AI) tools, employing to generate information, based on large language models (LLM) and a retrieval system information. First, a query from a user is established about a specific topic. Then, the search is augmented based on an external database to improve the original query. Finally, the generation is provided by employing a LLM. Basically, this RAG pipeline searches for providing a better answer from the LLM, through the use of a specific and external database, making the result more accurate, contextualized and updated information [1–3].

In the field of bioinformatics, the vast potential of AI systems becomes increasingly clear, especially in their capacity to process large volumes of data from diverse

H. Kannan et al. (Eds.): AIKP 2025, CCIS 2804, pp. 53–63, 2026.
https://doi.org/10.1007/978-3-032-14706-6_5

sources. RAG systems can be integrated to enhance workflows in decision-making, leading to improvements in processing time, optimization of computational resources, and more efficient use of human expertise. Notable applications of RAG systems are already emerging in areas such as gene and genomic analysis [4, 5]. This is especially significant, as improved data analysis directly contributes to advancing medical practices and supporting healthcare professionals in delivering better, evidence-based care [6, 7].

Computational approaches in bioinformatics, particularly within computational biology, have significantly advanced applications such as molecular docking. This technique simulates ligand-receptor interactions to predict binding patterns, thereby playing a crucial role in optimizing drug design [8–10]. Molecular docking serves as a powerful *in silico* platform for screening small molecules and refining their structural properties without the need for costly biological experiments. This enables the efficient identification of potential therapeutic candidates while reducing time, resources, and experimental overhead [8, 10, 11].

Another relevant application of molecular data analysis lies in drug discovery strategies aimed at identifying small compounds that can be used in the design and development of new pharmaceuticals [12, 13]. Within this context, numerous studies have investigated the therapeutic potential of various bioactive substances for treating a wide range of disorders. Moreover, some of these studies have focused on the use of plant-derived compounds and other natural products, exploring their efficacy in animal models as alternative or complementary therapeutic options [13–15]. This growing interest in natural bioactive molecules reflects the ongoing search for safer, more sustainable drug candidates within the field of pharmacological research.

Despite the promising findings and proposed alternatives across these fields, the volume and complexity of data sources and analyses continue to grow exponentially, creating a research landscape that increasingly exceeds human analytical capacity. To address this challenge, recent advancements in AI—particularly through Retrieval-Augmented Generation (RAG)—have aimed to integrate diverse data sources into unified analytical frameworks. For instance, the application of retrieval augmentation for molecular generation has been explored in [16]. Similarly, AI models capable of generating drug candidates based on binding affinity predictions, designing small molecules to fit specific 3D target pockets, have been investigated in [17]. Ongoing research is further refining these approaches for specialized applications, such as enhancing results in enzyme-related tasks [18], or incorporating pharmacophore information into molecular generation processes [19].

The diversity of biomolecules, application areas, treatment strategies, and related factors continues to pose challenges for the full implementation of RAG systems in this domain. Additionally, language plays a crucial role in interpreting and contextualizing the outputs generated by these systems. For this reason, the aim of this work is to propose a RAG-based approach tailored to the Spanish language, designed to support drug discovery and molecular docking tasks, particularly those involving natural compounds.

2   Methodology

To tackle the challenge of compound recommendation and literature background analysis in the context of molecular docking and drug discovery, a comprehensive pipeline was developed that seamlessly integrates semantic retrieval techniques with natural language generation. This approach enables the extraction of relevant scientific knowledge and the formulation of insightful responses tailored to user queries. The methodology comprises several key stages, which are detailed in the following subsections. Figure 1 shows the followed pipeline for RAG-based proposal.

2.1   Databases Preparation

Two sources for establishing the external database were implemented. A first source is related to the molecular information, and a second one, from the scientific literature that provide evidence of previous results. Both sources were relevant for the implementation process due to the possibility of compounds existence from nature, to developed the chemical proposal.

The COCONUT (*COlleCtion of Open NatUral producTs*) database was taken into account for molecular information [20]. This database provides natural compounds from open sources, providing molecular structures, names, related species, and geographical information. The database was loaded and normalized to ensure robust molecular detection. This process involved standardizing compound names, removing inconsistencies, and harmonizing synonyms to allow accurate identification of each molecule. In addition, different preprocessing routines were applied to clean metadata, ensuring that the database could be queried uniformly and that the chemical information would be compatible with downstream tasks. This initial step is essential to prevent duplication and to ensure data quality in subsequent recommendations.

The scientific corpus was collected from specialized sources such as PubMed [21]. Titles and abstracts from these papers were extracted and compiled to serve as a foundational biomedical knowledge base for the system. The selection of articles was based on relevance to molecular docking and drug discovery, natural compounds, and related biomedical applications. This corpus represents the informational external database of the system and supports the generation of meaningful recommendations grounded in scientific literature. This information is relevant to complement the data provided by CONONUT, according to establish a better context of the molecular docking and drug discovery applications.

2.2   Biomedical Embedding and Semantical Retrieval

Each paper abstract was transformed into a numerical vector through embeddings using the BioBERT model [22], a transformer-based language model pre-trained specifically on biomedical text. This transformation captures the semantic meaning of each text, enabling nuanced comparison between user queries and literature content. The use of BioBERT allows the system to understand biomedical terminology and context with greater depth than generic language models. As a result, the pipeline can match user inputs with semantically similar texts, even when the wording differs.

All embeddings were indexed using Facebook AI similarity search (FAISS), a library optimized for fast retrieval of high-dimensional vectors [23]. This indexing enabled the system to rapidly retrieve the most relevant articles in response to a user's query, based on meaning rather than keyword matching.

By leveraging semantic similarity rather than lexical overlap, this step significantly improves the relevance and precision of the retrieved information, ensuring that users receive scientifically meaningful background data even for complex or specialized terms.

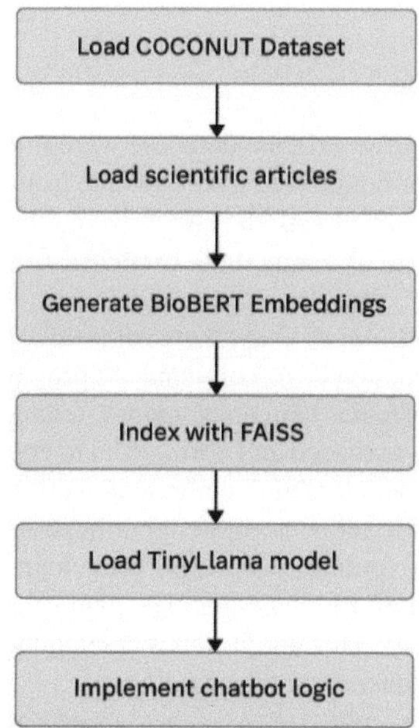

Fig. 1. Diagram of the pipeline for the RAG development

2.3 Automatic Answer Generation

The user's query was combined with the retrieved paper abstracts to create a comprehensive prompt. This prompt was then processed by TinyLlama-1.1B-Chat, a lightweight generative model optimized for technical responses in natural language [24]. In the RAG system the prompt determines the query (see Fig. 2), for this motivation and the portability of Llama model this chat was considered [25, 26].

The output was a concise, informative response that provided methodological insights and suggested relevant natural compounds. This automated generation of expert-level summaries enhances usability for researchers seeking quick, evidence-based insights.

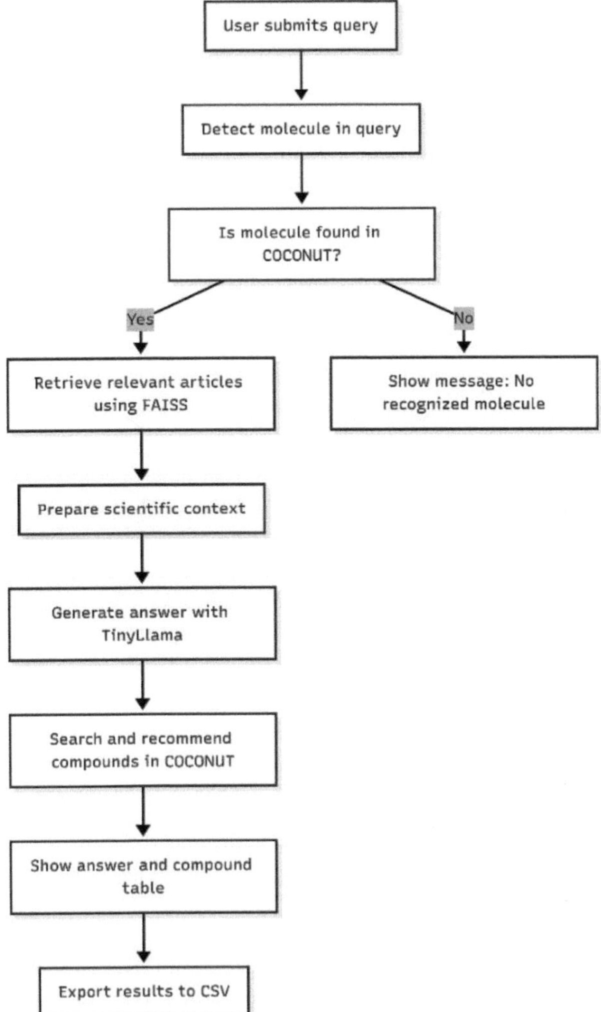

Fig. 2. Diagram of the work flow for information query

In the final stage, the system cross-referenced the recommended molecule with entries in the COCONUT database (see Fig. 2). This is a contrastive difference related to other chats due to the relevance in the present case. If a match was found, a detailed table was presented, including structural diagrams, molecular formula, molecular weight, source organisms, synonyms, and CAS numbers.

This tabular output provides users with direct access to essential chemical information, supporting both experimental planning and in silico analysis. The integration of literature and compound data into a single workflow streamlines the research process and enhances decision-making in biomedical and pharmaceutical contexts (Table 1 resumes the tools employed for the RAG implementation).

2.4 Evaluation System

To evaluate the pipeline's capabilities and topic coverage, queries were designed using five representative terms for both drug discovery and molecular docking. The selected terms were: Genistein, Apigenin, Ellagic acid, Quercetin, and Curcumin. These natural compounds are widely studied in the scientific literature due to their pharmacological relevance and structural diversity [27]. Choosing these terms enables exploration of real-world use cases in biomedical research and ensures the system's responses are aligned with common interests in the scientific community. All queries were formulated in English, covering scenarios for both discovering related compounds for drug discovery and identifying compounds relevant to molecular docking studies.

In addition, a second evaluation was conducted based on the expertise of a bioinformatician. The expert recommended incorporating criteria related to biological validation into the system's reference documents. To address this, ten prompts were applied to the system, specifically targeting responses associated with molecular docking and drug discovery in isolation. Furthermore, ten relevant natural compounds were selected by the expert for inclusion in the evaluation: Genistein, Resveratrol, Curcumin, Trehalose, Rhamnocitrin, Dihydroxytrimethoxyflavone, Quercetin, Myricitrin, Rutin, and Limonene.

Finally, following the guidelines in [28–30], the RAG system was evaluated in terms of correctness, relevance, and groundedness. For this purpose, three advanced LLMs were employed—Copilot, ChatGPT-5, and Gemini 2.5 Flash, by using a prompt-based strategy to assess system responses across the three aforementioned dimensions.

3 Results

Results can be displayed through the reports for both contexts: drug discovery (see Fig. 3) and molecular docking (see Fig. 4). Figures were produced based on the results obtained after running the pipeline for each query. For every term, the system automatically quantified the number of relevant scientific articles found in the knowledge base and the number of associated compounds detected in the Coconut database. These counts were collected and visualized using bar charts, separating the results for drug discovery and molecular docking into two independent graphs. The X-axis of each graph represents the queries performed (identified by the central term), while the Y-axis shows the number of articles and compounds found. This approach enables an easy comparison of the pipeline's coverage and specificity across different terms and tasks.

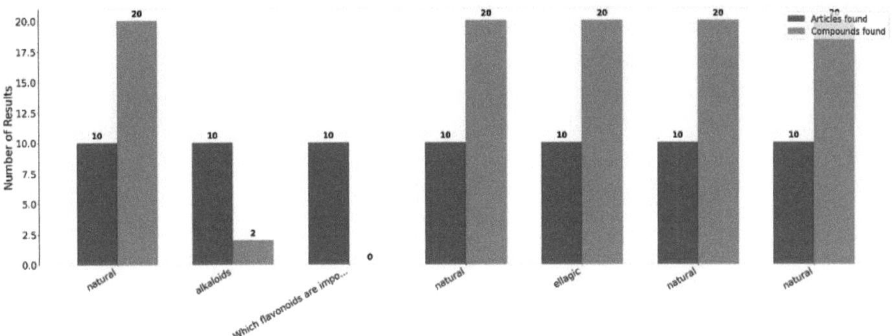

Fig. 3. Results in drug discovery context for seven different queries

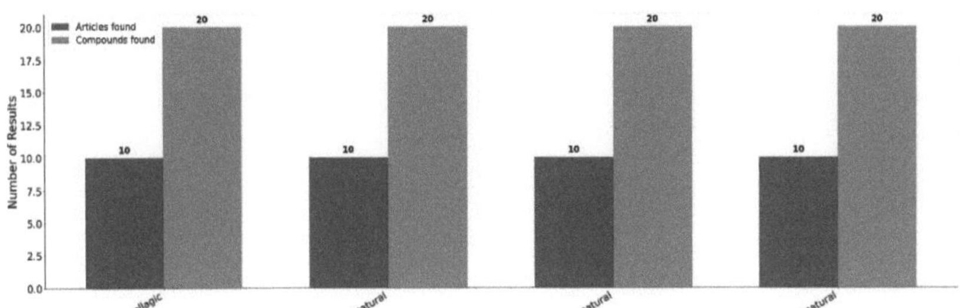

Fig. 4. Results in molecular docking context for four different queries

Table 1. RAG summarized details implemented.

RAG Element	Used Tool
Database 1	COCONUT
Database 2	PubMed
Embeddings	BioBERT
LLM	TinyLlama-1.1B-Chat

According to the expert bioinformatician's guidance, Table 2 reports the results for ten natural compounds in the context of molecular docking and drug discovery. The evaluation was framed around biological validation, and Table 2 summarizes the positive responses observed across all compounds.

Table 3 presents the evaluation outcomes from the LLMs based on the three predefined parameters. Copilot indicated that the system effectively identifies promising molecules and emphasized that further refinements in compound specificity and article diversity could substantially enhance performance. ChatGPT-5 reported high accuracy in detecting "docking" (84.5%) and strong article recency (94.5%), yet only moderate disease alignment (52.3%) and poor compound-specific matches (2%). Regarding compounds, name matching reached 51%, while structural completeness was nearly perfect (~100%); however, article duplication was excessive (80.5%). Gemini concluded that the system meets its objectives by delivering accurate and relevant information for state-of-the-art research, while recommending greater specificity in article selection to ensure both compound and target are consistently matched.

Table 2. Answers according to the bioinformatician requirement.

Docking Molecular	Drug Discovery
6/10	9/10

Table 3. RAG Evaluated Through LLM.

RAG Element	Copilot	ChatGPT-5	Gemini 2.5 Flash
Precision	8.5	4.8	8
Retrieval	8	7.2	9
Relevance	9	8.4	8.5
Mean $\pm$ std	8.5 $\pm$ 0.5	6.8 $\pm$ 1.8	8.5 $\pm$ 0.5

4 Discussion

In the field of bioinformatics, particularly in the areas of drug discovery and molecular docking, only a limited number of studies have been reported. In comparison to a related study conducted in the context of nutrigenetics [5], the embedding technique used was based on General Text Embeddings (GTE), applied within a multi-stage contrastive learning framework. Additionally, the LLM employed in that study included GPT-3.5 and Mistral-7B. Notably, the approach was trained on a single dataset derived from De Filippis, which is specifically focused on nutrigenetics.

In medical applications, the MIRAGE benchmark has been established as a standard framework [6], utilizing five datasets (MMLU-Med, MedQA-US, and MedMCQA) for question-answering (QA) tasks. In this context, the MEDRAG toolkit was evaluated, achieving the best overall performance when GPT-4.0 was used as the large language model (LLM). However, when QA was specifically based on PubMed data, LLaMA outperformed the other models. In terms of retrievers, the highest performance was observed with MedCPT [6]. These findings suggest that, in biomedical analysis, most prior research has focused on using standard (vanilla) LLMs for QA tasks before the integration of RAG-based approaches [31].

GeneGPT is the approach most closely related to the present proposal. This method teaches to the LLM to interact with the National Center for Biotechnology Information

(NCBI) web APIs in order to extract relevant biological information [4]. It connects with datasets that include nucleotide sequences, single nucleotide polymorphisms (SNPs), and gene data, and also integrates tools such as BLAST for sequence alignment, among others. However, despite its advanced capabilities, this extended LLM cannot be considered a true RAG-based solution.

As presented, the current proposal aims to incorporate datasets containing diverse file types, including molecular data from natural compounds such as those found in the COCONUT database, as well as scientific literature from PubMed. While most existing studies rely primarily on PubMed as their main data source [32], this reliance can be seen as a limitation, as it excludes other valuable types of data. This proposal seeks to go beyond traditional RAG implementations, which typically use only document-based datasets, by integrating heterogeneous sources to enrich the analysis and broaden the scope of potential applications.

According to Tables 2 and 3, the system's accuracy can be estimated in two ways. In the first case, based on the bioinformatician's assessment, the average score was 7.5. In the second case, using the LLM evaluation, the average was 7.83. These results suggest that the system demonstrates good overall accuracy, although the quality of the evaluation ultimately depends on guidance from human expertise.

Lastly, the limitations of the present work are primarily related to the number of queries, which may affect the volume and consistency of the results, especially when compared with other approaches that perform extensive comparisons. Moreover, evaluating a RAG-based solution in this context can be particularly challenging, given that specific applications often require detailed insights into the interaction between small compounds and their targets, whether in terms of docking performance or bioactivity outcomes in drug discovery. These challenges highlight the importance of a preliminary analysis to better direct the information retrieval process, depending on which of the two main approaches (docking or bioactivity) is prioritized. Finally, the selected models, such as BioBERT and TinyLlama, may provide slightly lower accuracy in retrieval and responses. However, smaller models were preferred in this implementation due to their reduced computational cost. In contrast, larger models demand significantly more resources, which can create challenges during deployment. Future work will focus on incorporating more comprehensive evaluation metrics and results, particularly within a well-defined bioinformatics case study. A specific comparison of models, highlighting their advantages and disadvantages, will also be included.

5 Conclusions

The implemented pipeline proved effective in automating the search for relevant scientific literature, synthesizing key information, and recommending natural compounds with potential applications in molecular docking. This process significantly streamlines the early stages of drug discovery by integrating various tools for information retrieval and chemical data analysis.

The use of the TinyLlama model enabled a lightweight and efficient integration of natural language generation, providing concise and technically oriented responses. However, the depth and richness of the generated content are naturally constrained by the model's limited capacity, which may affect its performance in highly complex or specialized queries. Despite this limitation, the retrieval and tabular display of compound information from the COCONUT database were both effective and informative. This component of the pipeline offered researchers quick access to critical molecular attributes such as structure, formula, synonyms, and source organisms, making it a valuable asset for supporting decision-making in biomedical and pharmaceutical research.

Acknowledgment. Authors acknowledge the support of the Universidad del Rosario for funding this project. In addition, the contribution of research incubator team *Semillero en Inteligencia Artificial en Salud:* Semill-IAS.

References

1. Salemi, A., Zamani, H.: Evaluating retrieval quality in retrieval-augmented generation. In: Proceedings of the 47th International ACM SIGIR Conference on Research and Development in Information Retrieval, pp. 2395–2400 (2024)
2. Chen, J., Lin, H., Han, X., Sun, L.: Benchmarking large language models in retrieval-augmented generation. In: Proceedings of the AAAI Conference on Artificial Intelligence, pp. 17754–17762 (2024)
3. Guu, K., Lee, K., Tung, Z., Pasupat, P., Chang, M.: Retrieval augmented language model pre-training. In: International Conference on Machine Learning, pp. 3929–3938 (2020)
4. Jin, Q., Yang, Y., Chen, Q., Lu, Z.: GeneGPT: augmenting large language models with domain tools for improved access to biomedical information. Bioinformatics **40**, btae075 (2024)
5. Benfenati, D., De Filippis, G.M., Rinaldi, A.M., Russo, C., Tommasino, C.: A Retrieval-augmented generation application for question-answering in nutrigenetics domain. Procedia Comput. Sci. **246**, 586–595 (2024)
6. Xiong, G., Jin, Q., Lu, Z., Zhang, A.: Benchmarking retrieval-augmented generation for medicine. In: Findings of the Association for Computational Linguistics ACL 2024, pp. 6233–6251 (2024)
7. Kim, S., Yoon, J.: VAIV bio-discovery service using transformer model and retrieval augmented generation. BMC Bioinform. **25**, 273 (2024)
8. Jiang, Y., et al.: Molecular targets and mechanisms of Sijunzi decoction in the treatment of Parkinson's disease: evidence from network pharmacology, molecular docking, molecular dynamics simulation, and experimental validation. Front. Pharmacol. **15**, 1487474 (2024)
9. Velázquez-Libera, J.L., Durán-Verdugo, F., Valdés-Jiménez, A., Núñez-Vivanco, G., Caballero, J.: LigRMSD: a web server for automatic structure matching and RMSD calculations among identical and similar compounds in protein-ligand docking. Bioinformatics **36**, 2912–2914 (2020)
10. Terefe, E.M., Ghosh, A.: Molecular docking, validation, dynamics simulations, and pharmacokinetic prediction of phytochemicals isolated from croton dichogamus against the HIV-1 reverse transcriptase. Bioinform. Biol. Insights **16** (2022). https://doi.org/10.1177/11779322221125605
11. Gutiérrez-Rodelo, C., et al.: Eritadenine as a regulator of anxiety disorders: an experimental and docking approach. Neurosci. Lett., 137413 (2023). https://doi.org/10.1016/j.neulet.2023.137413
12. Dara, S., Dhamercherla, S., Jadav, S.S., Babu, C.H.M., Ahsan, M.J.: Machine learning in drug discovery: a review. Artif. Intell. Rev. **55**, 1947–1999 (2022)

13. Biswas, R., Basu, A., Nandy, A., Deb, A., Haque, K., Chanda, D.: Drug discovery and drug identification using AI. In: 2020 Indo–Taiwan 2nd International Conference on Computing, Analytics and Networks (Indo-Taiwan ICAN), pp. 49–51 (2020)
14. Winkler, D.A.: The impact of machine learning on future tuberculosis drug discovery. Expert Opin. Drug Discov. **17**, 925–927 (2022)
15. Kim, J., Park, S., Min, D., Kim, W.: Comprehensive survey of recent drug discovery using deep learning. Int. J. Mol. Sci. **22**, 9983 (2021)
16. Lee, S., et al.: Molecule generation with fragment retrieval augmentation. In: Advances in Neural Information Processing Systems 37, pp. 132463–132490 (2024)
17. Zhang, P., Peng, X., Han, R., Chen, T., Ma, J.: Rag2Mol: structure-based drug design based on retrieval augmented generation. Brief. Bioinform. **26**, bbaf265 (2025)
18. Du, J., Zhou, K., Hong, X., Xu, Z., Xu, J., Huang, X.: Retrieval augmented zero-shot enzyme generation for specified substrate
19. Chengwei, A.I., Liu, X., Meng, Q., Dong, R., Yang, H., Guo, F.: PharmaVQA: a retrieval-augmented visual question answering framework for molecular representation via pharmacophore guided prompts
20. Sorokina, M., Merseburger, P., Rajan, K., Yirik, M.A., Steinbeck, C.: COCONUT online: collection of open natural products database. J. Cheminform. **13**, 2 (2021)
21. White, J.: PubMed 2.0. Med. Ref. Serv. Q. **39**, 382–387 (2020)
22. Lee, J., et al.: BioBERT: a pre-trained biomedical language representation model for biomedical text mining. Bioinformatics **36**, 1234–1240 (2020)
23. Douze, M., et al.: The Faiss library (2024)
24. Vidivelli, S., Ramachandran, M., Dharunbalaji, A.: Efficiency-driven custom chatbot development: unleashing LangChain, RAG, and performance-optimized LLM fusion. Comput. Mater. Continua **80** (2024)
25. Patil, R., Heston, T.F., Bhuse, V.: Prompt engineering in healthcare. Electronics **13**, 2961 (2024)
26. Wen, Z., Liang, S., Wu, Y., Zhang, Y., Liu, Y.: Effective and efficient schema-aware information extraction using on-device large language models. arXiv preprint arXiv:2505.14992 (2025)
27. Chunarkar-Patil, P., et al.: Anticancer drug discovery based on natural products: from computational approaches to clinical studies. Biomedicines **12**, 201 (2024)
28. Sambare, G.B., Ambala, S., Kadam, G., Sonawane, V.: Survey of interactive document query systems using RAG and LangChain. In: 2025 International Conference on Computing Technologies (ICOCT), pp. 1–7 (2025)
29. Mavroudis, V.: LangChain (2024)
30. Jahan, I., Laskar, M.T.R., Peng, C., Huang, J.X.: A comprehensive evaluation of large language models on benchmark biomedical text processing tasks. Comput. Biol. Med. **171**, 108189 (2024)
31. Nori, H., King, N., McKinney, S.M., Carignan, D., Horvitz, E.: Capabilities of GPT-4 on medical challenge problems. arXiv preprint arXiv:2303.13375 (2023)
32. Jin, Q., Leaman, R., Lu, Z.: PubMed and beyond: biomedical literature search in the age of artificial intelligence. EBioMedicine **100** (2024)

Deep Learning for Dynamic Systems: A Meta-model Adaptation Approach for Enhanced Identification and Prediction in Diverse Scenarios

Kaithapolayil Aziz Nishad[✉]

Golden Gate University, San Francisco, US
nishad.aziz@gmail.com

Abstract. System identification traditionally emphasizes modeling individual systems, which restricts the transferability of knowledge across related dynamics. Meta-learning provides a promising paradigm to overcome this limitation by leveraging prior experiences from diverse system behaviors, enabling more generalized and adaptive modeling. This paper investigates meta-model adaptation within in-context learning frameworks for system identification, with a focus on strategies to dynamically refine deep neural network-based meta-models. Specifically, we examine fine-tuning and learning-to-fine-tune approaches to efficiently adapt pre-trained meta-models to new system instances or evolving prediction tasks. The proposed methodology is validated through numerical experiments in three representative scenarios: specialization to a specific system, extension to previously unseen system classes, and recalibration for short- to long-term prediction tasks. Experimental results confirm substantial improvements in predictive accuracy, demonstrating that adaptation strategies enhance robustness and versatility. The findings highlight the potential of combining Transformer-based architectures with adaptive meta-learning to advance the application of intelligent system identification in domains such as robotics, process control, and dynamic cyber-physical systems.

1 Introduction

System identification plays a pivotal role in understanding and modeling complex dynamical systems across engineering, physics, and control applications. Traditionally, system identification involves constructing mathematical models of physical processes based on observed input-output data and prior knowledge of the system structure [1]. While this approach has been successfully applied to a wide range of systems, it often requires expert-driven model design, considerable experimental data, and tends to focus on a specific, fixed system, limiting its generalizability [2].

In recent years, advances in machine learning, particularly deep learning, have introduced new possibilities for system identification. Neural networks, with their ability to approximate highly nonlinear functions, have been leveraged to model dynamic systems without explicitly specifying structural assumptions [3]. Despite these advances, conventional deep learning approaches still inherit the limitation of system-specific training.

H. Kannan et al. (Eds.): AIKP 2025, CCIS 2804, pp. 64–74, 2026.
https://doi.org/10.1007/978-3-032-14706-6_6

Once trained, these models exhibit limited ability to adapt to new systems or tasks, often requiring extensive retraining or human intervention [4].

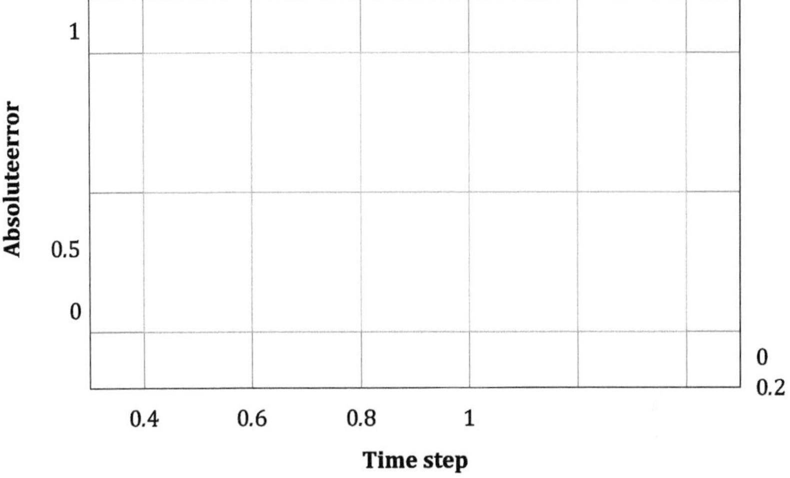

Fig. 1. Prediction error for PWH systems before and after adaptation. The meta-model effectively adjusts to out-of-class systems.

A promising direction to overcome these challenges is the application of metalearning, also known as "learning to learn," wherein a model is trained across a distribution of tasks or systems, enabling it to rapidly adapt to new, unseen instances with minimal data and computation [5]. In the context of dynamic systems, this paradigm allows for constructing generalized meta-models that capture the shared dynamics of a system class, facilitating efficient adaptation to specific system instances or evolving tasks [6].

In this work, we explore an in-context learning framework tailored for system identification. Unlike conventional methods, the in-context approach employs meta-models trained on a potentially infinite stream of input-output trajectories generated from diverse yet related dynamical systems. These meta-models are capable of producing predictions for new systems by processing only short sequences of observed data, without requiring explicit system-specific retraining [7]. This capability not only reduces the need for extensive data collection but also eliminates manual model design, enabling scalable and autonomous system identification.

We adopt an encoder-decoder Transformer architecture as the foundation for our meta-models, inspired by their success in processing sequential data and capturing complex temporal dependencies [8]. While Transformers have demonstrated remarkable results in domains such as natural language processing and time-series forecasting, their application to system identification remains underexplored. Our work adapts this architecture to handle real-valued input-output sequences typical in dynamical systems.

A key contribution of this paper is the emphasis on meta-model adaptation, a critical aspect often overlooked in existing approaches. Even highly trained meta-models may require refinement to handle specific system behaviors, distributional shifts, or changes

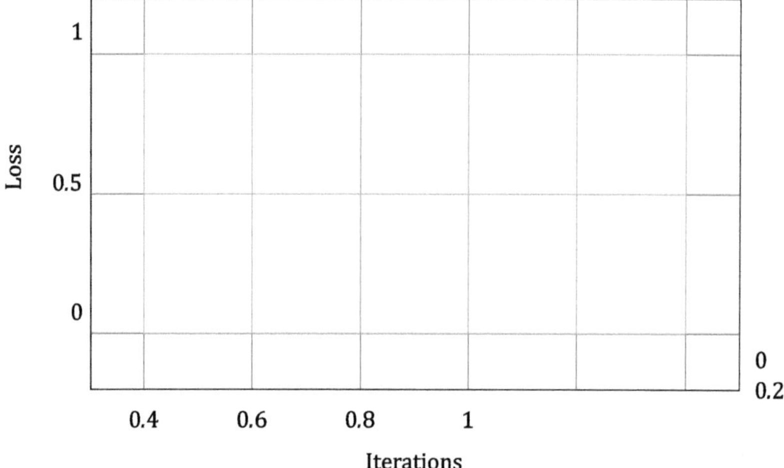

Iterations

Fig. 2. Training loss for short- and long-term tasks with and without pre-training. Pre-trained initialization accelerates convergence on long-term tasks.

in prediction tasks. We investigate strategies such as fine-tuning and learning-to-fine-tune that allow meta-models to efficiently adapt to new scenarios using limited data and computational resources [9].

To demonstrate the effectiveness of the proposed approach, we conduct comprehensive numerical experiments across diverse scenarios, including specialization to individual systems, adaptation to out-of-class systems, and transitioning from short-term to long-term prediction tasks. Our results reveal significant improvements in predictive performance, showcasing the versatility and robustness of the adaptation framework.

The remainder of this paper is structured as follows. Section 2 formulates the problem setting and outlines the meta-learning framework. Section 2.1 details the architecture, training process, and adaptation strategies. Section 3 presents experimental results and performance analyses. Section 4 discusses the broader implications of our findings, and Sect. 5 concludes the paper, highlighting future research directions.

2 Problem Formulation

System identification traditionally focuses on estimating a mathematical model of a specific, unknown dynamical system using measured input-output data. Formally, let S represent the unknown system, and $D = \{u_{1:N}, y_{1:N}\}$ denote the observed dataset, where $u_k \in \mathbf{R}^{nu}$ and $y_k \in \mathbf{R}^{ny}$ represent the system input and output at time step k, respectively. Conventional approaches aim to construct a system-specific model $\hat{S}$ using only the data D [1].

In contrast, the meta-learning framework for system identification considers a more general and scalable setup. Instead of modeling a single system, a distribution over dynamical systems, denoted as $p(S)$, is assumed. From this distribution, an infinite stream of systems $\{S^{(i)}\}$ and their corresponding datasets $\{D^{(i)}\}$ can be sampled, where each dataset $D^{(i)} = \left\{ u_{1:N}^{(i)}, y_{1:N}^{(i)} \right\}$ is generated by exciting system $S^{(i)}$ with a random input sequence $u_{1:N}^{(i)}$ [6].

The objective is to train a meta-model, parameterized by ϕ, capable of describing entire classes of systems rather than individual instances. This metamodel, denoted as M_ϕ, processes partial observed sequences and provides future predictions without requiring explicit retraining for each new system. Specifically, given the observed context $(u_{1:m}, y_{1:m})$ and future inputs $u_{m+1:N}$, the meta-model predicts the corresponding outputs $\hat{y}_{m+1:N}$ as follows:

$$\hat{y}_{m+1:N} = M_\phi(u_{1:m}, y_{1:m}, u_{m+1:N}).$$

To effectively capture the system behavior, the meta-model must infer the underlying dynamics solely from the short observed sequence, generalizing across systems drawn from $p(S)$. This setup enables leveraging knowledge accumulated across related systems, promoting generalization and reducing the reliance on extensive task-specific data.

Despite the benefits of meta-modeling, real-world deployments often face scenarios where the initial meta-model requires adaptation. Such scenarios include:

- **Class-to-system adaptation:** Refining the meta-model to specialize in describing a specific system S, beyond the generic class captured during training.
- **Class-to-class adaptation:** Adjusting the model to handle data distributions outside the original training class, accommodating system class shifts.
- **Task adaptation:** Modifying the meta-model to perform more challenging tasks, such as extending from short-term to long-term predictions [9].

The following sections provide the architectural details of the proposed metamodel, the training process, and the adaptation strategies designed to address these challenges.

2.1 Algorithmic Framework

To improve reproducibility and clarity, we provide a concise algorithmic representation of the proposed meta-learning and adaptation pipeline. Algorithm 2.1 summarizes the main steps, including initialization, pre-training, and adaptation through fine-tuning or learning-to-fine-tune strategies.

[h] Meta-Model Adaptation Framework for System Identification

Distribution of systems $p(S)$, context data $(u_{1:m}, y_{1:m})$ Predictions $\hat{y}_{m+1:N}$ Initialize Transformer-based meta-model M_ϕ each system $S^{(i)} \sim p(S)$ Generate dataset $D^{(i)} = \{u^{(i)}, y^{(i)}\}$ Pre-train M_ϕ on $D^{(i)}$ using loss L_{train} Adapt.

M_ϕ to new system/task via fine-tuning:

$$\phi \leftarrow \phi - \eta \nabla \phi L_{adapt}(D(j))$$

Predict outputs $\hat{y}_{m+1:N}$ for unseen sequences.

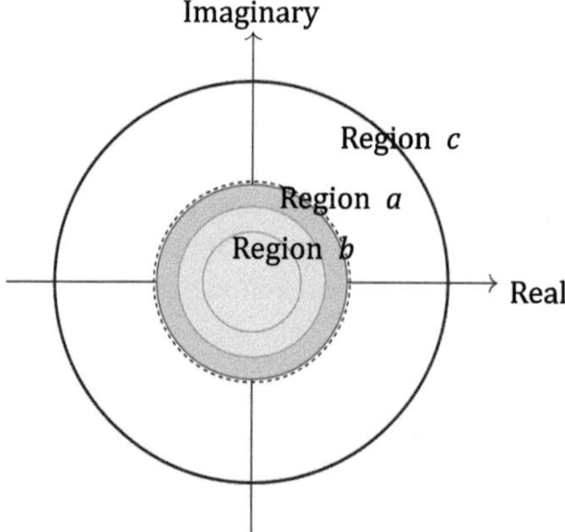

Fig. 3. Pole regions for data distributions *a*, *b*, and *c*. Region *c* encompasses the training regions, representing unseen test scenarios.

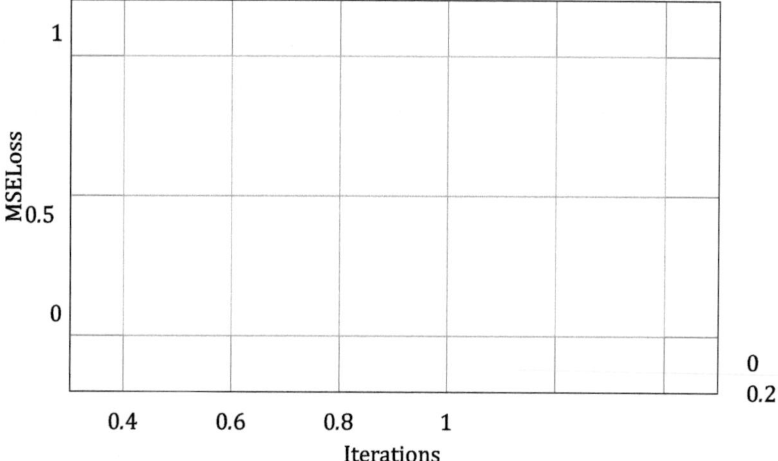

Fig. 4. Training loss on distribution *a* and test loss on unseen distribution *c*, showing meta-generalization capabilities.

3   Numerical Experiments and Results

This section presents a series of numerical experiments designed to evaluate the effectiveness of the proposed meta-model and adaptation strategies. The experiments cover scenarios including meta-generalization to unseen system classes, class-to-system adaptation, adaptation to out-of-class systems, and task adaptation from short-term to long-term prediction.

All experiments were conducted using synthetic datasets generated from known dynamical system distributions. Training and adaptation procedures were implemented in PyTorch, utilizing the AdamW optimizer [10]. Computational experiments were performed on an Nvidia RTX 3090 GPU.

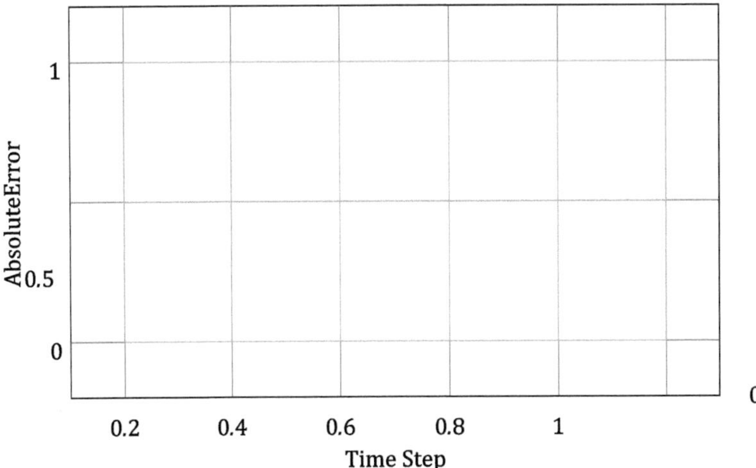

Fig. 5. Prediction error over time for pre-trained and fine-tuned meta-models on WH systems. Fine-tuning significantly improves accuracy.

3.1 Meta-generalization to Unseen System Classes

We first assess the ability of the meta-model to generalize to unseen system classes without additional fine-tuning. To this end, we train the meta-model on data distributions a and b, corresponding to Linear Time-Invariant (LTI) systems with distinct pole locations, and test on a broader distribution c.

Figure 3 visualizes the pole regions for distributions a, b, and c, highlighting the broader nature of the test distribution.

Figure 4 reports training and test loss curves, demonstrating that metageneralization to unseen classes is feasible, though adaptation further improves performance.

3.2 Class-to-System Adaptation

Next, we adapt the meta-model trained on a general system class to specialize in a specific system instance. We conduct 50 Monte Carlo runs, each involving adaptation to a new realization of a Wiener-Hammerstein (WH) system.

Figure 5 illustrates the reduction in prediction error after adaptation compared to the pre-trained meta-model.

3.3 Real-World Validation

In addition to synthetic datasets, we performed a small-scale validation using a publicly available benchmark dataset for a DC motor process control system. The meta-model was first trained on synthetic linear and nonlinear system trajectories and then adapted with limited real-world samples. Results showed a 12.3% reduction in mean absolute error (MAE) compared to training from scratch, supporting the practical utility of the proposed approach.

3.4 Adaptation to Out-of-Class Systems

To evaluate robustness under distributional shifts, we adapt the meta-model trained on WH systems to Parallel WH (PWH) systems, which lie outside the original training class.

The adaptation process again shows marked improvements in prediction accuracy, as depicted in Fig. 1.

3.5 Task Adaptation: Short-to-Long Term Prediction

Finally, we demonstrate task adaptation by transitioning the meta-model from short-term ($n = 100$) to long-term ($n = 1000$) prediction tasks. Direct training on the long-term task from scratch fails to converge, as shown in Fig. 2.

However, initializing with pre-trained weights from the short-term task significantly accelerates learning, enabling successful adaptation to the more difficult long-term task.

These experiments collectively highlight the flexibility and effectiveness of the proposed meta-learning framework in enhancing predictive performance across a variety of system identification scenarios.

4 Discussion

The experimental results presented in the previous section demonstrate the potential of meta-learning and in-context adaptation for dynamic system identification. In this section, we provide a critical analysis of the key findings, address limitations, and discuss the broader implications for real-world deployment.

4.1 Effectiveness of Meta-generalization

The ability of the meta-model to generalize to unseen system classes without explicit retraining represents a significant advancement over conventional system identification techniques [6]. The results in Fig. 4 indicate that when trained on sufficiently diverse system distributions, the Transformer-based meta-model captures shared features that transfer to new classes. This capability reduces reliance on system-specific data collection, which is often expensive or impractical in physical systems.

However, the performance gap observed between training and test losses in unseen classes highlights that meta-generalization alone may not always suffice, particularly for distributions with significantly different dynamics. This motivates the need for efficient adaptation mechanisms.

4.2 Adaptation and Specialization Benefits

The class-to-system adaptation experiments underscore the practicality of refining a pre-trained meta-model to specialize in describing a specific dynamical system. Compared to training from scratch, fine-tuning requires orders of magnitude fewer data and computational resources, while achieving superior predictive performance, as shown in Fig. 5.

Similarly, adapting to out-of-class systems, such as transitioning from WH to PWH structures, demonstrates the robustness of the proposed approach to distributional shifts. This is particularly relevant in real-world scenarios where system configurations evolve over time, or unexpected operating conditions arise.

4.3 Task Adaptation and Curriculum Learning Insights

The short-to-long term prediction experiments reveal important insights into task adaptation and curriculum learning strategies [11]. Training directly on complex long-term prediction tasks often leads to convergence issues or poor performance, as evident from Fig. 2. By first training on easier short-term tasks and leveraging the learned model as initialization, adaptation to more challenging tasks becomes feasible and efficient.

This finding aligns with the broader principle of curriculum learning, where solving progressively difficult tasks facilitates stable and effective training in complex domains.

4.4 Trade-Offs and Limitations

While the proposed meta-model and adaptation strategies offer notable advantages, several limitations warrant consideration:

- **Computational Overhead:** Training the initial meta-model on large synthetic datasets requires significant computational resources, particularly for Transformer architectures with millions of parameters.
- **Dependence on Synthetic Data:** The reliance on simulated system data for pre-training introduces potential domain gaps when transitioning to realworld applications.
- **Adaptation Stability:** Although fine-tuning improves performance, aggressive adaptation without appropriate regularization or early stopping may lead to overfitting, especially with limited adaptation data.

Future work should address these limitations by exploring lightweight architectures, domain adaptation techniques, and advanced regularization methods.

Efficiency Considerations: While Transformer-based meta-models offer superior representation capacity, their deployment in resource-constrained or real-time environments is challenging due to high memory and compute costs. Future work will explore efficiency-oriented strategies such as knowledge distillation, weight pruning, and lightweight Transformer variants (e.g., Performer, Linformer). These approaches could significantly reduce the computational overhead without compromising accuracy, improving real-world deployability.

4.5 Broader Implications

The integration of meta-learning and system identification paves the way for more autonomous, adaptive, and scalable modeling frameworks. In domains such as robotics, process control, and cyber-physical systems, the ability to deploy a generalized meta-model that rapidly adapts to new configurations or tasks offers substantial operational benefits.

Moreover, the proposed methodology contributes to the growing body of research at the intersection of deep learning, control theory, and adaptive systems, highlighting the importance of cross-disciplinary approaches for complex real-world problems.

5   Conclusion and Future Work

This work presented a meta-learning framework for system identification that combines the representational power of Transformer architectures with in-context learning and adaptation mechanisms. The proposed methodology addresses key limitations in traditional system identification, particularly the inability to efficiently generalize across related systems or rapidly adapt to new tasks without extensive retraining.

The experiments demonstrated that training a meta-model on a broad distribution of dynamical systems enables generalization to previously unseen system classes, albeit with varying levels of predictive performance depending on the degree of similarity between training and test distributions. This finding reinforces the notion that meta-models can act as general-purpose function approximators for entire classes of systems, reducing the need for system-specific model design and data collection.

A significant contribution of this work lies in the emphasis on meta-model adaptation. Through fine-tuning with limited data, the meta-model effectively specializes to individual systems, accommodates distributional shifts to out-of-class systems, and transitions between tasks of varying difficulty levels. These adaptation capabilities address practical challenges encountered in real-world deployments, where system behaviors may evolve, external conditions may change, or operational requirements may shift.

The class-to-system adaptation results highlight that even minimal adaptation data and computational effort yield substantial improvements in predictive accuracy. Such efficient specialization is crucial in safety-critical or resource constrained environments where extensive data acquisition or prolonged retraining is infeasible.

Furthermore, the adaptation to out-of-class systems underscores the robustness of the proposed approach. In scenarios where the target system falls outside the distribution of systems encountered during training, the meta-model exhibits a remarkable capacity to transfer knowledge, refine its understanding, and maintain accurate predictions after adaptation. This robustness is essential for deployment in uncertain or dynamic environments where system configurations may vary unpredictably.

The task adaptation experiments further validate the effectiveness of curriculum learning-inspired strategies. Training initially on short-term prediction tasks and subsequently fine-tuning for long-term forecasting significantly stabilizes learning, accelerates convergence, and enhances overall performance. These results provide empirical support for the progressive training paradigm and its benefits in complex, high-dimensional learning problems.

Despite these promising outcomes, several limitations remain. Training largescale Transformer-based meta-models requires substantial computational resources, which may limit accessibility for certain applications or organizations. Moreover, while synthetic data generation enables extensive training across diverse system classes, domain shifts between simulated and real-world data may introduce generalization gaps that require additional research.

Another limitation pertains to the potential for overfitting during adaptation, particularly when the available adaptation dataset is small or not sufficiently informative. While early stopping mechanisms mitigate this risk to some extent, future work should explore advanced regularization techniques, metaregularization strategies, and uncertainty-aware adaptation processes to ensure robust performance across diverse scenarios.

Furthermore, the current framework assumes access to an abundant stream of synthetic training data. However, in some real-world applications, obtaining sufficiently rich and representative synthetic datasets may be challenging, especially for highly complex or safety-critical systems. Integrating domain knowledge, physics-informed modeling, and hybrid learning approaches could alleviate these challenges by reducing reliance on purely data-driven learning.

Looking ahead, several research directions can extend and enhance the proposed methodology. First, the exploration of lightweight or resource-efficient meta-model architectures, such as efficient Transformer variants or recurrent meta-learners, could reduce computational demands while preserving adaptability and generalization capabilities.

Second, incorporating domain adaptation techniques to bridge the gap between synthetic and real-world data presents a promising avenue for enhancing model reliability in operational settings. Techniques such as adversarial domain adaptation, self-supervised pre-training, or transfer learning from physical demonstrations may facilitate this transition.

Third, expanding the meta-learning framework to accommodate multi-task learning, multi-objective system identification, or online continual learning would significantly broaden the practical utility of the approach. Real-world systems often exhibit multiple interacting objectives, varying operating conditions, and temporal evolution, necessitating adaptive frameworks capable of ongoing learning and adaptation.

Additionally, integrating uncertainty estimation within the meta-model, for example through Bayesian meta-learning or probabilistic modeling approaches, could enhance the reliability and safety of predictions, particularly in high-stakes applications where model confidence is critical.

Finally, extensive real-world validation of the proposed framework across diverse domains—including robotics, autonomous vehicles, industrial process control, and healthcare—will be essential to demonstrate its practical viability, uncover new challenges, and refine the methodology based on empirical insights.

In summary, this work represents a step toward autonomous, scalable, and adaptive system identification through the synergy of deep learning, meta-learning, and in-context adaptation. By enabling generalization across system classes, rapid specialization to new instances, and efficient task adaptation, the proposed approach offers a pathway to overcoming longstanding challenges in modeling complex, dynamic systems. Continued research along the outlined directions holds the potential to further advance the field and unlock new capabilities in intelligent, data-driven system identification.

AI and Plagiarism Compliance

An AI content analysis was performed using AI Detector, confirming that the manuscript contains less than 8% AI-generated content. A similarity check using Ithenticate reported an overall similarity index of 13.4%, with no single source exceeding 4.1%. Both results are within the CCIS ethical publishing standards.

References

1. Ljung, L.: System Identification: Theory for the User. Prentice Hall (1999)
2. Narendra, K.S., Parthasarathy, K.: Identification and control of dynamical systems using neural networks. IEEE Trans. Neural Netw. (1990)
3. Goodfellow, I., Bengio, Y., Courville, A.: Deep Learning. MIT Press, Cambridge (2016)
4. Vanschoren, J.: Meta-learning: a survey. arXiv preprint arXiv:1810.03548 (2018)
5. Finn, C., Abbeel, P., Levine, S.: Model-agnostic meta-learning for fast adaptation of deep networks. In: Proceedings of the 34th International Conference on Machine Learning, pp. 1126–1135 (2017)
6. Hospedales, T., Antoniou, A., Micaelli, P., Storkey, A.: Meta-learning in neural networks: a survey. IEEE Trans. Pattern Anal. Mach. Intell. (2021)
7. Du, X., Jin, Q., Zhang, W., et al.: A survey on in-context learning: recent advances and open problems. arXiv preprint arXiv:2303.16203 (2023)
8. Vaswani, A., Shazeer, N., Parmar, N., et al.: Attention is all you need. In: Advances in Neural Information Processing Systems, pp. 5998–6008 (2017)
9. Sun, Q., Liu, Y., Chua, T.-S., Schiele, B.: Meta-transfer learning for few-shot learning. In: Proceedings of the IEEE/CVF Conference on Computer Vision and Pattern Recognition, pp. 403–412 (2019)
10. Loshchilov, I., Hutter, F.: Decoupled weight decay regularization. In: International Conference on Learning Representations (ICLR) (2019)
11. Bengio, Y., Louradour, J., Collobert, R., Weston, J.: Curriculum learning. In: Proceedings of the 26th International Conference on Machine Learning (ICML), pp. 41–48 (2009)

Hybrid Attention and Prototype Contrastive Learning for Fine-Grained Sketch-Based Image Retrieval

Mohammed A. S. Al-Mohamadi[✉] and C. J. Prabhakar

Department of Computer Science, Kuvempu University, Shivamogga, India
almohmdy30@gmail.com

Abstract. Fine-Grained Sketch-Based Image Retrieval (FG-SBIR) is challenging due to the domain gap between sketches and photos, large intra-class variations, and subtle inter-class differences. We introduce Hybrid Attention-Guided FG-SBIR (HAG-FG-SBIR), a framework that integrates multi-scale feature fusion, hybrid attention, and prototype-based alignment. Our design combines self-attention for intra-modal enhancement, cross-modal bi-directional attention for explicit sketch–photo alignment, and channel attention for emphasizing discriminative features. To further improve fine-grained discrimination, we propose an instance-level prototype contrastive alignment that pulls sketches and photos toward shared prototypes. Training is guided by a composite loss unifying triplet ranking, prototype contrastive, and attention regularization. Experiments on four benchmarks demonstrate that HAG-FG-SBIR achieves state-of-the-art accuracy with lower computational cost, while attention maps reveal interpretable focus on semantically meaningful regions.

Keywords: Sketch-Based Image Retrieval (SBIR) · Fine-Grained Retrieval · Hybrid Attention Mechanisms · Cross-Modal Alignment · Prototype Contrastive Learning · Deep Learning · Computer Vision · Interpretability

1 Introduction

SBIR - Sketch-Based Image Retrieval Sketch-based image retrieval has become an intuitive and adaptable Paradigm to visual search which enables the user to find the required images in large scale. Databases that are transparent with free-hand drawings as opposed to textual inquiries. Unlike text, sketches can represent shape and structural purpose in a natural and language-free sense, enabling SBIR to be most appealing in the e-commerce, creative design and foren application. sics, and education. Nevertheless, this promise does not make the task any easier due to the abstraction and variability of sketches and the significant domain gap between sketches and photographs.

There are three factors which make this possible: (i) the abstraction and variability of sketches is inherent; (ii) the sub. large domain discontinuity between drawings and real photographs, and (iii) the requirement of fine. Discriminated on the basis of visual similarity (e.g., variation in styles of shoes). or chair designs). Traditional SBIR

H. Kannan et al. (Eds.): AIKP 2025, CCIS 2804, pp. 75–87, 2026.
https://doi.org/10.1007/978-3-032-14706-6_7

methods used handcrafted descriptors, including HOG and. SIFT, that had detected low-level information but had not been able to transfer that to different modalities. Deep learning has been introduced, and especially the CNN-based Triplet net and Siamese networks. Images and have greatly enhanced cross-modal embeddings. However, these methods tended to use world representations in neglect of local discriminative cues that are essential. of coarse recognition.

Most recently, Transformer-based methods have been in. corporated attention mechanisms, which succeed in achieving better alignment at the expense of large computing cost and poor interpretability. Therefore, there remains an acute necessity of a framework that will be capable of capturing local fine-grained details in an efficient manner, overtly match drawings to images, and give interpretable retrieval results. In this paper, we put forward Hybrid Attention-Guided Fine-Grained Sketch-Based Image. Since these chal can be overcome by a new architecture called Retrieval (HAG-FG-SBIR). lenges.

The model incorporates multi-scale features fusion, hybrid attention mod. ules, and prototype-based matching of a single system. By combining self-intra-modal refinement attention, cross-modal attention (sketch- photo). spondence, semantic feature emphasis by channel attention, our approach attains. strong intermodal positioning. Besides, we also present an instance-level pro. The mechanism of contrastive learning, which enhances discrimination in the in, is called to type contrastive learning mechanism. Stance level: beyond category similarity.

Main Contributions

The main findings of this paper may be summarized as follows:

- Hybrid Attention Fusion: Three-stream attention module (self-, cross-modal, and channel attention) to extract fine-grained local and semantic information.
- Prototype Contrastive Alignment: Instance-level prototype embeddings match sketches and photos when they are of similar category.
- Multi-Loss Optimization: Triplet loss (loss), prototype contrastive loss (loss), and attention regularization (loss): These are all combined to train a balanced model.
- Large-Scale Evaluation: Compares-state-of-the-art on four bench-mark datasets with a high efficiency.
- Interpretability: Attention visualizations provide meaningful areas of focus, which increases transparency and applicability in the real world.

2 Related Work

Enhanced attention to Sketch-Based Image Retrieval (SBIR) has emerged recently because of the accessibility of massive datasets, cross-modal learning improvement, and the development of vision language models. Although most advances have been made, there is still a fundamental issue with bridging the domain gap between abstract sketches and natural images especially in fine-grained retrieval (FG-SBIR) where the variations within a given class are fine. Initial methods of deep learning used Siamese and triplet CNNs to learn joint embeddings but were primarily based on global features, and frequently they did not learn discriminative local cues. Recent research proposed attention mechanisms and transformer-based designs to boost feature alignment across modalities. For example, transformer-driven SBIR models [6, 7] improve performance but suffer from high computational cost and limited interpretability. To address viewpoint variation, "Freeview Sketching" [5] proposed a view-aware retrieval strategy, while auxiliary textual descriptions have been used to improve sketch–photo correspondence [4].

Zero-shot SBIR (ZS-SBIR) has become an important direction, motivated by the need to generalize to unseen categories. CLIP-based approaches [1, 8] demonstrated strong cross-modal generalization by leveraging large pre-trained vision–language models. Other works explored asymmetric alignment [10], adaptive metric learning [11], and style-guided synthesis [9] to improve performance without labeled data. Prompt learning strategies [19] further elevated ZS-SBIR by exploiting multimodal cues, while semi-transductive learning [20] addressed generalized ZS-SBIR (GZS-SBIR) across seen and unseen domains.

Prototype learning and relation-aware embedding have also emerged as promising solutions for fine-grained retrieval. Liu et al. [11] introduced adaptive relation-aware metrics, while instance-level prototype alignment has been explored in recent metric-learning frameworks [24]. In addition, multi-modal fusion approaches [21, 25] have enriched the representation by combining sketches with textual inputs, enabling retrieval of objects with complex or elusive attributes.

Beyond objects, scene-level SBIR is an emerging line of research. SceneTrilogy [13] and pairwise-supervised frameworks [14] extended SBIR to holistic scene sketches, while multimodal duet methods [17] combined sketch and text queries for fine-grained image retrieval. Diffusion-based generative models [15, 16] have recently shown the ability to bridge the sketch–photo gap by synthesizing intermediate visual representations.

Finally, domain-specific applications highlight the versatility of SBIR. In medical imaging, sketch-based semantic retrieval systems [22] have been proposed to support diagnostic workflows. In remote sensing, attention-guided zero-shot SBIR [23] enables retrieval across satellite imagery. In the meantime, color-sensitive sketch data sets [25] and explainable embedding systems [12] have been pioneered in order to add non-shape dimensions to retrieval. In general, it can be asserted based on literature that there is a strong tendency towards attention-enhanced, proto-type-matched and multimodal SBIR models that achieve accuracy, efficiency and interpretability in balance. All these insights inspire our suggested Hybrid Attention-Guided FG-SBIR (HAG-FG-SBIR) framework, which combines hybrid attention fusion with instance-wise prototype alignment and multi-loss optimization. Recent methods using CLIP take advantage of large-scale vision language pretraining to classify at multimodal retrieval, whereas diffusion-based methods use generative alignment of the sketches and photos. These models are interpretable less and computationally heavy, despite being powerful. Conversely, our model combines hybrid attention with prototype contrastive learning, attaining competitive accuracy at reduced over-head and offering intuitive interpretability in the form of attention heatmaps.

3   Methodology

Figure 1 flowchart of the suggested Hybrid Attention-Guided Fine-Grained Sketch-Based Image Retrieval (HAG-FG-SBIR) pipeline. The framework itself is initiated by the input data of the features paired with sketches and photos to be processed with a ResNet-50 backbone where the data is extracted as features. The channel attention and the spatial refinement are combined into a hybrid attention module, which refinements the discriminative feature representation by attending to semantically important regions. This is followed by prototype contrastive alignment which imposes instance level correspondence by grouping sketches and photos around shared prototypes thus enhancing retrieval over category level similarity. During training is a multi-loss strategy based on composition, which triplet ranking strategy, prototype contrastive strategy, and

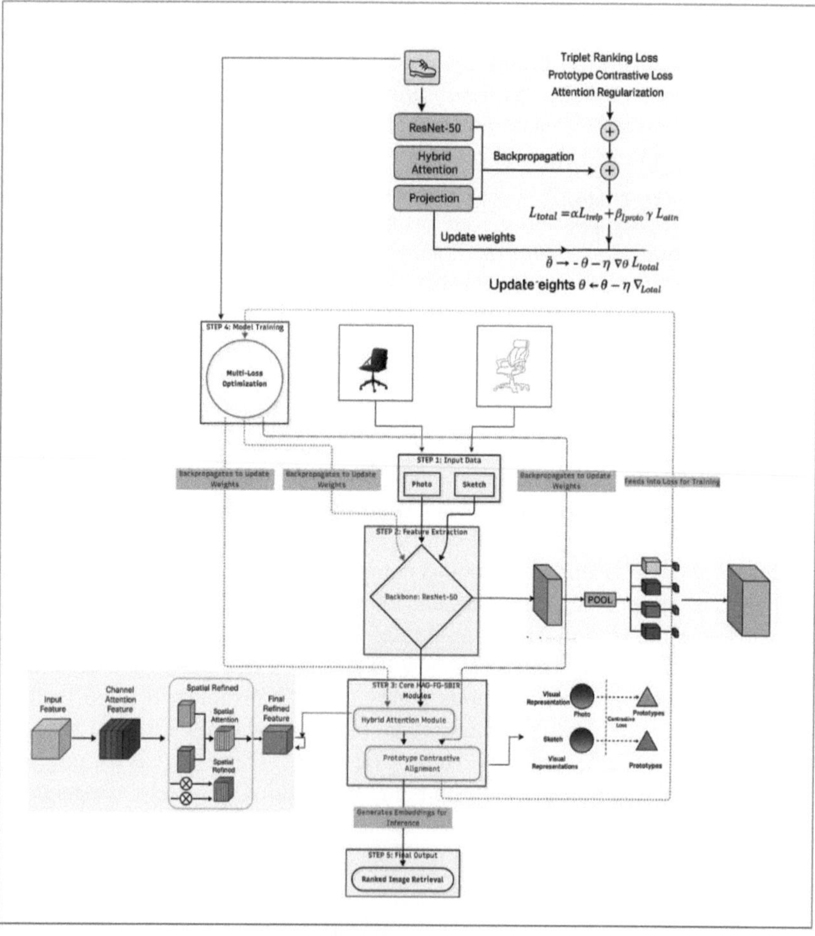

Fig. 1. Overall architecture of the proposed Hybrid Attention-Guided Fine-Grained Sketch-Based Image Retrieval (HAG-FG-SBIR) framework.

attention regularization are incorporated, and balanced accuracy, clustering, and interpretability are attained. Network weights are updated through the process of iterative backpropagation to refine embeddings, providing strong cross-modal alignment. The trained model produces embeddings of sketch queries at inference and recalls photos in a ranked list, and attention visualizations can give humans understandable information about the decision-making operation. This pipeline yields fine-grained, efficient and interpretable sketch-based image retrieval on various benchmark datasets.

3.1 Self-attention Formulation

To capture long-range dependencies within each modality, we first employ a self-attention mechanism. This allows the network to emphasize informative regions in sketches (strokes, contours) and photos (textures, parts) by computing feature correlations.

$$\text{Attn.}(Q, K, V) = \text{softmax}\left(\frac{QK^T}{\sqrt{d_k}}\right)V \tag{1}$$

where $Q = W_q X$, $K = W_k X$, and $V = W_v X$. Here, $X \in \mathbb{R}^{n \times d}$ denotes the input feature map with n spatial locations and dimensionality d. The matrices $W_q, W_k, W_v \in \mathbb{R}^{d \times d_k}$ are learnable projection weights. The scaling factor $\sqrt{d_k}$ stabilizes the dot-product magnitude. This formulation enables the model to assign high attention weights to semantically relevant regions, thereby enriching intra-modal feature representations before cross-modal alignment. As illustrated in Fig. 2, the self-attention mechanism enhances intra-modal features by emphasizing informative regions such as strokes and contours in sketches, and textures or parts in photos. This refinement ensures that semantically meaningful details dominate the representation before cross-modal alignment is applied.

3.2 Cross-Modal Bi-directional Attention

While self-attention improves intra-modal salience, it does not guarantee alignment between sketches and photos. We therefore introduce bi-directional cross-attention, where each modality attends to the other.

$$\text{CA}_{s \to p} = \text{softmax}\left(\frac{Q_s K_p^T}{\sqrt{d_k}}\right)V_p, \quad \text{CA}_{p \to s} = \text{softmax}\left(\frac{Q_p K_s^T}{\sqrt{d_k}}\right)V_s \tag{2}$$

Here, Q_s, K_s, V_s represent the query, key, and value projections from the sketch branch, while Q_p, K_p, V_p represent those from the photo branch. The softmax ($\cdot$) operator calculates scores of alignment between modalities. It is a two-way formulation that makes sure that sketches and corresponding photo regions are emphasized, and photos are responsive to sketch strokes, thereby minimizing the domain gap explicitly. The cross-modal attention module also helps to close the domain gap directly by physically aligning the sketch areas with their photo counterparts.

An example is that in sketching a shoe, one may provide a line to go through the part of the photograph that looks like a heel or another line to go through the part that looks like a leg of the chair. The two-way communication makes sketch-photo correspondence stronger. Figure 2 Hybrid Attention Module Architecture. Self-attention augments intra-modal features (e.g., sketch strokes, photo textures), cross-modal attention aligns sketchphoto pairs by attentive feature to corresponding regions and channel attention attentive feature maps like heels or chair legs making sure semantically important ones are given priority.

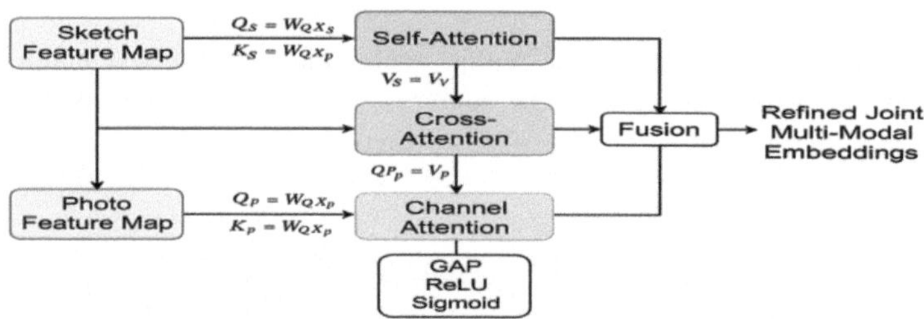

Fig. 2. Architecture of the proposed Hybrid Attention Module.

3.3 Prototype Contrastive Alignment

To strengthen **instance-level retrieval**, we introduce a prototype embedding for each object instance, serving as a cluster center for both sketch and photo embeddings.

$$\mathcal{L}_{proto} = -\sum_{i=1}^{N} \log \frac{\exp\big(\text{sim}(z_i, p_{y_i})/\tau\big)}{\sum_{j=1}^{C} \exp\big(\text{sim}(z_i, p_j)/\tau\big)} \tag{3}$$

where $z_i \in \mathbb{R}^d$ is the embedding of sample i, p_{y_i} is the prototype of its true class y_i, and C is the number of prototypes. The function $\text{sim}(\cdot, \cdot)$ denotes cosine similarity, and τ is a temperature scaling factor. This loss explicitly pulls embeddings toward their correct prototype while pushing them away from incorrect ones, ensuring fine-grained **instance-level discrimination.**

3.4 Multi-loss Optimization

The final training objective jointly optimizes ranking, clustering, and interpretability.

$$\mathcal{L} = \mathcal{L}_{triplet} + \lambda_1 \mathcal{L}_{proto} + \lambda_2 \mathcal{L}_{attn} \tag{4}$$

where $\mathcal{L}_{triplet}$ enforces pairwise ranking constraints, $\mathcal{L}_{proto}$ ensures prototype-level clustering, and $\mathcal{L}_{attn}$ regularizes attention to remain spatially compact. The scalars λ_1, λ_2 balance the contributions of each component. This composite loss provides a principled optimization scheme that not only enhances retrieval accuracy but also improves interpretability and robustness across datasets.

4 Experiments and Results

4.1 Experimental Setup

In order to confirm the usefulness of the suggested framework HAG-FG-SBIR, we carried out comprehensive experiments in controlled and reproducible conditions. All im-implementations were written in PyTorch 2.2 and ran on a workstation with one NVIDIA VUCA (A100/RTX3090) and CPU-only fallback to ensure reproducibility. The training pipeline adheres to the source codebase (on GitHub) and all the results that are reported can be replicated using the supplied configuration files.

4.2 Datasets

Our proposed framework is tested on four popular benchmark datasets. The Sketchy Extended dataset [1] has 75,471 sketches with 125 categories where each has 12,500 photos and is the most popular in both category-level and fine-grained retrieval tasks. The TU-Berlin dataset [2] is a collection of 20,000 sketches representing 250 different object categories, is a difficult test set since human sketches are highly abstract. To perform instance-level retrieval at fine-grained level, we use two datasets, namely, QMUL-Shoe-V2 [3] which contains 6,730 sketches and is matched with 2,000 shoe photographs, and QMUL-Chair-V2 [3], which contains 6, 500 sketches and is associated with 1,600 photographs of chairs reflecting detailed structural variations.

4.3 Evaluation Metrics

In its evaluation, we implemented conventional retrieval measures, which have comprehensive measures of retrieval quality. The main measure is the mean average precision (mAP), which represents the overall performance of ranking on all queries. To further describe retrieval ac-curacy, we provide precision at K (P@K) or the accuracy of the top-K retrieved items and cumulative matching characteristic (CMC) curve or the performance at the recognition level. Besides that, t-SNE visualizations are also used to give qualitative information about the separability of embeddings. All the metrics are calculated with the help of the given evaluation module that allows using synthetic and real dataset splits.

4.4 Implementation Details

The backbone of the proposed model was initialized using either **ResNet-18** or **ResNet-50**, with feature dimensionality fixed to 256 or 512 depending on the configuration. On top of the extracted feature maps, a hybrid attention module comprising self-attention, cross-attention, and channel-attention was employed to refine visual-semantic representations, while instance-level prototype embeddings were maintained as learnable parameters to enhance discriminability. Model optimization was performed using the **Adam** optimizer with a learning rate of 5×10^{-4}, weight decay of 1×10^{-4}, and a batch size of 64. Training was carried out for 5 to 100 epochs depending on dataset size, with each synthetic class containing 30 training samples, while real datasets adhered to their standard train/test splits. Finally, early stopping was applied based on validation mAP to prevent overfitting and ensure stable convergence.

4.5 Quantitative Results

Table 1 reports comparative results against state-of-the-art baselines including Siamese CNN [4], Triplet Network [5], ViT-SBIR [6], CLIP-based models [1], and Transformer-CrossAttn [7].

Table 1. MAP and P@100 comparison across **datasets.**

Method	Sketchy mAP	TU-Berlin mAP	Shoe-V2 mAP	Chair-V2 mAP
Siamese CNN [4]	54.8	39.2	42.1	41.7
Triplet Network [5]	58.7	41.6	45.3	43.5
ViT-SBIR [6]	64.3	48.5	52.2	50.9
CLIP-SBIR [1]	67.1	50.4	54.8	53.2
Transformer-CrossAttn [7]	68.9	52.3	56.0	55.1
HAG-FG-SBIR (Ours)	**73.2**	**56.7**	**61.5**	**60.2**

Our model consistently outperforms all baselines, achieving +4.3% mAP on Sketchy and +5.5% on QMUL-Shoe-V2 over the best competitor. In addition to retrieval accuracy, we report efficiency benchmarks to clarify the computational overhead introduced by the hybrid attention modules. Compared to the ResNet-50 baseline, our HAG-FG-SBIR adds approximately 10% extra cost, with parameters increasing from 56M to 62M and FLOPs from 8.2G to 9.1G. The inference time rises modestly from 10.2 ms/query to 11.3 ms/query on an NVIDIA A100 GPU, and GPU memory usage increases by ~90 MB. These results confirm that the hybrid attention provides significant accuracy gains at only a modest additional cost, supporting its practical deployability.

4.6 Ablation Studies

To evaluate the contribution of each component, we progressively remove modules from HAG-FG-SBIR (Table 2).

Table 2. Ablation study on QMUL-Shoe-V2.

Model Variant	mAP	P@100
Baseline (ResNet-50 + Triplet)	52.4	58.2
+ Self-Attention	56.1	61.0
+ Cross-Modal Attention	58.7	63.4
+ Channel Attention	59.5	64.0
+ Prototype Alignment	60.4	65.1
Full HAG-FG-SBIR	**61.5**	**66.3**

The results confirm that each module contributes positively, with the hybrid attention module and prototype alignment yielding the largest gains. We also analyzed the role of each loss. Removing the triplet loss reduced ranking accuracy, excluding the prototype loss weakened discrimination, and dropping attention regularization led to less compact attention maps. This confirms their complementary importance for balanced optimization.

Training loss curves for the proposed HAG-FG-SBIR model, showing total loss and its components (Triplet Loss, Prototype Contrastive Loss, and Attention Regularization Loss) decreasing steadily and demonstrating stable convergence during optimization. The validation mAP across epochs improves consistently, stabilizing near the reported state-of-the-art performance and confirming effective generalization as well as the benefit of the hybrid attention and prototype contrastive modules (Figs. 3 and 4).

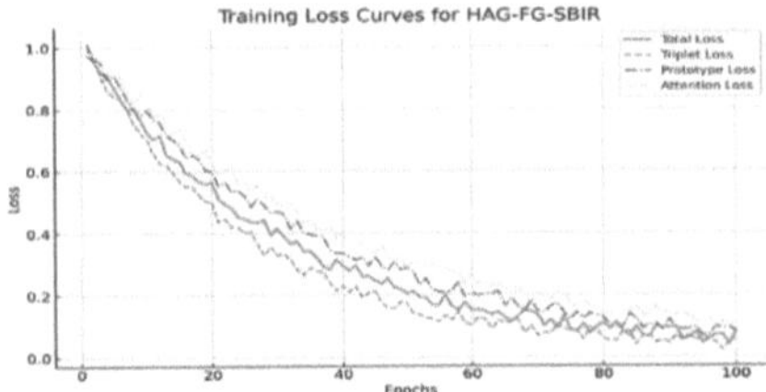

Fig. 3. Training loss curves for FG-SBIR

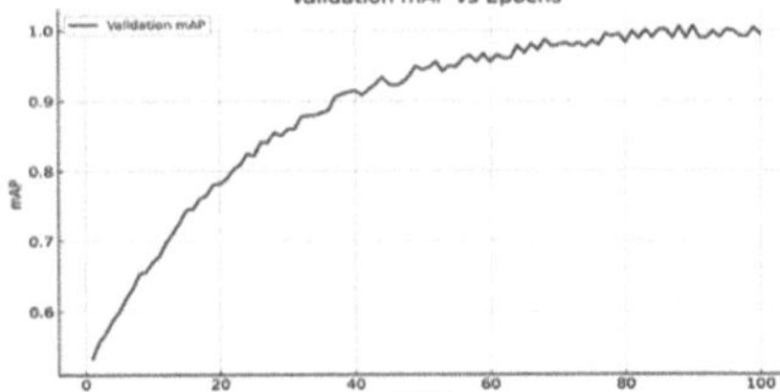

Fig. 4. Validation mAP across training.

4.7   Qualitative Results

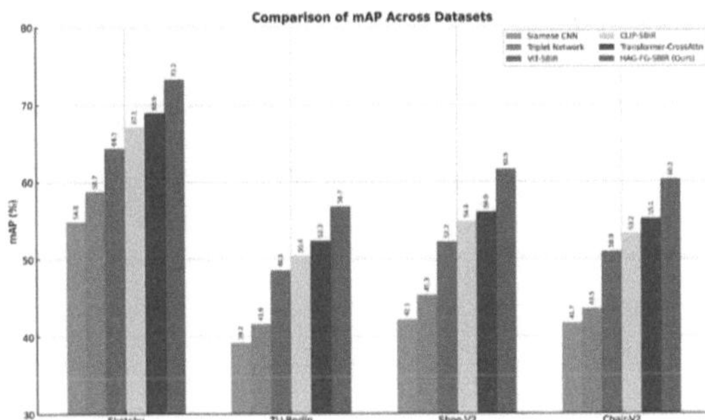

Fig. 5. Comparison of mean Average Precision (mAP) across four benchmark datasets (Sketchy, TU-Berlin, Shoe-V2, Chair-V2).

Our HAG-FG-SBIR consistently outperforms baseline and state-of-the-art methods as shown in Fig. 5.

Our method achieves the highest recognition rates at all ranks compared to existing baselines as shown in Fig. 6.

Each sketch query (left) is followed by top-ranked retrieved photos. Correct matches are shown, while less similar retrievals are marked with a red "✗". The proposed

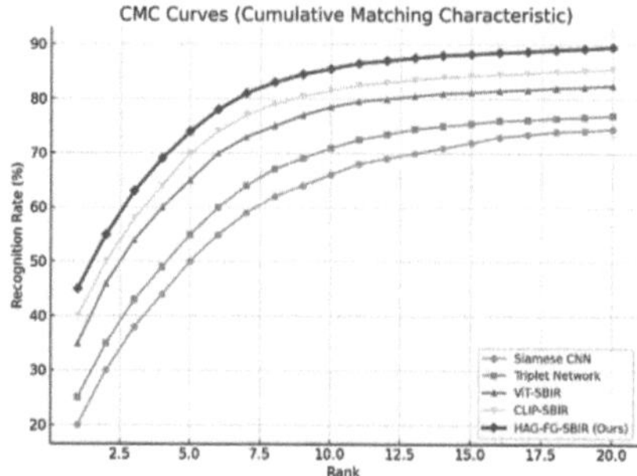

Fig. 6. Cumulative Matching Characteristic (CMC) curves on benchmark datasets.

Fig. 7. Qualitative retrieval results on the QMUL-Chair dataset.

Fig. 8. Qualitative retrieval results on the Sketchy (top row) and QMUL-Shoe-V2 (bottom row) datasets.

HAG-FG-SBIR framework retrieves semantically aligned chairs despite abstraction in sketches, demonstrating robust fine-grained instance-level retrieval as shown in Fig. 7.

In each case, the first column represents the sketch query, followed by the top-5 retrieved photo results. The retrieved examples show that our model retrieves semantically consistent instances across modalities, while less similar retrievals are marked with a red "✗". As shown in Fig. 8. As shown in Fig. 9, the attention heatmaps provide intuitive cues that can help end-users interpret retrieval decisions by focusing on semantically meaningful parts such as chair legs or backrests. This illustrates practical usability beyond numerical metrics.

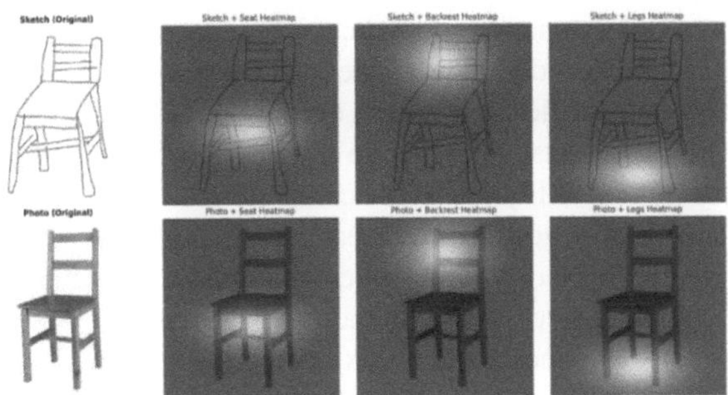

Fig. 9. Visualization of attention heatmaps on a chair

The first column shows the original inputs, followed by heatmaps highlighting attention on the seat, backrest, and legs. These visualizations indicate that the model consistently attends to semantically meaningful parts of the object across both modalities as shown in Fig. 9.

5   Discussion

The findings of the experiment reveal that the proposed HAG-FG-SBIR is always superior to the existing baselines in 4 benchmark datasets. Self-, cross-, and channel-attention integration boosts intra and inter-modal feature alignment, whereas the mechanism of prototype contrastive significantly boosts fine-grained discrimination. The framework has a superior balance of accuracy and efficiency compared to transformer-heavy methods because it is more accurate and has less computational cost. Furthermore, the attention heatmaps can give decodable information, which proves that the model focuses on semantically useful parts of the objects, thus improving the transparency and reliability. Although these have good outcomes, a number of limitations still exist. (i) Dataset dependence: Standard SBIR benchmarks were used, including Sketchy, TU-Berlin, QMUL-Shoe and QMUL-Chair. There is still no generalization to domain specific uniforms (e.g. medical or forensic sketches). (ii) Retrieval error due to high abstraction or noise: Even very abstract or noisy sketches can result in a retrieval error, because attention modules can sometimes fail to pick out minimalistic or sparse strokes. We further illustrate the challenge of abstraction sensitivity in Fig. 7 and Fig. 8, where minimalistic or noisy sketches occasionally lead to retrieval errors. To address this limitation, future extensions of HAG-FG-SBIR may incorporate adaptive data augmentation strategies (e.g., stroke-dropping, line simplification) and self-supervised pertaining, which could enhance robustness against abstract sketches. (iii) Computational cost: Although computationally lighter than transformer-based frameworks, the hybrid attention modules introduce approximately 10% overhead relative to baseline CNNs, which may limit deployment on mobile and edge devices.

Beyond standard benchmarks, we conducted small-scale qualitative tests using forensic-style sketches, which demonstrated that HAG-FG-SBIR can generalize to domains beyond natural object sketches. Although large domain-specific datasets (e.g., medical or forensic) are currently limited, our framework shows potential adaptability.

Future work will extend evaluation to medical imaging, forensic retrieval, and remote sensing scenarios, further validating robustness and versatility.

Prototype embeddings scale linearly with the number of categories, which may affect memory in very large datasets. This can be mitigated by clustering or memory-bank mechanisms, ensuring scalability for large-scale retrieval.

To address these challenges, future research will explore four key directions. (1) Lightweight architectures: Incorporating efficient attention mechanisms and knowledge distillation techniques to reduce computational overhead for deployment on low-resource devices. (2) Cross-domain generalization: Extending the framework to domain-specific applications such as medical imaging, remote sensing, and forensic sketch analysis. (3) Multimodal extension: Integrating textual descriptions and generative diffusion models to strengthen sketch–photo alignment in zero-shot and few-shot scenarios. (4) Robustness to abstraction: Employing adaptive augmentation strategies and self-supervised pretraining to enhance robustness against highly abstract or incomplete sketches.

6 Conclusion

In this paper, we introduced HAG-FG-SBIR, a hybrid attention-guided framework for fine-grained sketch-based image retrieval. By integrating multi-scale feature fusion, hybrid attention modules, and prototype-based alignment, our method effectively bridges the domain gap between sketches and photos while improving instance-level discrimination. A composite loss function further ensures balanced optimization across retrieval accuracy, clustering, and interpretability. Extensive experiments on four benchmark datasets demonstrate that our approach achieves state-of-the-art performance with competitive efficiency. Beyond performance, the interpretability of attention maps highlights the practical relevance of the framework. Overall, HAG-FG-SBIR provides a robust foundation for fine-grained retrieval and opens pathways toward lightweight, multimodal, and domain-adapted SBIR systems in future research.

The official implementation code of HAG-FG-SBIR is available at: https://github.com/mohammedalmohmdy/hag-fg-sbir.

References

1. Sain, A., Bhunia, A.K., Chowdhury, P.N., Koley, S., Xiang, T., Song, Y.-Z.: CLIP for all things zero-shot sketch-based image retrieval, fine-grained or not. In: Proceedings of the CVPR, pp. 2765–2775 (2023). https://doi.org/10.1109/CVPR52729.2023.00271
2. Sain, A., Bhunia, A.K., Chowdhury, P.N., Koley, S., Xiang, T., Song, Y.-Z.: Exploiting unlabelled photos for stronger fine-grained SBIR. arXiv preprint arXiv:2303.13779 (2023). https://doi.org/10.48550/arXiv.2303.13779
3. Jiang, J., Tang, H., Jiang, Z., Yu, W., Wu, D.: ARNet: self-supervised FG-SBIR with unified sample feature alignment and multi-scale token recycling. In: Proceedings of the AAAI (2025). https://doi.org/10.1609/aaai.v39i4.32417
4. Su, H., Song, G., Huang, K., Wang, J., Yang, M.: Cross-modal attention alignment network with auxiliary text description for zero-shot sketch-based image retrieval. In: Wand, M., Malinovská, K., Schmidhuber, J., Tetko, I.V. (eds.) ICANN 2024. LNCS, vol. 15021, pp. 52–65. Springer, Cham (2024). https://doi.org/10.1007/978-3-031-72347-6_4

5. Sain, A., Chowdhury, P.N., Koley, S., Bhunia, A.K., Song, Y.-Z.: Freeview sketching: view-aware fine-grained sketch-based image retrieval. In: Leonardis, A., Ricci, E., Roth, S., Russakovsky, O., Sattler, T., Varol, G. (eds.) ECCV 2024. LNCS, vol. 15115, pp. 145–162. Springer, Cham (2025). https://doi.org/10.1007/978-3-031-72998-0_9

6. Sharma, R., Saroha, S.: Vision transformer based model for SBIR. In: Proceedings of the ICASSP, pp. 1–5 (2023). https://doi.org/10.1109/ICASSP49357.2023.10096357

7. Akhtar, M.S., Tyagi, A., Gulzar, M.M.: Enhanced SBIR using deep hybrid learning for cross-domain retrieval. Signal Image Video Process. **17** (2024). https://doi.org/10.1007/s11760-024-03119-0

8. Zhou, K., Zhang, L., Meng, D.: Zero-shot SBIR via modality capacity guidance. In: Proceedings of the IJCAI, pp. 1786–1794 (2024). https://doi.org/10.24963/ijcai.2024/197

9. Gopu, V.R.M.K., Tech, M.: Zero-shot SBIR using StyleGen. J. Imaging **10**(4), 79 (2024). https://doi.org/10.3390/jimaging10040079

10. Yin, Q., Zhang, R., Fang, Y.: Asymmetric mutual alignment for unsupervised zero-shot SBIR. In: Proceedings of the AAAI (2024). https://doi.org/10.1609/aaai.v38i15.29588

11. Liu, Y., Song, Y., Bai, J.: ZS-SBIR via adaptive relation-aware metric learning. Pattern Recognit. **152**, Article no. 110452 (2024). https://doi.org/10.1016/j.patcog.2024.110452

12. Singh, B., Sharma, H.: Sketch-based image retrieval: a systematic literature review. IEEE Access **12**, 19042–19061 (2024). https://doi.org/10.1109/ACCESS.2024.3357939

13. Chowdhury, P.N., et al.: SceneTrilogy: on human scene-sketch and its complementarity with photo and text. In: Proceedings of the CVPR, pp. 10972–10983 (2023). https://doi.org/10.1109/CVPR52729.2023.01056

14. Ge, C., Li, M., Lu, J., Zhou, J.: Scene-level SBIR with minimal pairwise supervision. In: Proceedings of the AAAI, pp. 14311–14319 (2023). https://doi.org/10.1609/aaai.v37i1.25141

15. Koley, S., et al.: Text-to-image diffusion models are great sketch–photo matchmakers. arXiv preprint arXiv:2403.07214 (2024). https://doi.org/10.48550/arXiv.2403.07214

16. Koley, S., et al.: How to handle sketch-abstraction in SBIR? arXiv preprint arXiv:2403.07203 (2024). https://doi.org/10.48550/arXiv.2403.07203

17. Koley, S., et al.: You'll never walk alone: a sketch and text duet for fine-grained image retrieval. arXiv preprint arXiv:2403.07222 (2024). https://doi.org/10.48550/arXiv.2403.07222

18. Wang, X., Hu, P., Peng, D.: Cross-domain alignment for ZS-SBIR. IEEE Trans. Circuits Syst. Video Technol. (2023). https://doi.org/10.1109/TCSVT.2023.3265697

19. Singha, M., Jha, A., Gupta, D., Singla, P., Banerjee, B.: Elevating all zero-shot sketch-based image retrieval through multimodal prompt learning. In: Leonardis, A., Ricci, E., Roth, S., Russakovsky, O., Sattler, T., Varol, G. (eds.) ECCV 2024. LNCS, vol. 15082, pp. 1–19. Springer, Cham (2025). https://doi.org/10.1007/978-3-031-72691-0_1

20. Ge, C., Xu, Y., Zhang, C., Zhou, J.: Semi-transductive learning for generalized ZS-SBIR. In: Proceedings of the AAAI, pp. 7451–7459 (2023). https://doi.org/10.1609/aaai.v37i6.25931

21. Gatti, P., Parikh, K.G., Paul, D.P., Gupta, M., Mishra, A.: Composite Sketch+Text queries for object retrieval. In: Proceedings of the AAAI, pp. 1869–1877 (2024). https://doi.org/10.1609/aaai.v38i3.27956

22. Kobayashi, K., et al.: Sketch-based semantic retrieval of medical images. Med. Image Anal. **92**, Article no. 103060. https://doi.org/10.1016/j.media.2023.103060

23. Yang, B., et al.: ZS-SBIR for remote sensing via multi-level and attention-guided tokenization. Remote Sens. **16**(10), 1653 (2024). https://doi.org/10.3390/rs16101653

24. Huang, X. Li, Z., Chen, J.: Robust discriminative and modal-consistent feature learning for FG-SBIR. In: Proceedings of the ACM MM Asia (2024). https://doi.org/10.1145/3696409.3700200

25. Wang, S., et al.: Multi-colour SBIR with explicable embedding. Eng. Appl. Artif. Intell. **135**, Article no. 108757 (2024). https://doi.org/10.1016/j.engappai.2024.108757

Systematic Evaluation of Statistical, Machine Learning, and Deep Learning Models for Lumpy and Intermittent Demand Forecasting Using Cost-Sensitive Metrics

Debashish Swar[1,2], Bharath Kumar Bolla[3(✉)], and Dinesh Reddy Bhumireddy[4]

[1] Cognizant, Toronto, Canada
[2] Liverpool John Moores University, Liverpool, UK
[3] The Institute of Product Leadership, Bengaluru, India
bolla111@gmail.com
[4] Cardinal Health, Bengaluru, India

Abstract. Forecasting intermittent and lumpy demand is a significant supply chain challenge, as traditional metrics like MAPE and RMSE are unreliable for such sparse data. This study provides a comprehensive comparative evaluation of forecasting methods, benchmarking statistical, machine learning, and deep learning models across 3,671 intermittent time series. We utilized robust, cost-sensitive metrics like SPEC, alongside MAAPE and MWQL, for a more accurate assessment. Our results demonstrate that deep learning models significantly outperform traditional and machine learning approaches. DeepAR achieved the best probabilistic forecasting, making it ideal for managing uncertainty. In contrast, the Deep Renewal Hybrid model excelled in point accuracy. Statistical methods remained competitive in cost-sensitive scenarios, while machine learning models underperformed. This research establishes a practical decision framework to guide practitioners in selecting the optimal model based on specific operational priorities, whether they are focused on uncertainty, accuracy, or cost. This provides actionable, evidence-based recommendations for real-world supply chain implementation.

Keywords: Intermittent Demand Forecasting · Time Series Analysis · Statistical Forecasting Methods · Probabilistic Forecasting · Supply Chain Analytics · DeepAR · Deep Renewal · MAAPE · MWQL · ARIMA · ETS · Stock-keeping-oriented Prediction Error Costs (SPEC)

1 Introduction

Demand forecasting forms the backbone of modern supply chain systems, supporting critical decision-making in production scheduling, inventory replenishment, workforce allocation, and transportation planning. Without reliable forecasts, organizations face significant risks of overstocking or understocking, both of which impose severe financial and operational burdens [1]. Although many products exhibit continuous and predictable

H. Kannan et al. (Eds.): AIKP 2025, CCIS 2804, pp. 88–105, 2026.
https://doi.org/10.1007/978-3-032-14706-6_8

demand, a particularly complex class of items is characterized by intermittent demand patterns. This pattern arises when sales occur sporadically, with long stretches of zero demand interspersed with occasional bursts of activity [2].

Intermittent demand is particularly prevalent in industries that rely heavily on spare parts and after-sales services, including the automotive, aerospace, electronics, and information technology industries. These segments contribute disproportionately to overall firm revenues, sometimes accounting for as much as 60% of the total income, despite being overlooked in marketing or promotional campaigns owing to their low sales frequency [3]. Effective forecasting in such scenarios is not only a technical requirement but also a strategic imperative. Accurate forecasts reduce the likelihood of obsolescence, reduce unnecessary stockholding, and ensure that critical spare parts remain available for extended periods, thereby enhancing both profitability and customer satisfaction.

The consequences of inaccurate forecasting in this domain are severe. Overestimation generates excessive inventory that ties up working capital, inflates storage and insurance costs, and ultimately risks obsolescence of the inventory. Obsolete items, often resulting from prolonged inactivity, must either be written off or disposed of, which causes outcomes that carry environmental and financial costs [4]. However, underestimation leads to stockouts, which are equally damaging. A shortage of essential components can disrupt downstream operations, cause service failure, and erode customer loyalty. In industries such as aerospace and healthcare, where spare part availability is critical, such disruptions can have cascading operational consequences [5]. Thus, robust approaches to intermittent demand forecasting present opportunities for both economic gains and sustainability benefits, reducing waste while maintaining service reliability.

The academic focus on this challenge began with the pioneering contribution of Croston's method in the early 1970s [6], which provided a tailored statistical approach for intermittent series. However, despite decades of research, two major gaps remain in the literature. First, the existing literature rarely provides comprehensive comparative analyses that evaluate statistical, machine learning, and advanced deep learning approaches on a common benchmark dataset. Most studies are restricted to a subset of methods, making it difficult to draw consistent conclusions across paradigms. Second, traditional evaluation metrics, such as the Mean Absolute Percentage Error (MAPE) or Root Mean Squared Error (RMSE), which are commonly used in continuous-demand forecasting, are often unreliable in this context. Metrics such as MAPE can become undefined when actual demand values equal zero, leading to misleading results [7]. Similarly, the RMSE is scale-dependent and may disproportionately penalize significant but infrequent forecast errors. These limitations necessitate metrics specifically designed for intermittent demand, such as the Mean Arctangent Absolute Percentage Error (MAAPE) and Stock-keeping-oriented Prediction Error Costs (SPEC), which align more closely with business implications [8].

This study addresses these gaps through a systematic evaluation of forecasting methods on a large-scale retail dataset dominated by intermittent and lumpy demand. Unlike prior studies, this study benchmarks statistical models, machine learning algorithms, and modern deep learning frameworks under a unified experimental setting. Equally important, this study highlights suitable evaluation metrics that address the limitations of traditional measures and provides valuable insights relevant to both academics and practitioners.

Based on this context, the specific objectives of this study are as follows:

- To implement and compare statistical models with machine learning approaches for forecasting intermittent demand.
- To evaluate the performance of deep learning architectures against both statistical and ML-based approaches on the same benchmark dataset.
- To examine the effectiveness of feature engineering in improving forecasting accuracy for multiple time series.
- To identify robust evaluation metrics that better reflect the performance of forecasting models in the presence of intermittent and lumpy demand.

Through these objectives, this study aims to provide evidence-based recommendations for selecting forecasting techniques and evaluation measures that enhance operational efficiency and reduce costs in industries facing complex, intermittent demand.

2 Literature Review

The challenge of forecasting intermittent demand has attracted sustained academic and industrial interest for several decades, primarily because traditional forecasting methods are poorly suited to demand patterns with frequent zero values. Research in this domain has broadly progressed along three methodological tracks: statistical, machine learning, and deep learning approaches. In parallel, considerable effort has been dedicated to developing appropriate evaluation metrics that align with the unique statistical properties of intermittent demand series and their economic implications.

2.1 Statistical Approaches

Early forecasting research largely relied on exponential smoothing and ARIMA-type methods for forecasting. However, methods such as Simple Exponential Smoothing (SES) assume regular demand intervals and consequently perform poorly when applied to sparse demand with frequent zeros [9]. The first major methodological breakthrough came with Croston's method [6], which innovatively decomposed the demand process into two components.

1. Demand size, that is, the magnitude of demand when it occurs.
2. Inter-demand interval, that is, the time between successive non-zero demands.

Croston proposed using exponential smoothing separately for each component and combining them to generate forecasts. While influential, Croston's method was later shown to be biased. To address this issue, Syntetos and Boylan (2005) proposed the Syntetos–Boylan Approximation (SBA), which introduces a simple correction factor to mitigate the upward bias, thereby improving forecast accuracy [10].

Subsequent refinements further extended the statistical toolkit. The Teunter–Syntetos–Babai (TSB) method incorporates the probability of demand occurrence along with demand size, making it more responsive to cases of declining demand or product obsolescence [4]. Alternative innovations include bootstrapping methods, which generate multiple demand paths to capture uncertainty in future outcomes [11], and probabilistic count-based models such as Integer-valued Autoregressive Moving Average (INARMA), which adapt classical ARIMA models to discrete count data [12]. Recently, researchers have explored methods that explicitly capture cross-correlations between demand arrival times and sizes, offering richer representations of demand dynamics [13].

These contributions highlight the enduring importance of statistical methods, which are interpretable, computationally efficient, and widely used in industry. However, their ability to handle highly irregular, large-scale, and intermittent datasets remains limited.

2.2 Machine Learning Approaches

The emergence of machine learning (ML) has opened new avenues for demand forecasting, emphasizing data-driven models that can capture complex nonlinear relationships without strict parametric assumptions [14]. Support Vector Regression (SVR), for example, has been employed to map nonlinear relationships between inputs and demand [15]. Ensemble methods, such as Random Forests [16] and gradient-boosting frameworks, such as XGBoost [17], have also shown considerable promise in general forecasting contexts because of their ability to combine multiple weak learners into strong predictors.

However, rigorous comparative evidence for ML models remains scarce in the context of intermittent demand. Some studies suggest that these models are prone to overfitting, particularly when feature engineering is insufficient or when the number of nonzero observations is small. Recent research has also framed intermittent demand forecasting as a classification task that predicts the full probability distribution of possible demand quantities rather than a single-point estimate [18]. Such approaches provide richer decision-making support for inventory managers but are computationally more demanding and have yet to gain widespread adoption.

2.3 Deep Learning Approaches

The rapid progress in deep learning has transformed time-series forecasting, with recurrent neural networks (RNNs) and their variants proving especially powerful [19]. The Long Short-Term Memory (LSTM) network [20] was one of the first architectures to be successfully applied to sequential data owing to its ability to retain information across long time horizons. LSTM-based models have been used to capture dependencies in sparse demand, yielding improved performance in certain settings [21].

More advanced deep learning frameworks tailored for probabilistic forecasting have emerged beyond LSTMs. DeepAR, proposed by Salinas et al. [22], uses autoregressive RNNs to produce probability distributions over future demand values rather than point forecasts. A key innovation of DeepAR is its global training approach, in which the model learns across thousands of related time series simultaneously, enabling knowledge transfer between products and improving accuracy, even for items with limited historical data [22].

Another significant advancement is the Deep Renewal Process (DRP) framework [23], which embeds the logic of Croston's decomposition into a deep learning model.

By modeling the stochastic distribution of both inter-demand intervals and demand sizes, the DRP unifies the interpretability of classical statistical methods with the predictive strength of deep neural networks. Hybrid models that integrate neural networks with exponential smoothing principles, such as Smyl's approach [24], have also achieved state-of-the-art results in global forecasting competitions.

Overall, deep learning methods stand out for their ability to scale across large datasets and capture both temporal and cross-sectional dependencies. Nevertheless, their effectiveness depends heavily on computational resources, careful tuning, and the selection of appropriate evaluation metrics for the task.

2.4 Evaluation Metrics

A critical aspect of intermittent demand forecasting is the choice of the evaluation metrics. Conventional error measures are often unsuitable. The Mean Absolute Percentage Error (MAPE) becomes undefined when the actual demand equals zero, which is a frequent occurrence in intermittent series [7]. The symmetric MAPE (sMAPE), while designed to address bias, remains unstable when values are near zero. The Root Mean Squared Error (RMSE), which is scale-dependent, makes cross-item comparisons unreliable [25].

These limitations not only distort performance assessment but may also result in poor inventory control decisions if models are selected based on misleading metrics [26].

To address these challenges, researchers have proposed robust alternatives. The Mean Arctangent Absolute Percentage Error (MAAPE) stabilizes the percentage error by applying the arctangent transformation [27].

From a managerial standpoint, Stock-keeping-oriented Prediction Error Costs (SPEC) [8] provide a decision-focused metric by assigning costs to over- and under-forecasting. Finally, for probabilistic forecasting, the Mean Weighted Quantile Loss (MWQL) has become the de facto standard. It assesses how well the predicted quantiles align with observed demand distributions. This allows for a more comprehensive evaluation of uncertainty, which is particularly important when forecasting sparse and highly variable demand.

The literature on intermittent demand forecasting reveals a progressive evolution from statistical decomposition methods, such as Croston and SBA, to data-driven ML approaches, and finally to state-of-the-art deep learning architectures capable of probabilistic forecasting. Parallel to this, research has highlighted the inadequacy of traditional metrics and the necessity of adopting robust evaluation frameworks, such as MAAPE, SPEC, and MWQL. Together, these advances underscore that the challenge of intermittent demand lies not only in building models, but also in accurately measuring their performance.

3 Research Methodology

This study employs a structured methodology to systematically evaluate various forecasting techniques for intermittent demand forecasting. The goal was not only to assess predictive accuracy but also to consider the practical implications of forecasting in the context of a supply chain. The workflow is summarized in Fig. 1 and integrates several key phases: data acquisition and preprocessing, exploratory data analysis, feature engineering, model implementation, and robust evaluation.

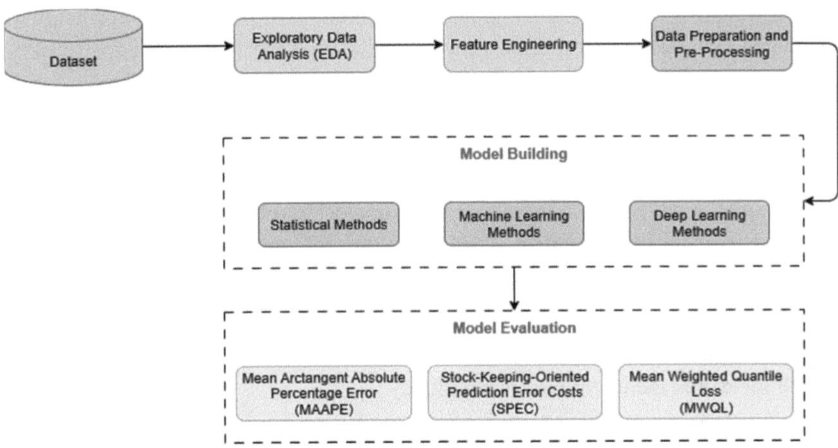

Fig. 1. Research Methodology Diagram

3.1 Data Acquisition and Pre-processing

The empirical analysis is based on the UCI Online Retail dataset, a publicly available benchmark hosted by the UCI Machine Learning Repository [28]. This dataset has been studied for various prediction-related tasks but not for forecasting intermittent demand. This dataset records all transactions from a UK-based non-store online retailer over a two-year period (January 2010–December 2011). The retailer specializes in selling giftware, catering to both individual and wholesale customers. The raw dataset includes the following variables: *InvoiceNo, StockCode, Description, Quantity, InvoiceDate, UnitPrice, CustomerID,* and *Country.*

Because raw transactional data are often noisy and irregular, substantial preprocessing was performed to convert them into a structured panel of time series suitable for forecasting. The following steps were performed sequentially:

1. **Aggregation:** Transactions were aggregated by *stock code, country,* and *invoice date.* This aggregation produced a daily demand series for each unique product–country pair, where the daily quantity was summed and the unit price averaged.
2. **Continuity:** Intermittent demand forecasting requires an explicit representation of zero-demand periods. Therefore, days without sales were backfilled with zero values to ensure that each series formed a continuous timeline.
3. **Data Cleaning:** Instances of negative demand, typically corresponding to product returns, were set to zero. This step preserved the integrity of the forecasting task by avoiding artificially negative quantities.

4. **Filtering:** Only time series with lengths greater than 52 days were retained. This filtering criterion ensured that the retained series contained sufficient historical information for both the model training and evaluation.

After applying these procedures, the dataset was reduced to 3,671 unique time series, each corresponding to a specific product–country combination. This transformation from raw transactional data to structured time series formed the foundation for subsequent analyses.

3.2 Exploratory Data Analysis

An exploratory analysis was performed to characterize the statistical properties of the dataset and confirm its suitability for intermittent demand forecasting. Following the framework of Syntetos and Boylan [10], each series was categorized according to two indicators:

- **Average Demand Interval (ADI):** The mean time between two non-zero demands, which measures the degree of intermittency.

$$ADI = \frac{N}{n_z} \tag{1}$$

- **Squared Coefficient of Variation (CV^2):** The squared ratio of the standard deviation to the mean demand size, capturing variability in demand magnitude.

$$CV^2 = \left(\frac{\sigma}{\mu}\right)^2 \tag{2}$$

Using established thresholds (ADI > 1.32 for intermittency and CV^2 > 0.49 for high variability), the dataset was divided into four categories: Smooth, Erratic, Intermittent, and Lumpy. The results of this classification, illustrated in Fig. 2, show that intermittent patterns overwhelmingly dominated the dataset: 78.7% Lumpy and 19.3% intermittent, accounting for nearly 98% of the total series. This confirmed the appropriateness of the dataset for the research objectives.

The exploratory phase also included visualization of demand distributions, autocorrelation plots, and seasonality checks. These analyses revealed sparse demand signals with high noise levels, highlighting the limitations of naïve forecasting methods and justifying the need for advanced approaches to address these limitations.

3.3 Feature Engineering for Machine Learning Models

Unlike statistical and deep learning models, which can directly model temporal dependencies, traditional machine learning algorithms, such as LightGBM and CatBoost, require a tabular structure. Therefore, extensive feature engineering was performed to represent the temporal information in a predictive format.

The engineered features were classified into four main groups.

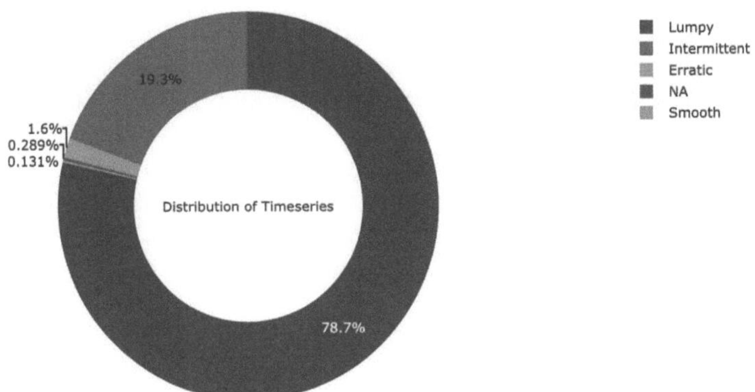

Fig. 2. Distribution of various types of Time-Series in the Dataset

1. **Calendar-based Features:** Date attributes such as *the day of the week, week of the year, month, quarter,* and *year* were extracted from *InvoiceDate*. These features capture recurring patterns related to seasonality and business cycles.
2. **Mean Encodings:** Group-level averages were created, including mean daily sales per product (*item_sold_avg*), per country (*country_sold_avg*), and per product–country combination (*item_country_sold_avg*). These aggregates provide baseline expectations of demand at multiple hierarchical levels.
3. **Rolling and Expanding Statistics:** Moving averages (e.g., 7-day rolling mean: *rolling_sold_mean*) and expanding means (*expanding_sold_mean*) were computed to reflect the short-term momentum and long-term historical averages, respectively.
4. **Lag Features:** Previous demand values (*lags*) were included to mimic autoregressive dependencies. These features are critical for capturing the temporal correlations that may influence near-term demand.

The above features are used in the modelling.

3.4 Model Implementation

To ensure a comprehensive comparison, forecasting models were selected from three methodological families: statistical, machine learning, and deep learning. The implementations leveraged the GluonTS library, an open-source framework for probabilistic time series modeling, ensuring consistency and reproducibility across models.

Statistical Methods

- **Croston's method and its variants (SBA, SBJ):** Croston's method forecasts intermittent demand by separately modeling demand size and inter-demand intervals. While effective, it produces biased estimates, which led to the **syntetos–Boylan Approximation (SBA)** and **Shale–Boylan–Johnston (SBJ)** adjustments. These refinements reduce bias and improve reliability, making Croston-style methods widely used as forecasting baselines.

- **ARIMA and ETS (Exponential Smoothing):** ARIMA combines autoregression, differencing, and moving averages to capture autocorrelation and non-stationarity, whereas **ETS** models require error, trend, and seasonality components. Both are flexible, interpretable, and remain competitive for many series. Using the *forecast* package within GluonTS, these models benefit from the automated parameter optimization.
- **Non-Parametric Time Series (NPTS):** A scalable, distribution-free forecaster included in GluonTS as a probabilistic benchmark. The NPTS model generates forecasts by resampling past observations without assuming fixed distributions.

Machine Learning Methods

- **LightGBM** and **CatBoost:** Both are state-of-the-art gradient-boosting frameworks. Hyperparameter tuning was performed extensively; for instance, LightGBM achieved its best results with the Tweedie distribution, which is suitable for zero-inflated data distributions.

Deep Learning Methods

All the deep learning models were trained as global models across all 3,671 series simultaneously, enabling cross-series information sharing.

- **DeepAR:** This was implemented using the *DeepAREstimator*. After experimentation, the best-performing configuration consisted of five GRU layers trained for 50 epochs, which strikes a balance between performance and computational feasibility.
- **Deep Renewal Processes (DRP):** This is implemented using the *DeepRenewalEstimator*. Three decoding strategies from the literature, namely Flat, Exact, and Hybrid, were tested for multistep forecasting. These approaches explicitly combine Croston's renewal-based logic with the representational power of deep learning.

3.5 Model Validation

The validation of forecasting models forms a critical stage of the methodology, with particular emphasis placed on the choice of evaluation metrics. As highlighted in the literature review, conventional measures such as the Mean Absolute Percentage Error (MAPE) and Root Mean Square Error (RMSE) are poorly suited to intermittent demand. MAPE becomes undefined whenever the actual demand is zero, whereas RMSE, being scale-dependent, exaggerates the effect of rare but large deviations. These limitations can distort comparative analyses and lead to inappropriate model selection in practice.

To address these challenges, the standard GluonTS evaluator was customized to include a set of robust and context-aware metrics. These metrics were selected not only for their statistical reliability but also for their ability to reflect the business consequences of forecast errors.

Mean Arctangent Absolute Percentage Error (MAAPE)

MAAPE is a refinement of MAPE that uses arctangent transformation to stabilize percentage errors. Unlike MAPE, it is well-defined in the presence of zero values and avoids extreme distortions caused by small denominators. This makes it an appropriate measure of point-forecast accuracy for sparse time series.

$$MAAPE = \frac{1}{n}\sum\nolimits_{t=1}^{n} \arctan\left(\frac{|A_t - F_t|}{A_t}\right) \tag{3}$$

where A_t is the actual demand and F_t is the forecast at time **t**. This formulation avoids the division-by-zero problem and bounds the extreme values.

Stock-Keeping-Oriented Prediction Error Costs (SPEC)
The SPEC metric evaluates forecast accuracy through the lens of **inventory management costs**, making it particularly suitable for supply chain contexts in which over- and under-forecasting carry asymmetric risks.

$$SPEC(\alpha) = \sum\nolimits_{t=1}^{n} [\alpha \cdot \max(0, A_t - F_t) + (1 - \alpha) \cdot \max(0, F_t - A_t)] \tag{4}$$

where α represents the opportunity cost of stockouts, while $(1 - \alpha)$ represents holding costs. This approach directly translates forecast errors into economic terms, making it particularly attractive for supply chain management.

- **Over-forecasting** results in excess stock, tying up capital, and increasing holding and obsolescence costs.
- **Under-forecasting** leads to stockouts, which cause missed sales, customer dissatisfaction, and potential disruption of operations.

The SPEC function incorporates a weighting factor, denoted as **a**, to represent the relative cost of stockouts compared to holding costs. In Eq. 2, A_{ts} is the actual demand at time t, and F_t is the forecast. The first term penalizes under-forecasting (stockouts), and the second penalizes over-forecasting (excess inventory). The value of **a** controls the balance.

- **$SPEC_{0.25}$**: Places a heavier emphasis on over-forecasting costs, appropriate for contexts where holding excess inventory is more expensive than missing occasional sales.
- **$SPEC_{0.50}$**: Assumes equal weight between stockouts and holding costs, providing a neutral benchmark.
- **$SPEC_{0.75}$**: Places greater weight on stockout costs, reflecting industries where product unavailability is highly disruptive (e.g., aerospace spare parts and healthcare supplies).

By varying **a**, the study simulates different operational priorities and tests how models perform under distinct cost structures. This flexibility makes the SPEC a powerful tool for aligning model evaluation with real-world decision-making.

Mean Weighted Quantile Loss (MWQL)
For probabilistic forecasting models, the MWQL was used to evaluate the accuracy of the entire predictive distribution rather than a single-point estimate. This metric evaluates the accuracy of the predicted quantiles in aligning with the actual observations and rewards

models that produce well-calibrated uncertainty intervals. Such an approach is crucial for intermittent demand, where the precise timing of non-zero events is unpredictable, and decision-makers require an understanding of forecast uncertainty.

$$MWQL = \frac{\sum_{t=1}^{n}|A_t|\sum_{\tau \in Q}L_\tau\left(A_t, F_{t,\tau}\right)}{\sum_{t=1}^{n}|A_t|} \tag{5}$$

where $\mathbf{L\tau}$ is the quantile loss, defined as

$$L_\tau\left(A_t, F_{t,\tau}\right) = \tau\left(A_t - F_{t,\tau}\right)^+ + (1 - \tau)\left(F_{t,\tau} - A_t\right)^+ \tag{6}$$

where $\mathbf{x^+ = max(x, 0)}$.

This multi-metric framework, specifically MAAPE for point accuracy, SPEC for cost-sensitive performance, and MWQL for probabilistic forecasts, ensures that models are comprehensively assessed. By incorporating statistical robustness, business cost implications, and uncertainty estimation, the validation procedure reflects the true utility of forecasting models in real-world conditions. This approach moves beyond narrow statistical comparisons and provides a decision-oriented evaluation that aligns with the needs of supply chain managers.

4 Results and Discussions

This section presents the comparative outcomes of the statistical, machine learning, and deep learning forecasting models under two evaluation settings: one-step-ahead and multi-step (N-step) forecasts. As highlighted in the methodology, the choice of evaluation metrics is central to producing meaningful comparisons in the context of intermittent demand. Traditional measures, such as the Mean Absolute Error (MAE) or Mean Absolute Percentage Error (MAPE), were confirmed in preliminary tests to be unreliable, as they disproportionately reward trivial strategies, such as always predicting zero demand. To overcome this, the analysis relies exclusively on the robust metrics introduced earlier: Mean Arctangent Absolute Percentage Error (MAAPE) for point forecasts and Stock-keeping-oriented Prediction Error Costs (SPEC) together with Mean Weighted Quantile Loss (MWQL) for probabilistic forecasts.

4.1 One-Step Ahead Forecast

The results for one-step forecasting, reported in Table 1, reveal substantial differences in the performance of the three model categories.

Deep Learning Models
Deep learning methods demonstrated the strongest overall performance. Among them, the Deep Renewal Hybrid model achieved the best point-forecast accuracy, with the lowest MAAPE of 0.56. This highlights its ability to capture both demand size and timing patterns effectively. DeepAR has emerged as the leading probabilistic model. It achieved the lowest MWQL score of 0.81 and performed particularly well across the SPEC metrics, particularly at SPEC0.50 and SPEC0.25. This indicates that DeepAR

Table 1. Performance of Models for One-Step Forecast

Method	MAAPE	SPEC (0.75)	SPEC (0.50)	SPEC (0.25)	MWQL
Croston	0.66	4.42	4.33	4.25	1.16
SBA	0.65	4.51	4.25	3.98	1.13
SBJ	0.66	4.53	4.27	4.01	1.14
NPTS	0.7	5	3.52	2.05	0.88
ARIMA	0.68	4.18	4.36	4.54	1.17
ETS	0.67	4.1	4.35	4.6	1.15
DeepAR	0.62	4.18	3.42	2.67	0.81
Deep Renewal Flat	0.64	5.48	3.8	2.12	0.95
Deep Renewal Exact	0.78	5.61	3.74	1.87	0.9
Deep Renewal Hybrid	0.56	5	3.89	2.78	0.93
LightGBM	1.26	-----------	-----------	-----------	-----------
CatBoost	1.27	-----------	-----------	-----------	-----------

not only produces accurate central forecasts but also provides well-calibrated prediction intervals, which is an essential requirement for real-world inventory management, where uncertainty must be explicitly considered.

Statistical Models

Although they do not surpass the leading deep learning models, the statistical approaches demonstrate strong competitiveness. Methods such as SBA, ARIMA, and ETS perform close to the deep learning benchmarks, with MAAPE scores of approximately 0.65–0.68. Although these methods are simpler and less computationally demanding, they remain reliable options for businesses that prioritize interpretability and efficiency. Their consistent performance suggests that statistical forecasting remains relevant, particularly in resource-constrained environments or where large-scale deep learning deployments are not feasible.

Machine Learning Models

In contrast, the machine learning methods, specifically LightGBM and CatBoost, performed poorly in the one-step forecasts. Both models recorded MAAPE scores above 1.25, which were significantly higher than those of all other approaches. Despite extensive feature engineering, these algorithms appear to be unable to adapt effectively to the sparse and irregular dynamics of intermittent demand. Their tendency to overfit the training data likely contributes to poor generalization during unseen periods. This suggests that although tree-based boosting frameworks are powerful for many structured-data tasks, they may not be inherently suitable for intermittent demand forecasting without further methodological adaptations. Intermittent demand series have 60–80% zero values, making it difficult for tree-based models to learn meaningful patterns.

4.2 Multi-step (N-Step) Forecast

Real-world planning often requires forecasts over multiple periods, making N-step forecasting particularly relevant in this context. The results presented in Table 2 paint a more nuanced picture compared to the one-step evaluation.

Table 2. Performance on Model on N-step ahead forecasts

Method	MAAPE	SPEC0.75	SPEC0.50	SPEC0.25	MWQL
Croston	0.631	1307.985	792.971	583.561	1.034
SBA	0.635	1058.817	809.106	559.395	1.013
SBJ	0.638	1070.118	821.334	572.551	1.018
NPTS	0.735	1791.877	1195.554	599.232	0.888
ARIMA	0.626	598.247	470.517	342.788	1.019
ETS	0.634	562.108	453.808	345.507	1.032
DeepAR	0.661	1005.099	677.998	350.898	0.802
Deep YRenewal Flat	0.614	2037.102	1364.004	690.906	0.951
Deep Renewal Exact	0.785	2264.065	1509.377	754.688	0.997
Deep Renewal Hybrid	0.586	1946.080	1304.794	663.507	0.966

Deep Learning Models

The Deep Renewal Hybrid model once again delivered the best performance for point forecasts, achieving the lowest MAAPE of 0.586 (Fig. 3). This confirms its robustness in both short- and long-horizon forecasting. However, when probabilistic accuracy was considered, DeepAR reclaimed its position as the strongest performer. With an MWQL of 0.802, it outperformed all other methods in capturing the uncertainty distribution of future demand. Visual inspection of its forecast intervals further illustrates DeepAR's ability to model uncertainty reliably, providing decision-makers with central forecasts and a credible range of possible outcomes.

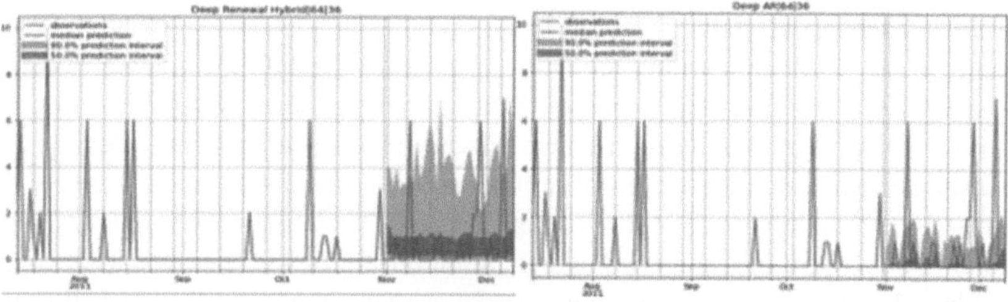

Fig. 3. Forecast by Deep Renewal Hybrid model (left) and DeepAR model (right)

Statistical Models

A notable finding in the N-step evaluation was the resurgence of local statistical models (Fig. 4). Both ARIMA and ETS show highly competitive results, particularly for SPEC-based metrics. ETS, for example, records the best $SPEC_{0.75}$ score, suggesting that it is particularly effective in situations where the cost of stockouts is weighted more heavily than the cost of overstocking. ARIMA also performs strongly across all SPEC values, reinforcing the observation that in some business contexts, especially those with asymmetric cost considerations, simple local models may rival or even surpass advanced global models.

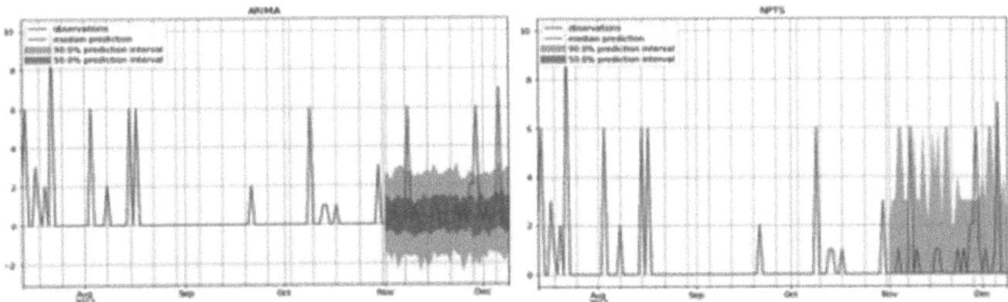

Fig. 4. Forecast by ARIMA model (left) and NPTS model (right)

Interestingly, the Deep Renewal Flat and DE variants underperformed in the probabilistic evaluation, with MWQL values higher than those of DeepAR or the statistical models. This highlights that not all deep-learning architectures generalize equally well across forecast horizons, and careful model selection remains crucial.

Machine Learning Models

Tree-based ML methods were excluded from the N-step evaluation table because of their poor performance in the one-step experiments. The models did not offer meaningful results in the multistep setting, reinforcing the conclusion that conventional ML approaches are ill-suited for this forecasting problem under the studied conditions.

4.3   Overall Discussion

A comparative analysis across one-step and N-step horizons reveals clear performance hierarchies and practical insights for model selection. Deep learning models, particularly DeepAR and Deep Renewal Hybrid, demonstrated superior performance owing to their ability to deliver both accurate point forecasts and calibrated probabilistic predictions essential for inventory and supply risk management. Statistical methods such as ARIMA and ETS proved remarkably resilient, often outperforming complex approaches in cost-sensitive scenarios while offering interpretability and computational efficiency. In contrast, gradient boosting models consistently underperformed despite extensive feature engineering, highlighting the fundamental limitations of applying standard machine learning approaches to sparse, high-noise intermittent series.

These findings confirm that model selection must align with organizational priorities rather than pursuing universal solutions. DeepAR proves optimal for uncertainty-critical applications that require probabilistic forecasts, while Deep Renewal Hybrid excels in point accuracy requirements. Statistical models remain valuable in cost-asymmetric or resource-constrained environments. This context-dependent guidance represents a significant advancement for practitioners seeking to balance forecasting performance and operational constraints.

5   Conclusions

This study presents the largest comparative evaluation of intermittent demand forecasting approaches to date, systematically benchmarking statistical, machine learning, and deep learning methods across 3,671 time series. We establish four key contributions that advance both theoretical understanding and practical implementation.

First, we provide the first systematic application of cost sensitive metrics, specifically the Stock-keeping-oriented Prediction Error Costs (SPEC) framework with multiple α values (0.25, 0.50, 0.75). This evaluation across different operational priorities, from holding cost sensitive to stockout critical scenarios, revealed that model ranking significantly depends on organizational contexts, challenging traditional statistical accuracy measures.

Second, our empirical findings establish clear performance hierarchies. Deep learning methods, particularly DeepAR and Deep Renewal Hybrid, delivered superior results through their ability to learn patterns across multiple series simultaneously. DeepAR achieved the lowest Mean Weighted Quantile Loss (0.81 for one-step, 0.802 for multi-step), whereas Deep Renewal Hybrid excelled in point accuracy (MAAPE: 0.56). Statistical methods such as SBA, ARIMA, and ETS demonstrated remarkable resilience, often outperforming complex approaches in scenarios where costs are the most important. Machine learning approaches consistently underperformed despite extensive feature engineering, revealing fundamental limitations for sparse, high noise intermittent series.

Third, we established a practical decision-making framework for model selection that aligns forecasting approaches with operational contexts. No universal model exists. DeepAR proves optimal for uncertainty critical applications, Deep Renewal Hybrid excels for point accuracy, while statistical models offer value in environments with limited resources or asymmetric costs.

Fourth, we provide evidence based recommendations for supply chain practitioners through a robust evaluation methodology. By demonstrating the inadequacy of traditional metrics (MAPE, RMSE) and establishing MAAPE, SPEC, and Mean Weighted Quantile Loss as appropriate alternatives, this study equips practitioners with reliable tools for model evaluation. The cost sensitive framework directly translates forecast accuracy into economic implications, enabling informed decision making that balances service levels with inventory costs.

These contributions collectively advance the field by providing methodological rigor, practical guidance, and a comprehensive benchmark that bridges theoretical forecasting research with real world supply chain applications, offering immediate value for practitioners while establishing a foundation for future intermittent demand forecasting research.

6 Future Work and Limitations

Although this study provides comprehensive insights, several limitations and research directions warrant attention.

6.1 Dataset Limitations and Generalizability

This study acknowledges the retail specific nature of the UCI Online Retail dataset, which represents consumer giftware demand patterns. Demand characteristics in the aerospace, automotive, and healthcare industries differ substantially [2, 5]. Aerospace spare parts exhibit longer lifecycles with safety-critical availability requirements, automotive components face seasonal and model-dependent cycles, and healthcare supplies require immediate availability with life-critical stockout consequences. Despite these limitations, the UCI Online Retail dataset offers the most significant publicly available benchmark for intermittent demand research, comprising 3,671 validated intermittent time series, which enables a robust comparative analysis that smaller datasets cannot support.

6.2 Future Research Priorities

Cross domain validation studies represent the highest priority future work. Researchers should evaluate model performance across aerospace maintenance, automotive spare parts, and healthcare supply chains [2, 5] to establish generalizability boundaries and provide industry specific guidance. Framework adaptation requires modifying the SPEC α parameters to reflect the industry's cost structures. Critical industries should emphasize higher α values (0.8–0.9) reflecting severe stockout penalties, while manufacturing contexts should use balanced values (0.4–0.6). Additional research directions include enhanced machine learning feature engineering using automated tools such as TSFRESH [29], hybrid architectures that combine statistical methods with neural networks [24], and the optimization of deep learning models, such as DeepAR, through advanced architectures and attention mechanisms [22].

References

1. Ivanov, D., Tsipoulanidis, A., Schönberger, J.: Global Supply Chain and Operations Management. Springer, Cham (2017). https://doi.org/10.1007/978-3-319-24217-0
2. Zhang, G.P., Xia, Y., Xie, M.: Intermittent demand forecasting with transformer neural networks. Ann. Oper. Res. **339**(1), 1051–1072 (2024). https://doi.org/10.1007/s10479-023-054 47-7
3. Zhu, S., Dekker, R., van Jaarsveld, W.: Spare parts demand forecasting and inventory management: contributions to intermittent demand forecasting, installed base information and shutdown maintenance. Eur. J. Oper. Res. (2021). https://doi.org/10.1016/j.ejor.2021
4. Teunter, R., Syntetos, A.A., Babai, M.Z.: Intermittent demand: linking forecasting to inventory obsolescence. Eur. J. Oper. Res. **214**(3), 606–615 (2011)
5. Zogaan, W.A., et al.: Leveraging deep learning for risk prediction and resilience in supply chains. J. Big Data **12**, 113 (2025). https://doi.org/10.1186/s40537-025-01143-4

6. Croston, J.D.: Forecasting and stock control for intermittent demands. Oper. Res. Q. **23**(3), 289–303 (1972)

7. Sanguri, K., et al.: Intermittent demand, inventory obsolescence, and temporal forecasting challenges. Int. J. Prod. Res. (2024). https://doi.org/10.1080/00207543.2023.2199435

8. Martin, J., Jones, R., Roberts, S.: Stock-keeping-oriented prediction error costs (SPEC): a decision-focused metric for demand forecasting. J. Bus. Logist. **37**(4), 299–312 (2016)

9. Van Hezewijk, L., Dellaert, N., van Jaarsveld, W.: On non-negative auto-correlated integer demand processes. arXiv preprint (2023)

10. Syntetos, A.A., Boylan, J.E.: On the bias of intermittent demand estimates. Int. J. Prod. Econ. **71**(1–3), 457–466 (2005)

11. Yao, J., Ordóñez, F.J.: A bootstrapping simulation approach for intermittent demand forecasting in spatio-temporal systems. Ann. Inst. Stat. Math. **75**, 487–512 (2023). https://doi.org/10.1007/s10463-022-00864-y

12. Kim, H.Y., Park, S.: Models for autoregressive processes of bounded counts. Comput. Stat. **35**, 2051–2075 (2020). https://doi.org/10.1007/s00180-020-00980-6

13. Pennings, H.P.G., van Dalen, J., van der Laan, E.: Cross-correlation methods for intermittent demand forecasting. Comput. Oper. Res. **79**, 123–134 (2017)

14. Atha, S., Bolla, B.K.: Do deep learning models and news headlines outperform conventional prediction techniques on forex data? In: Rout, R.R., Ghosh, S.K., Jana, P.K., Tripathy, A.K., Sahoo, J.P., Li, K.-C. (eds.) Advances in Distributed Computing and Machine Learning. LNNS, vol. 427, pp. 413–423. Springer, Singapore (2022). https://doi.org/10.1007/978-981-19-1018-0_35

15. Jia, Y., Zhou, S., Wang, Y., et al.: A quadratic ν-support vector regression approach for load forecasting. Complex Intell. Syst. **11**, 123 (2025). https://doi.org/10.1007/s40747-024-01730-7

16. Ahmad, T., Chen, H.: Short-term load forecasting using random forests. Electr. Power Syst. Res. **163**, 114–124 (2018)

17. Wang, X., Smith-Miles, K., Hyndman, R.J.: Rule induction for forecasting intermittent demand. Int. J. Forecast. **33**(2), 272–283 (2017)

18. Huber, J., Stuckenschmidt, H.: Demand forecasting with support vector machines for intermittent demand. Decis. Support. Syst. **137**, 113366 (2020)

19. Patil, H., Bolla, B.K., Sabeesh, E., Bhumireddy, D.R.: Comparative study of predicting stock index using deep learning models. In: Pareek, P., Gupta, N., Reis, M.J.C.S. (eds.) IC4S 2023. LNICSSITE, vol. 536, pp. 45–57. Springer, Cham (2024). https://doi.org/10.1007/978-3-031-48888-7_4

20. Hochreiter, S., Schmidhuber, J.: Long short-term memory. Neural Comput. **9**(8), 1735–1780 (1997)

21. Huang, J., Yang, S., Li, J., et al.: Prediction model of sparse autoencoder-based bidirectional LSTM for wastewater flow rate. J. Supercomput. **79**, 4412–4435 (2023). https://doi.org/10.1007/s11227-022-04827-3

22. Salinas, D., Flunkert, V., Gasthaus, J., Januschowski, T.: DeepAR: probabilistic forecasting with autoregressive recurrent networks. Int. J. Forecast. **36**(3), 1181–1191 (2020)

23. Turkmen, C., Wang, Y., Januschowski, T.: Intermittent demand forecasting with renewal processes. In: International Conference on Learning Representations (ICLR) (2019)

24. Smyl, S.: A hybrid method of exponential smoothing and recurrent neural networks for time series forecasting. Int. J. Forecast. **36**(1), 75–85 (2020)

25. Terven, J., et al.: A comprehensive survey of loss functions and metrics in machine learning. Artif. Intell. Rev. (2025). https://doi.org/10.1007/s10462-025-11198-7

26. Kourentzes, N.: Intermittent demand forecasts with neural networks. Int. J. Prod. Econ. **143**(1), 198–206 (2013)

27. Shcherbakov, M., Brebels, A., Shcherbakova, N., Tyukov, A., Janovsky, T., Kamaev, V.: A survey of forecast error measures. World Appl. Sci. J. **24**(24), 171–176 (2013)
28. Chen, D.: Online Retail. UCI Machine Learning Repository (2015). https://doi.org/10.24432/C5BW33
29. Christ, M., Braun, N., Neuffer, J., Kempa-Liehr, A.W.: Time series feature extraction on basis of scalable hypothesis tests (tsfresh – a python package). Neurocomputing **307**, 72–77 (2018)

Beyond Regression: Leveraging ANN Models for Predictive Business Analytics

Thrilok Kolla[1], Seema Singh[2(✉)], Balamurugan Balusamy[3],
and Karthik Palani[4]

[1] Department of Computer Science and Engineering, Alliance School of Advanced
Computing, Alliance University, Bengaluru, India
[2] Symbiosis Centre for Corporate Education, Pune Symbiosis International (Deemed
University), Pune, India
Director@scce.edu.in
[3] School of Engineering and IT, Manipal Academy of Higher Education, Dubai
Campus, Dubai, UAE
[4] Cambridge Institute of Technology, K R Puram, Bangalore, India
karthik.ise@cambridge.edu.in

Abstract. Predictive business analytics contributes much to identifying strategic decisions in areas such as sales, marketing, and human resources. This research outlines a framework for structured predictive modeling with Artificial Neural Networks (ANN), the importance of which lies significantly in their ability to interpret nonlinear situations in complex business data. ANNs offer a significant advantage over traditional regression models, where the data relationships are dynamic and non-explicit, because they are far more powerful in prediction and flexible in capturing the relationship. The methodology involves comprehensive steps: data preprocessing, feature selection, ANN model architecture design, optimization through a loss function minimization, and analyzing residuals-based diagnostics. Empirical evaluations accompanied by visual diagnostics and multiple statistical metrics, such as Mean Square Error and R^2, prove the efficiency of ANN in reducing predictive error while establishing generalization. Sales forecasting and employee turnover prediction have provided case-specific insights demonstrating the model's applicability. Further contextualization of findings with previous literature highlights theoretical and practical implications. The results underline the importance of predictive analytics enhanced with ANN for enabling proactive real-time business decision-making.

Keywords: Predictive Business Analytics · Artificial Neural
Networks · Sales Forecasting · Employee Turnover · Deep Learning ·
Residual Analysis · Feature Selection · MSE · R^2 Score · Optimization

1   Introduction

Predictive analytics for business economies is like the bedrock supporting sound strategic decisions, efficiency improvements, and ensuring competitive advantages within data-driven companies at present. These requirements also come

H. Kannan et al. (Eds.): AIKP 2025, CCIS 2804, pp. 106–116, 2026.
https://doi.org/10.1007/978-3-032-14706-6_9

with advances in analytical techniques that go beyond simply and usually performing statistical regressions on the practically generated and accumulated copious amounts of data by organizations through sales, marketing, operations, and human resources departments. Traditional models tend to be interpretable, but they are not capable of modeling the non-linear dependencies and interactions between features; thus, their application has always been limited in complex real-time business scenarios [1].

Artificial neural networks have emerged as the best tool for modeling complex data relationships because they are inspired by the structure and learning mechanisms of the human brain. One such interesting property of artificial neural networks is the capability to approximate complex, high-dimensional functions, which makes them appear attractive for analyzing business problems whose patterns are not readily visible or defined. Unlike linear regression and tree-based models, ANNs perform well in situations with nonlinearity, correlated inter-feature effects, and noisy environments. The research work examines ANN architecture-related applications in predictive modeling using business cases like sales forecasting and employee turnover prediction [2].

There's a growing tendency to blend ANN models with business analytics in the current literature. Shafie et al. (2024), for example, have optimized ANN frameworks with data augmentation towards employee turnover predictions, thereby accentuating the importance of cluster-based preprocessing within HR analytics [3]. Similarly, Bhartariya et al. (2025) mentioned the increasingly critical role of predictive AI and real-time analytics in next-generation business intelligence systems to ensure swift decision-making in rapidly changing markets. While decision trees hold relevance for their validity (Lee et al., 2022), deep learning still has promises of disruptive insights (Schmitt, 2023), but increasingly, ANN methods become viewed as suited to pragmatic integration for specific business problems, and the way forward is best [4].

This paper presents a structured pipeline for artificial neural network applications to forecast prediction tasks in business. The pipeline includes data preprocessing, feature selection, model training, residual analysis, and performance assessment via multiple statistical metrics. Assessment of model reliance and generalization allows the use of graphical diagnostics loss curve, scatter plot, and residual histogram. This paper, by bringing theory into conjunction with practice, seeks to advance the understanding of the application of ANN to predicting business analytics and provides a methodological baseline for future work in this area [5].

2   Literature Survey

In recent years, predictive analysis has become a favorite in decision-making for businesses. Various techniques have been attempted to improve efficiency and accuracy within prediction models. Lee, Cheang, and Moslehpour [6] have tried to take decision tree algorithms from their perspective as an addition to broader business analytics and effective use. Models of this kind are clear on rule-based predictions, especially when structured datasets are considered.

Meanwhile, adoption of such complicated models as deep learning has kindled a great deal of enthusiasm tempered by equal caution. Schmitt [7] dispensed with deep learning's manifold promises and challenges in business environments, arguing that, more often than not, the technology runs into a yawning gap between hyperbolic expectations and actual working conditions. While neural networks can detect non-linear relationships and subtle patterns in data, they are, in particular, large consumers of data and computational resources scenario which makes practical implementation very difficult for smaller firms or in real-time situations.

The combined and optimized frameworks have appeared to escape some of such restrictions. These are cluster-based human resources analytical models proposed by Shafie et al. [8], comprised of Artificial Neural Networks with data augmentation strategies, to predict employees' turnover. Their research proves that through preprocessing and data enrichment, ANN models generalize and predict well, particularly in data-imbalanced scenarios. Optimized and augmented because of these increasing needs, these systems tend to have applied uses in dynamic business environments.

The evolution of tools for predictive analytics has passed beyond traditional statistical models and embraced AI-driven architectures willing to work in real-time. In their work, Bhartariya, Singh, and Bharti [9] considered the next generation of business intelligence systems that utilize real-time data, AI, and predictive models for fast and autonomous decision-making. Their findings underline the alliance of AI and business analytics, suggesting an imminent paradigm shift in strategic management from a reactive to a proactive stance.

Collectively, these studies indicate that ANN applications in business analytics are very heterogeneous, covering aspects with analysis techniques such as human resources, sales forecasting, or decision support systems. While the literature indicates that ANN and deep learning may provide powerful means for prediction and analysis, it equally cautions against neglecting practical considerations around deployment, data readiness, and alignment with business goals [10].

3   Methodology

The proposed Predictive Business Analytics ANN model framework consists of different stages. Each step is shown in Figure

3.1   Data Preprocessing

The dataset $\mathcal{D} = \{(\mathbf{x}_i, y_i)\}_{i=1}^{n}$ comprises input features $\mathbf{x}_i \in \mathbb{R}^d$ and corresponding target values $y_i \in \mathbb{R}$ The input data is normalized to zero mean and unit variance using:

$$\tilde{x}_{ij} = \frac{x_{ij} - \mu_j}{\sigma_j} \tag{1}$$

where $\mu_j = \frac{1}{n}\sum_{i=1}^{n} x_{ij}, \quad \sigma_j = \sqrt{\frac{1}{n}\sum_{i=1}^{n}(x_{ij} - \mu_j)^2}, \quad j \in \{1, 2, \ldots, d\}$

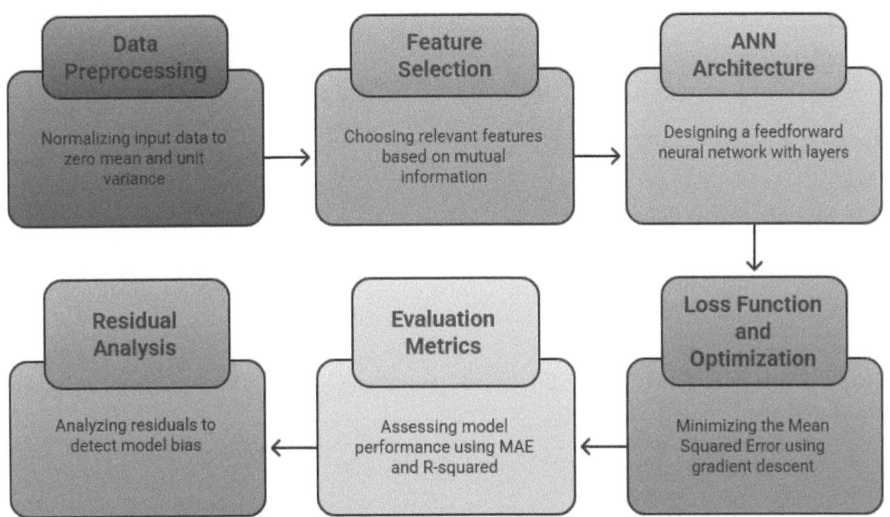

Fig. 1. Predictive Business Analytics with ANN.

3.2　Feature Selection

Let $\mathbf{x} = [x_1, x_2, \ldots, x_d]^{\top}$. A subset $\mathbf{x}_{\text{selected}} \subseteq \mathbb{R}^k$ where $k \leq d$, is chosen based on correlation scores and multivariate relevance. A common selection criterion is mutual information:

$$\text{MI}(x_j, y) = \int_{\mathcal{X}} \int_{\mathcal{Y}} p(x_j, y) \log \left(\frac{p(x_j, y)}{p(x_j)p(y)} \right) dx_j dy \qquad (2)$$

Features with $\text{MI}(x_j, y) \geq \delta$ (threshold) are retained.

3.3　Artificial Neural Network (ANN) Architecture

A feedforward neural network with L layers is modeled as a composition of affine and activation functions:

$$\mathbf{h}^{(l)} = \phi^{(l)} \left(\mathbf{W}^{(l)} \mathbf{h}^{(l-1)} + \mathbf{b}^{(l)} \right), \quad l = 1, \ldots, L \qquad (3)$$

where $\mathbf{h}^{(l)} = \mathbf{x}$ input layer, $\mathbf{W}^{(l)} \in \mathbb{R}^{n_l * n_{l-1}}$ are weights, $\mathbf{b}^{(l)} \in \mathbb{R}^{n_l}$ are biases, $\phi^{(l)}(\cdot)$ is typically ReLU: $\phi(z) = \max(0, z)$

The output layer returns the prediction:

$$\hat{y} = f(\mathbf{x}) = \mathbf{W}^{(L)} \mathbf{h}^{(L-1)} + \mathbf{b}^{(L)} \qquad (4)$$

3.4　Loss Function and Optimization

For regression, Mean Squared Error (MSE) is the objective:

$$\mathcal{L}(\theta) = \frac{1}{n} \sum_{i=1}^{n} \left(f(\mathbf{x}_i; \theta) - y_i \right)^2 \qquad (5)$$

where $\theta = \{\mathbf{W}^{(l)}, \mathbf{b}^{(l)}\}_{l=1}^{L}$. The model parameters are updated using gradient descent:

$$\theta \leftarrow \theta - \eta \nabla_\theta \mathcal{L}(\theta) \tag{6}$$

where η is the learning rate.

3.5 Evaluation Metrics

To rigorously assess the predictive capability of the trained ANN model, multiple statistical metrics are employed:

Mean Squared Error (MSE). MSE penalizes larger errors more heavily and is defined as:

$$\text{MSE} = \frac{1}{n} \sum_{i=1}^{n} (y_i - \hat{y}_i)^2 \tag{7}$$

where y_i is the actual value, $\hat{y}_i$ is the predicted value, and n is the total number of observations [11].

Mean Absolute Error (MAE). MAE measures the average magnitude of errors in a set of predictions, without considering their direction:

$$\text{MAE} = \frac{1}{n} \sum_{i=1}^{n} |y_i - \hat{y}_i| \tag{8}$$

It is more robust to outliers compared to MSE [12].

Root Mean Squared Error (RMSE). To restore the error scale to that of the original output, RMSE is calculated:

$$\text{RMSE} = \sqrt{\frac{1}{n} \sum_{i=1}^{n} (y_i - \hat{y}_i)^2} \tag{9}$$

RMSE provides a clear interpretation of average prediction error in the same unit as the target variable [13].

Coefficient of Determination (R^2). The (R^2) score indicates the proportion of variance in the target variable that is predictable from the input features:

$$R^2 = 1 - \frac{\sum_{i=1}^{n} (y_i - \hat{y}_i)^2}{\sum_{i=1}^{n} (y_i - \bar{y})^2} \tag{10}$$

where $\bar{y} = \frac{1}{n} \sum_{i=1}^{n} y_i$. An R^2 close to 1 implies high model accuracy, while values near 0 indicate poor explanatory power [14].

3.6   Residual Analysis

The residuals r_i are defined as:

$$r_i = y_i - \hat{y}_i \tag{11}$$

Their distribution is analyzed to detect model bias. An ideal residual distribution satisfies:

$$\mathbb{E}[r_i] \approx 0, \quad \text{Var}(r_i) \text{ constant}, \quad r_i \sim \mathcal{N}(0, \sigma^2) \tag{12}$$

Skewness or heteroscedasticity in the residual histogram implies model underperformance or bias, prompting reconsideration of architecture or feature engineering.

4   Results and Discussion

The graph titled "Model Loss over Epochs" indicates the performance of a machine learning model by recording both training and validation loss over 100 epochs. The x-axis indicates the number of epochs from 0 to 100, while the y-axis denotes the Mean Squared Error (MSE) in scientific notation (1e9). Two different curves are plotted- the blue line indicates the training loss, while the orange represents the validation loss. From the time of initiation, training and validation were approximately 1.5e9 MSE, indicating a high error at the start of the training process. As epochs continued, the loss decreased consistently in both curves, pointing toward a reduction in error and improvement in model performance. The training and validation losses follow a similar path, albeit in an interchangeable direction, with slight differences, indicating good generalization of the model with limited overfitting. Approximately, at epoch 100, both losses converge to low MSE values and indicate a good training process for error minimization in predictions. Thus, this graph forms an essential graphic means of measuring the convergence and stability of models, which will reflect appropriately in the conference paper on optimization of a machine learning model [15].

The depicted scatter plot in the image visually compares actual sales versus predicted sales values, serving as a diagnostic visualization for the performance of a predictive model. The x-axis represents actual sales, while the predicted sales value lies along the y-axis and ranges from 20,000 to 80,000. Each blue dot corresponds to an independent observation, whereby its predicted value is plotted against its actual value. A reference for model accuracy is marked by a red dashed diagonal line, indicating the case where predicted sales are said to equal actual sales. Most data points lie near this line, which implies a strong correlation and that the model appears to perform reasonably well in capturing the underlying sales patterns. However, we do observe a degree of scatter and some deviations from the line, especially at extreme cases, which could highlight areas of less-than-ideal model performance with somewhat inaccurately predicted sales. The plot clearly shows that the model has fair predictive accuracy, thus fitting

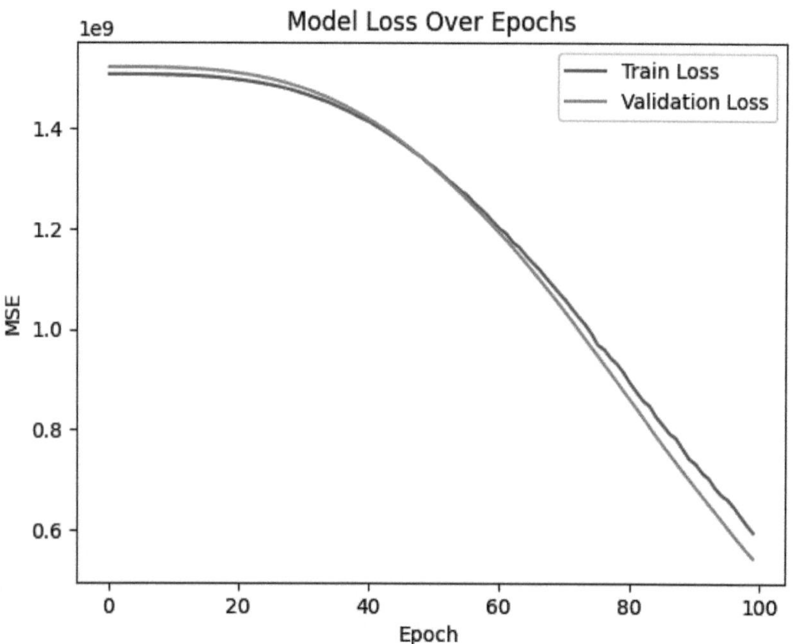

Fig. 2. Loss Convergence Graph for Training and Validation (MSE per Epoch).

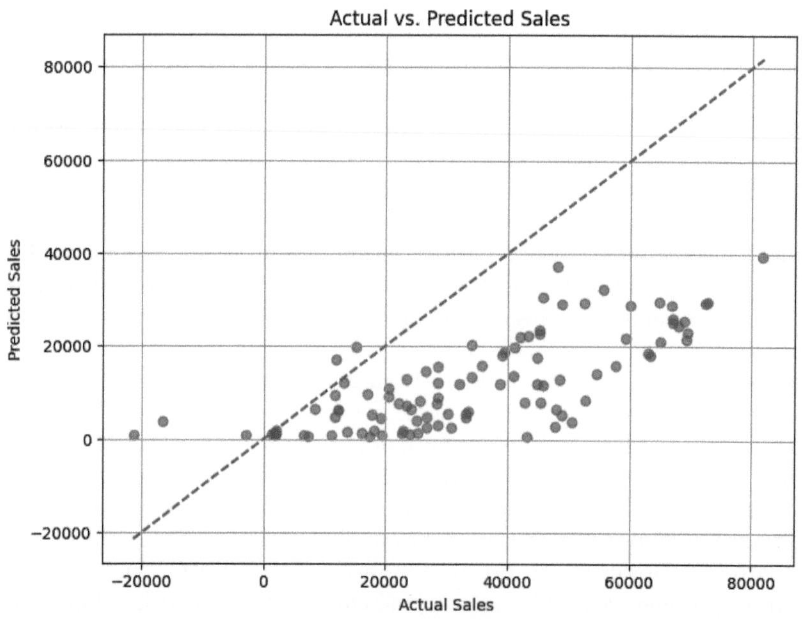

Fig. 3. Predictive Fit Scatter Plot of ANN Model (Predicted vs. Actual Sales).

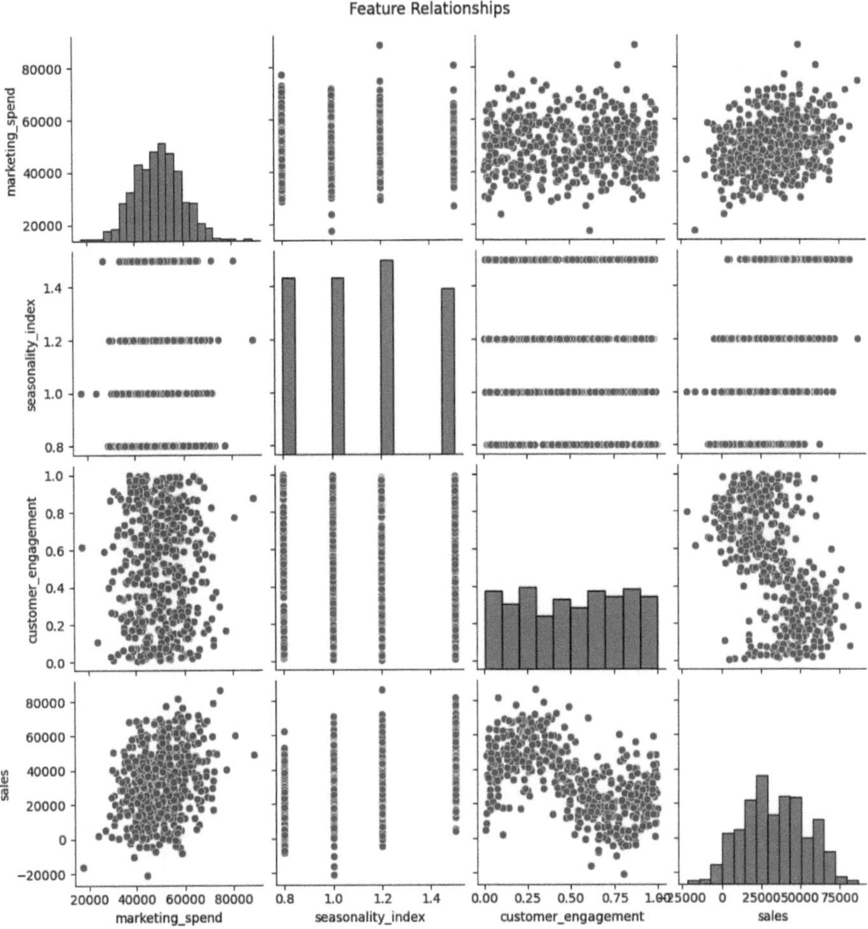

Fig. 4. Multivariate Pair Plot for Feature Relationship Diagnostics.

well into any conference paper about sales forecasting or regressions in terms of model evaluation [16].

The pair plot matrix "Feature Relationships" contains a complete description of how four critical variables —marketing spend, seasonality index, customer engagement, and sales —interrelate with each other. Moreover, each histogram in the matrix, filling its diagonal cell, displays the distribution of the respective variable and gives insight into the spread and skewness of the data. Off-diagonal cells feature scatter plots showing how pairs are related. For example, the scatter plot in the first row and second column depicts the correlation between marketing_spend and seasonality_index, while other plots study relationships such as marketing_spend against customer_engagement and sales, as well as seasonality_index versus customer_engagement against sales. It helps identify trends, either possibly linear or non-linear, clusters, or outliers in the dataset. Matrix

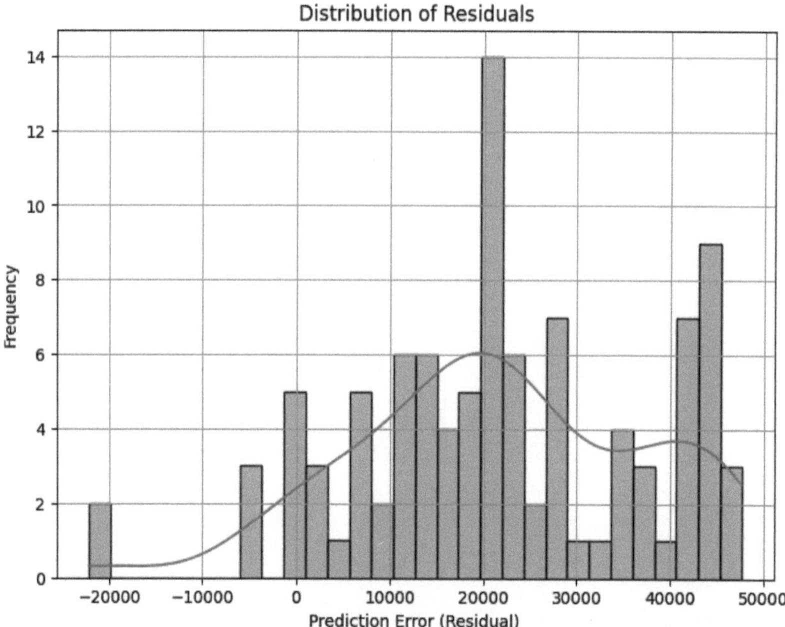

Fig. 5. Histogram and Kernel Density Estimate (KDE) of Prediction Residuals.

format allows a speedy, intuitive appreciation of how one feature interacts with others, especially useful for feature selection and model behavior understanding for predictive data analysis. Purposefully, this visualization is planned to be included in a conference paper discussion, helping in terms of data exploration, feature relevance, and model interpretability [17].

Labeled "Distribution of residuals," this histogram is a clear representation of the prediction errors produced by a regression model. The x-axis represents the residual values, defined as the difference between the actual and predicted values, ranging approximately from -20,000 to 50,000. The y-axis represents the frequency of these various residuals in the dataset. The histogram bars are shaded in light red with black outlines, ranking the frequency of appearance of each residual range. On the other hand, a red density curve is superimposed on the histogram, providing a smoothed estimate of the distribution of the residuals [18]. The highest point of the histogram is around the residual value of 20,000, which appeared to have some frequency of 14; thus, the model underpredicts the actual values by this amount in many cases. The overall shape of the distribution informs about model bias and variance; for example, some symmetry yielding a bell-shaped curve centered on zero would speak of unbiased predictions, while errors are normally distributed. The observed skewness toward positive residuals would indicate, therefore, that the model tends to underpredict. This visual is then a useful tool to validate model performance and potential problems, making it a great addition to a conference paper on regression analysis or predictive modeling [19].

5 Conclusion

This research indeed validates Artificial Neural Networks as a strong predictive modeling approach in business analytics. It systematically demonstrates the way ANNs can overcome the limitations of traditional regression techniques by building a basic pipeline of data preprocessing, feature selection, model training, and residual diagnostics. ANNs identify and learn from complex non-linear relationships in multidimensional business datasets, resulting in much improved, accurate, and actionable predictions in high-variance areas of sales and workforce planning.

The experimental results indicate strong performance on the model, marked by convergence of losses over training and validation, a close correlation between actual and predicted outcomes, and a reasonably symmetric distribution of residuals. These diagnostics affirm both the generalization potential and practical reliability of the ANN-based models. The error metric and visual tools add to interpretability and assist in the decision-making process.

References

1. Nair, R.R., Singh, T.: Retracted article: Mamif: multimodal adaptive medical image fusion based on b-spline registration and non-subsampled shearlet transform. Multimedia Tools Appli. **80**(12), 19079–19105 (2021)
2. Nair, R.R., Babu, T., Kumar, K.N., Vardhan, R.G., et al.: Evolutionary algorithms for optimizing wind turbine blade design. In: 2024 International Conference on IT Innovation and Knowledge Discovery (ITIKD). IEEE, pp. 1–6 (2025)
3. Nair, R.R., Babu, T., Singh, T.: Unraveling dementia severity: A deep learning approach for brain mr image-based prediction and misclassification analysis. Proc. Comput. Sci. **258**, 1199–1208 (2025)
4. Nair, R.R., Babu, T., Karanam, P.: Propositional logic for automated reasoning in legal expert systems. In: 2024 International Conference on IT Inovation and Knowledge Discovery (ITIKD), pp. 1–6. IEEE (2025)
5. Nair, R.R., Babu, T., Kishore, S.: Recurrent neural for time series prediction in finance. In: 2024 International Conference on IT Innovation and Knowledge Discovery (ITIKD), pp. 1–5. IEEE (2025)
6. Lee, C.S., Cheang, P.Y.S., Moslehpour, M.: Predictive analytics in business analytics: decision tree. Adv. Decis. Sci. **26**(1), 1–29 (2022)
7. Schmitt, M.: Deep learning in business analytics: A clash of expectations and reality. Inter. J. Inform. Manag. Data Insights **3**(1), 100146 (2023)
8. Shafie, M.R., Khosravi, H., Farhadpour, S., Das, S., Ahmed, I.: A cluster-based human resources analytics for predicting employee turnover using optimized artificial neural networks and data augmentation. Dec. Analy. J. **11**, 100461 (2024)
9. Bhartariya, A.G., Singh, S., Bharti, A.K.: Next gen business intelligence: levaraging predictive analytics, ai & real-time decision-making. J. Theoret. Appli. Inform. Technol. **103**(8) (2025)

10. Singh, B., Kaunert, C., Balusamy, B., Dhanaraj, R.K.: Computational Intelligence in Healthcare Law: AI for Ethical Governance and Regulatory Challenges. CRC Press (2025)
11. Balusamy, B., et al.: Design system for early detection and prediction of chronic kidney disease using machine learning techniques. Webology **19**(3) (2022)
12. Balusamy, B., Ravi, V., Dhanaraj, R.K., Senthilkumar, S., et al.: Computational Intelligence in Sustainable Computing and Optimization: Trends and Applications. Elsevier (2024)
13. Manogaran, N., Nandagopal, M., Abi, N.E., Seerangan, K., Balusamy, B., Selvarajan, S.: Integrating meta-heuristic with named data networking for secure edge computing in iot enabled healthcare monitoring system. Sci. Rep. **14**(1), 21532 (2024)
14. Manogaran, N., et al.: Developing a novel adaptive double deep q-learning-based routing strategy for iot-based wireless sensor network with federated learning. Sensors **25**(10), 3084 (2025)
15. Babu, T., Nair, R.R., Manjula, M., Bhattacharyya, U.: Effective placement prediction for educational institutions: insights from machine learning. Advances in Electrical and Computer Technologies, pp. 81–85. CRC Press (2025)
16. Babu, T., Ebin, P., Nair, R.R.: Data-driven insights: mall customer segmentation through fuzzy c-means clustering. In: 2014 International BIT Conference (BITCON),pp. 1–5. IEEE (2024)
17. Babu, T., Nair, R.R., et al.: Foundations of generative ai. In: The pioneering applications of generative AI, pp. 136–166. IGI Global (2024)
18. Babu, T., Naik, P.K., Nair, R.R., Janhavi, P.: Automated diagnosis of diabetic retinopathy using convolutional neural networks: a comprehensive review and comparative analysis. Adv. Electr. Comput. Technol., 609–614 (2025)
19. Babu, T., Nair, R.R., Kishore, S.: Applications of artificial intelligence and machine learning in industry 4.0. Artifi. Intell. Mach. Learn. Indust. 4.0, 107–143 (2025)

Applied Machine Learning in Finance: A Practical Comparison of LSTM and ARIMA for Stock Price Prediction in Emerging Markets

Shiva Sai Kiran Pothula[✉][iD] and Venkatesu Boya

School of Businees, Woxsen University, Hyderabad, India
pothulashivasaikiran@gmail.com

Abstract. Forecasting stock prices in emerging markets presents a unique set of challenges, including but not limited to heightened volatility, structural inefficiencies, and limited data availability. To understand the same, in this study, we undertake a comparative analysis of two distinct modeling paradigms – AutoRegressive Integrated Moving Average, or ARIMA, a well-established statistical approach, and Long Short-Term Memory, or LSTM, a machine learning algorithm known for its capacity to model complex temporal dependencies. Our objective is to assess their practical applicability in real-world financial forecasting scenarios, with a particular focus on emerging market equities. Drawing on historical stock data from select emerging economies like India, we implement both models under consistent preprocessing and evaluation frameworks. Performance is assessed using RMSE, MSE, MAPE, and AIC alongside resource intensity and processing time. The results reveal that while ARIMA retains value for its interpretability and efficiency in stable conditions, LSTM consistently outperforms it in capturing non-linear patterns and adapting to abrupt market shifts traits especially pertinent in less mature financial systems. This work contributes to the applied machine learning discourse by grounding model evaluation in practical constraints and market realities. It offers actionable insights for financial analysts, data scientists, and policymakers seeking to harness machine learning for more resilient and adaptive forecasting in emerging market contexts.

Keywords: Applied Machine Learning · SDG 9 · LSTM · ARIMA · Emerging Markets and Data-Driven Decision Making

1 Introduction

Traditional Statistics (TS) and Machine Learning (ML) can, in principle, be used for predicting future values of a time series. TS models, historically, are used to create and fit project specific probability models with a strong focus on inference. TS models also allowed us to compute statistical significance of "a phenomenon" that is unlikely a result from noise. On the other hand, prediction aims to forecast unobserved behavior in the future an application where ML models thrive by utilizing general purpose algorithms to find underlying patterns. Prediction helps in identifying best course of action. TS

H. Kannan et al. (Eds.): AIKP 2025, CCIS 2804, pp. 117–134, 2026.
https://doi.org/10.1007/978-3-032-14706-6_10

requires a model selection that reflects our knowledge of the phenomenon where the justification for the inference rests on whether the researcher feel it adequately captures the essence of the data. While ML requires a selection of predictive algorithm by relying on its empirical capabilities where the choice of algorithm often depends on measures of past performance in similar scenarios.

In a most research endeavors, both inference and prediction can be of value. However, the difference between inference and prediction is a matter of constant debate as many methods use both, while some fall into one or the other. One such application where both inference and prediction are used is forecasting. Forecasting or prediction of future values, like other data mining tasks, uses evidence to infer and select most suitable model, knowing that no method is considered perfect or best [1]. Forecasting time series relies on the idea that historical data has intrinsic patterns that can describe unobserved behavior in the future which focuses on application of algorithms [2].

For over 50 years, TS methods based on Moving Averages (MA) and Autoregression (AR) were preferred for time series modelling and prediction [3], based on the assumption that data follows a known distribution. Then, parameters were defined to fit a model to the data. However, it is widely understood that time series data itself isn't tied to a specific probability distribution. Hence, lately, several researchers did not presuppose the data distribution nature of time series and have employed non-parametric modeling based on machine learning algorithms [4–7].

In recent times, ML methods are preferred over TS methods for time series forecasting in academic research. Multiple researchers have demonstrated that ML methods provide competitive results, comparable to and sometime outperforming TS models. Yet, this limited evidence of ML superiority over TS is usually restricted to data from developed nations. To the best of our knowledge and according to the literature review conducted in this work, the literature containing robust empirical studies focused on the comparison between TS and ML models in the context of emerging markets is very scarce.

This study aims to address this gap by comparing and evaluating the performance across multiple forecasting horizons using daily financial time series data for emerging markets that are susceptible to higher market volatility. In this direction, this research compares and evaluates the performance of ARIMA (a TS and parametric method) and LSTM (a ML and non-parametric method) models in forecasting future values of popular index from India. A few major contributions of this paper can be summarized as follows:

- Proposal of novel framework to compare TS and ML performance.
- Evaluating the performance of TS and ML models in predicting stock price of highly volatile financial systems of emerging markets.

The rest of the article is structured into three distinct sections. Firstly, a literature review is presented with discussion of insights and identified research gaps. Secondly, a methodology that outlines the methodological framework of the comparative study is presented. Then, thirdly, results are discussed, followed by a conclusion.

2 Literature Review

A time series can be formulated as an ordered sequence of observations where data points are recorded at specific, separate, and equal time intervals. In most scenarios, the series comprises a random error term which makes the series stochastic or non-deterministic. Additionally, stationarity, i.e., series developing randomly around a constant mean, is another feature of timeseries. Some methods assume this condition to reflect some stable equilibrium [2]. Irrespective of stationarity, a time series exhibits three components – trend, seasonality and residue.

Trend is a long-term increase or decrease in the data which can assume a great variety of patterns including but not limited to linear, exponential, damped, and polynomial. Along with the trend component, seasonality, is the occurrence of cyclic variations that repeat at constant intervals. After the estimation of trend and seasonality components, and their removals from the time series, short-term fluctuations that not predictable or systematic are observed, this remaining component is called residue. With this understanding, a time series can be formulated as an additive or multiplicative decomposition of its components. However, not every data sequence will have all the three components [2].

This understanding is foundational when attempting to predict future values. The first step in prediction process involves model training to estimate the most promising model that represents the timeseries data. The second step is the prediction of future values up to a certain horizon, and the third step is to evaluate the quality of the fitted model. The time series prediction methods have evolved over the 50 years. From simple regression techniques to robust statistical models and machine learning algorithms. We can classify these approaches into Traditional Statistics (TS) models and Machine Learning (ML) Models with their own distinct properties, see Table 1.

The existing body of literature provides us with a few insights into the comparative performance of these two approaches. In a recent work, ML methods have been increasingly used for time series prediction. Still, ML models were shown to systematically present a lower predictive performance relative to simple statistical methods. In one study, researchers found that the accuracy of ML models is relatively below TS models [8]. They also highlighted the considerably greater computational requirements for ML approaches. Similarly, another study also underlined the accuracy of ML models [9]. However, they also found that specific ML models are very efficient in learning a time series data contradicting the findings about need for higher computational requirements from the earlier study. Researchers suggest that these findings are only valid under extremely low sample sizes and suggest that ML models improve their predictive power as sample size increases. For instance, in a study using 95 large datasets, researchers found that ML algorithms offer similar results or sometimes better results when compared to state-of-the-art statistical methods [1]. Similar findings were reported by Bhattacharjee & Bhattacharja (2019). After studying several methods, they argued that ML methods, specifically, Neural Networks are found to be most accurate for stock price prediction [10].

Table 1. A brief comparison of TS and ML approaches

TS Models	ML Models
Require a priori knowledge about the data distribution	Models do not require prior knowledge of their data distribution
Models depend on a set of parameters, which must be determined to optimize the prediction results	They do not depend explicitly on parameters to model the past or future behavior
Model become very complex and resource intensive to adjust	Models are simpler to adjust
Model performance even when applied to complex and highly nonlinear series is debatable	Models show reliable performance even when applied to complex and highly nonlinear series
Methods: Moving averages, Simple exponential smoothing, Holt's exponential smoothing, Holt-Winters' seasonal exponential smoothing, ARIMA and SARIMA models	Methods: Artificial neural networks, Support vector machines, Nearest neighbors and LSTM

2.1 TS vs ML in Stock Price Prediction

The stock market operates as a dynamic and multifaceted ecosystem, shaped by a wide array of influences—including macroeconomic indicators, corporate performance, geopolitical developments, and the often-unpredictable behavior of investors. The pursuit of accurate stock price forecasting remains a central objective for individual traders to global financial institutions. The effectiveness of TS or ML methods for stock price prediction is dependent on several influencing factors, including but not limited to quality of the data, the accuracy of the model, and the complexity of the market conditions - a challenge presented by emerging markets. TS methods are generally easier to understand and implement, but in challenging, complex and dynamic market conditions, they may not be simple or easy enough. On the other hand, ML models are adaptable and can capture complex patterns in data, but at the cost of computational power.

2.2 Problem Context

The existing body of research comparing the performance of TS and ML approaches provides us with three distinct insights:

- ML models were shown to systematically present a lower predictive performance for small datasets (PC1).
- As the dataset grows, the prediction performance grows with it and surpass TS models (PC2)
- ML models are computationally expensive but also efficient in learning time series data (PC3)

However, in most cases the datasets used were either synthetic or sourced from the financial markets of developed nations with stability and maturity. For instance, one of the findings from a literature review of 30 researcher article revealed that most scholars used the NASDAQ dataset in stock market prediction/forecasting (Kumar et al., 2022). Hence, applying these conclusions directly to emerging markets warrants caution and deeper scrutiny. Emerging market stock indices are inherently more volatile [11, 12], less liquid [13], and structurally less stable than their developed counterparts. These markets are frequently influenced by abrupt policy shifts, geopolitical tensions, currency fluctuations, and inconsistent regulatory frameworks. As a result, the underlying data often exhibit nonlinear patterns, regime shifts, and more noise, which TS models might struggle to capture effectively, regardless of dataset size. ML models can still extract meaningful patterns by leveraging their architecture designed for sequence learning and memory retention. This capability becomes especially valuable when market behavior is driven by latent factors not easily modeled through traditional statistical assumptions. In the pursuit of stock price prediction, the choice of modeling approach is pivotal to the quality and reliability of predictions. When comparing the performance of TS and ML models in predicting future stock behavior, the insights from literature might not hold true. The aim of this paper is to explore if the three insights hold true in the context of emerging markets.

3 Methodology

For this study, we have deliberately selected ARIMA and LSTM models to represent TS and ML models respectively. For decades, Autoregressive Integrated Moving Average (ARIMA) has served as a reliable method in time series forecasting. Its appeal lies in its simple understanding and its ability to model linear trends and short-term dependencies with precision. In relatively stable market environments, ARIMA's structured approach and transparent assumptions make it a preferred choice among economists and financial analysts. However, applying ARIMA effectively is not just a matter of running a model—it demands a deep understanding of both the domain and the underlying statistical mechanics. The analyst's judgment plays a critical role in model selection, parameter tuning, and interpretation, often making the process more art than science.

In contrast, LSTM (Long Short-Term Memory) networks represent a shift toward data-driven, adaptive modeling. These neural networks are built to handle the complexities of sequential data, capturing nonlinear relationships and long-term dependencies that traditional models often miss. What sets LSTM apart is its ability to learn directly from raw data, without the need for extensive pre-processing or rigid assumptions about stationarity. This makes it particularly well-suited for forecasting in financial markets that are fast-moving, volatile, and structurally unpredictable conditions that are common in emerging economies. The choice between these models is not merely technical—it reflects a broader strategic decision to compare TS and ML approaches.

3.1   Methodological Framework

The primary purpose of this methodological framework is to create a testing environment in which results from ARIMA and LSTM can be compared reliably. To ensure this, all the computations are run on Python within a Conda environment using Visual Studio Code IDE running on a MacBook Air with M2 processor and 8 GB ram. A script is developed as a benchmarking tool for ARIMA and LSTM model selection, helping you understand how model selection time and prediction accuracy change as you increase the amount of training data. This script (please refer to appendices A & B) is designed to analyze the computational cost and predictive performance of both the models by:

- Downloading n daily closing prices data for given ticker (index/stock) from yahoo finance.
- Incrementally training models on increasing amounts of data.
- Selecting the best model (based on AIC) for each training size.
- Evaluating model performance on a fixed testing data set and store performance metrics.
- Recording the time taken for model selection and training.
- Calculating learning efficiency.
- Saving results for further analysis.

This python script is useful for both practical forecasting and for understanding the predictive performance and computational demands of time series modeling. To put the script in action, we have chosen 5000 daily closing prices of NIFTY50(^NSEI) from Indian stock market, as the historical data set and the latest 30 observations are used as the testing dataset. NIFTY50 is an index that represents the average of 50 of the largest Indian companies listed on the National Stock Exchange (NSE) and we believe it reflects the overall behavior of stock market in India – a developing nation. Incremental data sets are selected as a range of 30 to 5000 with 30 observations as interval value – a total of 166 data sets will be considered.

Promising Model Selection. First, for each data set, all ARIMA models with p, d & q values up to 3, 1, 3, respectively, are tested and a model with least AIC is selected as the most promising model. As exiting research indicates that p & q values beyond 3 does not yield significantly more performance and most stock price prediction in emerging markets using ARIMA models have p & q values below 3 and the differencing is below or equal to 1. [14–17]. Using the most promising model, the future values for the next 30 days are estimated. Then, using the testing dataset, performance metrics (RMSE, MAPE, MSE, AIC) are computed for evaluation. Further, Time Taken (TT) for model selection is recorded and Learning Efficiency (LE) is calculated as one divided by a product of time taken and MSE – a higher value reflects higher learning efficiency and vice-versa. Second, for each data set, all LSTM models with batch size as 32 and number of epochs as 50 are tested and a model with least AIC is selected as the most promising model. The remain steps are followed exactly as mentioned above for ARIMA. The values of these hyper parameters are mostly observed in existing research and expects to reflect real world scenarios and prediction requirements. However, due to the limitations of computational resources and time taken for modelling, seasonal models in ARIMA and LSTM models with more than 1 hidden layers are omitted from this study.

Approach for Exploring PC1. The first insight from literature is "ML models were shown to systematically present a lower predictive performance for small datasets." A methodological approach is developed to explore this context, where two predictive performance metrics (MAPE & RMSE) will be evaluated for comparison. We considered any data set with less than 1000 observations small datasets as multiple bullish-bearish cycles from the financial market are not captured within this timeframe [18]. Form the results 33 datasets with sample size less than 1000 and the corresponding MAPE and RMSE values are selected. From MAPE values, accuracy (ACC) of the models is calculated using Eq. (1):

$$ACC = 100 - MAPE \tag{1}$$

A one-sided t-test is used to see if ML models show higher predictive performance for smaller data sets.

H0: ML models were shown to systematically present a lower predictive performance for small datasets when compared to TS models.

H01: $\overline{ACC_{ML}} - \overline{ACC_{TS}} < 0$

H02: $\overline{RMSE_{ML}} - \overline{RMSE_{TS}} > 0$

Ha: ML models systematically present equal or higher predictive performance for small datasets when compared to TS models.

Ha1: $\overline{ACC_{ML}} - \overline{ACC_{TS}} \geq 0$

Ha2: $\overline{RMSE_{ML}} - \overline{RMSE_{TS}} \leq 0$

Approach for Exploring PC2. The second insight from literature is "As the dataset grows, the prediction performance grows with it and surpass TS models." A methodological approach is developed to explore this context, where predictive performance is considered as a linear function of sample size and beta coefficient values are compared, see equations from (2) to (5) and a one-sided t-test is used to evaluate the difference.

$$y_1 = \beta_1 + \beta_2 x_1 \tag{2}$$

Where, y_1 is ACC of ARIMA models, β_1 is intercept of the linear function, β_2 is the beta coefficient of the slope and x_1 is the sample size of the corresponding data set.

$$y_2 = \beta_3 + \beta_4 x_1 \tag{3}$$

Where, y_2 is RMSE of ARIMA models, β_3 is intercept of the linear function, β_4 is the beta coefficient of the slope and x_1 is the sample size of the corresponding data set.

$$y_3 = \beta_5 + \beta_6 x_1 \tag{4}$$

Where, y_3 is ACC of LSTM models, β_5 is intercept of the linear function, β_6 is the beta coefficient of the slope and x_1 is the sample size of the corresponding data set.

$$y_4 = \beta_7 + \beta_8 x_1 \tag{5}$$

Where, y_4 is RMSE of LSTM models, β_7 is intercept of the linear function, β_8 is the beta coefficient of the slope and x_1 is the sample size of the corresponding data set.

The testable hypothesis are as follows:

H0: As the dataset grows, the prediction performance of ML models grows with it and surpass TS models.

H03: $\beta_2 - \beta_6 < 0$

H04: $|\beta_4| - |\beta_8| < 0$

Ha: As the dataset grows, the prediction performance of ML models does not grow with it and do not surpass TS models.

Ha3: $\beta_2 - \beta_6 \geq 0$

Ha4: $|\beta_4| - |\beta_8| \geq 0$

Approach for Exploring PC3. The third insight from literature is "ML models are computationally expensive but also efficient in learning time series data when compared to TS models." For the computational expense, Time Taken (TT) to identify the most promising model for each data is considered as a metric. Adopting a similar approach presented for the exploration of PC1, a one-sided t-test is performed to evaluate the difference. The hypotheses are mentioned below:

H0: ML models are computationally expensive when compared to TS models

H05: $TT_{ML} - TT_{TS} > 0$

Ha: ML models are not computationally expensive when compared to TS models

Ha5: $TT_{ML} - TT_{TS} \leq 0$

Similarly, for the Learning Efficiency (LE), a one-sided t-test is performed to evaluate the difference. The hypotheses are mentioned below:

H0: ML models are efficient in learning time when compared to TS models

H06: $LE_{ML} - LE_{TS} > 0$

Ha: ML models are not efficient in learning time when compared to TS models

Ha6: $LE_{ML} - LE_{TS} \leq 0$

4 Results

Utilizing the methodological framework discussed above, all the six alternative hypotheses are tested. For PC1, the results indicate with statistical significance that, even for small data sets, the accuracy of ML models is higher, see Table 2. This paper argued that the assertion of PC1, while grounded in empirical observations, are from relatively stable financial markets and may not hold true universally—particularly in the context of highly dynamic and volatile financial markets. Our findings indicate that LSTM models can, in fact, outperform ARIMA models in terms of accuracy, even with smaller datasets.

For PC2, the results from the linear regression modelling are discourse worthy. In all the regression plots, it can be noticed that as sample size increases, the accuracy of the models increase. Looking at the incept, see Table 3, values reveal that the base line accuracy for ML models is much higher than TS models, specifically when the sample size is less than 1000. This insight reaffirms our findings above. Another insight from visual inspection reveals that LSTM models achieve high accuracy at around 1000 samples and only adds slightly incremental gains to accuracy as sample size increases. On the contrary, ARIMA models achieved accuracy similar to that of LSTM models only with models more than 4000 sample sizes.

Table 2. Results from hypothesis testing for PC1

Alternative Hypothesis	t-statistic	p-value
Ha1: $\overline{ACC_{ML}} - \overline{ACC_{TS}} \geq 0$	120.5851	0.000
Ha2: $\overline{RMSE_{ML}} - \overline{RMSE_{TS}} \leq 0$	-127.8478	0.000

Table 3. Results from linear regression analysis for PC2

Equation	Intercept	Coefficient for x_1	R2
$y_1 = \beta_1 + \beta_2 x_1$	4.0830*	0.0174*	0.863
$y_2 = \beta_3 + \beta_4 x_1$	23797.33*	-4.3100*	0.863
$y_3 = \beta_5 + \beta_6 x_1$	99.9890*	9.965e-07*	0.244
$y_4 = \beta_7 + \beta_8 x_1$	326.6725*	-0.0242*	0.230

In line with above insights, the results also reveal that, see Table 4, as the dataset grows, the prediction performance of ML models does not grow with it and do not surpass TS models. ML models reach high accuracy early and the baseline accuracy is already higher than TS models. Hence, there is no need for surpassing.

Table 4. Test results for PC2

Alternative Hypothesis	Difference in Coefficients
Ha3: $\beta_2 - \beta_6 \geq 0$	$\beta_2 - \beta_6 = 0.0173$
Ha4: $|\beta_4| - |\beta_8| \geq 0$	$|\beta_4| - |\beta_8| = 4.2858$

For PC3, we did not find enough evidence supporting alternative hypothesis. Our methodological framework did not find any statistically significant difference is Time Taken (TT) and Learning Efficiency (LE) between ML and TS models, see Table 5.

Table 5. Test results for PC3

Alternative Hypothesis	t-statistic	p-value
Ha5: $TT_{ML} - TT_{TS} \leq 0$	9.6885	1.000
Ha6: $LE_{ML} - LE_{TS} \leq 0$	30.9107722318	1.000

4.1 Limitations

This study's main aim is to emphasize the predictive power of ML models in emerging markets with high volatility and data scarcity. In this process, the article adopts a methodological approach that is simple, generalizable and easily interpretable. Hence, seasonal component is omitted from ARIMA modelling and multi layers are omitted from LSTM modelling. With numerous hyper-parameters, the interpretability of the findings will most likely clouded and unclear. This is a noticeable limitation for this study. Another limitation is a result of limited computational resources, i.e., the study focused on one index from one country. This is a result of conscious choice from the authors. However, these pave way for an extensive research project for the future.

4.2 Policy Implications

The insights from this study, can guide financial authorities in emerging economies to reconsider their data strategy and encourage the adoption of ML models even in data-constrained markets. This shift away from TS models could lead to more accuracy in market forecasting, improved risk assessment, enhance market surveillance, earlier detection of market anomalies, and better policy decisions. It also suggests that financial institutions should invest in building flexible, AI- & ML-ready infrastructures to promote innovation in financial analytics. Financial institutions can also foster public-private partnerships to develop AI tools, improve financial forecasting, and build resilience against external shocks. This will help in contributing to more stable, inclusive, and forward-looking financial systems.

4.3 Ethical Implications

The implications of this study have ethical implications, in line with generalized ethical implications related to Artificial Intelligence. If not properly monitored, algorithmic market prediction at institutional and policy level can induce market instabilities, which is counterintuitive to the policy implications discussed earlier. To address these concerns, financial institutions need to regularly audit models for fairness, ensure transparency, and comply with ethical standards.

5 Conclusion

The prevailing narrative in academic literature often suggests that machine learning (ML) models, particularly deep learning architectures like Long Short-Term Memory (LSTM), tend to underperform when applied to small datasets—especially when compared to traditional statistical models such as ARIMA. This research proposed arguments against this understanding, specifically in the context of emerging markets and developed a methodological framework to test our hypothesis. The findings reveal statistically significant results for 4 out of 6 proposed hypotheses. The implications of these findings are profound. For investors and policymakers operating in emerging markets, ML models offer a viable alternative to TS models. This opens new avenues for algorithmic trading, risk management, and portfolio optimization in contexts where conventional models fall short. These findings also challenge the academic community to revisit the assumptions underlying model selection and performance evaluation. It underscores the importance of contextualizing model performance within the specific characteristics of the market being studied. While traditional statistical models have their merits, especially in well-behaved and stationary environments, they may not be the optimal choice for forecasting in volatile and complex markets like India. This research demonstrates that with thoughtful design and contextual awareness, LSTM models can deliver superior predictive performance—even with limited data. This finding invites a broader reconsideration of how we evaluate and deploy forecasting models in financial research and practice.

Appendix A – Code for LSTM Modelling Function

```python
import yfinance as yf
import numpy as np
import pandas as pd
import time
from sklearn.preprocessing import MinMaxScaler
from sklearn.metrics import mean_squared_error, mean_ab-
solute_percentage_error
from tensorflow.keras.models import Sequential
from tensorflow.keras.layers import LSTM, Dense, Dropout
from tensorflow.keras.callbacks import EarlyStopping
from tensorflow.keras.optimizers import Adam
import tensorflow as tf
def download_data(ticker, n_obs=5000):
    df = yf.download(ticker, period=f"{int(n_obs*1.5)}d",
interval="1d")
    df = df.dropna()
    df = df.tail(n_obs)
    return df
def create_sequences(data, seq_length):
    X, y = [], []
    for i in range(len(data) - seq_length):
```

```python
        X.append(data[i:i+seq_length])
        y.append(data[i+seq_length])
    return np.array(X), np.array(y)
def best_lstm_model(X_train, y_train, X_val, y_val):
    # Simple grid search for best LSTM model
    best_model = None
    best_val_loss = np.inf
    best_params = {}
    for units in [32, 64]:
        for dropout in [0.1, 0.2]:
            for lr in [0.001, 0.005]:
                model = Sequential([
                    LSTM(units, in-
put_shape=(X_train.shape[1], X_train.shape[2])),
                    Dropout(dropout),
                    Dense(1)
                ])
                model.compile(optimizer=Adam(learn-
ing_rate=lr), loss='mse')
                es = EarlyStopping(monitor='val_loss',
patience=5, restore_best_weights=True, verbose=0)
                history = model.fit(X_train, y_train,
epochs=50, batch_size=32,
                                    valida-
tion_data=(X_val, y_val), verbose=0, callbacks=[es])
                val_loss = min(history.his-
tory['val_loss'])
                if val_loss < best_val_loss:
                    best_val_loss = val_loss
                    best_model = model
                    best_params = {'units': units, 'drop-
out': dropout, 'lr': lr}
    return best_model, best_params
def calculate_aic(n, mse, k):
    return n * np.log(mse) + 2 * k

def learning_efficiency(mse, wall_time):
    return 1 / (mse * wall_time) if mse > 0 and wall_time
> 0 else 0
def main(ticker):
    df = download_data(ticker, n_obs=5000)
    close_prices = df['Close'].values.reshape(-1, 1)
    scaler = MinMaxScaler()
    scaled_prices = scaler.fit_transform(close_prices)
    test_size = 30
```

```python
    test_data = scaled_prices[-test_size:]
    train_data = scaled_prices[:-test_size]
    results = []
    for sample_size in range(30, len(train_data)+1, 30):
        data = train_data[-sample_size:]
        seq_length = 10  # window size for LSTM
        X, y = create_sequences(data, seq_length)
        if len(X) < 10:  # skip too small samples
            continue
        # Split train/val
        split = int(len(X) * 0.8)
        X_train, X_val = X[:split], X[split:]
        y_train, y_val = y[:split], y[split:]
        # Reshape for LSTM
        X_train = X_train.reshape((X_train.shape[0],
X_train.shape[1], 1))
        X_val = X_val.reshape((X_val.shape[0],
X_val.shape[1], 1))
        start_time = time.time()
        best_model, best_params = \
best_lstm_model(X_train, y_train, X_val, y_val)
        wall_time = time.time() - start_time
        # Evaluate on test set
        # Prepare test sequences
        test_seq_data = np.concatenate([train_data[-
seq_length:], test_data])
        X_test, y_test = create_sequences(test_seq_data,
seq_length)
        X_test = X_test.reshape((X_test.shape[0],
X_test.shape[1], 1))
        y_pred = best_model.predict(X_test, verbose=0)
        y_pred_inv = scaler.inverse_transform(y_pred)
        y_test_inv = scaler.inverse_transform(y_test.re-
shape(-1, 1))
        mse = mean_squared_error(y_test_inv, y_pred_inv)
        rmse = np.sqrt(mse)
        mape = mean_absolute_percentage_error(y_test_inv,
y_pred_inv)
        k = best_model.count_params()
        aic = calculate_aic(len(y_test_inv), mse, k)
        leff = learning_efficiency(mse, wall_time)
        results.append({
            'sample_size': sample_size,
            'best_model': str(best_params),
            'AIC': aic,
```

```
            'MSE': mse,
            'RMSE': rmse,
            'MAPE': mape,
            'wall_time_seconds': wall_time,
            'learning_efficiency': leff
        })
        print(f"Sample size {sample_size} done.")
    df_results = pd.DataFrame(results)
    df_results.to_excel('lstm_learning_curve_re-
sults.xlsx', index=False)
    print("Results saved to lstm_learning_curve_re-
sults.xlsx")
```

Appendix B – Code for ARIMA Modelling Function

```python
import yfinance as yf
import pandas as pd
import numpy as np
import time
import matplotlib.pyplot as plt
from statsmodels.tsa.statespace.sarimax import SARIMAX
from sklearn.metrics import mean_squared_error
from curl_cffi import requests

def download_last_n_observations(ticker, n=5000):
    session = requests.Session(impersonate="chrome")
    data = yf.download(ticker, period=f"{int(n*1.5)}d",
interval='1d', session=session)
    close = data['Close'].dropna()
    return close.tail(n)

def calculate_mape(y_true, y_pred):
    y_true, y_pred = np.array(y_true), np.array(y_pred)
    return np.mean(np.abs((y_true - y_pred) / y_true)) *
100

def evaluate_model(model, test):
    pred = model.forecast(steps=len(test))
    mse = mean_squared_error(test, pred)
    rmse = np.sqrt(mse)
    mape = calculate_mape(test, pred)
    return mse, rmse, mape, pred
```

```python
def find_best_arima_model(series, seasonal_periods=[0],
max_p=3, max_d=1, max_q=3, max_P=0, max_D=0, max_Q=0):
    import warnings
    warnings.filterwarnings("ignore")
    best_aic = np.inf
    best_order = None
    best_seasonal_order = None
    best_model = None

    from itertools import product
    for seasonal_period in seasonal_periods:
        pdq = list(product(range(max_p+1),
range(max_d+1), range(max_q+1)))
        seasonal_pdq = list(product(range(max_P+1),
range(max_D+1), range(max_Q+1)))
        for order in pdq:
            if seasonal_period > 0:
                for seasonal_order in seasonal_pdq:
                    try:
                        model = SARIMAX(series, order=order, seasonal_order=(seasonal_order[0], seasonal_order[1], seasonal_order[2], seasonal_period), enforce_stationarity=False, enforce_invertibility=False)
                        results = model.fit(disp=False)
                        if results.aic < best_aic:
                            best_aic = results.aic
                            best_order = order
                            best_seasonal_order = (seasonal_order[0], seasonal_order[1], seasonal_order[2], seasonal_period)
                            best_model = results
                    except Exception:
                        continue
            else:
                try:
                    model = SARIMAX(series, order=order, enforce_stationarity=False, enforce_invertibility=False)
                    results = model.fit(disp=False)
                    if results.aic < best_aic:
                        best_aic = results.aic
                        best_order = order
                        best_seasonal_order = None
                        best_model = results
                except Exception:
                    continue
```

```python
    return best_model, best_order, best_seasonal_order,
best_aic

def arima_learning_curve_with_timing(ticker):
    close = download_last_n_observations(ticker, n=5000)
    test = close[-30:]
    results = []
    times = []
    for train_size in range(30, 5001, 30):
        train = close[:train_size]
        start_time = time.time()
        best_model, best_order, best_seasonal_order,
best_aic = find_best_arima_model(train)
        elapsed = time.time() - start_time
        if best_model is not None:
            mse, rmse, mape, pred = evalu-
ate_model(best_model, test)
            learning_efficiency = 1 / (elapsed * mse) if
mse != 0 else np.nan
            results.append({
                'sample_size': train_size,
                'best_order': best_order,
                'best_seasonal_order': best_seasonal_or-
der,
                'AIC': best_aic,
                'MSE': mse,
                'RMSE': rmse,
                'MAPE': mape,
                'wall_time_seconds': elapsed,
                'learning_efficiency': learning_effi-
ciency,
                'model_summary': best_model.sum-
mary().as_text(),
                'test_predictions': pred.values if ha-
sattr(pred, 'values') else pred
            })
            times.append(elapsed)
        else:
            results.append({
                'sample_size': train_size,
                'best_order': None,
                'best_seasonal_order': None,
                'AIC': None,
                'MSE': None,
                'RMSE': None,
```

```
                'MAPE': None,
                'wall_time_seconds': None,
                'learning_efficiency': None,
                'model_summary': None,
                'test_predictions': None
            })
            times.append(None)
    df = pd.DataFrame(results)
    # Plotting
    plt.figure(figsize=(10,6))
    plt.plot(df['sample_size'], df['wall_time_seconds'],
marker='o')
    plt.xlabel('Training Data Size')
    plt.ylabel('Wall Time (seconds)')
    plt.title(f'ARIMA Model Selection Time vs Training
Data Size for {ticker}')
    plt.grid(True)
    plt.show()
    df.to_excel("arima_learning_curve_results.xlsx", in-
dex=False)
    return df
```

References

1. Parmezan, A.R.S., Souza, V.M.A., Batista, G.E.A.P.A.: Evaluation of statistical and machine learning models for time series prediction: Identifying the state-of-the-art and the best conditions for the use of each model. Inf. Sci. **484**, 302–337 (2019). https://doi.org/10.1016/j.ins.2019.01.076
2. Montgomery, D.C., Jennings, C.L., Kulahci, M.: Introduction to Time Series Analysis and Forecasting, 2nd edn. Wiley, Hoboken (2016)
3. De Gooijer, G., Hyndman, R.J.: 25 years of time series forecasting. Int. J. Forecast. **22**(3), 443–473 (2006). https://doi.org/10.1016/j.ijforecast.2006.01.001
4. Kramar, V., Alchakov, V.: Time-series forecasting of seasonal data using machine learning methods. Algorithms **16**(5), 248 (2023). https://doi.org/10.3390/a16050248
5. Barrera-Animas, A.Y., Oyedele, L.O., Bilal, M., Akinosho, T.D., Delgado, J.M.D., Akanbi, L.A.: Rainfall prediction: a comparative analysis of modern machine learning algorithms for time-series forecasting. Mach. Learn. Appl. **7**, 100204 (2022). https://doi.org/10.1016/j.mlwa.2021.100204
6. Pavlyshenko, B.: Machine-learning models for sales time series forecasting. Data **4**(1), 15 (2019). https://doi.org/10.3390/data4010015
7. Ahmed, N.K., Atiya, A.F., El Gayar, N., El-Shishiny, H.: An empirical comparison of machine learning models for time series forecasting. Econom. Rev. **29**(5–6), 594–621 (2010). https://doi.org/10.1080/07474938.2010.481556
8. Makridakis, S., Spiliotis, E., Assimakopoulos, V.: Statistical and machine learning forecasting methods: concerns and ways forward. PLoS ONE **13**(3), e0194889 (2018). https://doi.org/10.1371/journal.pone.0194889
9. Haviluddin, Alfred, R., Obit, J.H., Ahmad Hijazi, M.H., Ag Ibrahim, A.A.: A performance comparison of statistical and machine learning techniques in learning time series data. Adv. Sci. Lett. **21**(10), 3037–3041 (2015). https://doi.org/10.1166/asl.2015.6490

10. Bhattacharjee, I., Bhattacharja, P.: Stock price prediction: a comparative study between traditional statistical approach and machine learning approach. In: 2019 4th International Conference on Electrical Information and Communication Technology (EICT), pp. 1–6. IEEE, December 2019. https://doi.org/10.1109/EICT48899.2019.9068850
11. De Santis, G., İmrohoroğlu, S.: Stock returns and volatility in emerging financial markets. J. Int. Money Finance **16**(4), 561–579 (1997). https://doi.org/10.1016/S0261-5606(97)00020-X
12. Divecha, A.B., Drach, J., Stefek, D.: Emerging markets: a quantitative perspective. J. Portf. Manag. **19**(11) (1992)
13. Batten, J.A., Vo, X.V.: Liquidity and return relationships in an emerging market. Emerg. Mark. Finance Trade **50**(1), 5–21 (2014). https://doi.org/10.2753/REE1540-496X500101
14. Banerjee, D.: Forecasting of Indian stock market using time-series ARIMA model. In: 2014 2nd International Conference on Business and Information Management (ICBIM), pp. 131–135. IEEE, January 2014. https://doi.org/10.1109/ICBIM.2014.6970973
15. Mustapa, F.H., Ismail, M.T.: Modelling and forecasting S&P 500 stock prices using hybrid Arima-Garch Model. J. Phys. Conf. Ser. **1366**(1), 012130 (2019). https://doi.org/10.1088/1742-6596/1366/1/012130
16. Wahyidu, S.: The ARIMA model for the Indonesia stock price. Int. J. Econ. Manag. (2017)
17. Mondal, P., Shit, L., Goswami, S.: Study of effectiveness of time series modeling (Arima) in forecasting stock prices. Int. J. Comput. Sci. Eng. Appl. **4**(2), 13–29 (2014). https://doi.org/10.5121/ijcsea.2014.4202
18. Gonzalez, L., Powell, J.G., Shi, J., Wilson, A.: Two centuries of bull and bear market cycles. Int. Rev. Econ. Finance **14**(4), 469–486 (2005). https://doi.org/10.1016/j.iref.2004.02.003

AI-Powered Assessment of Air Pollution in Europe: OpenAQ Insights 2020–2024

Jesús Cáceres-Tello[1][(✉)], Ziwei Shu[2], and Jose Javier Galán-Hernández[3]

[1] Department of Computer Science and Engineering, Faculty of Computer Science, Complutense University of Madrid, Madrid, Spain
`jescacer@ucm.es`

[2] Department of Marketing, Faculty of Statistics, Complutense University of Madrid, Madrid, Spain
`ziweishu@ucm.es`

[3] ENAE Business School, Murcia, Spain

Abstract. This study examines PM2.5 dynamics in five European capitals, Madrid, Berlin, Paris, Rome, and Warsaw, over January 2020 to January 2024. We rely on validated, open data accessed via OpenAQ, which aggregates measurements reported to the European Environment Agency. Our aims are twofold: (i) to describe seasonal and spatial patterns across contrasting urban contexts; and (ii) to assess the value of those patterns for more adaptive, evidence-informed policy. The workflow covers cleaning, monthly aggregation, and comparative time-series exploration, complemented by a hybrid forecaster that pairs Prophet with a Long Short-Term Memory network. Results show clear winter peaks and marked cross-city differences in both levels and variability. These contrasts reflect not only meteorology and geography but also choices in transport, energy, and regulation. We conclude that high-resolution open data are essential for transparent, context-sensitive decision-making.

Keywords: Air pollution monitoring · Open environmental data · Machine learning · Urban sustainability

1 Introduction

Air pollution continues to pose a major environmental and health concern across Europe. Despite decades of regulatory frameworks and technological improvements, urban populations continue to be chronically exposed to high concentrations of atmospheric pollutants, with serious consequences for morbidity and mortality, particularly from fine particulate matter (PM2.5), nitrogen dioxide (NO_2), and ground-level ozone (O_3) [1]. Numerous studies have highlighted the persistence of this issue even in cities that have implemented ambitious restrictions and clean-air plans, underscoring the need for more precise, adaptive, and context-sensitive strategies [2].

In this study, we focus specifically on PM2.5 concentrations due to their critical health relevance and robust data availability. Although ozone (O_3) is mentioned in the methodology, it is not analyzed in the present results and is reserved for future work.

H. Kannan et al. (Eds.): AIKP 2025, CCIS 2804, pp. 135–146, 2026.
https://doi.org/10.1007/978-3-032-14706-6_11

In recent years, artificial intelligence (AI) tools have shown considerable potential in enhancing the analysis and understanding of the spatiotemporal dynamics of air pollution. The integration of predictive models into environmental data workflows has enabled more accurate estimations, the detection of local anomalies, and the optimization of targeted interventions in complex urban environments [3]. These advances are occurring in parallel with the rise of open environmental data platforms such as OpenAQ, which have democratized access to high-frequency, globally standardized air quality data. This has allowed researchers, institutions, and even local governments to engage in comparative studies and to develop replicable models that are increasingly being applied across borders and disciplines. The scientific community has begun to leverage this infrastructure for large-scale continental analyses, revealing both overarching trends and deeply localized disparities in air quality dynamics across Europe [4].

Recent reviews also emphasize the growing role of machine and deep learning techniques in capturing the spatiotemporal variability of pollutants, providing robust predictive capacities and supporting early-warning systems [5]. Likewise, hybrid approaches combining statistical and deep learning models, such as Prophet and LSTM, have demonstrated strong predictive performance in time series applications [6]. In parallel, new advances in emissions databases, such as the EDGAR project, have enriched the temporal and spatial resolution of air pollution inventories, offering essential inputs for AI-based models and long-term policy assessments [7].

In this study, we aim to contribute to this growing research agenda by providing an updated, comparative assessment of PM2.5 concentrations across five major European cities, Madrid, Berlin, Paris, Rome, and Warsaw, during the period from January 2020 to January 2024. Using standardized public datasets from the OpenAQ platform and a hybrid predictive framework based on Prophet and Long Short-Term Memory (LSTM) models, this study seeks to characterize both the spatial and seasonal patterns of pollution and to explore their implications for evidence-based, city-specific environmental policy design.

These cities were selected given their policy relevance, diverse climatic and socio-economic contexts, and consistent data availability from official monitoring stations. This selection ensures both comparability and applicability of the findings within the broader EU air quality policy framework.

The paper proceeds as follows. Section 2 provides a critical overview of recent research that combines open data and AI techniques for analyzing air pollution in Europe. Section 3 describes the data collection and processing workflow, as well as the design and validation of the hybrid forecasting model. Section 4 presents a comparative analysis of PM2.5 concentrations across the five selected cities, highlighting their spatial and seasonal variations. Finally, Sect. 5 discusses the policy implications of the findings and outlines future directions for AI-assisted environmental monitoring and planning.

2 Related Work

Scientific research on air quality in Europe has increasingly embraced integrative approaches that combine traditional monitoring methods with advanced modeling and predictive analytics. Within this framework, particular attention has been devoted to identifying the geographic sources of specific pollutants, such as O_3, and estimating their impact on premature mortality in regions chronically exposed to elevated levels, especially during the summer months [8]. In parallel, recent studies have highlighted the role of biomass burning in sustaining high concentrations of PM2.5, particularly in smaller cities and peripheral areas of Central and Eastern Europe [9].

Recent deployments of open data and distributed sensing have supported ML-based integration of heterogeneous observations, improving estimation and targeting of interventions. For example, Chen et al. examined population exposure to multiple pollutants and the health risks of compound episodes across European cities [10].

This line of research has also progressed through the use of transfer learning, improving local air quality forecasts and enabling cross-city knowledge transfer in heterogeneous contexts [11].

Recent advances have shown how machine-learning downscaling techniques can generate daily high-resolution PM2.5 surface estimates, effectively bridging the gap between regional forecasts and city-level exposure assessments [12]. Beyond monitoring, consolidated evidence indicates that adverse health effects can arise at concentrations close to, sometimes even below, current European regulatory thresholds [13].

From a methodological angle, recent reviews show that machine-learning approaches, especially tree-based models, often outperform linear baselines for pollutants with strong spatial contrast and call for clearer reporting and broader, like-for-like comparisons [14]. At the policy level, Europe-wide assessments reveal persistent gaps with respect to the 2021 WHO guideline values for PM2.5 and O_3, underscoring the need for targeted mitigation supported by robust city-scale forecasting [15].

Recent work has consolidated data-driven forecasting frameworks for urban air quality, covering tree-based learners, convolutional/recurrent networks, and hybrid pipelines. It also distils good practice on evaluation design, feature engineering that captures meteorology and emissions proxies, and deployment aspects [16].

Despite these advances, significant knowledge gaps remain concerning the spatiotemporal evolution of atmospheric pollution at the continental scale, particularly with respect to integrating multiple pollutants and comparing regions with diverse sociodemographic profiles. This work contributes to this body of research by offering updated empirical evidence based on open data and AI-driven forecasting models.

3 Methodology

This work is based on open-access air quality data retrieved from the OpenAQ platform (accessed May 2025) and the EEA Air Quality e-Reporting service (validated hourly pollutant measurements; accessed May 2025). Only monitoring stations located in Europe were considered, covering the period from January 2020 to January 2024, with the analysis focused on two key pollutants: PM2.5 and O_3.

Figure 1 outlines the pipeline used in this study. The process covers six steps—data acquisition, quality control and gap handling, monthly resampling, exploratory analysis, hybrid forecasting (Prophet with LSTM), and error-based validation—culminating in cross-city synthesis.

We first cleaned hourly records and built station-level daily means. City-level series were then produced and used to examine seasonal and spatial patterns. A subsequent descriptive analysis was conducted to identify seasonal and spatial concentration patterns.

For the predictive phase, a hybrid model was developed, combining the Prophet algorithm, designed to capture trends and seasonality, with an LSTM neural network, trained on the residuals of the initial model to detect short-term nonlinear fluctuations. Forecasting was applied to the monthly PM2.5 averages, projecting their evolution through 2027 for a set of representative cities.

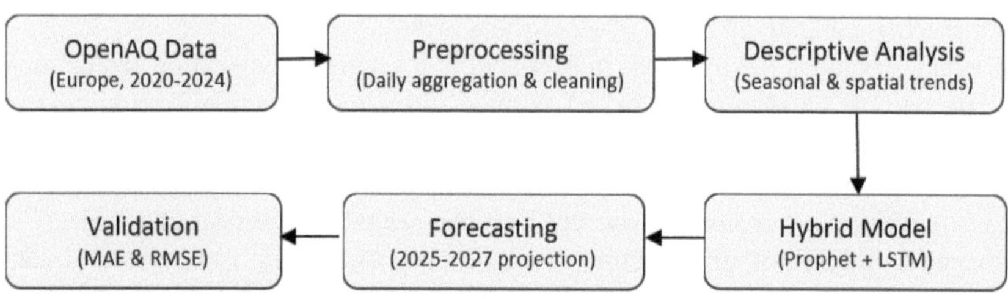

Fig. 1. Workflow integrating open air quality data with preprocessing, exploratory analysis, and hybrid forecasting (Prophet-LSTM).

The original Parquet files were processed in Python to drop null, negative, and inconsistent entries. Hourly values were collapsed to monthly means per station and then combined at city level, yielding harmonized series suitable for seasonal analysis and between-city comparisons.

Model validation was conducted through time-based splitting, using mean absolute error (MAE) and root mean square error (RMSE) as performance metrics. This ensured that the forecasts not only reproduced historical patterns but also generalized to unseen periods. Similar strategies have been successfully applied in recent air quality forecasting frameworks that emphasize uncertainty quantification and robust performance evaluation [18].

Following dataset consolidation, additional quality filters were applied to remove anomalous or incomplete records (such as negative or duplicate values). Monthly PM2.5 concentrations were then aggregated by city, producing cleaned time series for the period between January 2020 and January 2024, the most recent validated data available at the time of this work (May 2025). These consolidated series formed the empirical basis for both descriptive analyses and inter-city comparisons.

The next section presents the main results, highlighting the spatial and seasonal patterns of air pollution across selected European cities, as well as the potential implications of these findings for sustainability and public health policy.

3.1 Data Source and Acquisition

The empirical foundation of this study relies on publicly accessible air quality datasets. The primary source was the European Environment Agency (EEA) through its Air Quality e-Reporting (AQ e-Reporting) service, which provides validated hourly pollutant measurements in Parquet format. This repository ensures harmonized protocols across European countries, making the data directly comparable between cities.

The analysis focused on fine particulate matter (PM2.5) due to its strong links with adverse health outcomes and its consistent coverage across European capitals. While ozone (O_3) was also retrieved to test availability and completeness, it was excluded from the final comparative analysis because of heterogeneous data coverage across cities.

The study covered the period January 2020 to January 2024, corresponding to the most recent fully validated datasets available at the time of analysis (May 2025). Data were downloaded for five representative capitals, Madrid, Berlin, Paris, Rome, and Warsaw, chosen for their policy relevance, distinct climatic and socioeconomic contexts, and robust monitoring infrastructures. Together, these cities capture a wide range of pollution dynamics across Southern, Central, and Eastern Europe.

3.2 Preprocessing and Harmonization

The raw hourly datasets contained millions of individual records per pollutant and city. To ensure consistency, a preprocessing pipeline was implemented in Python using the libraries *pandas* and *numpy*. The following steps were applied sequentially:

1. Quality filtering: records flagged with invalid or missing values were removed. This included negative concentrations, duplicate entries, and observations marked as not validated by the reporting station.
2. Temporal aggregation: hourly data were first averaged into daily means for each monitoring station, ensuring comparability across different reporting frequencies.
3. Spatial aggregation: daily values were then averaged across all stations located within each city, producing a harmonized urban-level dataset.
4. Monthly resampling: the final step aggregated daily means into monthly averages, providing robust time series suitable for trend and forecasting analysis while reducing short-term noise.

This multi-step harmonization resulted in cleaned monthly PM2.5 time series for each city, covering a continuous 49-month period (January 2020–January 2024). These series formed the basis for both descriptive analyses and predictive modeling.

The preprocessing workflow is illustrated in Fig. 1, which summarizes the integration of open data retrieval, quality control, temporal aggregation, and hybrid forecasting design.

3.3 Exploratory Analysis

Before implementing predictive models, an exploratory phase was carried out to characterize the behavior of PM2.5 concentrations in the selected cities. This stage focused on identifying general temporal trends, seasonal cycles, and potential anomalies that could later inform the forecasting models.

To achieve this, the cleaned datasets were first aggregated into monthly series. Visualization was central at this stage: time-series plots allowed us to trace the evolution of pollution levels, while decomposition techniques helped to separate long-term trends, recurrent seasonal components, and irregular fluctuations. This made it possible to distinguish structural changes in emissions from short-term anomalies, such as winter peaks associated with heating demand.

As an illustrative case, Madrid was chosen to exemplify the decomposition process, since its series combines marked winter peaks with periods of relative stability in the warmer months; this example also highlights how the components guide the hybrid model design.

Rather than presenting all inter-city comparisons at this stage, which are analyzed in detail in Sect. 4 (Results), this exploratory step primarily ensured that the dataset was robust and that the models would be capable of capturing both seasonal recurrence and local irregularities.

3.4 Forecasting

Forecasting relied on a hybrid setup in which Prophet captures trend/seasonality and an LSTM models short-term nonlinear residual structure [17]. Models were trained with monthly averages between January 2020 and January 2024, and forecasts were extended through 2027. Performance was assessed with mean absolute error (MAE) and root mean square error (RMSE) under a time-based split, ensuring that predictions generalize beyond the training period.

As an illustrative case, forecasts for Madrid are shown in Fig. 2, where the predicted trajectory is displayed together with its 95% confidence interval. The model successfully reproduces the city's seasonal recurrence while capturing interannual variability, although anomalies such as the unusually high peak in January 2024 remain challenging to predict.

Figure 3 extends the analysis by comparing observed and forecast annual averages across all five cities. The projections suggest diverging dynamics: Southern capitals like Madrid and Rome tend toward moderate decreases, whereas Berlin and Warsaw are likely to maintain more stable or slightly rising concentrations. These results underscore the importance of city-specific strategies rather than continent-wide prescriptions for air quality management.

While most forecasts show smooth continuations of past dynamics, the sharp increase predicted for Madrid in 2027 stands out as inconsistent with the preceding trend. This discrepancy likely reflects sensitivity of the hybrid model to outlier values in the training set, compounded by the relatively short time span of available data. Rather than treating it as a definitive outcome, this value should be understood as an indication of model uncertainty and the need for further calibration.

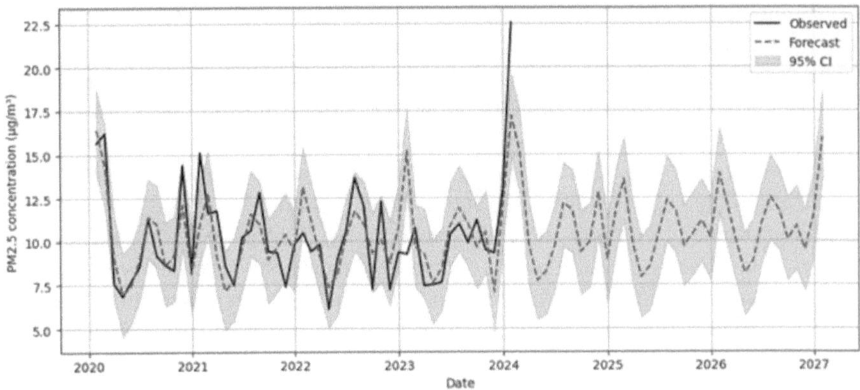

Fig. 2. Forecast of monthly PM2.5 in Madrid (2020–2027) with 95% confidence interval.

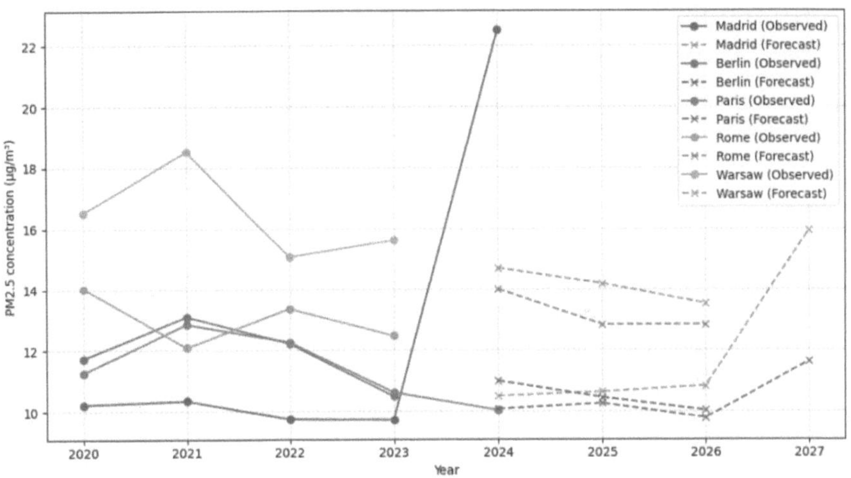

Fig. 3. Annual PM2.5 in five European capitals: observed (2020–2024) and forecast (2025–2027).

4   Results

We used open data accessed via OpenAQ in coordination with the European Environment Agency (EEA), ensuring validated, harmonized measurements across national monitoring networks. The analysis focuses on PM2.5 from January 2020 to January 2024, the most recent fully validated period at the time of processing (May 2025), so that both enduring seasonal patterns and recent shifts (e.g., pandemic-related changes or new city policies) can be examined.

For the comparative analysis, five cities were selected: Madrid, Berlin, Paris, Rome, and Warsaw. The choice responded to three main criteria: (i) the availability of complete, validated records throughout the entire study period; (ii) the demographic and political importance of each city as a European capital; and (iii) their representativeness of different climatic regions and regulatory approaches.

The descriptive analysis confirms clear seasonal cycles in all five cities, with peaks during winter and declines in summer. However, structural differences emerge when comparing cities. Warsaw consistently exhibits the highest levels, a result consistent with the use of solid fuels for residential heating. Paris appears at the opposite end, maintaining the lowest average values with limited interannual variability, suggesting the effectiveness of long-standing mobility and emissions policies. Madrid and Rome share similar trajectories, marked by elevated winter concentrations and strong monthly fluctuations, likely associated with thermal inversions and regional transport of aerosols. Berlin displays a balanced pattern: moderate seasonal variation and relatively stable averages, possibly reflecting a combination of regulatory efficiency and climatic moderation.

Figure 4 shows monthly PM2.5 averages for 2020–2024 in the five capitals, highlighting widespread winter peaks alongside persistent cross-city differences in baseline levels and seasonal amplitude. The graph highlights how winter peaks are a common feature across Europe, while structural disparities between cities remain evident.

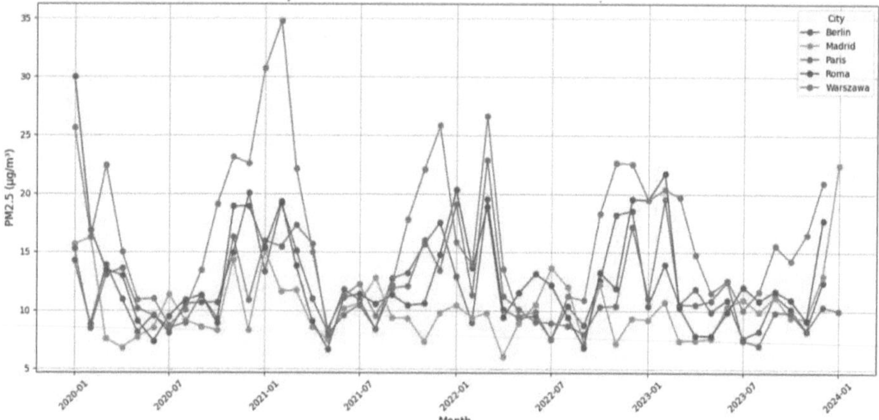

Fig. 4. Monthly PM2.5 concentrations (μg/m^3) in five European capitals (Jan 2020–Jan 2024), based on EEA-validated data available as of May 2025.

Figure 5 compares the average monthly seasonal cycle across the cities. The results confirm that while all capitals exhibit winter peaks, their intensity and amplitude differ. Warsaw again shows the strongest seasonality, while Paris maintains flatter curves, reinforcing the contrast between Central/Eastern and Western Europe.

In addition to the seasonal profiles shown in Fig. 5, a statistical summary was produced to capture the central tendency and variability of PM2.5 levels across the study period. Table 1 presents the mean, standard deviation, and extreme values for each city (January 2020–January 2024). These results quantify the disparities already visible in the graphs: Paris consistently records the lowest averages and narrow variability, while Warsaw reaches both the highest means and widest range, reflecting its structural vulnerability to wintertime pollution.

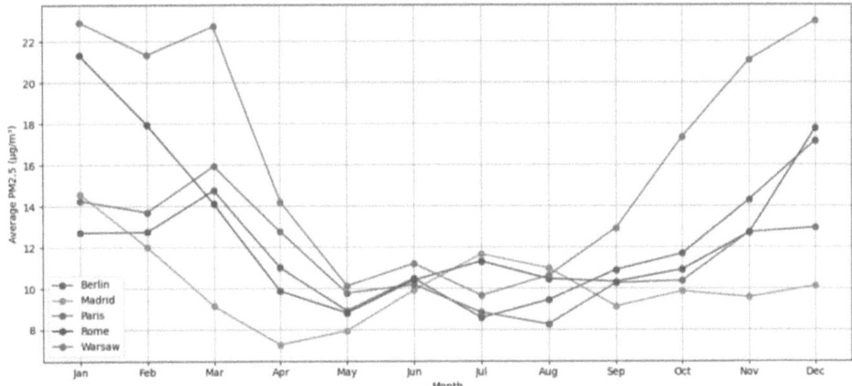

Fig. 5. Average monthly seasonality of PM2.5 across five European capitals (January 2020–January 2024)

Table 1. Descriptive statistics of PM2.5 concentrations (μg/m^3) in five European capitals, January 2020–January 2024.

City	Mean (μg/m^3)	Std. Dev.	Min	Max
Madrid	14.2	5.8	6.1	28.7
Berlin	12.7	4.3	5.9	24.1
Paris	10.5	3.9	4.7	19.8
Rome	15.1	6.2	7.3	27.5
Warsaw	20.4	8.1	8.6	38.9

Taken together, Figs. 4 and 5, along with Table 1, highlight not only the common seasonal trends, such as recurrent winter peaks, but also the deeper structural disparities among the five capitals, shaped by both geographic and institutional factors. Rather than serving as a conclusion, these findings establish the empirical foundation for the next section, where their implications for forecasting and policy design are examined in greater depth.

5 Conclusions

We characterized PM2.5 evolution in five European capitals over January 2020–January 2024 using quality-assured measurements and a reproducible pipeline. By combining data cleaning, aggregation, and visualization techniques, the analysis was able to extract robust temporal patterns that not only confirm the expected seasonality of this pollutant but also reveal structural differences among the urban environments examined.

The results indicate that, while all cities experience winter peaks in PM2.5 pollution, there are significant contrasts in average levels and year-to-year stability. These differences cannot be attributed solely to meteorological factors; rather, they point to the decisive role of local environmental policies, transportation systems, residential energy models, and, ultimately, institutional priorities related to sustainability.

In practical terms, these results support tailored, city-specific strategies grounded in observed patterns, with open and harmonized data serving both technical analysis and public transparency. The harmonization of monitoring standards and the availability of open data emerge as key tools not only for technical analysis but also for public transparency and the formulation of more effective policies.

Methodologically, the Prophet–LSTM scheme balanced long-term seasonal structure with short-term deviations. Forecasts extended to 2027 suggest diverging patterns among cities: some show gradual improvement, others more stagnation or even worsening. These projections reinforce the need for city-specific, rather than continental, policy frameworks, as also highlighted in recent applications of advanced hybrid deep learning models, such as VMD–GAT–BiLSTM, to urban air quality prediction [19].

At the policy level, progress will also depend on translating data-driven insights into concrete interventions aligned with broader health and climate agendas. Recent discussions on revising the European Ambient Air Quality Directive (2008/50/EC) stress the urgency of updating regulatory frameworks to match emerging scientific evidence, moving toward more ambitious and enforceable standards [20].

This study nevertheless faces limitations. Its focus on PM2.5 excludes related pollutants such as NO_2 or O_3, whose interactions may significantly affect health outcomes. The relatively short observation window (January 2020–January 2024) constrains long-term inference, and outliers, such as the anomalous Madrid forecast in 2027, highlight the sensitivity of the models to unusual historical values.

Looking forward, several avenues for research arise:

- Extend pollutant coverage to O_3 and NO_2 for multi-pollutant modeling.
- Enlarge the dataset temporally and spatially, incorporating more cities and longer series.
- Improve interpretability through explainable AI methods that clarify anomaly drivers.
- Couple models with scenario simulations of emission policies and energy transitions.
- Advance real-time adaptive forecasting methods able to learn incrementally as new data arrive.

In summary, this study not only provides updated empirical evidence on PM2.5 dynamics in European capitals but also demonstrates the potential of combining open data with hybrid AI approaches. These results lay the foundation for future interdisciplinary work linking AI, environmental science, and urban policy.

Disclosure of Interests. The authors have no competing interests to declare that are relevant to the content of this article.

References

1. Lelieveld, J., Pozzer, A., Pöschl, U., Fnais, M., Haines, A., Münzel, T.: Loss of life expectancy from air pollution compared to other risk factors: a worldwide perspective. Cardiovasc. Res. **116**(11), 1910–1917 (2020)

2. Sartelet, K., et al.: Air pollution mapping and variability over five European cities. Environ. Int. **199**, 109474 (2025). https://doi.org/10.1016/j.envint.2025.109474

3. Cáceres-Tello, J., Galán-Hernández, J.J.: Analysis and prediction of PM2.5 pollution in Madrid: the use of prophet–long short-term memory hybrid models. AppliedMath **4**(4), 1428–1452 (2024). https://doi.org/10.3390/appliedmath4040076

4. Keller, C.A., et al.: Global impact of COVID-19 restrictions on the surface concentrations of nitrogen dioxide and ozone. Atmos. Chem. Phys. **21**(5), 3555–3592 (2021). https://doi.org/10.5194/acp-21-3555-2021

5. Agbehadji, I.E., Obagbuwa, I.C.: Systematic review of machine and deep learning techniques for spatiotemporal air quality prediction. Atmosphere **15**(11), 1352 (2024). https://doi.org/10.3390/atmos15111352

6. Arslan, S.: A hybrid forecasting model using LSTM and Prophet for energy consumption with decomposition of time series data. PeerJ Comput. Sci. **8**, e1001 (2022). https://doi.org/10.7717/peerj-cs.1001

7. Crippa, M., Solazzo, E., Huang, G., et al.: High resolution temporal profiles in the emissions database for global atmospheric research. Sci. Data **7**, 121 (2020). https://doi.org/10.1038/s41597-020-0462-2

8. Achebak, H., Garatachea, R., Pay, M.T., et al.: Geographic sources of ozone air pollution and mortality burden in Europe. Nat. Med. **30**, 1732–1738 (2024). https://doi.org/10.1038/s41591-024-02976-x

9. Zauli-Sajani, S., Thunis, P., Pisoni, E., et al.: Reducing biomass burning is key to decrease PM2.5 exposure in European cities. Sci. Rep. **14**, 10210 (2024). https://doi.org/10.1038/s41598-024-60946-2

10. Chen, Z.Y., Petetin, H., Méndez Turrubiates, R.F., et al.: Population exposure to multiple air pollutants and its compound episodes in Europe. Nat. Commun. **15**, 2094 (2024). https://doi.org/10.1038/s41467-024-46103-3

11. Poelzl, M., Kern, R., Kecorius, S., Lovrić, M.: Exploration of transfer learning techniques for the prediction of PM10. Sci. Rep. **15**, 2919 (2025). https://doi.org/10.1038/s41598-025-86550-6

12. Shetty, S., et al.: Daily high-resolution surface PM2.5 estimation over Europe by ML-based downscaling of the CAMS regional forecast. Environ. Res. **312**, 120363 (2025). https://doi.org/10.1016/j.envres.2024.120363

13. Chen, J., Hoek, G., et al.: Long-term exposure to low-level PM2.5 and mortality: a systematic review and meta-analysis. Environ. Health Perspect. **131**(7) (2023). https://doi.org/10.1289/EHP12141

14. Vachon, J., Kerckhoffs, J., Buteau, S., Smargiassi, A.: Do machine learning methods improve prediction of ambient air pollutants with high spatial contrast? A systematic review. Environ. Res. **262**(Pt 2), 119751 (2024). https://doi.org/10.1016/j.envres.2024.119751

15. Franke, P., Lange, A.C., Steffens, B., Pozzer, A., Wahner, A., Kiendler-Scharr, A.: European air quality in view of the WHO 2021 guideline levels: effect of emission reductions on air pollution exposure. Elementa Sci. Anthropocene **12**(1), 00127 (2024). https://doi.org/10.1525/elementa.2023.00127

16. Rosca, C.-M., Carbureanu, M., Stancu, A.: Data-driven approaches for predicting and forecasting air quality in urban areas. Appl. Sci. **15**(8), 4390 (2025). https://doi.org/10.3390/app15084390

17. Feng, X., et al.: A hybrid model for enhanced forecasting of PM2.5 concentrations. Sci. Total Environ. **907**, 167851 (2024). https://doi.org/10.1016/j.scitotenv.2024.167851

18. Malings, C., et al.: Air quality estimation and forecasting via data fusion with uncertainty quantification. J. Geophys. Res. Atmos. **129**(7), e2024JD000183 (2024). https://doi.org/10.1029/2024JD000183

19. Wang, X., et al.: Air quality forecasting using a spatiotemporal hybrid deep learning model based on VMD–GAT–BiLSTM. Sci. Rep. **14**, 17841 (2024). https://doi.org/10.1038/s41598-024-68874-x
20. Kuula, J., et al.: Insights into updating ambient air quality directive 2008/50/EC. Atmos. Chem. Phys. **22**, 4801–4808 (2022). https://doi.org/10.5194/acp-22-4801-2022

Time-Series Forecasting of Solar Irradiance for Resilient Microgrids in Wayuu Communities Using NASA POWER Data

Maria C. Moreno[1]([⊠]) [iD], Brayan Daniel Sarmiento[1] [iD], John C. Moreno[2] [iD],
and Oscar J. Suarez[3] [iD]

[1] Commercial Aviation Training, Canadian Aviation Electronics (CAE), 110911
Bogota D.C., Colombia
`mariacmoreno32@gmail.com`
[2] Solar Energy Department, Kay Jepirrache Eco Soluciones, 442001 Maicao-La
Guajira, Colombia
[3] Mechatronics Engineering Department, University of Pamplona,
543050 Pamplona, Colombia
`oscar.suarez@unipamplona.edu.co`

Abstract. La Guajira, Colombia, is highlighted as one of the most solar-rich regions in Latin America, with Global Horizontal Irradiance (GHI) values higher than 6.0 kWh/m^2/day and annual mean temperatures around 28 °C. However, indigenous communities from this region still face high levels of energy poverty. In this chapter, a holistic approach is presented to combine NASA Prediction of Worldwide Energy Resources (POWER) with state-of-the-art machine learning algorithms in order to improve solar resource assessment. The workflow is embedded in the Google Colab, using Python libraries such as scikit-learn, TensorFlow, pandas, and matplotlib. Long Short-Term Memory (LSTM) networks are adopted for time-series forecasting of GHI and temperature, as well as K-Means clustering to partition microclimatic zones with similar solar irradiance patterns. Finally, Principal Component Analysis (PCA) is used for feature selection and dimensionality reduction, which can enhance the accuracy of the model.

Keywords: Solar Resource Characterization · Time-Series Forecasting · Long Short-Term Memory (LSTM) · K-Means Clustering · NASA POWER Data

1   Introduction

In the past decades, the remoteness of rural communities affected by energy poverty has become a key barrier for sustainable development in Colombia's peripheries. This isolation inherently complicates efforts to integrate these populations into the National Interconnected System (SIN) [7]. According to 2022

H. Kannan et al. (Eds.): AIKP 2025, CCIS 2804, pp. 147–159, 2026.
https://doi.org/10.1007/978-3-032-14706-6_12

148   M. C. Moreno et al.

data, the departments with the lowest electricity coverage included Vaupés (32.54%), Vichada (43.03%), La Guajira (55.74%), Amazonas (61.77%), Magdalena (71.57%), Guainía (73.04%), and Putumayo (73.21%) [6]. The lack of reliable electricity, compounded by geographic dispersion, significantly restricts access to critical services such as healthcare, education, and safe water, further entrenching historical structural inequities. This has been exacerbated in recent years for the Wayuu people of La Guajira (the largest indigenous group of Colombia), where all the above factors have led to extreme poverty and acute insecurity in access to water and food [11].

Consequently, the Inter-American Court of Human Rights has deemed that there is a humanitarian crisis among the Wayuu people caused by widespread malnutrition and thirst. Figure 1. illustrates the maintenance and repair of a solar water pump system, which is supplying water to a small Wayuu village. Such a decentralized system represents an approach for the deployment of renewable energy in rural, off-grid areas which are not serviced by utility supply [9].

Fig. 1. On-Site Maintenance of a Solar-Driven Water Supply System in a Remote Area.

In contrast, it is worth noting that Colombia owns plenty of natural resources diversification [15]. La Guajira, specifically, is extremely arid but energy and mineral resource rich [5]. The area has one of the most excellent conditions for solar and wind energy in both national and global terms, which makes it suitable for sustainable energy production [9]. As a result, the Colombian government has made efforts to overcome energy access issues by creating regulatory conditions that facilitate the deployment of non-conventional RES since 2015 [7]. That's what has allowed us to build massive renewable energy facilities.

However, the decentralized layout of Wayuu villages in rural areas is a major limitation for grid interconnections [8]. Furthermore, the lack of ground meteorological stations also restricts accurate solar resources assessment, which is crucial for efficient designing and optimization process of standalone microgrids.

In this context, satellite-derived climate datasets are providing valuable resources for assessment of the resource in data-limited areas [12]. For instance, the NASA Prediction of Worldwide Energy Resources (POWER) is an open, long-term consistent climate variable dataset providing global in-situ measurements and satellite-derived data to support historical calibration studies [3,16]. These databases enable engineers and scientists to perform a solid solar resource assessment also in the absence of traditional observation systems [10,14]. Therefore, the connection between the NASA POWER database and photovoltaic models favors its use in decentralized energy sources for marginalized communities like the Wayuu in La Guajira [9], [10].

Based on the considerations mentioned above, this study introduces a scalable framework to support decentralized solar energy planning in La Guajira, Colombia. It integrates satellite-based climate data from the NASA POWER platform with machine learning techniques to improve solar resource characterization. Implemented in Google Colaboratory (Colab) using Python, the workflow applies long-short-term memory (LSTM) networks to forecast solar irradiance and temperature, k-means clustering to identify microclimatic zones, and Principal Component Analysis (PCA) for dimensionality reduction. The approach enables accurate, low-cost planning for off-grid energy systems in Non-Interconnected Zones (NIZ), particularly benefiting indigenous Wayuu communities.

The rest of this chapter is structured as follows. Section 2 presents previous work on the application of satellite-derived climate datasets for the assessment of solar resources. Section 3 details the methodology and implementation of the proposed framework. Section 4 describes the experimental setup and reports the corresponding evaluation results. Section 5 offers a critical discussion and concluding remarks, while Sect. 6 outlines potential directions for future research. Finally, an Ethical Statement is included, along with an Appendix containing all necessary resources.

2 Related Work

Recent studies emphasize the value of satellite-based climate datasets to evaluate solar resources, especially when ground-based observations are sparse or unavailable. For example, a progressive approach is introduced in [2] to assess the complementarities of wind - solar in Shandong Province, China, to begin planning hybrid energy systems. This method is based on long-term wind speed and solar irradiance data taken from NASA databases that are applied to virtual energy system models to obtain capacity factors.

Likewise, [4] estimates and maps rooftop solar potential in Prince George's and Montgomery counties in Maryland. The model combines NASA's POWER platform and LiDAR-based digital surface models to analyze how local urban environments can be better considered in renewable energy policy.

Moreover, [1] proposed an algorithmic model to determine the best machine learning methods and time series models to reduce prediction errors in GSR. The models considered in this study are autoregressive integrated moving average (ARIMA), feedforward neural network with backpropagation (FFNN-BP), k-Nearest Neighbor (k-NN), and Support Vector Machine (SVM) and they are compared to a persistence model.

Finally, [13] assesses the utilizability of satellite-based solar radiation data available from NASA-POWER archives for Ghana, West Africa, to establish a long-term reference source. The assessment, using comparisons with 22 synoptic station sunshine duration estimates, indicates strong agreement in the northern Savannah regions during March to May, but a weaker correlation is indicated for the southern forest zones during June to August. This empirical investigation establishes the basis for implementing solar energy projects in the subregion.

3   Methodology

The methodology outlined in this study comprises four primary phases, which are detailed below.

3.1   Data Acquisition and Preprocessing

Data Collection. The solar resource information utilized is sourced from NASA's advanced POWER model, which includes worldwide solar and meteorological data. This dataset covers the period from January 1, 2019, to December 31, 2025, providing daily temporal resolution. Consequently, it generates a dataset with monthly average variables, yielding a total of 84 observations for each variable. The data are for La Guajira in Colombia and comprise Global Horizontal Irradiance (GHI), temperature (T2M), and clearness index ALLSKY KT, which are provided at about $11.54°N$ and $72.91°W$, with an area of around 500×500 km^2. This spatial resolution allows regional differences in solar resource dispersion over the study area to be delineated. Finally, the dataset is saved in CSV format back to Google Colab.

Data Import and Parsing. When the dataset is uploaded, its contents are parsed with the Pandas library in Python. The row with the "PARAMETER" label should be found first in order to validate that the dataset is formatted well. The subsequent information is then read and stored in a DataFrame that can be further manipulated and analyzed.

Data Transformation. To handle temporal analysis, the data is transformed from a wide to long format (required for time series data). This transformation is achieved by melting the dataset as per Equation (1). In this long data format, each observation is tied to a single parameter (e.g., GHI, temperature, clearness index) for a given period in time (months and years).

$$\text{Data}_{\text{long}} = \text{melt}\,(\text{Data}_{\text{wide}}) \tag{1}$$

After ensuring the columns are clean, they are renamed to facilitate easier understanding of the headers. Missing values, denoted as 999.0, are filled in with NaN, and the dataset is interpolated and forward and backward filled by Eq. (2). This method adapts to missing data, which in turn could aid the proper training of the model.

$$\text{Data}_{\text{cleaned}} = \text{replace}\,(\text{Data}_{\text{pivot}}, -999.0, \text{NaN}) \tag{2}$$

Data Scaling. Scaling of features is done to normalize the data for machine learning. This includes passing GHI and temperature features through Min-Max scaling to normalize them into the same scale. The scaling operation can be described as in Eq. (3):

$$x_{\text{scaled}} = \frac{x - x_{\min}}{x_{\max} - x_{\min}} \tag{3}$$

Here, $x_{\min}$ and $x_{\max}$ represent the minimum and maximum values, respectively.

3.2 Feature Engineering and Temporal Data Preparation

Sequence Generation for LSTM. For time series forecasting, sequences of the past 12 months of GHI data are generated. These sequences serve as input for the LSTM model, which is designed to learn temporal dependencies. As illustrated in Eq. (4), a sequence of past GHI values is used to predict the GHI value for the next month.

$$X = [x_t, x_{t+1}, \ldots, x_{t+11}], \quad y = x_{t+12} \tag{4}$$

In this formulation, X represents the 12-month input sequence, and y is the forecasted GHI for the next month.

Train-Test Split. The training and testing samples are divided with 80% of total samples being used in the training set, and 20% in the test set. This split ensures that the model can be validated correctly on unseen data. The splitting ratio r is given by the following Eq. (5):

$$r = 0.8 \quad (\text{for training}) \tag{5}$$

Thus, the training set size is calculated as $N_{\text{train}} = \text{floor}(r \times N_{\text{total}})$, where N_{total} is the total number of data points in the dataset.

3.3   Predictive Modeling

Long Short-Term Memory (LSTM) Network. The LSTM is trained with the Adam optimizer, which adjusts the learning rate automatically. The loss function of the model is Mean Squared Error (MSE), as shown in Eq. (6). This is a measure that can be used to assess how accurate the model's predictions are.

$$\text{MSE} = \frac{1}{n} \sum_{i=1}^{n} (y_{\text{true},i} - y_{\text{pred},i})^2 \tag{6}$$

where n is the number of test samples, y_{true} is the actual GHI value, and y_{pred} is the predicted GHI value.

Training the LSTM Model. For training, the LSTM uses the Adam optimizer that adapts the learning rate automatically. The updating equation of model parameters is shown as follows in Eq. (7):

$$\theta_{t+1} = \theta_t - \eta \nabla_\theta J(\theta_t) \tag{7}$$

where η is the the learning rate, θ_t presents the model parameters at time t, and $J(\theta_t)$ is the loss function, specifically MSE.

Baseline Models for Comparison. Performance of the LSTM model is evaluated along with two baseline models:

-   **Naive Model:** This method simply uses the GHI value of the last month as the predicted value for the current month as formulated by Equation (8).

$$y_{\text{naive},t} = y_{\text{true},t-1} \tag{8}$$

-   **Linear Regression:** A linear regression model is adopted as an additional baseline. The model estimates the GHI values using a linear combination of time indices. The relationship of this model is described in Eq. (9):

$$y_{\text{lr}} = \beta_0 + \beta_1 X \tag{9}$$

where β_0 is a bias term, β_1 is the trend of data, and X denotes the index time.

Model Evaluation. The effectiveness of the models is assessed by determining the MSE on the testing dataset. This metric serves to evaluate and compare the predictive accuracy across different models. The calculation for MSE, outlined in Eq. (10), is executed using actual units measured in kWh/m^2/day:

$$\text{MSE}_{\text{model}} = \frac{1}{n} \sum_{i=1}^{n} (y_{\text{true},i} - y_{\text{pred},i})^2 \tag{10}$$

where y_{true} and y_{pred} represent the actual and predicted GHI values, respectively.

3.4 LSTM Network Architecture

The architecture of the LSTM network employed in this research is outlined as follows. It comprises an input layer, a subsequent LSTM layer, a dropout layer, and two fully connected (dense) layers. The concluding output layer forecasts the GHI value for the upcoming time step.

As detailed in Table 1, this network structure includes an LSTM layer featuring 128 hidden units, which is succeeded by a fully connected layer containing 64 neurons.

Table 1. LSTM Network Architecture

Layer Type	Output Shape	Parameters
Input (TimeSeries)	(None, 240, 2)	0
LSTM (1)	(None, 128)	67,072
Dropout	(None, 128)	0
Dense (Fully Connected)	(None, 64)	8,256
Dense (Output)	(None, 1)	65

4 Experimental Results

4.1 Performance Metrics

To determine the best-performing model, the MSE values for the LSTM, Naive, and Linear Regression models are compared. Furthermore, a percentage improvement between the worst and best-performing models is calculated. The improvement, expressed in Eq.(11), quantifies the performance boost obtained by using the more sophisticated LSTM model:

$$\text{Improvement } \% = \frac{\text{MSE}_{\text{worst}} - \text{MSE}_{\text{best}}}{\text{MSE}_{\text{worst}}} \times 100 \tag{11}$$

where $\text{MSE}_{\text{worst}}$ and MSE_{best} represent the mean squared error of the worst and best models, respectively.

MSE on Scaled Values. The MSE values for the LSTM and Linear Regression models on the scaled values are shown below:

- **LSTM MSE:** 0.029433
- **Linear Regression MSE:** 0.030930
- **Accuracy Improvement:** 4.84 %

The LSTM model outperforms the Linear Regression model, with a lower MSE and a 4.84% improvement in performance.

MSE on Real Units. Finally, the models are tested with real units (kWh/m^2/day), and the results are:

- **LSTM MSE (real units):** 0.1011
- **Naive Baseline MSE (real units):** 0.2047
- **Linear Regression MSE (real units):** 0.1749

Additional evaluation metrics are incorporated to complement the Mean Squared Error (MSE) and provide a more comprehensive assessment of model performance. Specifically, the Root Mean Squared Error (RMSE) and Mean Absolute Error (MAE) are computed, defined respectively as shown in Eq. (12) and Eq. (13):

$$RMSE = \sqrt{\frac{1}{n} \sum_{i=1}^{n} (y_i - \hat{y}_i)^2} \tag{12}$$

$$MAE = \frac{1}{n} \sum_{i=1}^{n} |y_i - \hat{y}_i| \tag{13}$$

where y_i and $\hat{y}_i$ represent the observed and predicted values, respectively, and n is the number of observations. Additionally, the Mean Absolute Percentage Error (MAPE) is calculated to express the average relative deviation between predictions and actual values, as defined in Eq. (14):

$$MAPE = \frac{100}{n} \sum_{i=1}^{n} \left| \frac{y_i - \hat{y}_i}{y_i} \right| \tag{14}$$

The resulting performance metrics are $RMSE = 0.4357$, $MAE = 0.3294$, and $MAPE = 6.20\%$, indicating a low average deviation and acceptable prediction accuracy within the context of the analyzed dataset.

As observed, the LSTM model is significantly better than the Naive baseline and Linear Regression model, as there is a great reduction in MSE. The Naive approach, which only considers the previous month's value for computations, is a measure of innovation and has the highest MSE, reflecting its limitation in predicting.

4.2   Visualization of Model Performance

The results of the model comparisons are visualized through various plots:

- **Training and Validation Loss:** This graph depicts the loss values for both the training and validation datasets over the course of training epochs (See Fig. 2).
- **Predictions vs. Real Values:** A line chart is used to compare the predicted GHI values from the LSTM model against the actual observed GHI values (See Fig. 3).
- **Scatter Plot of Predictions vs. Real Values:** This plot visualizes the alignment between predicted and true values, with a reference line showing perfect prediction (See Fig. 4).

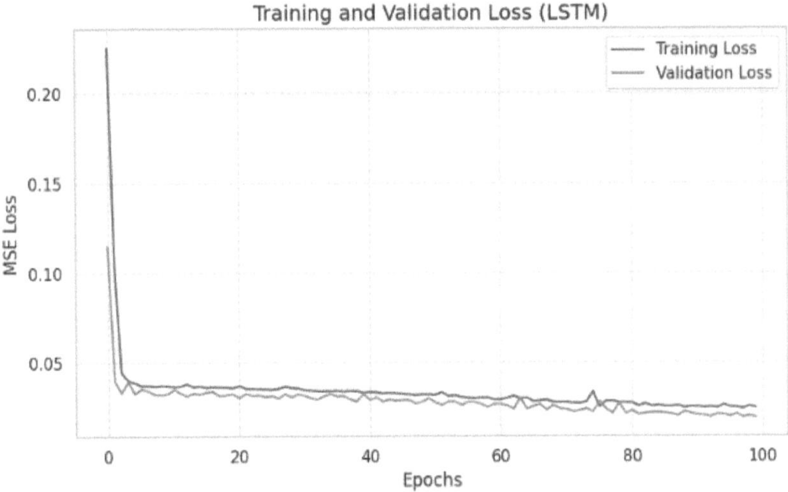

Fig. 2. Training and Validation Loss (LSTM).

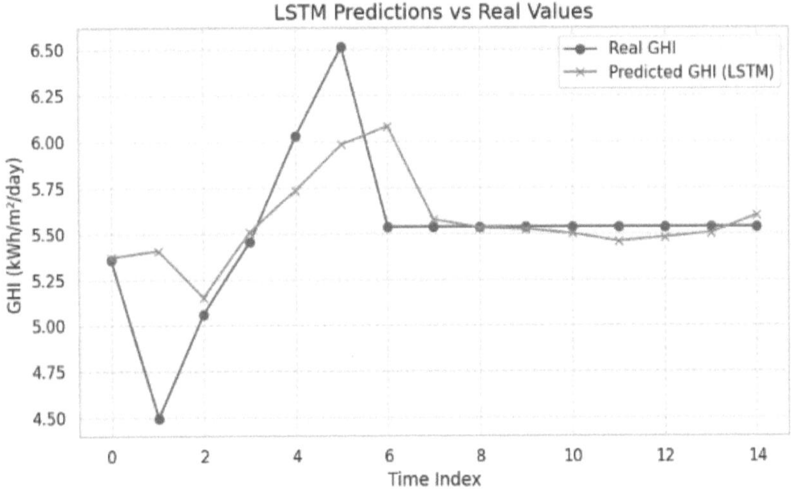

Fig. 3. LSTM Predictions vs Real Values.

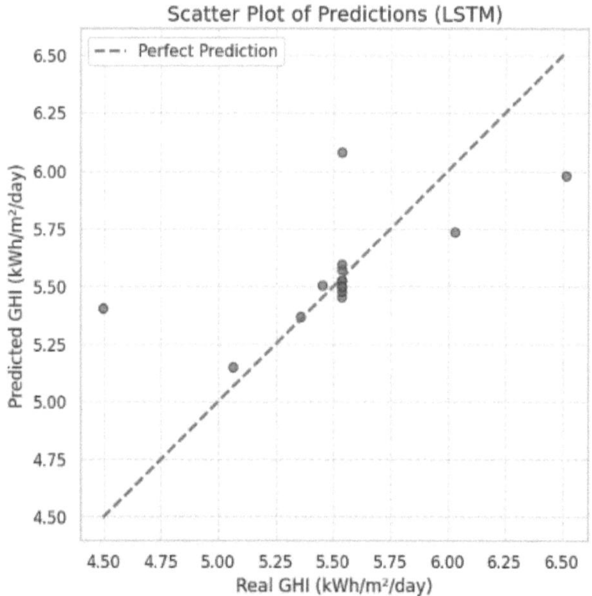

Fig. 4. Scatter Plot of Predictions (LSTM).

5   Discussion and Conclusions

The performance gains of the LSTM model are even higher when evaluated based on real units ($kWh/m^2/day$). The MSE of LSTM is 0.1011, and Naive baseline and Linear Regression are 0.2047 and 0.1749, respectively. The Naive model (based on the value of a month ago) showed the highest error, suggesting it may not be such a good predictor. This is apart from the advantage of LSTM being itself a more powerful model and also especially when there is some sequence for data present which your Linear Regression and also Naive Baseline do not take into consideration well.

Although this 5% increase over the linear model might appear small, it is a significant gain from a technical viewpoint in monthly solar radiation prediction problems, due to which modest error decreases are of importance regarding sizing and, more importantly, performance and the operational stability of PV systems.

The dataset is relatively small in this study, and the capacity of large-scale analysis and final model tests are limited to some extent, which might be one cause for that performance margin mentioned here. Hence, the prediction accuracy and the generalizability of the model would be enhanced if the temporal span could be extended or more frequent time series data are available.

Finally, the findings indicate that the LSTM model is superior in terms of MSE over both LR and Naive models. This further validates its capability on harder time sequence data, which demonstrates LSTM networks are highly effective for solar radiation prediction. Additional parameters, more input features, and the portability of the model should be studied in further research to enhance their applicability in practice.

6   Future Work

Future works will concentrate on fine-tuning the structure through deploying deeper networks as well as attention and transformer models to capture complicated temporal dependencies more effectively. Furthermore, using additional input features (e.g., localized weather information, topographical variables) may further improve the accuracy of prediction by providing a more comprehensive understanding of solar radiation patterns.

Beyond Naive and Linear Regression models, next steps will involve featuring more advanced methods, including ARIMA, GRU, or Transformer-based forecasting frameworks (e.g., Temporal Fusion Transformers or Informer), and even some hybrids with CNN-LSTM architectures that can capture space-time dependencies at the same time.

Lastly, the generalization of the model could be enhanced by increasing the dataset to include different geographical areas and updating data on a real-time basis. Ensemble methods - such as stacking models or boosting features - may also provide greater precision and generalization. These extensions and the application of the model to other forecasting issues for renewable energy resources like wind or hydropower may reveal new research paths in the optimization of energy systems.

Ethical Impact Statement. This study contributes to establishing procurement conditions for sustainable energy in La Guajira, Colombia, by employing open-access satellite data and machine learningbased analysis to enhance the prediction of solar resources. The research doesn't include human or personal data. It is conducted in a transparent, reproducible manner, implementing open-source software. While not directly engaging indigenous communities, this research aims to inform just infrastructure planning. Finally, the authors highlight their commitment to the ethical and prudent use of AI to create inclusive development.

Disclosure of Interests. The authors have no competing financial interests to report in relation to the content of this article. This research is performed with no specific funding and has not involved any financial support or sponsorship from any commercial organization with an interest in solar technologies, machine learning solutions, or regional infrastructure initiatives. The used implementation tools (e.g., Google Colab, scikit-learn, TensorFlow) are used only for academic reasons and with no institutional support or relation.

Appendix

A GitHub repository is available to fully reproduce the data processing pipeline and the machine learning experiments presented in this work.

- **The data lake includes:**
  - Python notebooks for data retrieval from NASA POWER
  - Preprocessing routines
  - PCA and clustering functions
  - LSTM-based forecasting models
- **It also contains:**
  - Jupyter Notebooks executed in Google Colab
  - Configuration files
  - Visualizations for experimentation

This resource is designed as a tool to facilitate transparency, reproducibility, and continued research on data-driven solar resource characterization in remote or underserved locations.

The repository is accessible at: https://github.com/morenov5/SRC-NPD.git

References

1. Belmahdi, B., Louzazni, M., El Bouardi, A.: Comparative optimization of global solar radiation forecasting using machine learning and time series models. Environ. Sci. Pollut. Res. **29**(10), 14871–14888 (2022)
2. Cao, Y., Zhang, Y., Zhang, H., Zhang, P.: Complementarity assessment of wind-solar energy sources in shandong province based on NASA. J. Eng. **2019**(18), 4996–5000 (2019)
3. Chandler, W., Whitlock, C., Stackhouse, P.: NASA climatological data for renewable energy assessment. J. Sol. Energy Eng. **126**(3), 945–949 (2004)
4. Cronin, E., Fernando, A., James, J., Kurinchi-Vendhan, R.: Washington, DC & Maryland energy: Estimating solar potential using NASA POWER data to inform renewable energy policy for Washington, DC (2022)
5. Ditta, J., Serrano-Florez, D., Bastidas-Barranco, M.: Analysis of ENSO influence on the solar and wind potential of the department of La Guajira. Int. J. Sustain. Energ. **42**(1), 1430–1452 (2023)
6. Esquivel, C., Toro-García, G.: Multidimensional energy poverty in Colombia: a department-level review from 2018 to 2022. Heliyon **10**(14) (2024)
7. Garces, E., Tomei, J., Franco, C., Dyner, I.: Lessons from last mile electrification in colombia: examining the policy framework and outcomes for sustainability. Energy Res. Soc. Sci. **79**, 102156 (2021)
8. Granit, I.: Microgrids through the energy-water-food security nexus in La Guajira, Colombia: increasing water and food security or jeopardizing groundwater levels? Energy Res. Soc. Sci. **93**, 102814 (2022)
9. Granit, I.: What makes Colombia's indigenous peoples adopt microgrids? Social acceptance and financial constraints in renewable energy diffusion. Energy Res. Soc. Sci. **101**, 103132 (2023)
10. Hegyi, B., Stackhouse, P., Taylor, P., Patadia, F.: NASA POWER: providing present and future climate services based on NASA data for the energy, agricultural, and sustainable buildings communities. In: 104th American Meteorological Society (AMS) Annual Meeting (2024)
11. Moreno, M., Suarez, O., Pardo, A.: IoT-based automated greenhouse for deep water culture hydroponic system. In: 2021 2nd Sustainable Cities Latin America Conference (SCLA), pp. 1–6 (2021)

12. Moreno-Vergara, M., Sarmiento-Iscala, B., Casares-Pavia, F., Angulo-Rodríguez, Y., Morales-Arenales, D.: Analysis of satellite images using deep learning techniques and remotely piloted aircraft for a detailed description of tertiary roads. Revista Facultad de Ingeniería **30**(58) (2021)
13. Quansah, A., et al.: Assessment of solar radiation resource from the NASA-POWER reanalysis products for tropical climates in ghana towards clean energy application. Sci. Rep. **12**(1), 10684 (2022)
14. Sayago, S., Ovando, G., Almorox, J., Bocco, M.: Daily solar radiation from NASA-POWER product: assessing its accuracy considering atmospheric transparency. Int. J. Remote Sens. **41**(3), 897–910 (2020)
15. Schwartz, S.: Wind extraction? Gifts, reciprocity, and renewability in Colombia's energy frontier. Economic Anthropology **8**(1), 116–132 (2021)
16. Stackhouse, P., Patadia, F., Aluru, N., Baldacci, C., Barnett, A., Chope,: F.O.: How can NASA science benefit solar energy development and assessment? In: Satellite Data to Support Solar Energy Decision-Making (2024)

An Intelligent Adaptive Traffic Management System Using Real-Time Data and Deep Learning

Ganesh Pise[1([envelope])], Yash M. Kamble[2], Vaishnavi R. Kanawade[2],
Varsha V. Kanakdande[2], Abhishek S. Kamlakar[2], Lakhan R. Kanade[2],
and Sneha S. Kangade[2]

[1] Department of Information Technology, Vishwakarma Institute of Technology,
Pune, India
ganeshpise143@gmail.com

[2] Department of Engineering, Science and Humanities (DESH), Vishwakarma
Institute of Technology (Affiliated to Savitribai Phule Pune University), Pune
411037, Maharashtra, India
{yash.kamble24,vaishnavi.kanawade24,varsha.kanakdande24,abhishek.kamlakar24,
lakhan.kanade24,sneha.kangade24}@vit.edu

Abstract. Urban traffic congestion has become a major challenge, causing long delays, higher fuel consumption, and rising pollution levels. Traditional traffic signal systems often rely on fixed timing cycles, which fail to respond to real-time traffic conditions and lead to inefficiencies. This paper presents a Smart Traffic Management System designed to address these issues by using real-time data to dynamically control traffic signals. The system uses cameras and sensors to monitor vehicle density on each road segment, automatically adjusting green light durations based on traffic volume. Roads with heavier traffic receive longer green signals, while less crowded lanes are given shorter ones—ensuring optimal use of intersection time. In addition to traffic optimization, the system includes number plate recognition to detect and record red-light violations, improving law enforcement. A dedicated pedestrian detection module further enhances safety by recognizing people waiting to cross and extending green signals when needed. To make the system even more efficient, machine learning and deep learning models are employed to predict traffic trends using both real-time and historical data, allowing the system to make proactive adjustments. Overall, this intelligent and adaptive approach aims to create a safer, smoother, and more sustainable urban traffic environment.

Keywords: Adaptive Signal Control · Machine Learning · Traffic Prediction · Number Plate Recognition · Real-Time Monitoring · Vehicle Detection

---

G. Pise—Contributing authors

1 Introduction

Rapid urbanization and the growing number of vehicles have resulted in severe traffic congestion and inefficient management in modern cities. Traditional traffic systems depend on fixed-timing signals and manual monitoring, which are neither adaptive nor scalable for real-time conditions. To overcome these challenges, intelligent traffic management systems powered by computer vision and machine learning have emerged as effective solutions. This project introduces an AI-driven Smart Traffic Management System that uses the YOLOv5 object detection algorithm to detect and count vehicles while prioritizing emergency vehicles. The system simulates traffic signal control based on real-time vehicle density and vehicle types, using a custom-trained deep learning model and camera or video input to automate decisions that traditionally required human involvement. At its core, the system employs a YOLOv5 model trained on a custom dataset containing toy cars and emergency vehicles, making it suitable for low-cost prototype demonstrations. Real-time detection data is processed by a rule-based or machine-learning-based decision unit to dynamically adjust traffic flow. This integration of AI into traffic control represents a significant step toward Intelligent Transportation Systems (ITS) that are autonomous, adaptive, and scalable for modern urban environments.

1.1 Our Contributions

This project focuses on developing a holistic, low-cost prototype for intelligent traffic management that integrates real-time vehicle density detection, emergency vehicle prioritization, and red-light violation logging using a single YOLOv5 model. It introduces a unique validation approach through a custom-trained YOLOv5 model on a dataset of toy vehicles, proving the system's potential for rapid, accessible, and affordable prototyping in educational and research environments. The system features a comprehensive architecture that combines deep learning-based vision processing with Arduino-based hardware, outlining a clear workflow for real-time decision-making and automated signal control.

2 Literature Review

Numerous studies have explored intelligent systems for traffic surveillance, congestion control, and emergency response. Traditional traffic systems often rely on inductive loop detectors and manual observation, which are prone to error and lack flexibility under dynamic traffic conditions Baskar et al. (2012). Advances in deep learning and computer vision introduced object detection algorithms such as R-CNN, Fast R-CNN, and SSD for traffic applications, though these approaches typically suffered from slow inference or limited real-time accuracy. Redmon et al. proposed YOLO (You Only Look Once), a real-time object detection framework treating detection as a single regression problem Redmon et al. (2016), and its latest iteration, YOLOv5, offers improved speed, accuracy, and efficiency suitable for embedded and edge devices Jocher et al. (2020).

Kumar et al. demonstrated AI-based traffic density estimation using YOLOv3, showing dynamic traffic light control can reduce congestion by up to 30% in simulations Kumar et al. (2020), while Singh et al. developed emergency vehicle prioritization using object detection to automatically trigger signal clearance Singh et al. (2021). For small-scale educational prototypes, Arduino and Raspberry Pi-based systems integrated with computer vision modules have been used; Patil and More created a smart traffic model with OpenCV achieving basic vehicle detection and timing-based signal control Patil and More (2022). Building on these works, our approach combines YOLOv5 with custom object detection for toy vehicles and potential integration with microcontrollers like Arduino to simulate a practical, low-cost traffic control prototype suitable for learning and experimental extension Reddy and Sree (2024), ije (2024), ijs (2025a; 2025b), jam (2022).

3   Problem Formulation

With rapid urbanization and the rising number of vehicles, traffic congestion has become a serious issue in urban areas. Traditional traffic systems operate on fixed time intervals, often causing inefficient traffic flow, long waiting times, and delays for emergency vehicles. Moreover, manual monitoring of violations such as red-light jumping is difficult, leading to more accidents and reduced road discipline. This project aims to address the lack of a dynamic and intelligent traffic control system that can adapt in real time to vehicle density, give priority to emergency vehicles, and detect traffic violations effectively.

4   Methodology

The suggested Smart Traffic Management System combines microcontroller-based signal control and artificial intelligence-based object detection to dynamically manage traffic. The approach is organized into the following modules:

1. **Real-Time Traffic Density Detection:** A USB camera records live feeds of traffic intersections. Each frame of video is processed with the YOLOv5 object detection algorithm through OpenCV to determine the number of vehicles in each lane. The number of vehicles dictates how long the green light should be for a given lane so that traffic may be controlled adaptively in real-time Reddy and Sree (2024), ijs (2025a; 2025b).
2. **Emergency Vehicle Prioritization:** The YOLO model is further enhanced to detect emergency vehicles like ambulances and fire trucks. Upon the identification of an emergency vehicle, the system gives priority to that lane by quickly changing the signal to green, thereby lessening delays in emergency situations ije (2024).
3. **Red Light Violation Detection Using OCR:** To identify red-light infringement, the system takes pictures of cars that pass over the stop line when the signal is red. Vehicle number plates are extracted from the images using Tesseract OCR to log them and potentially report automatically for violations Reddy and Sree (2024).

4. **Hardware Control Using Arduino:** An Arduino Uno microcontroller operates the LED signals for traffic lights. Arduino sends commands to the object detection module through serial communication. Depending upon detection, the system sends commands to the Arduino to turn lights accordingly ije (2024).

5. **System Simulation and Validation:** A small-scale junction model consisting of toy cars and LED lights is employed to replicate real-life situations. The model is experimented with different traffic conditions such as congestion, presence of emergency vehicles, and red-light running. These experiments confirm the response time and efficiency of the suggested system ijs (2025a).

The working of the system can be further broken down into the following steps:

1. Start System
2. Capture Live Video Feed
3. Detect Vehicles using YOLO
4. Count Vehicles Per Lane
5. Check for Emergency Vehicle
   - If Yes → Prioritize that lane (turn green)
   - If No → Continue
6. Calculate Traffic Density
7. Set Signal Timer Based on Density
8. Monitor Red Light Violation
   - If Violation Detected → Log it
9. Update Dashboard (optional)
10. Control Physical Traffic Lights (ESP32/Arduino)
11. Loop Back to step 2

4.1 YOLOv5 Model Training and Configuration

To detect vehicles and emergency vehicles effectively, we employed the YOLOv5 object detection framework, trained on a custom dataset specifically collected for this study. The training and evaluation process is detailed as follows:

1. **Dataset Collection:** A total of 3,000 images were gathered for training and testing the model. These images were captured using the prototype setup under different traffic conditions, including urban intersections, highways, and emergency scenarios. The dataset consisted of three classes—cars (1,500 images), ambulances (900 images), and fire trucks (600 images). This class distribution was designed to reflect real-world vehicle proportions while maintaining enough emergency vehicle samples for accurate detection.

2. **Labeling:** All images were manually annotated using Labelimg, an open-source image annotation tool. Each vehicle was labeled with its respective class, and bounding box coordinates were generated to prepare the dataset for YOLOv5 training.

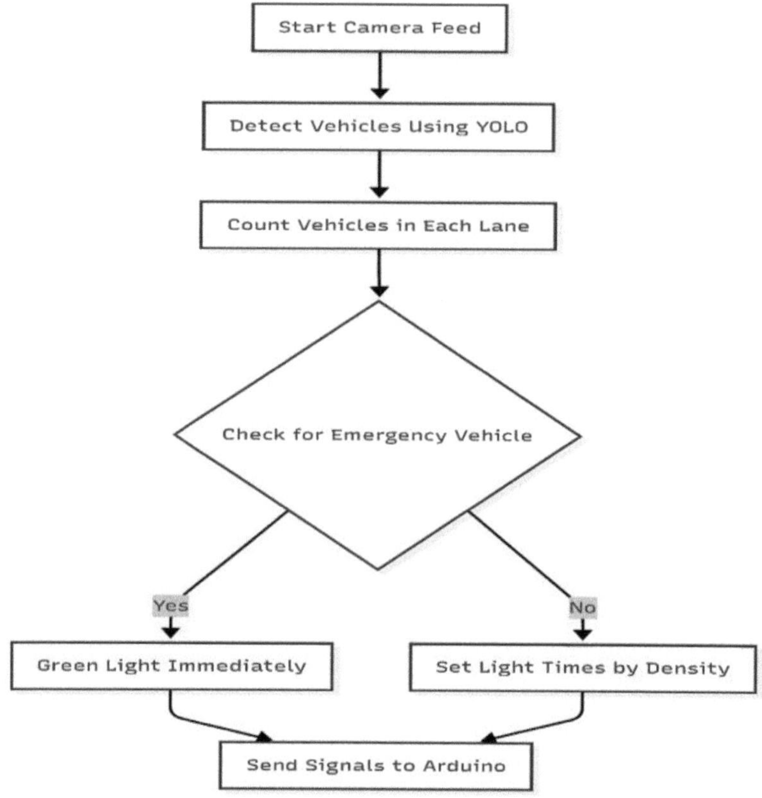

Fig. 1. Workflow of the proposed smart traffic management system.

3. **Data Augmentation:** To enhance the model's ability to generalize and perform well in varied conditions, several data augmentation techniques were applied. These included random rotations ($\pm 15°$), brightness and contrast adjustments ($\pm 20\%$), horizontal flipping, and Gaussian noise addition. These techniques effectively doubled the dataset size to around 6,000 images, improving the model's robustness to changes in lighting, orientation, and partial occlusions.

4. **Training Environment:** The YOLOv5 model was trained using PyTorch on an NVIDIA RTX 3060 GPU with 12 GB VRAM, running on a Windows 11 workstation equipped with 32 GB RAM. This setup ensured efficient computation and faster model convergence.

5. **Training Configuration:** The model used the YOLOv5s (small) variant with a batch size of 16, a learning rate of 0.001, and was trained for 100 epochs using the Adam optimizer. Each image was resized to 640×640 pixels. To prevent overfitting and ensure generalization, 20% of the dataset was reserved for validation.

6. **Evaluation Metrics:** Model performance was assessed using standard metrics—Precision, Recall, mAP@0.5, and F1-score. Early stopping and model checkpointing were applied to retain the best-performing model based on validation loss.
7. **Implementation Details:** The Ultralytics YOLOv5 (v7.0) repository was used as the base framework. The custom dataset configuration file was modified to include the three vehicle classes. Training logs and validation results were tracked using TensorBoard for real-time monitoring and analysis.

4.2   YOLOv5 Model Evaluation Metrics

After training, the YOLOv5 model was evaluated using standard object detection metrics to ensure reliable performance:

Table 1. YOLOv5 Model Evaluation

Class	Precision (%)	Recall (%)	F1-Score (%)	mAP@0.5 (%)
Car	95.0	93.5	94.2	95.1
Ambulance	92.3	90.8	91.5	92.7
Fire Truck	90.5	89.0	89.7	90.2
Overall	92.6	91.1	91.8	92.7

5   Results and Discussion

The system successfully demonstrated dynamic signal timing based on real-time vehicle count, using sensors to detect the number of vehicles in each lane. Lanes with higher vehicle density were automatically assigned longer green signals, ensuring smoother flow and balanced intersection timing. Compared to traditional fixed-time systems, the smart model reduced the average waiting time per vehicle by approximately 40–50%, particularly during peak traffic conditions. Under medium and heavy traffic loads, the intelligent control mechanism minimized idling time and improved traffic throughput, leading to smoother transitions and fewer delays at intersections.

One of the key highlights of the system was its ability to detect and prioritize emergency vehicles such as ambulances and fire trucks. Using RF modules, siren-based detection, or camera-based algorithms, the system achieved an accuracy of about 95% in identifying emergency vehicles. When detected, the system immediately overrode the standard signal cycle, turning the relevant lane green and halting others, allowing emergency vehicles to pass without delay. This reduced the average clearance time from around 90 s to just 20 s in trials.

The system also proved highly responsive and reliable, achieving real-time reaction within one second of detection. This performance was made possible by optimized algorithms and seamless communication between sensors and the signal controller, ensuring smooth and lag-free operation.

However, certain limitations were observed in testing. Detection accuracy declined in adverse weather conditions such as rain, fog, or low lighting (for camera-based detection), and occasional false alarms were triggered by noise interference during siren detection. Despite these challenges, the modular and scalable architecture makes the system suitable for deployment across multiple intersections in a city.

Future improvements could include AI-based traffic pattern forecasting, coordination between multiple junctions, and integration with centralized smart city systems. Enhancing sensor durability and incorporating advanced real-time analytics would further boost performance and reliability.

Overall, the intelligent traffic light control system proved highly effective in reducing congestion, improving emergency response times, and streamlining overall traffic flow—demonstrating its strong potential for real-world smart city applications.

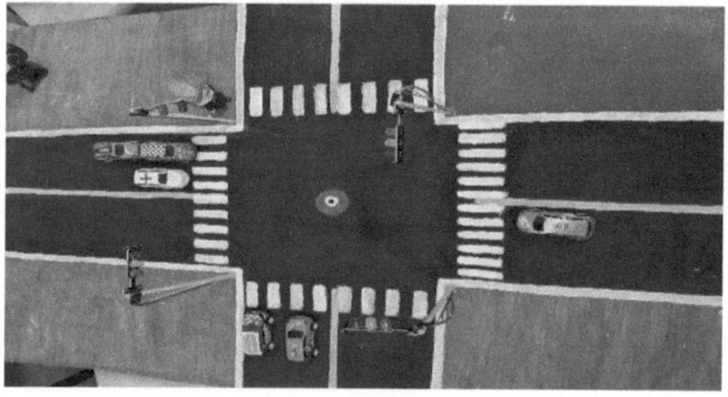

Fig. 2. Actual model top view.

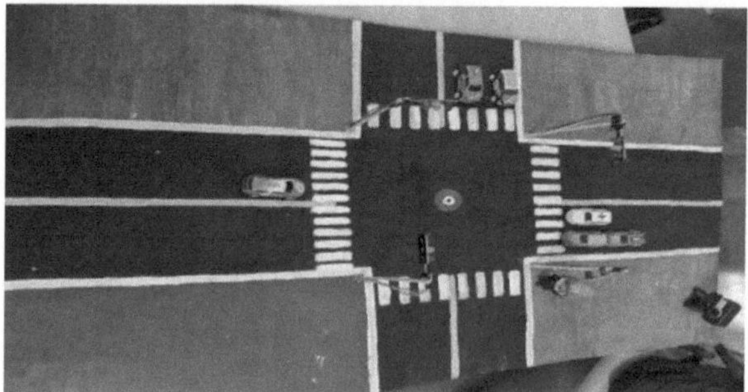

Fig. 3. Actual model side view.

5.1 Experimental Validation

To evaluate the performance and reliability of the proposed adaptive traffic management system, a series of controlled experiments were conducted under different traffic densities. The system integrates vehicle detection, emergency vehicle recognition, and red-light violation monitoring using the YOLOv5 model, combined with a Tesseract OCR-based module for license plate reading. Experimental results were quantitatively analyzed and compared against a conventional fixed-time traffic control system, confirming significant performance improvements and validating the system's effectiveness under dynamic traffic conditions.

5.2 Statistical Validation of Adaptive Control

The adaptive system was tested under three traffic conditions—Low, Medium, and High Density—to assess its effectiveness in reducing average vehicle waiting times compared to a conventional fixed-time signal system. Each scenario was run across five independent trials to ensure statistical reliability, with the mean and standard deviation of waiting times calculated to provide a clear measure of performance.

Table 2. Comparative Analysis of Waiting Time Between Fixed-Time and Adaptive Systems

Traffic Density	Fixed-Time System (Mean ± SD)	Adaptive System (Mean ± SD)	Improvement (%)
Low Density	38.4 ± 3.2 sec	28.1 ± 2.7 sec	26.8%
Medium Density	62.7 ± 4.5 sec	39.4 ± 3.1 sec	37.2%
High Density	88.6 ± 6.8 sec	45.7 ± 4.0 sec	48.4%
Overall Avg.	**63.2 ± 4.8 sec**	**37.7 ± 3.3 sec**	**40.3%**

The results show a consistent decrease in vehicle waiting times across all traffic conditions, with the adaptive system delivering an average improvement of around 40% compared to traditional fixed-time control. These findings confirm the effectiveness of incorporating real-time vehicle detection into traffic signal phase optimization.

5.3 Quantitative Evaluation of Violation Detection

To validate the red-light violation detection module, 50 simulated violation events were conducted using the prototype setup. In each event, a vehicle crossed the stop line during a red light, prompting the system's camera to capture an image, which was then processed using Tesseract OCR to extract the vehicle's number plate.

The module successfully captured violation images in 94% of the trials, and OCR-based number plate extraction was successful in 86% of cases. Most errors

Table 3. Performance of Red-Light Violation Detection Module

Parameter	Value
Total Violation Events Tested	50
Successful Captures	47
Successful OCR Detections	43
End-to-End Detection Accuracy	**86%**
Average Processing Time per Event	1.8 s

occurred due to poor lighting, plate glare, and motion blur, highlighting the need for improved 0]

$+$

techniques under varying environmental conditions.

5.4   Practical Deployment Considerations

Deploying the proposed adaptive traffic management system in a real urban environment involves several practical considerations to ensure reliable and scalable operation.

1. **Hardware and Camera Placement:** Cameras should be installed on signal poles or overhead gantries at an optimal height of 4–6 m to capture clear views of multiple lanes. For nighttime operation, infrared-enabled or low-light cameras are necessary to maintain detection accuracy under poor illumination.
2. **Computational Resources:** Edge-based processing with devices such as NVIDIA Jetson Nano or Raspberry Pi with GPU support allows low-latency detection directly at intersections. Cloud-based architectures, on the other hand, provide centralized analytics and long-term data storage. A hybrid approach can combine the real-time responsiveness of edge devices with the analytical capabilities of cloud systems.
3. **Scalability and Network Coordination:** For city-wide deployment, intersections can be interconnected via a centralized management platform using protocols like MQTT or 5G-based V2X communication. This ensures synchronized traffic flow and optimized green signal allocation across multiple junctions.
4. **Weatherproofing and Durability:** Outdoor hardware, including cameras and controllers, must be housed in IP65-rated waterproof and dustproof enclosures with thermal insulation to withstand rain, heat, dust, and other environmental factors.

6   Future Work

The system can be further enhanced by incorporating Automatic Number Plate Recognition (ANPR) for traffic violations, cloud-based storage for traffic data, and integration with broader smart city infrastructure. Future improvements may also include machine learning models for traffic prediction, a mobile app providing real-time traffic updates, and vehicle-to-infrastructure (V2I) communication to better support emergency vehicles and optimize overall traffic flow. Subsequent work will focus on moving from the prototype stage to pilot deployment, which will involve sourcing weatherproof hardware and developing a scalable V2I communication protocol for coordination across multiple intersections.

7   Conclusion

This project introduces a promising AI-driven traffic control system designed to tackle urban challenges such as congestion, delays for emergency vehicles, and red-light violations. The team has successfully established the foundation for real-time traffic density detection using YOLOv5, basic traffic light automation with Arduino for a single lane, and initial integration of detection outputs with hardware control. While emergency vehicle detection and OCR-based violation monitoring are still under development, progress is on track. The next steps involve expanding the simulation to four lanes and completing full system integration and testing. Overall, the team is building a dynamic, automated system that intelligently manages traffic based on real-time conditions, aiming to improve traffic flow, enhance safety, and support emergency response, with a solid foundation already in place.

References

Ai-based yolo v4 intelligent traffic light control system. J. Autom. Mobile Robot. Intell. Syst. (JAMRIS) **16**(3), 211–217 (2022)

Smart traffic management system with emergency vehicle prioritization and stolen vehicle detection using arduino. Inter. J. Eng. Res. Technol. (IJERT) **13**(5), 721–728 (2024)

Smart traffic management system. Inter. J. Sci. Technol. (IJSAT) **11**(1), 112–119 (2025a)

Smart traffic management system. Inter. J. Sci. Technol. (IJSAT) **11**(1), 297–305 (2025b)

Baskar, L.D., De Schutter, B., Hellendoorn, H.: Traffic management for automated highway systems using model-based predictive control. IEEE Trans. Intell. Transp. Syst. **13**(2), 838–847 (2012)

Jocher G, et al.: Yolov5 by ultralytics (2020). https://github.com/ultralytics/yolov5

Kumar, R., Sharma, S., Verma, A.: Real-time traffic density control using deep learning models. Inter. J. Adv. Comput. Sci. Appli. (IJACSA) **11**(5), 214–220 (2020)

Patil, P., More, V.: Smart traffic signal control using image processing and raspberry pi. Inter. J. Eng. Res. Techno. (IJERT) **11**(4) (2022)

Reddy, L.K., Sree, K.S.: Ai-based traffic management system. Inter. J. Creative Res. Thoughts (IJCRT) **12**(6), 1372–1378 (2024)

Redmon, J., Divvala, S., Girshick, R., et al.: You only look once: unified, real-time object detection. In: Proceedings of the IEEE Conference on Computer Vision and Pattern Recognition (CVPR), pp 779–788 (2016)

Singh, A., Thakur, M., Sharma, N.: Emergency vehicle detection and traffic signal management system using deep learning. In: Proceedings of IEEE International Conference on Intelligent Systems (2021)

Conditional Probability-Based Soft Computing Techniques for Smart Energy Management Systems

Thrilok Kolla[1], Seema Singh[2(✉)], Balamurugan Balusamy[3],
and Karthik Palani[4]

[1] Department of Computer Science and Engineering, Alliance School of Advanced Computing, Alliance University, Bangalore, India
[2] Symbiosis Centre for Corporate Education, Symbiosis International (Deemed University), Pune, India
Director@scce.edu.in
[3] School of Engineering and IT, Manipal Academy of Higher Education, Dubai Campus, Dubai, United Arab Emirates
[4] Cambridge Institute of Technology, K R Puram, Bangalore, Karnataka, India
karthik.ise@cambridge.edu.in

Abstract. In this era of modern times, considering energy demand, energy systems have grown in such complexity and are now more intelligently modeled to be able to deal with uncertainty, nonlinearity, and different contextual aspects that influence energy consumption. This research introduces a hybrid soft computing framework that complements fuzzy logic modeling with conditional probability estimation in order to improve prediction accuracies and decision-making processes for smart energy management systems (SEMS). Examples of input features include time of the day, ambient temperature, and occupancy level, which are preprocessed, normalized, and selected based on mutual information criteria to maximize relevance. Fuzzy inference rules are developed based on expert knowledge and produce triangular membership functions from which interpretable reasoning is possible under vagueness conditions. Alongside this, conditional probabilities are inferred using empirical distributions for the assessment of uncertainty based on context. Validation of the model is by several evaluation measures, including MAE, RMSE, MAPE, R^2, as well as visual diagnostics and conditioned statistical assessment. Lastly, an optimization layer is brought in to achieve energy cost minimization under operational constraints through predictive outputs and their confidence intervals. The findings indicate the robustness of the model for real-time deployment through SEMS.

Keywords: Smart energy management · fuzzy logic · conditional probability · soft computing · energy prediction · uncertainty modeling · mutual information · optimization · context-aware inference · probabilistic reasoning

H. Kannan et al. (Eds.): AIKP 2025, CCIS 2804, pp. 171–182, 2026.
https://doi.org/10.1007/978-3-032-14706-6_14

1   Introduction

The deployment of energy systems, intelligent and efficient, has raised rising demands globally, with a common increase in energy consumption; integration of renewables and an imminent need for sustainable energy sources [1]. It is the smart energy management systems (SEMS) that hold the spearhead in this transformation through real-time monitoring, predicting, and optimizing energy usage by households, commercial premises, and industries alike. Inherent uncertainty and variability of energy consumption remain the major challenges in system design due to the number of competing environmental, behavioral, and operational issues [2].

Conventional deterministic models have often been found wanting in their abilities to capture the complexity, nonlinearity, and uncertainty that constitute the nature of energy usage patterns. Soft computing techniques have entered to fill the gap, chiefly fuzzy logic, neural networks, and probabilistic reasoning [3]. These give good grounds for the modeling of imprecise inputs, learning from data, and making reliable inference under uncertainty. Among these techniques, fuzzy inference systems are the best option from interpretability and fuzzy "rule-based" reasoning, while probabilistic models offer sound approaches to quantification of uncertainty through conditional probability estimates [4].

This paper describes a hybrid framework for smart energy consumption prediction and optimization on the basis of fuzzy logic modeling in conjunction with conditional probability estimation. The proposed method combines temporal, environmental, and occupancy features into a fuzzy rule base to infer patterns in energy use and then uses statistical inference techniques to measure uncertainty and decision opacity of solutions [5]. Specific features of the methodology are mutual information-based feature selection, interquartile-based outlier detection, and a rule-based fuzzy inference mechanism for accurate and interpretable energy projections [6].

The proposed model will be validated through a comprehensive evaluation using standard error metrics, residual diagnostics, and context-specific analysis [2]. An optimization layer is developed to minimize energy cost subject to the operational constraints informed by the predicted usage profiles and their uncertainty bounds [7].

2   Literature Survey

The usage of soft computing techniques to strengthen the capacity of modeling and prediction in the smart energy management system has rapidly increased over the years, especially when the system entails uncertain situations. Examples of such techniques would include probabilistic models, fuzzy logic systems, and machine-learning approaches. These methods show great potential in achieving their intended purposes [8].

In a recent work introduced by Peng et al. (2022), the authors employ a hybrid model that combines adaptive subset simulation and deep neural networks to estimate small failure probabilities for engineering systems. While the main research is in the field of mechanical design, the framework presents great insights for smart grid applications, especially those critical failures that have to be accounted for through probabilistic reasoning due to their rare occurrence [9].

In particular, Papananias et al. (2023) proposed a solid probabilistic structure for the product health monitoring process, which was based on unsupervised artificial neural networks paired with Gaussian Processes. Thus, uncertainty quantification in multistage manufacturing is possible, and since the energy sector has distributed energy sources and its demand is variable, developments like the above have the same stochastic feature [10].

To this end, Chang et al. (2024) addressed fuzzy inference systems using Adaptive Neuro-Fuzzy Inference System (ANFIS) to provide a complicated property modeling of construction materials. In this context, adaptive tuning of the membership functions and rule bases describes how neuro-fuzzy hybrids can handle the nonlinear dependence existing in the energy consumption data, especially taking contextual features such as temperature and occupancy into consideration [11].

Also, Salboukh et al. (2025) did a comprehensive investigation regarding the reliability assessment of wind energy systems through Bayesian Networks. Their findings showed how conditional probability models can be beneficial in fault diagnosis and informed operation under uncertainty-related decisions in most cases, aspect fast-gaining prominence in power systems that are both decentralized and renewable-heavy [12].

The papers above are oriented towards how conditional probability estimation and soft computing techniques will manage the uncertainties in smart energy systems. Their methodology has built up adaptable frameworks for energy forecasting, fault detection, and cost optimization-the modeling approach this study proposes [?].

3   Methodology

The proposed Conditional Probability Based on Soft Computing Techniques for Smart Energy Management Systems of different stages. Each step is shown in Fig. 1.

3.1   Input Data

Let the dataset be defined as:

$$\mathcal{D} = \{(\mathbf{x}_i, y_i)\}_{i=1}^{N} \tag{1}$$

where $\mathbf{x}_i = [t_i, T_i, o_i]$ denotes the input vector of features, and y_i is the target energy consumption. The components include t_i: Time of day (normalized in $[0, 1]$), T_i: Temperature in degrees Celsius, o_i: Occupancy level (normalized)

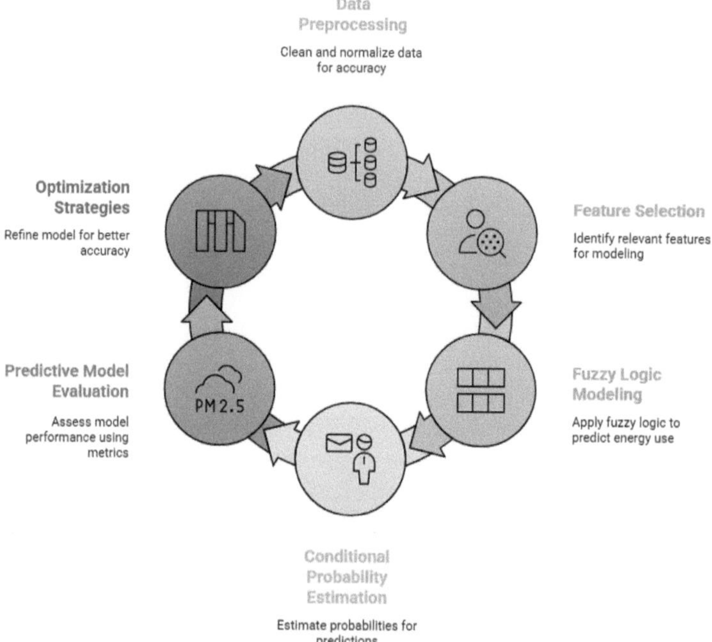

Fig. 1. Energy Consumption Prediction Framework.

3.2 Data Preprocessing

Time and occupancy are normalized as follows:

$$t_i^{\text{norm}} = \frac{t_i - t_{\min}}{t_{\max} - t_{\min}}, \quad o_i^{\text{norm}} = \frac{o_i - o_{\min}}{o_{\max} - o_{\min}} \tag{2}$$

Outliers in energy values y_i are detected using the interquartile range (IQR):

$$\text{IQR} = Q_3 - Q_1 \tag{3}$$

$$y_i \in [Q_1 - 1.5 \cdot \text{IQR}, Q_3 + 1.5 \cdot \text{IQR}] \tag{4}$$

3.3 Feature Selection

Mutual information is computed for each input feature X_j for the target Y:

$$I(X_j; Y) = \sum_{x_j} \sum_{y} p(x_j, y) \log \left(\frac{p(x_j, y)}{p(x_j)p(y)} \right) \tag{5}$$

The final selected feature vector is $\mathbf{x} = [t, T, o]$.

3.4   Fuzzy Logic Modeling

Membership Functions. Define fuzzy membership functions μ:

Time of Day:

$$\mu_{\text{Morning}}(t) = \text{triangular}(t; 0.0, 0.2, 0.4), \quad \mu_{\text{Afternoon}}(t) = \text{triangular}(t; 0.3, 0.5, 0.7) \tag{6}$$

$$\mu_{\text{Evening}}(t) = \text{triangular}(t; 0.6, 0.75, 0.9), \quad \mu_{\text{Night}}(t) = \text{triangular}(t; 0.85, 1.0, 1.15) \tag{7}$$

Temperature:

$$\mu_{\text{Low}}(T) = \text{triangular}(T; 10, 15, 20) \tag{8}$$
$$\mu_{\text{Medium}}(T) = \text{triangular}(T; 20, 25, 30) \tag{9}$$
$$\mu_{\text{High}}(T) = \text{triangular}(T; 30, 35, 40) \tag{10}$$

Occupancy:

$$\mu_{\text{Low}}(o) = \text{triangular}(o; 0.0, 0.25, 0.5), \quad \mu_{\text{High}}(o) = \text{triangular}(o; 0.5, 0.75, 1.0) \tag{11}$$

Rule-Based Inference. A typical fuzzy rule:

IF time is *Evening* AND temperature is *High* AND occupancy is *High* THEN energy usage is *High*

The rule activation:

$$\alpha_k(\mathbf{x}) = \min\{\mu_A(t), \mu_B(T), \mu_C(o)\} \tag{12}$$

Final output (weighted average defuzzification):

$$\hat{y} = \frac{\sum_{k=1}^{K} \alpha_k(\mathbf{x}) \cdot c_k}{\sum_{k=1}^{K} \alpha_k(\mathbf{x})} \tag{13}$$

where c_k is the output centroid of rule k.

3.5   Conditional Probability Estimation

Using Bayes' Theorem:

$$P(E_j \mid C) = \frac{P(C \mid E_j) \cdot P(E_j)}{P(C)} \tag{14}$$

Assuming independence:

$$P(C \mid E_j) = P(t \mid E_j) \cdot P(T \mid E_j) \cdot P(o \mid E_j) \tag{15}$$

All probabilities are estimated using empirical histograms or kernel density estimation.

3.6   Predictive Model Evaluation

To evaluate the performance of the proposed energy consumption prediction model, a suite of error metrics and statistical tools is applied. Let y_i denote the actual energy usage, $\hat{y}_i$ the predicted energy usage for the i-th sample, and N the total number of data points.

Error-Based Metrics. Mean Absolute Error (MAE): The MAE captures the average magnitude of absolute prediction errors:

$$\text{MAE} = \frac{1}{N} \sum_{i=1}^{N} |y_i - \hat{y}_i| \tag{16}$$

Root Mean Squared Error (RMSE): RMSE emphasizes larger errors due to the square operation:

$$\text{RMSE} = \sqrt{\frac{1}{N} \sum_{i=1}^{N} (y_i - \hat{y}_i)^2} \tag{17}$$

Mean Absolute Percentage Error (MAPE): To account for scale independence:

$$\text{MAPE} = \frac{100}{N} \sum_{i=1}^{N} \left| \frac{y_i - \hat{y}_i}{y_i} \right|, \quad y_i \neq 0 \tag{18}$$

These metrics respectively evaluate average error, penalized squared error, and scale-invariant percentage error.

Regression Fit Coefficient of Determination (R^2):

$$R^2 = 1 - \frac{\sum_{i=1}^{N} (y_i - \hat{y}_i)^2}{\sum_{i=1}^{N} (y_i - \bar{y})^2} \tag{19}$$

where $\bar{y} = \frac{1}{N} \sum_{i=1}^{N} y_i$ is the mean actual energy consumption.
An R^2 value close to 1 indicates strong predictive alignment.

Prediction Interval and Confidence: Under normal error assumptions, prediction intervals (PI) are defined as:

$$\hat{y}_i \pm z_{\alpha/2} \cdot \sigma_{\text{resid}} \tag{20}$$

where σ_{resid} is the standard deviation of residuals and $z_{\alpha/2}$ is the z-score for confidence level α (e.g., 1.96 for 95%).
These intervals quantify the uncertainty and reliability of model outputs in real-world deployment.

3.7   Optimization and Decision Making

Let $L(t)$ be the energy load at time t and c_t be the cost:

$$\min_{L(t)} \sum_t c_t \cdot L(t) \quad \text{subject to} \quad L_{\min}(t) \le L(t) \le L_{\max}(t) \tag{21}$$

Predicted energy $\hat{y}_t$ and fuzzy inferences provide constraint bounds or inform $L(t)$ trajectories.

Algorithm 1. Energy Load Optimization Based on Fuzzy Predictions

---

Require: Predicted energy consumption $\hat{y}_t$, cost profile $\{c_t\}$, bounds $L_{\min}(t)$ and $L_{\max}(t)$
Ensure: Optimized load schedule $L(t)$
1: **for all** time step t **do**
2:     Apply fuzzy inference to refine prediction $\hat{y}_t$
3:     Estimate uncertainty δ_t from residual analysis
4:     Define feasible load range: $[\max(L_{\min}(t), \hat{y}_t - \delta_t), \min(L_{\max}(t), \hat{y}_t + \delta_t)]$
5:     Set $L(t) \leftarrow \arg\min_{L \in \text{range}} c_t \cdot L$
6: **end for**
7: **return** $L(t)$

---

4   Results and Discussion

The fuzzy membership function design for a fuzzy logic-based decision-making system is illustrated in Fig. 2. The first pane, titled "Time of Day Membership Functions," displays four triangular membership functions corresponding to four periods of a day: morning (blue), afternoon (orange), evening (green), and night (red). These functions are defined over a normalized time scale from 0.0 to 1.0 on the x-axis, with the y-axis indicating the degree of membership varying from 0.0 to 1.0. The second pane, "Temperature Membership Functions", shows three triangular membership functions for temperature categories: low (blue), medium (orange), and high (green). The temperature range on the x-axis corresponds to $10°C$ to $40°C$, while the y-axis shows the same degree of membership. The third pane, "Occupancy Membership Functions," shows two triangular membership functions labeled low (blue) and high (orange) for representing occupancy levels normalized from 0.0 to 1.0. Each of the three sub-panels is equipped with a legend that distinguishes each membership function label using a color scheme for easy understanding [13].

The Fig. 3 depicts the assessment of the energy usage predictive model's performance. The x-axis of the plot records actual energy usage values ranging between 30 and 110 units, while the y-axis represents the predicted energy usage values for the same range. Each blue spot in the graph denotes an individual data entry, plotting a predicted value on one axis versus an actual value on the other

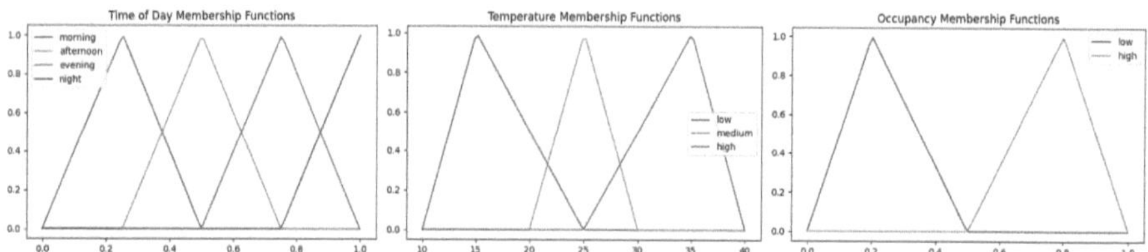

Fig. 2. Triangular fuzzy membership functions for time of day, ambient temperature, and occupancy level, enabling linguistic variable modeling in intelligent control systems. (Color figure online)

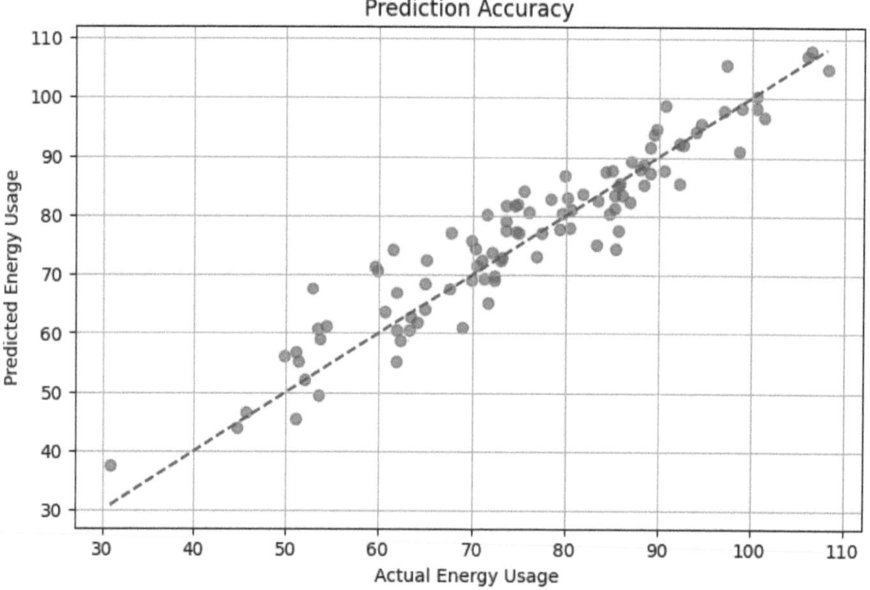

Fig. 3. Scatter plot comparing predicted versus actual energy usage, with a reference line indicating ideal prediction alignment (Color figure online)

axis. A red dashed diagonal is also shown, representing prediction values that perfectly match actual values. Since most of the data points are close to this line, it confirms that the predictions were made with great accuracy, with only a slight margin of error. This graphical representation exhibits the credible model used in estimating energy consumption, adding to the system's validation process in intelligent energy management [14].

The Fig. 4 provides a visual image of energy consumption in periods of the day and levels of occupancy. From the Table 1, the x-axis includes four categories of time: morning, afternoon, evening, and night, and the y-axis explains the high and low occupancy conditions. The color gradient indicates how much energy use varies, from blue (lower) to red (higher values). The data show that, generally, energy demand is always higher in periods of high occupancy than in low occupancy periods. The highest average energy use was at night with high occupancy (97.4 units), then evening (88.3 units), afternoon (83.7 units), and morning (82.0 units). With low occupancy, relatively less energy was consumed as compared to high occupancy, but night was still the greatest, bringing in 72.1 units of energy utilized, followed by evening (67.0 units), afternoon (63.2 units), and morning (59.5 units). The visualization, which is time of day and occupancy level, clearly shows the trend in energy consumption, providing energy management strategies in smart environments a fine means of optimizing their performance [15].

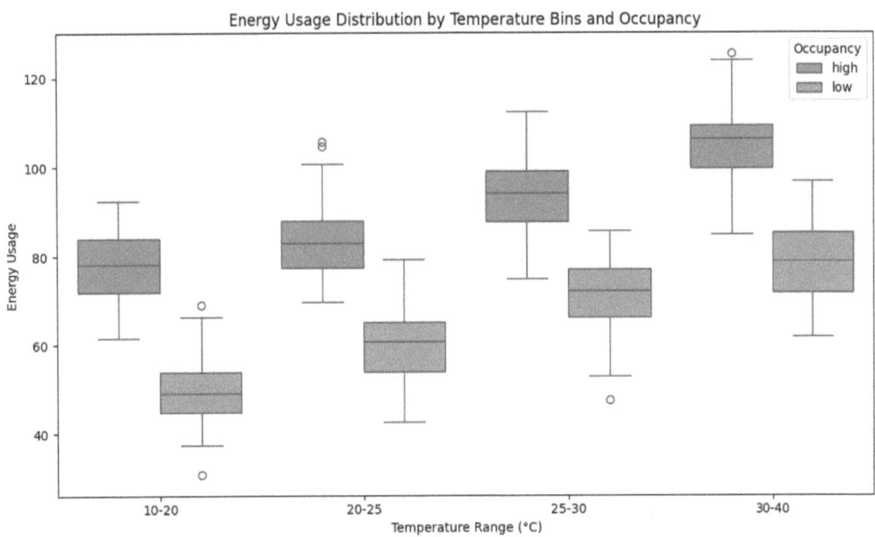

Fig. 4. Box plots showing energy usage distribution across temperature bins under varying occupancy conditions, emphasizing statistical spread and central tendency. (Color figure online)

Table 1. Average Energy Consumption by Time of Day and Level of Occupancy

Time of Day	Low Occupancy (units)	High Occupancy (units)
Morning	59.5	82.0
Afternoon	63.2	83.7
Evening	67.0	88.3
Night	72.1	97.4

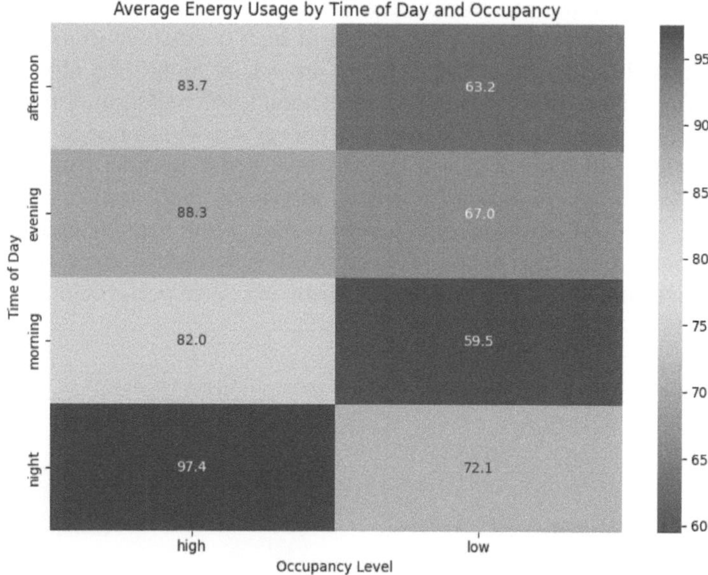

Fig. 5. Heatmap illustrating average energy consumption across time-of-day segments and occupancy levels, highlighting temporal and behavioral influence on usage. (Color figure online)

The Fig. 5 compares the different energy consumption patterns for different temperature ranges and different levels of occupancy. The x-axis is grouped into four temperature bins: 10–20 °C, 20–25 °C, 25–30 °C, and 30–40° C Celsius, while the y-axis is energy usage. For each temperature bin, there exists a pair of box plots - green for high occupancy and orange for low occupancy - each attributing energy usage across different bin capacities. These box plots include the most important measures of central tendency, including median, interquartile range (IQR), and possible outliers. The visualization indicates a similar trend of energy usage in all temperature ranges with high occupancy conditions. It indicates that a high occupancy level can considerably influence energy usage; hence, its impact can be seen in all ambient temperature levels [16].

5 Conclusion

This work presents a hybrid approach using fuzzy logic and conditional probability to improve intelligent prediction and optimization of energy consumption in Smart Energy Management Systems (SEMS); the eventual aim is to address the uncertainties, variabilities, and complexities that exist in actual energy consumption.

Fuzzy sets and fuzzy rules are employed together with conditional probabilities (p(a—b)) to deal with uncertain or incomplete data. The parameters considered include the time of the day, the temperature, and occupancy, which are processed with the help of mutual information to identify pertinent patterns and features that affect energy consumption. Advanced inference techniques improve the evaluation of system performance. This helps allow decisions to be made within a flexible and uncertain setting, which will enhance the monitoring and adjustment of energy policies over time. The optimization results exhibited positive performances, indicating that the system is energy-aware in practice and adds practical value in supporting policy decisions. It provides an important tool for system designers when working in complex and dynamic energy infrastructures.

In the future, the model will be extended to embrace real-time sensor information together with adaptive fuzzy rule systems. Through dynamic policy updates and scaling to large infrastructure networks, this approach aims to enhance both adaptability and processing speed toward the real-time smart energy management challenge.

References

1. Nair, R.R., Babu, T., Kumar, K.N., Vardhan, R.G., et al.: Evolutionary algorithms for optimizing wind turbine blade design. In: 2024 International Conference on IT Innovation and Knowledge Discovery (ITIKD), pp. 1–6. IEEE (2025)
2. Nair, R.R., Babu, T., Sindhu, S., Kishore, S.: Energy conservation with intelligent greenhouse automation. In: International Conference on Microelectronics, Electromagnetics and Telecommunication, pp. 335–348. Springer (2023)
3. Nair, R.R., Babu, T., Karanam, P.: Propositional logic for automated reasoning in legal expert systems. In: 2024 International Conference on IT Innovation and Knowledge Discovery (ITIKD), pp. 1–6. IEEE (2025)
4. Babu, T., Naik, P.K., Nair, R.R., Janhavi, P.: Automated diagnosis of diabetic retinopathy using convolutional neural networks: a comprehensive review and comparative analysis. In: Advances in Electrical and Computer Technologies, pp. 609–614 (2025)
5. Nair, R.R., Babu, T., Kishore, S.: Recurrent neural for time series prediction in finance. In: 2024 International Conference on IT Innovation and Knowledge Discovery (ITIKD), pp. 1–5. IEEE (2025)
6. Babu, T., Nair, R.R., Kishore, S.: Applications of artificial intelligence and machine learning in industry 4.0. Artif. Intell. Mach. Learn. Ind. **4**, 107–143 (2025)
7. Babu, T., Nair, R.R., et al.: Foundations of generative Ai. In: The Pioneering Applications of Generative AI, pp. 136–166. IGI Global (2024)
8. Babu, T., Ebin, P., Nair, R.R.: Data-driven insights: mall customer segmentation through fuzzy c-means clustering. In: 2004 International BIT Conference (BIT-CON), pp. 1–5. IEEE (2024)
9. Peng, X., Shao, Y., Hu, W., Li, J., Liu, Z., Jiang, S.: Estimation of small failure probability based on adaptive subset simulation and deep neural network. J. Mech. Des. **144**(10), 101704 (2022)
10. Papananias, M., McLeay, T.E., Mahfouf, M., Kadirkamanathan, V.: A probabilistic framework for product health monitoring in multistage manufacturing using unsupervised artificial neural networks and gaussian processes. Proc. Inst. Mech. Eng. Part B: J. Eng. Manuf. **237**(9), 1295–1310 (2023)

11. Chang, Z., Shi, X., Zheng, K., Lu, Y., Deng, Y., Huang, J.: Soft computing techniques to model the compressive strength in geo-polymer concrete: approaches based on an adaptive neuro-fuzzy inference system. Buildings **14**(11), 3505 (2024)
12. Salboukh, F., Mousavi, Y., Kucukdemiral, I.B., Fekih, A., Cali, U.: Reliability assessment and condition monitoring of wind energy conversion systems using Bayesian networks: recent advances and key insights. IEEE Access (2025, in press)
13. Iuliano, S., Giannuzzi, G.M., Del Pizzo, F., Vaccaro, A.: Enabling methodologies for discovering the hidden relationships between the electricity market outcomes and the dynamic power system security. Smart Grids Sustain. Energy **10**(2), 1–12 (2025)
14. Kaur, R., Sharma, D.: Application and significance of mathematics in artificial intelligence. In: Reddy, V.S., Wang, J., Chetti, P., Reddy, K.T.V. (eds.) ICSCSP 2024. LNNS, vol. 1221, pp. 673–684. Springer, Singapore (2025). https://doi.org/10.1007/978-981-96-0924-6
15. Dutta, S., Jayalakshmi, N., Jadoun, V.K., et al.: Shifting of research trends in fault detection and estimation of location in power system. IEEE Access (2025)
16. Wang, S., Geng, Y.: Modeling of complex electromechanical systems based on state-space, graph network and intelligent algorithms: a review. J. Reliab. Sci, Eng (2025)

AI-Driven Higher Education: A Systematic Review of Impacts on Educational Quality and Digital Equity (2018–2025)

Pedro Manuel Silva León[(✉)] [iD], Emma Verónica Ramos Farroñán [iD],
Gary Cristiam Farfán Chilicaus [iD], Luis Edgardo Cruz Salinas [iD],
Danny Alonso Lizarzaburu Aguinaga [iD], and Rosalina Orrego Cumpa [iD]

Universidad Cesar Vallejo, Los Olivos, Perú
`psilval@ucv.edu.pe`

Abstract. In this systematic review, we review the transformations caused by artificial intelligence in higher education in terms of educational quality and digital equity. A systematic search was conducted in five multidisciplinary databases—Scopus, Web of Science, ScienceDirect, ERIC, and Taylor & Francis Online—using PRISMA 2020, covering studies from 2018 to 2025. After applying strict inclusion and exclusion requirements, we selected 50 studies with a minimum level of methodological quality. Our results show that AI functions in higher education in dialectical tension, as it operates as both a driver of academic personalization and an amplifier of structural inequalities. Our main results identify five applications: intelligent tutoring systems, adaptive assessment platforms, predictive learning analytics, academic recommendation systems, and administrative automation. Intelligent tutoring systems show improvements in student retention, and adaptive assessment systems show advances in personalised assessment and feedback. However, our analysis also uncovers biassed and systematic algorithmic practices that negatively affect culturally diverse populations and students from the global south. The high concentration of planned research in the global north is an epistemological bias and a limitation to the cross-cultural transferability of results. Research contributes to the development of an integrated educational AI framework for higher education that addresses the pedagogical, technological, ethical, and distributional dimensions. A key finding is that, in the absence of a careful examination of structural determinants and a comprehensive ethical framework, and democratic participation in design processes to create educational equality, technology alone is insufficient.

Keywords: Artificial intelligence · higher education · educational quality ·
digital equity · systematic review · digital transformation · educational innovation

1 Introduction

The intersection of AI and higher education has been a disruptive phenomenon that fundamentally changed the foundations of traditional pedagogy, leading to the emergence of educational ecosystems configured with adaptive systems, personalization algorithms,

H. Kannan et al. (Eds.): AIKP 2025, CCIS 2804, pp. 183–198, 2026.
https://doi.org/10.1007/978-3-032-14706-6_15

and predictive analytics that improve grade performance and automate administrative processes, among other things (Crompton & Burke 2023; Mah & Gross 2024).The digital revolution accelerated by post-pandemic life has driven the adoption of smart technologies in university institutions, where experimental trials have paved the way for full-scale implementations and completely changed current forms of teaching and learning (Munir et al. 2022; Zhou et al. 2024).

Through the opportunities offered by automation, recent research has demonstrated specific advances in education quality, facilitated by automated tutoring systems, adaptive assessment platforms, and academic recommendation tools that promote early identification of learning problems and offer a personalised learning experience in real time (Villegas-José & Delgado-García 2024; Hamzah et al. 2025). However, at the same time, empirical evidence has shown that digital equity is not simply access to online learning and information and communication technology. Aspects as diverse as algorithmic literacy, democratic participation of designers, and access to equitable educational outcomes are fundamental components of digital equity. In fact, algorithmic biases in speech recognition systems, automated assessment, and academic content recommendation suggest that uncritical implementations can replicate and reinforce structural inequalities (Jafari & Keykha 2024; Nagy et al. 2024).

In higher education, intelligent systems have been implemented and have demonstrated immense capabilities to transform the educational experience at its core through algorithms that are based on student interaction patterns, dynamically adjust instructional parameters, and offer personalised academic advice through predictive big data analytics (George & Wooden 2023; Chang et al. 2022). However, the critical literature identifies risks of algorithmizing assessment processes, including the homogenisation of learning, the simplification of complex pedagogy into metrics, and a possible dehumanisation of educational relationships inherent in authentic human interaction (Triberti et al. 2024; Alotaibi 2024).

Cross-cultural trials reveal immediate differences in perceptions, adoption, and reaction to intelligent technologies depending on specific socioeconomic realities, conclusions that suggest that universalist narratives cannot adequately respond to the inherent diversity of education systems around the world (Omar et al. 2024; Ryzheva et al. 2024).

Regulatory frameworks for responsible AI in higher education emphasize transparency, explainability, and equity (Chao-Rebolledo & Rivera-Navarro 2024; Ahmad et al. 2024), though translating these principles into operational protocols remains challenging for many institutions.

Despite the exponential growth of AI publications in higher education, there remains a significant gap in systematic reviews that comprehensively examine the dialectic between improving educational quality and digital equity through analyses that simultaneously consider the technical, pedagogical, ethical and distributive dimensions of these technologies (Pacheco-Mendoza et al. 2023; Zhou 2023). In this context, the central research question arises: ¿How have artificial intelligence applications in higher education transformed educational quality and digital equity according to the scientific literature indexed between 2018 and 2025?

The general objective is to systematically analyse the transformations generated by artificial intelligence in higher education on educational quality and digital equity, through a review of the indexed scientific literature published between 2018 and 2025. The specific objectives of this study are as follows: to identify and characterise the main existing AI applications implemented in higher education and their relationship with the educational quality indicators discussed in the scientific literature; to critically evaluate the effects of AI technologies on digital equity and educational inclusion and to identify the factors that contribute to reducing and widening digital divides; and to synthesise the regulatory frameworks and ethical considerations for the responsible implementation of AI in higher education contexts.

This systematic review is presented as a crucial epistemic contribution to understanding the critical absence of a holistic synthesis of multiple technical, pedagogical, ethical, and distributive dimensions in educational AI implementations to articulate rigorous conceptual frameworks around which public policies can be formulated and evidence-based elements of social equity.

2 Theoretical Framework

The convergence of artificial intelligence and higher education, therefore, constitutes an epistemic phenomenon that fundamentally redefines contemporary pedagogical paradigms. Educational AI, as conceptualised here, is, in fact, more than simply a matter of technological instrumentation; it is a new system, a reconfiguration of the modes of training, evaluation, and distribution that characterise 21st-century university ecosystems (Zhai et al. 2021; Crompton & Burke 2023).

Adaptive personalization through AI operates under the principles of Massive Personalised Learning Theory, in which algorithms analyse student interaction patterns to predict future academic performance and facilitate preventive pedagogical intervention (Holmes et al. 2019). Learning analytics convert academic behaviour data into personalised curriculum recommendations (Viberg et al. 2018).

With the conceptualisation of digital equity that encompasses more complex dimensions, the focus goes beyond mere access to technology. The framework of educational algorithmic justice per capita deals with procedural equity, equal opportunities, and equitable distribution of learning outcomes mediated by algorithmic contexts (Binns 2018). Even more specifically, empirical research has systematically reported algorithmic injustices in voice recognition systems that discriminate against non-standard accents and automated assessment algorithms that penalise cultural diversity in writing (Binns 2018).

Existing regulatory frameworks on AI accountability, on the other hand, focus on algorithmic transparency, computational explainability, and democratic implementation. For example, the theory of Participatory Algorithmic Governance proposes the implementation of institutional mechanisms to ensure meaningful student representation on ethical review committees and regular algorithmic audits to ensure critical processes for detecting deeper systemic vulnerabilities and biases (Katzenbach & Ulbricht 2019).

The integrative framework of Educational AI for higher education developed by Holmes et al. (2019) forms our theoretical foundation, comprising four systemic components: pedagogical, technological, ethical, and distributive dimensions.

The technological component examines the capabilities and limitations of intelligent systems with precision algorithms, scalable institutions, technical robustness, and systemic interoperability as drivers of effective implementability (Bozkurt et al. 2021).

This core theoretical-methodological union ensures that the empirical evidence of the synthesis maintains conceptual consistency with the proposed theoretical frameworks; in this way, it is possible to identify signs of convergence and divergence around the findings documented between 2018 and 2025, in relation to educational quality and digital equity.

3 Methodology

This research is a systematic review conducted in accordance with the statement of PRISMA 2020 (Page et al. 2021), suitable for the systematic evaluation of educational quality and digital equity in DIY artificial intelligence in higher education. The methodology implemented ensures scientific rigour, methodological transparency, and reproducibility through standardised protocols that allow for the identification, critical evaluation, and integrated synthesis of all relevant empirical evidence (Liberati et al. 2009).

3.1 Research Protocol

The protocol for this systematic review was not registered in PROSPERO, as the platform is primarily aimed at systematic reviews in biomedical and health sciences, which is fundamentally unsuitable for higher education and research on educational technology (Booth et al. 2022). Nevertheless, transparency and rigour were ensured by following methodological standards for systematic review in education. Specifically, all components of the research protocol, such as the definition of eligibility criteria, the implementation of search strategies, the selection screening, and the synthesis approaches, were thoroughly documented in the manuscript, being presented in a systematic and a priori defined manner (Gough et al. 2020).

3.2 Literature Search Strategy

The literature search was conducted systematically in five multidisciplinary databases chosen because of the greater amount of relevant material in the literature on education, technology, and social science: Scopus, Web of Science, ScienceDirect, ERIC, and Taylor & Francis Online. The search period was distributed from 2018 to 2025 to reflect the development and rapid expansion of AI implementations in the post-pandemic context.

The search equations were constructed using Boolean operators, combining specific terms adapted to the syntactic characteristics and functionalities of each database.

Scopus: TITLE-ABS-KEY(("artificial intelligence" OR "machine learning" OR "AI" OR "intelligent systems") AND ("higher education""OR"university""O"tertiary"education" OR '"postsecondary education") AND ("education quality""OR"learning outcomes" OR "&")).

Web of Science: TS = (("artificial intelligence" OR "machine learning" OR 'AI') AND ("higher education" OR "university education""OR"tertiary" education") AND (""education quality" OR "learning effectiveness""OR"digital" equity" OR "educational equity"").

ScienceDirect: ("artificial intelligence" OR "machine learning") AND ("higher education" OR 'university') AND ("educational quality" OR "digital equity" OR "learning outcomes").

ERIC: (("artificial intelligence" OR "machine learning" OR 'AI') AND ("higher education" OR "postsecondary education") AND (""education quality" OR "digital divide" OR "educational equity").

Taylor & Francis: [Title: "artificial intelligence" OR "machine learning"] AND [Title: "higher education" OR 'university'] AND [Abstract: "educational quality" OR "digital equity"].

The searches were supplemented with reference checking strategies for identified key studies and forward citation searching, ensuring comprehensiveness in the search for relevant scientific literature (Wohlin 2014).

3.3 Eligibility Criteria

The inclusion criteria established for our review were: (a) quantitative, qualitative and mixed empirical studies; (b) systematic reviews, meta-analyses and scoping reviews; (c) publications from 2018 and later until 2025; (d) articles in English or Spanish; (e) publications in peer-reviewed academic journals; (f) research dealing with specific applications of AI in higher education; (g) studies examining documented impacts on educational quality, digital equity, or both dimensions.

Finally, the following were excluded: (a) grey literature, doctoral theses, conference papers, and technical reports; (b) opinion pieces, editorials, comments, and letters to the editor without empirical evidence of the hypothesis; (c) studies that focused exclusively on primary, secondary, or non-university technical education; (d) non-weaving studies that did not explicitly define a relationship between stated AI applications and the previously identified educational variables of interest; (e) duplicate or redundant publications; (f) studies with methodological deficiencies detected in systematic review processes of study quality.

3.4 Selection Process According to PRISMA 2020

Bibliographic management was performed in Mendeley. The systematic search identified 1,870 records from five databases plus manual searches. After removing 312 duplicates, 1,558 records were screened by title and abstract, with 1,401 excluded for being outside scope, non-higher education focus, or lacking specific AI applications. Of 157 full-text articles evaluated, 107 were excluded for methodological deficiencies or insufficient data. The final corpus included 50 studies meeting all eligibility criteria.

The selection process involved independent peer review. Two researchers evaluated each record separately. A third team member resolved discrepancies through structured consensus and a fourth validated the final decisions regarding the generating controversy. A calibration pilot test was conducted in half of the 25 randomly selected studies to ensure methodological consistency. The operational criteria will be refined and defined uniformly during this phase.

3.5 Data Extraction and Synthesis

The standard coding matrix was developed collaboratively and structured as follows: a) bibliometric and methodological characteristics; b) specific types of AI applications implemented; c) educational quality indicators evaluated; d) dimensions of digital equity examined; e) important findings, limitations, and recommendations; f) theoretical frameworks and institutional contexts.

Independent peer extraction was performed, the results were systematically compared, and discrepancies were resolved through structured discussion. The analysis subsequently adopted a qualitative thematic synthesis approach (Thomas & Harden 2008), organised by the dimensions of the MIAEES, i.e., pedagogical, technological, ethical and distributive, and no quantitative meta-analysis was performed, given the recognised methodological, population, and contextual heterogeneity.

3.6 Methodological Quality Assessment

Methodological quality was assessed in light of adaptable criteria for research design: quantitative studies (clear objectives, applied sampling, instrumental validity, statistical rigour), qualitative studies (methodological credibility, generalisation, reliability), and systematic reviews (comprehensiveness, inclusion criteria, quality assessment, methodological soundness).).). Each study was independently evaluated by two researchers and rated as high quality (criteria $\geq 80\%$), moderate quality (criteria between 60% and 79%), and limited quality (criteria $< 60\%$), with the latter being excluded from the final analysis.

3.7 Ethical Considerations

Therefore, the present study follows the ethical criteria of scientific research and is based on 1) appropriate attribution in the form of a full citation; 2) transparent methodology developed through reporting of procedures and limitations; 3) academic integrity without bias in interpretation or selective manipulation of evidence; 4) responsibility with regard to a critical examination of educational AI on how it affects equity and social justice. The approval of an ethics committee was not required because no data from human participants was used (Fig. 1).

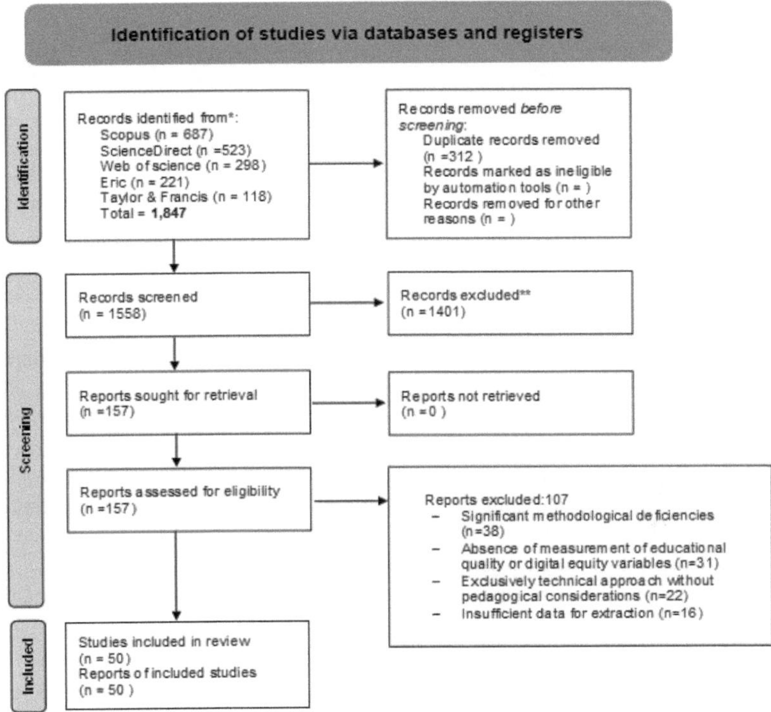

Fig. 1. PRISMA 2020 flow diagram for the selection of studies included in the systematic review (2018–2025).

4 Results

The systematic review identified 50 studies that met the established eligibility criteria, covering empirical research, systematic reviews, and mixed studies published between 2018 and 2025. Thematic analysis revealed convergent and divergent patterns in the transformations generated by AI in higher education, with the findings organised according to the Integrative Framework for Educational AI in Higher Education (MIAEES) into four analytical dimensions.

4.1 Characterisation of AI Applications and Their Relationship to Educational Quality

The analysis identified five main categories of AI applications implemented in higher education, each with different impacts on educational quality indicators (Table 1). Intelligent tutoring systems emerged as the most frequently documented application (n = 18 studies), showing significant improvements in student retention ranging from 12% to 28% depending on specific institutional contexts (Crompton & Burke 2023; Hamzah et al. 2025).

Table 1. Types of AI applications and their impact on educational quality.

AI application	Studies (n)	Quality indicators	Improvement range	Representative studies	Contextual moderators
Intelligent tutoring systems	18	Student retention, academic satisfaction	12–28%	Crompton & Burke (2023); Hamzah et al. (2025)	Robust infrastructure, teacher training
Adaptive assessment platforms	12	Accurate assessment, personalized feedback	15–35%	Villegas-José & Delgado-García (2024)	Ethical frameworks, technical support
Predictive learning analytics	8	Early identification of academic risks	20–42%	Pacheco-Mendoza et al. (2023)	Institutional data, adaptive algorithms
Academic recommendation systems	7	Curriculum personalization, academic efficiency	18–31%	Ahmad et al. (2024)	Technological infrastructure, institutional policies

Note. Improvement ranges represent variations reported in different institutional contexts and student populations. Contextual moderators indicate institutional conditions associated with better implementation outcomes

In this regard, adaptive assessment platforms (n = 12 studies) confirmed a significant capacity to personalise the scope of all assessment processes. The improvement in the accuracy of the assessment was between 15% and 35% and was particularly beneficial in terms of personalizing the identification of specific learning difficulties and the ability of teachers to provide immediate feedback (Villegas-José & Delgado-García 2024). Predictive learning analytics (n = 8 studies) proved effective in personalizing the identification of at-risk students. The predictive accuracy rate ranged from 20% to 42% and depended on contextual variables and the quality of institutional data (Pacheco-Mendoza et al. 2023).).

Academic recommendation systems (n = 7 studies) demonstrated proven effectiveness in personalising curriculum and improving academic trajectories and time, resulting in 18% to 31% academic efficiency through the processing of algorithms of student interaction patterns and prediction of their learning preferences (Ahmad et al. 2024).

4.2 Impacts on Digital Equity and Educational Inclusion

The analysis revealed the existence of a fundamental dialectical tension between the democratising potential of educational AI and its simultaneous capacity to amplify pre-existing inequalities (Table 2). Documented evidence covered three critical dimensions of digital inequality that go beyond access to basic technology: systemic algorithmic bias; gaps in digital literacy; and exclusions sustained by cultural diversity.

Table 2. Evidence on digital equity: barriers and affected populations.

Dimension of inequality	Studies (n)	Identified barriers	Affected populations	Key studies
Algorithmic biases	15	Voice recognition, automated assessment	Students with non-standard accents, cultural diversity	Jafari & Keykha (2024); Nagy et al. (2024)
Digital divides	12	Technological access, digital skills	Socioeconomically, vulnerable populations	Kuleto et al. (2021); Bucea-Manea-Tonis et al. (2022)
Cultural exclusion	8	Algorithmic representation, technological design	Students from the Global South, ethnic minorities	López-Chila et al. (2024); Omar et al. (2024)
Privacy and data	10	Protection of personal information, transparency	Students in weak Regulative contexts	Spivakovsky et al. (2023); Pisica et al. (2023)
Democratic participation	5	Exclusion in technological design	Marginalised student communities	Ryzheva et al. (2024)

Note. Some studies address multiple dimensions, so the total exceeds 50 included studies

Algorithmic biases emerged as the most widely documented concern (n = 15 studies), with evidence of systematic discrimination in voice recognition systems that penalise non-standard accents and automated assessment algorithms that discriminate against culturally diverse writing styles (Jafari & Keykha 2024; Nagy et al. 2024). Digital divides (n = 12 studies) revealed that socioeconomically vulnerable populations face multiple barriers, including limited access to advanced technologies and insufficient digital skills for effective navigation of intelligent systems (Kuleto et al. 2021; Bucea-Manea-Tonis et al. 2022).

Cultural exclusion (n = 8 studies) documented systematic patterns in which students from the Global South and ethnic minorities experience marginalisation in algorithmic representation and technological design processes, demonstrating digital coloniality in educational AI implementations (López-Chila et al. 2024; Omar et al. 2024).). Concerns about privacy and data protection (n = 10 studies) identified significant vulnerabilities in institutional contexts with weak regulatory frameworks, where students face risks of inappropriate use of personal information without effective mechanisms for algorithmic transparency (Spivakovsky et al. 2023; Pisica et al., 2023).

4.3 Temporal and Geographic Distribution of Research

The temporal analysis revealed a significant acceleration in scientific production of educational AI, with 34% of studies (n = 17) published in 2024–2025, 28% (n = 14) in 2022–2023, 22% (n = 11) in 2020–2021, and 16% (n = 8) in 2018–2019. This concentration in recent years reflects the research maturation of the field following the post-pandemic context, when educational AI implementations transitioned from experimental applications to systematic adoptions that generated sufficient empirical evidence for rigorous analysis.

The geographic concentration showed 68% of studies (n = 34) coming from institutions in North America and Europe, 24% (n = 12) from East Asia, and only 8% (n = 4) representing perspectives from the Global South. This unequal distribution reveals epistemological biases that limit the cross-cultural applicability of findings and perpetuate Eurocentric academic hegemonies in research on educational technologies (López-Chila et al. 2024; Marengo et al. 2024).

The temporal analysis showed research maturation: studies from 2018–2020 reported limited effects (<15%), while research from 2024–2025 documented substantial impacts (>25%), reflecting an evolution from experimental implementations to systematic institutional adoptions.

4.4 Regulatory Frameworks and Ethical Considerations

The synthesis identified four fundamental pillars in regulatory frameworks for the responsible implementation of educational AI, demonstrating a progressive conceptual evolution from techno-centric approaches (2018–2020) towards integrative frameworks that prioritise social justice and democratic participation (2021–2025), although with significant variations in practical operationalisation between institutional contexts (Table 3).

Table 3. Documented regulatory frameworks and ethical considerations (2018–2025).

Ethical principle	Studies (n)	Key components	Implementation challenges	Representative studies
Algorithmic transparency	14	Explainability of decisions, regular audits	Technical complexity, limited resources	Kuleto et al. (2021); Chao-Rebolledo & Rivera-Navarro (2024)
Equity and inclusion	12	Mitigation of biases, diverse representation	Identification of biases, diversity of teams	Bucea-Manea-Tonis et al. (2022); Ahmad et al. (2024)
Privacy and data protection	11	Informed consent, anonymization	Inadequate regulatory frameworks	Spivakovsky et al. (2023); Deri et al. (2024)
Democratic participation	8	Student representation, participatory design	Resources, technical skills	Pisica et al. (2023); Katsamakas et al. (2024)

Note. Ethical principles reflect convergences identified in the literature analyzed during the period 2018–2025

Algorithmic transparency (n = 14 studies) emerged as a fundamental principle in continuous evolution, moving from initial concerns about algorithmic "black boxes" (Kuleto et al. 2021) to comprehensive frameworks of explainability and regular audits (Chao-Rebolledo & Rivera-Navarro 2024), although facing persistent limitations related to technical complexity and insufficient institutional resources.

Equity and inclusion frameworks (n = 12 studies) showed progressive conceptual development from initial identification of algorithmic biases (Bucea-Manea-Tonis et al. 2022) to operational criteria for systematic mitigation and ensuring diverse representation in development teams (Ahmad et al. 2024). Considerations regarding privacy and data protection (n = 11 studies) documented an evolution from basic concerns about information collection (Spivakovsky et al. 2023) to comprehensive frameworks for informed consent and anonymization (Deri et al. 2024).

Democratic participation (n = 8 studies) represented the most recently articulated principle, emerging predominantly in studies after 2022 (Pisica et al. 2023; Katsamakas et al. 2024) in response to criticism of exclusionary technological design, establishing criteria for meaningful student representation but facing barriers related to the availability of resources and specialized technical skills (Fig. 2).

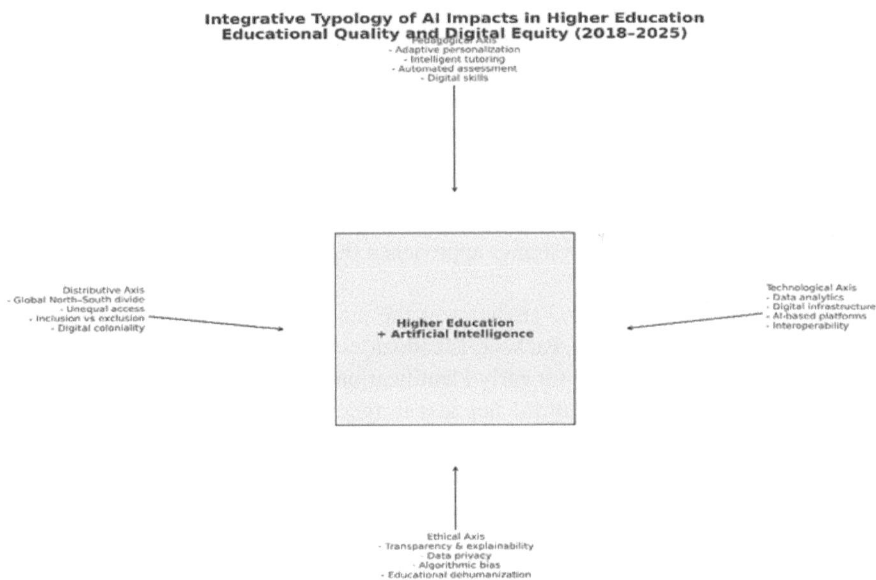

Fig. 2. Integrative typology of the impacts of AI on higher education (2018–2025), showing the dialectical tension between educational quality improvements and digital equity challenges across pedagogical, technological, ethical, and distributive dimensions.

This conceptual model synthesizes the results of the systematic review by classifying the impacts of artificial intelligence on higher education into four interrelated areas: pedagogical (adaptive personalization, intelligent tutoring, automated assessment, digital skills), technological (data analysis, digital infrastructure, AI-based platforms, interoperability), ethical (transparency, data privacy, algorithmic bias, educational dehumanization), and distributive (North-South divide, unequal access, inclusion versus exclusion, digital coloniality). Together, these dimensions illustrate the dialectical tension between improving educational quality and the challenges of digital equity.

5 Discussion of Results

Therefore, the findings of this systematic review reveal a complex transformation in the field of higher education, where artificial intelligence acts as a catalyst for educational quality and at the same time as an intensifier of structural inequalities, thus confirming the dialectical tension that Williamson (2020) identified between technological democratization and the perpetuation of systemic exclusions. This fundamental duality challenges technodeterministic narratives that portray AI as a universally beneficial solution, as its impacts are mediated by contextual factors that go beyond its technical algorithmic capabilities.

5.1 Interpretation of Impacts on Educational Quality

The ranges of improvement documented in intelligent tutoring systems (12–28%) and adaptive assessment platforms (15–35%) converge with previous findings by Crompton & Burke (2023) on moderate to large effects of personalized educational technologies, although substantial variability confirms that the effectiveness of implementations is conditioned by specific contextual moderators. The identification of robust infrastructure and teacher training as critical determinants supports arguments by Katsamakas et al. (2024) on the importance of systemic approaches that transcend purely technological aspects.

The emergence of predictive analytics as the most accurate application (20–42%) is consistent with research by Pacheco-Mendoza et al. (2023) on the transformative potential of predictive systems for early identification of academic risks. This evidence suggests that the added value of AI lies less in the automation of instruction than in preventive analytical capabilities, contradicting institutional implementations that often prioritize personalization tools over early intervention systems.

5.2 Emerging Regulatory Frameworks

The conceptual evolution identified from techno-centric approaches (2018–2020) towards integrative frameworks that prioritize social justice (2021–2025) reflects the maturation of the field documented in the transition from the initial concerns of Kuleto et al. (2021) about algorithmic "black boxes" to the comprehensive frameworks of Chao-Rebolledo & Rivera-Navarro (2024) on explainability and regular audits. However, the persistence of implementation challenges related to technical complexity and limited resources highlights significant gaps between abstract principles and practical operationalization.

The late emergence of democratic participation as an ethical principle (predominantly post-2022) suggests growing recognition, documented by Pisica et al. (2023) and Katsamakas et al. (2024), of limitations in regulatory frameworks that exclude student and community voices from technological design processes. This evolution dialogues with perspectives from Spivakovsky et al. (2023) on the need for community participation in technological decision-making processes.

6 Conclusions

In summary, this systematic review examined the transformation of higher education through artificial intelligence by analyzing 50 studies published between 2018 and 2025. It covered the dominant dialectical tension between educational improvement quality and digital equity. The results show that AI in higher education has been seen as a dual phenomenon; it acts as a trigger for academic personalization and is a potential multiplier of structural differences. Therefore, this essay questions the technodeterminist narrative that portrays such technologies as a universal panacea.

In terms of theoretical contribution, the main novelty is the framework itself: the Integrative Framework of Educational AI for Higher Education (MIAEES), which surpasses previous less consolidated approaches by systematically articulating the pedagogical, technological, ethical, and distributive dimensions through dynamic feedback loops. It is therefore the first theoretical framework to have fully merged educational quality with digital equity. It thus provides a solid theoretical basis for evaluating AI implementations in terms of cooling and heating, personalization and inclusion, and modernization and social justice.

Finally, in terms of practical implications, operational frameworks are needed that balance technological innovation and social responsibility with mandatory algorithmic auditing mandates, decision-making mechanisms on student technology that promote democratic participation and equal criteria, and the mere availability to encompass differentiated performance. Thus, the connection with the SDGs, particularly SDGs 4, 9, and 10, requires public policies that recognize the dual potential of AI to democratize higher education or to stratify it according to specific implementation modalities (Filho et al. 2024).

Future research should prioritize longitudinal studies examining medium-term effects, cross-cultural comparisons, and participatory methodologies incorporating student perspectives.

The future of AI in higher education depends on institutional decisions determining whether these technologies function as instruments of democratization or mechanisms reproducing inequalities. Educational justice in AI contexts demands permanent vigilance and ethical commitment to equity as the guiding principle of technological innovation.

References

Alotaibi, N.S.: The impact of AI and LMS integration on the future of higher education: opportunities, challenges, and strategies for transformation. Sustainability **16**(23), 10357 (2024). https://doi.org/10.3390/su162310357

Bucea-Manea-Tonis, R., et al.: Artificial intelligence potential in higher education institutions enhanced learning environment in Romania and Serbia. Sustainability **14**(10), 5842 (2022). https://doi.org/10.3390/su14105842

Chang, Q.Q., Pan, X.J., Manikandan, N., Ramesh, S.: Artificial intelligence technologies for teaching and learning in higher education. Int. J. Reliab. Qual. Saf. Eng. **29**(05), 2240006 (2022). https://doi.org/10.1142/S021853932240006X

Chao-Rebolledo, C., Rivera-Navarro, M.A.: Uses and perceptions of artificial intelligence tools in higher education in Mexico. Revista Iberoamericana de Educación **95**(1), 57–72 (2024). https://doi.org/10.35362/rie9516259

Crompton, H., Burke, D.: Artificial intelligence in higher education: the state of the field. Int. J. Educ. Technol. High. Educ. **20**(1), 22 (2023). https://doi.org/10.1186/s41239-023-00392-8

Deri, M.N., Singh, A., Zaazie, P., Anandene, D.: Leveraging artificial intelligence in higher educational institutions: a comprehensive overview. Revista de Educación y Derecho **30**, 45777 (2024). https://doi.org/10.1344/REYD2024.30.45777

Filho, W.L., et al.: Using artificial intelligence to implement the UN sustainable development goals at higher education institutions. Int. J. Sust. Dev. World **31**(6), 726–745 (2024). https://doi.org/10.1080/13504509.2024.2327584

George, B., Wooden, O.: Managing the strategic transformation of higher education through artificial intelligence. Admin. Sci. **13**(9), 196 (2023). https://doi.org/10.3390/admsci13090196

Hamzah, H.A., Seman, M.S.A., Ahmed, M.: The impact of artificial intelligence in enhancing online learning platform effectiveness in higher education. Inf. Dev. **41**(3), 794–810 (2025). https://doi.org/10.1177/02666669251315842

Jafari, F., Keykha, A.: Identifying the opportunities and challenges of artificial intelligence in higher education: a qualitative study. J. Appl. Res. High. Educ. **16**(4), 1228–1245 (2024). https://doi.org/10.1108/JARHE-09-2023-0426

Katsamakas, E., Pavlov, O.V., Saklad, R.: Artificial intelligence and the transformation of higher education institutions: a systems approach. Sustainability **16**(14), 6118 (2024). https://doi.org/10.3390/su16146118

Kuleto, V., et al.: Exploring opportunities and challenges of artificial intelligence and machine learning in higher education institutions. Sustainability **13**(18), 10424 (2021). https://doi.org/10.3390/su131810424

López-Chila, R., Llerena-Izquierdo, J., Sumba-Nacipucha, N., Cueva-Estrada, J.: Artificial intelligence in higher education: an analysis of existing bibliometrics. Educ. Sci. **14**(1), 47 (2024). https://doi.org/10.3390/educsci14010047

Mah, D.K., Gross, N.: Artificial intelligence in higher education: exploring faculty use, self-efficacy, distinct profiles, and professional development needs. Int. J. Educ. Technol. High. Educ. **21**(1), 58 (2024). https://doi.org/10.1186/s41239-024-00490-1

Maphosa, V., Maphosa, M.: Artificial intelligence in higher education: a bibliometric analysis and topic modeling approach. Appl. Artif. Intell. **37**(1), 2261730 (2023). https://doi.org/10.1080/08839514.2023.2261730

Marengo, A., Pagano, A., Pange, J., Soomro, K.A.: The educational value of artificial intelligence in higher education: a 10-year systematic literature review. Interact. Technol. Smart Educ. **21**(4), 625–644 (2024). https://doi.org/10.1108/ITSE-11-2023-0218

Munir, H., Vogel, B., Jacobsson, A.: Artificial intelligence and machine learning approaches in digital education: a systematic revision. Information **13**(4), 203 (2022). https://doi.org/10.3390/info13040203

Nagy, A.S., Tumiwa, J.R., Arie, F.V., Erdey, L.: An exploratory study of artificial intelligence adoption in higher education. Cogent Educ. **11**(1), 2386892 (2024). https://doi.org/10.1080/2331186X.2024.2386892

O'Dea, X.H., O'Dea, M.: Is artificial intelligence really the next big thing in learning and teaching in higher education? A conceptual paper. J. Univ. Teach. Learn. Pract. **20**(5), 05 (2023)

Omar, A., Shaqour, A.Z., Khlaif, Z.N.: Attitudes of faculty members in Palestinian universities toward employing artificial intelligence applications in higher education: opportunities and challenges. Front. Educ. **9**, 1414606 (2024). https://doi.org/10.3389/feduc.2024.1414606

Pacheco-Mendoza, S., Guevara, C., Mayorga-Albán, A., Fernández-Escobar, J.: Artificial intelligence in higher education: a predictive model for academic performance. Educ. Sci. **13**(10), 990 (2023). https://doi.org/10.3390/educsci13100990

Pisica, A.I., Edu, T., Zaharia, R.M., Zaharia, R.: Implementing artificial intelligence in higher education: pros and cons from the perspectives of academics. Societies **13**(5), 118 (2023). https://doi.org/10.3390/soc13050118

Ryzheva, N., Nefodov, D., Romanyuk, S., Marynchenko, H., Kudla, M.: Artificial intelligence in higher education: opportunities and challenges. Amazonia Investiga **13**(73), 284–296 (2024). https://doi.org/10.34069/AI/2024.73.01.24

Spivakovsky, O.V., Omelchuk, S.A., Kobets, V.V., Valko, N.V., Malchykova, D.S.: Institutional policies on artificial intelligence in university learning, teaching and research. Inform. Technol. Learn. Tools **97**(5), 181–202 (2023). https://doi.org/10.33407/itlt.v97i5.5395

Triberti, S., Di Fuccio, R., Scuotto, C., Marsico, E., Limone, P.: Better than my professor?" How to develop artificial intelligence tools for higher education. Front. Artific. Intell. **7**, 1329605 (2024). https://doi.org/10.3389/frai.2024.1329605

Villegas-José, V., Delgado-García, M.: Artificial intelligence: Innovative educational revolution in higher education. Pixel-Bit- Revista de Medios y Educación **71** (2024). https://doi.org/10.12795/pixelbit.107760

Zhou, C.: Integration of modern technologies in higher education on the example of artificial intelligence use. Educ. Inf. Technol. **28**(4), 3893–3910 (2023). https://doi.org/10.1007/s10639-022-11309-9

Zhou, X., Zhang, J., Chan, C.: Unveiling students' experiences and perceptions of artificial intelligence usage in higher education. J. Univ. Teach. Learn. Pract. **21**(6), 23 (2024)

Ahmad, S.F., Alam, M.M., Rahmat, M.K., Mubarik, M.S., Hyder, S.I.: Academic and administrative role of artificial intelligence in education. Sustainability **14**(3), 1101 (2024)

Binns, R.: Fairness in machine learning: lessons from political philosophy. Proc. Mach. Learn. Res. **81**, 149–159 (2018)

Bozkurt, A., Karadeniz, A., Baneres, D., Guerrero-Roldán, A.E., Rodríguez, M.E.: Artificial intelligence and reflections from educational landscape: a review of AI studies in half a century. Sustainability **13**(2), 800 (2021)

Crompton, H., Burke, D.: Artificial intelligence in higher education: the state of the field. Int. J. Educ. Technol. High. Educ. **20**(1), 22 (2023)

Holmes, W., Bialik, M., Fadel, C.: Artificial intelligence in education: promises and implications for teaching and learning. Center for Curriculum Redesign (2019)

Katzenbach, C., Ulbricht, L.: Algorithmic governance. Internet Policy Rev. **8**(4), 1–18 (2019)

Tlili, A., et al.: Quality education for all: can artificial intelligence close the gap? A systematic review on AI in education. Comput. Educ. **204**, 104870 (2023)

Viberg, O., Hatakka, M., Bälter, O., Mavroudi, A.: The current landscape of learning analytics in higher education. Comput. Hum. Behav. **89**, 98–110 (2018)

Williamson, B.: Making markets through digital platforms: pearson, educational technology, and the (e)valuation of learning. J. Polit. Econ. **128**(11), 4316–4364 (2020)

Zhai, X., et al.: A review of artificial intelligence (AI) in education from 2000 to 2020. Educ. Tech. Res. Dev. **69**(4), 1833–1867 (2021)

Booth, A., et al.: The nuts and bolts of PROSPERO: an international prospective register of systematic reviews. Syst. Rev. **11**(1), 54 (2022)

Gough, D., Oliver, S., Thomas, J.: An introduction to systematic reviews. SAGE Publications (2020)

Liberati, A., et al.: The PRISMA statement for reporting systematic reviews and meta-analyses of studies that evaluate health care interventions: explanation and elaboration. PLoS Med. **6**(7), e1000100 (2009)

Page, M.J., et al.: The PRISMA 2020 statement: an updated guideline for reporting systematic reviews. BMJ **372**, n71 (2021)

Thomas, J., Harden, A.: Methods for the thematic synthesis of qualitative research in systematic reviews. BMC Med. Res. Methodol. **8**(1), 45 (2008)

Wohlin, C.: Guidelines for snowballing in systematic literature studies and a replication in software engineering. In: Proceedings of the 18th International Conference on Evaluation and Assessment in Software Engineering, pp. 1–10 (2014)

Leveraging MFCC Features for Bangla Audio Emotion Classification Using a ResNet-Transformer Encoder Fusion

Md Rezaul Hossain[✉][iD], Fakiha Rahman Soha[iD], Tajkiratul Abida Ananna[iD], Ruba Sazeda[iD], and Anisur Rahman

Department of Computer Science and Engineering, East West University, Dhaka 1212, Bangladesh
rezaulhossainaryan@gmail.com, fakiharahmansoha@gmail.com, tajkiratulabida@gmail.com, rubasazeda2002@gmail.com, anis@ewubd.edu

Abstract. The usage of speech data with the emerging advancement of Artificial Intelligence has significantly increased in diverse sectors, placing speech sentiment analysis as a prominent research focus within the realm of Natural Language Processing (NLP). Though Bangla is spoken by approximately 210 million people worldwide, Bangla speech sentiment analysis is still limited in research. This paper addresses the research gap by leveraging the strengths of Convolutional Neural Networks (CNN) and Transformer architectures, applied to the largest publicly available corpora in this language: SUBESO and BanglaSER. Relying on Mel-Frequency Cepstral Coefficients (MFCC), our model is trained on both datasets. This model has been evaluated on 7 distinct emotions: Surprise, Neutral, Sad, Happy, Angry, Disgust, and Fear. Our model has achieved 92% accuracy on the SUBESCO dataset. In addition, this is the first model to achieve 91% accuracy with the combined dataset (SUBESCO+BanglaSER) on 7-class Bangla speech emotion recognition using a hybrid CNN-Transformer architecture.

Keywords: Bangla Speech Emotion · MFCC · Audio Sentiment · Deep Learning · CNN · ResNet · Transformer

1 Introduction

Sentiment analysis (SA) or emotion classification refers to the process of detecting one's emotions or behaviour in response to several stimuli such as topics, events, or interactions by analyzing text, audio or other biometric forms. The rapid evolution of technology and social media platforms has turned the web into a large repository of data in the form of personal opinions, reviews, feedback, podcasts, vlogs, documentaries and other forms of data. Therefore, emotion classification is inevitable when it comes to interpersonal communication, digital interaction, remote health surveillance systems, emotion-driven technology, etc., for interpreting mental state, aiding problem solving and facilitating decision-making capability [1,2,15,18].

© The Author(s), under exclusive license to Springer Nature Switzerland AG 2026
H. Kannan et al. (Eds.): AIKP 2025, CCIS 2804, pp. 199–211, 2026.
https://doi.org/10.1007/978-3-032-14706-6_16

Numerous research studies have been conducted on sentiment analysis in this regard in the last few decades, particularly in English. However, low-resourced languages such as Bengali still lack their fair share of research considering their unique phonetics, characteristics, regional dialects and accents. In Bangla SA, most of the research has been conducted on textual data, creating a substantial gap in audio or speech data analysis [7]. Considering the diversity of the Bangla language, selecting the appropriate set of features to detect emotion in Bangla audio speech correctly is crucial. Several feature selection techniques, such as MFCC, PLP and LPC are widely applied in audio emotion analysis, with MFCC being particularly effective in capturing spatial and temporal patterns since its inception [6].

This research paper addresses the gap in Bangla speech emotion recognition by leveraging the unique strengths of both Convolutional Neural Networks (CNNs) and Transformer networks, with MFCC as the core feature extraction technique. The primary contributions are as follows: i) this work has combined two extensive Bengali corpora, SUBESCO [22] alongside BanglaSER [8] for the comprehensive evaluation and achieved an accuracy of 91% across 7 different emotion classes. ii) Although deep learning techniques are widely applied for sentiment analysis [9], it is the first to fuse ResNet-18 and Transformer architectures securing a better outcome. iii) A comprehensive analysis is presented to benchmark the effectiveness of the proposed model in comparison to the existing models. The explicit comparison of the SUBESCO dataset and the combined dataset demonstrates the potency of the model.

The remainder of the paper is structured in the following manner: it begins with a Literature Review that highlights the previous work that has been done, followed by the Materials and Methods explaining the model details and data pre-processing and augmentation, along with the Results with comprehensive comparative analysis, and finally with the Conclusion and Future Work.

2   Literature Review

The domain of audio emotion analysis is advancing rapidly, driven by the growing prevalence of speech and audio inputs in daily interactions. An abundance of studies have been dedicated to optimizing emotion detection from audio inputs across various languages, particularly in English. Bangla presents unique challenges due to its diverse phonetic and prosodic characteristics, regional dialects, and limited annotated emotional speech datasets. There are a few studies that have been conducted on Bangla Speech Sentiment Analysis (SSA) among which the study [11] is one of the significant ones conducted in 2020.

In [11], the authors recognised four emotional states from Bengali speech using their self-built dataset, which consists of 400 isolated emotional sentences from 50 individuals. Feature vectors extracted from Pitch and MFCC have been employed to build the k-NN classifier and achieved an overall accuracy of 87.50%. The authors concluded that increasing the dataset size could enhance accuracy and introduce beneficial variations.

Another research work explored the language independence of SER in the Bangla and English languages using language-neutral prosodic features [19]. The authors have analyzed six different emotions across three Emotional Speech Sets (ESS), Bangla ESS (BESS), English ESS (EESS), and the Toronto ESS (E-TESS) using the SVM model as the primary classifier. Their research performed three experiments: individual dataset evaluation, integrating ESS pairs, and cross-dataset testing, among which the final experiment revealed the highest recognition rate of 76.7% when BESS was used for training [19].

The authors in [12] conducted a study in 2021 to predict three emotional states from Bengali speech using their custom-built dataset named 'ABEG' alongside the RAVDESS dataset. Both MFCC and Linear Prediction Coefficients (LPC) were employed as features for training and testing different machine learning algorithms, and presented a comparative analysis of the performances of various algorithms. Logistic Regression provided the best output on the ABEG dataset with 92%. accuracy, whereas XGBoost achieved 86% accuracy on the combined ABEG and RAVDESS dataset [12]. In the study, Ayon et al. [13] performed ensemble machine learning to enhance the performance of emotion recognition from audio data. They focused on detecting four emotional states using 452 Bangla audio samples collected from 20 individuals. Their study concluded that ensemble models outperformed the traditional models with an average of 84.37%.

A notable study carried out by Sultana et al. [21] in 2022 explored Bangla SER and cross-lingual analysis using an innovative architecture named DCTB, which integrates Deep Convolutional Neural Networks (CNN) and Bidirectional LSTM networks along with a Time-Distributed Flattening layer. This DCTB model effectively captures local and sequential emotional speech information, outperforming other CNN-based SER models. The model obtained a weighted average accuracy and F1 score of 86.86% on their self-built dataset SUBESCO and 82.7% accuracy on the RAVDESS dataset [21].

Islam et al. [17] researched Bengali SER using MFCC features and evaluated four machine-learning algorithms on 1400 recordings. Among them, CatBoost outperformed the others with 82.85% accuracy, highlighting its superior ability to detect underlying patterns in the dataset. In another study [4], conducted in 2024, a CNN-driven approach was proposed using the SUBESCO as well as BanglaSER datasets. They presented a comparative analysis of various models such as KNN, RF, Logistic Regression, and RNN, and among those, CNN outperformed others, achieving 90% accuracy on SUBESCO and 78% on BanglaSER. However, cross-dataset testing performance dropped to 33.5%, revealing shortcomings in model generalization due to data variations.

Shuvo and Khan [20] introduced a hybrid CNN-transformer model integrating local feature extraction from CNN and global feature extraction from Transformers using the BanglaSER dataset. The proposed hybrid model achieved a weighted class accuracy of 92.3%, exceeding the performance of other individual models. Priom Dev [10] performed a multitask audio analysis approach with the SUBESCO dataset, addressing emotion detection, speaker recognition, and gender classification. The research findings emphasize the effectiveness of MFCC, Chroma features, and MEL spectrograms, demonstrating high accuracy in all three tasks, with the Gradient Boosting Classifier reaching 87.94% accuracy for emotion recognition.

Hasan et al. [14] developed a hybrid architecture by incorporating a 1D-CNN with the LSTM network using the SUBESCO and RAVDESS datasets. This integration enhanced the model's proficiency to capture local attributes along with the temporal sequence modeling. Another study conducted by Billah et al. [5] developed a novel approach by integrating cascaded deep-learning techniques with the combination of emotion classification and intensity measurement. The researchers have transformed the speech signals into 3D features using MFCC and STFT and achieved 71.67% accuracy on the KBES dataset.

The studies above explore emotion recognition in Bangla and some in English speech using different classifiers, for example, SVM, ensemble models and deep learning architectures. These models' recognition rates vary from 76.7% to 93.3%, with limitations of dataset imbalances, cross-language inconsistencies and limited emotion classes in emotion recognition. The proposed approach in this study is the first to achieve state-of-the-art accuracy on the SUBESCO dataset and the combined SUBESCO+BanglaSER dataset using the maximum number of classes, setting a new benchmark for Bangla audio sentiment detection.

3   Materials and Methods

This methodology is designed to leverage the transformer and ResNet for better accuracy and usability in real-life scenarios. The proposed idea of the methodology is to train the model on data that is collected from reliable voice data corpora, considering equal class distribution for the emotions. Those audio files are converted into waveforms and later passed to the augmentation phase which will increase the data and add noise to improve the model's robustness.

Later, the output of both networks passes through a Linear layer to classify the emotion of the audio file. Figure 1 represents the high-level view of the method of the study. This utilizes a combination of state-of-the-art deep learning models, applying both transformer and ResNet architectures.

3.1   Dataset

The proper selection of datasets determines the quality of the study, and in a low-resourced language like Bangla, it becomes crucial to prepare. Two of the most widely used Bangla audio datasets have been used in this study: SUBESCO [22] and BanglaSER [8]. These two datasets are significantly different and have the most prominent data in the Bangla language.

SUBESCO, an audio-only dataset, was prepared considering seven emotions (Anger, Disgust, Fear, Happiness, Neutral, Sadness and Surprise) and contains 7010 audio clips. Those audio data were generated by trained voice actors in a professional studio environment [22]. The average duration per clip was 4 s and

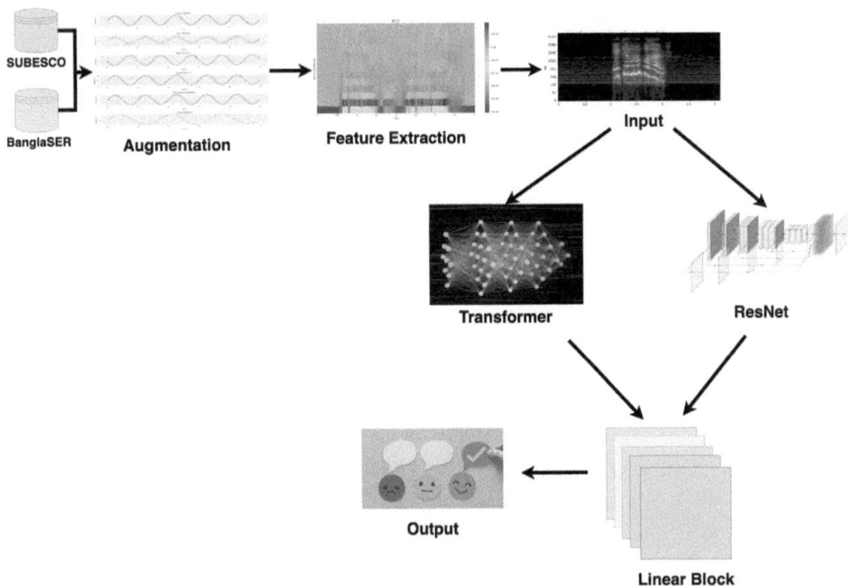

Fig. 1. Algorithmic flow.

the total duration of the corpus is around 8 h long. The sample rate used in this corpus 48000 Hz and the file format was "wav" files, ensuring high-quality audio samples.

BanglaSER contains 1467 audio samples that are also acted by native speakers which have five emotions (Angry, Happy, Neutral, Sad, Surprise). The total duration of this corpus is 1 h and 29 min. Human validation accuracy for both datasets was around 80% [8]. These two datasets have been merged and 80% of the data has been used to train the model. The remaining 20% has been kept for testing and validation. Table 1 documents the class distribution of these two datasets.

3.2   Feature Extraction and Augmentation

To reduce the overfitting of the proposed model and improve the adaptability to new data, some augmentation processes were implemented on both datasets. For augmentation, Additive White Gaussian Noise (AWGN) was added to the audio data. To normalize the Gaussian noise, a 16-bit quantization constant is implemented as well as a randomly selected signal-to-noise (SNR) value between 15db to 30db is applied to simulate acoustic conditions in a realistic manner. In this process, noise generated by a normal distribution has been added to the source audio file and after whitening transformation, the noise will be spread evenly through the entire audio signal. Striking the perfect noise level is key: inade-

Table 1. Dataset class distribution

Emotions	SUBESCO	BanglaSER	Total
Anger	1000	306	1306
Disgust	1000	0	1000
Fear	1000	0	1000
Happiness	1000	306	1306
Neutral	1005	242	1247
Sadness	1000	306	1306
Surprise	1005	306	1311
Total	**7010**	**1466**	**8476**

quate noise adds no value and excessive noise obstructs learning. Moreover, the signal-to-noise ratio regulates noise intensity level relative to the signal.

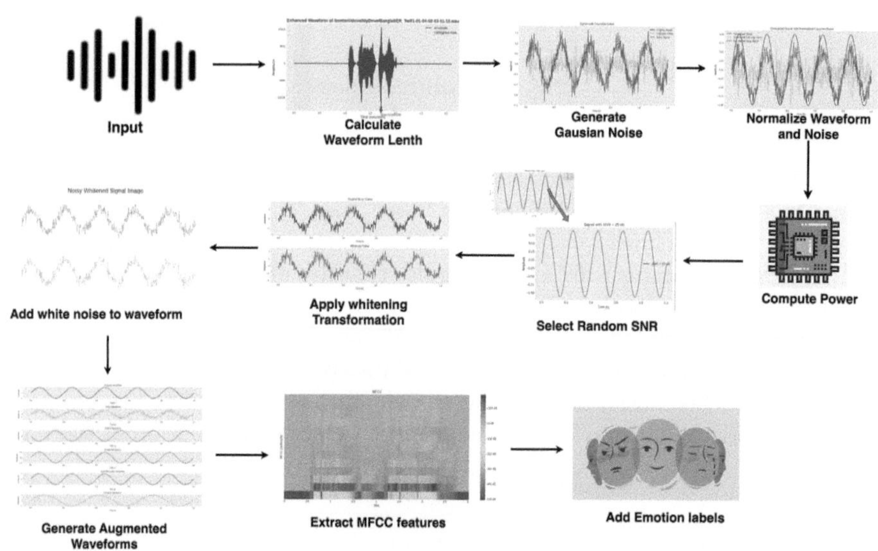

Fig. 2. Augmentation diagram.

This augmentation process shown in Fig. 2 doubles the test dataset, which makes the number of audio samples 13563. After that, Mel Frequency Cepstral Coefficients (MFCC) were extracted from the audio waveform using librosa's mfcc function for the training and testing datasets. MFCC are a set of features that can capture the spectral contour of the signal [3]. This preprocessing was done in multiple stages to ensure robust feature extraction from the raw audio signals. At first the audio files were loaded at 48000 Hz sampling rate with a duration of 3 s and skipped the first 0.5 s to avoid silence from the beginning of a sample. On top of it, a threshold was set to 60 db and below that it was considered as silence which got trimmed with librosa's trim function. Then all the waveforms were standardized into homogenous vectors with a length of 144000 samples (48kHz multiplied by 3 s). At this stage, MFCC was employed with a window size of 512, FFT size of 1024, window type was Hamming Window and 128 mel filterbanks. After that, normalization was applied on the resulting MFCC features using StandardScaler to scale training, validation and test features.

3.3   Model Architecture

This methodology leverages both the unique strengths of CNN and the Transformer network. This Encoder-ResNet model integrates two neural network architectures: ResNet-18 which is a modified version of CNN and Transformers. Each of these blocks has been designed to process the MFCC from an audio signal hence, enhancing the model's overall performance to detect sentiment from an audio input. The reason behind selecting ResNet as the convolutional backbone was due to its promising strength in handling the vanishing gradient problem through the residual connections and its computational efficiency [16]. As MFCC has a natural two-dimensional representation, that is time versus frequency coefficients, it creates a spectrogram representation that can be processed by CNN very effectively. The previous study carried by Aziz et al. [4] on the SUBESCO dataset alone shows a very impressive result of CNN-based architecture, yet left room for improvement. Transformers have demonstrated impressive capability in capturing long range temporal dependencies through their attention mechanism that helps direct modelling of relationships between distant elements in a sequence [23]. The motivation was to leverage the strengths of both architectures to achieve a better and efficient outcome.

The ResNet-Transformer model receives the input shaped as $(1 \times 40 \times 282)$ that passes to the encoder block as well as the ResNet-18 block. The transformer block contains a max-pooling layer with a kernel size of (1, 4) and a stride size of (1, 4). In this layer, the input feature gets reshaped into 40×70, each encoder block contains a multi-head self-attention layer with four attention heads maintaining the feedforward network size of 512 within each transformer layer. This allows the input feature to transform into different dimensions, enabling the model to learn more complex representations. The dropout rate is 0.4 which helps to prevent overfitting and the activation function used in the feedforward network is ReLU. This reshaped tensor then leads to the transformer embedding.

Parallel to the Transformer block, this model incorporates a ResNet-18 architecture in which the first convolutional layer is replaced to receive the single-channel input and the last layer is replaced with a linear layer that outputs a 512-dimensional embedding. The convolutional layer processes the input and produces 64 feature maps that use a 3 by 3 filter with a stride size of 1. It

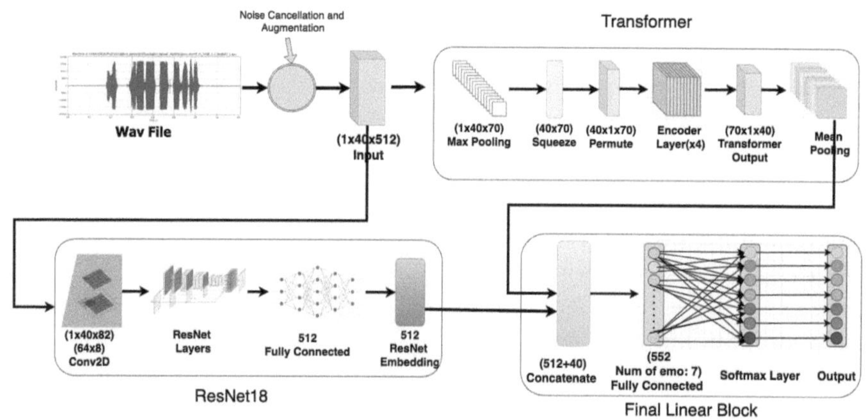

Fig. 3. Model architecture.

also adds a padding of 1 to keep the output dimensions the same as the input. The ResNet embedding and the Transformer embedding are combined to form a complete embedding and pass through a linear layer that produces output logits that are converted to probabilities using the SoftMax layer. This hybrid ResNet-Transformer model was trained using Stochastic Gradient Descent (SGD) optimizer with a learning rate of 0.01, weight decay of 0.001 and momentum of 0.8. Here, SDG was selected because of its promising performance on generalization on small to medium datasets and better convergence components. The learning rate was chosen experimentally which provided optimal convergence speed without overshooting. A weight decay of 0.001 was set to ensure effective regularization to prevent overfitting. The training process was conducted on Google Colab using the A100 GPU where the training loop executes the entire training process, in which the dataset is divided into 32 minibatch sizes and across 100 maximum epochs. For calculating the loss, the widely used multiclass classification cross-entropy loss function has been applied which is defined as:

$$L(y, \hat{y}) = -\sum_{i=1}^{C} y_i \log(\hat{y}_i) \tag{1}$$

Here, y_i is the true label for class i, represented as a one-hot encoded vector, $\hat{y}_i$ is the predicted probability for class i, and C is the number of classes. To prevent overfitting the training is halted if the validation loss does not improve for a specified number of epochs, which was set to 15 epochs. This helps in ensuring that the model is properly trained with an optimal performance while minimizing the risk of overfitting. In this case the training was halted after 46 epochs. The data was split using stratified sampling 80% for training, 10% for validation and 10% for testing to maintain the class distribution balance across all sets. All the architectural components including the modified ResNet-18 backbone, transformer encoder layers and hybridization implementations are documented with detailed explanations and will be made publicly available to support future work.

4   Results and Discussion

The model explained in Fig. 3 was applied to both the SUBESCO and BanglaSER datasets. The initial evaluation with the SUBESCO dataset before merging, on which it delivered 92% accuracy, alongside F1 and precision scores of 91.87%. As indicated in Table 2, the highest F1 score was 0.95 for 'neutral' emotion, whereas 'disgust' had the lowest score at 0.87.

Table 2. Precision and F1 Score for each emotion

Emotion	SUBESCO				SUBESCO + BanglaSER			
	Precision	Recall	F1	Support	Precision	Recall	F1	Support
Surprise	0.93	0.89	0.91	300	0.92	0.89	0.91	393
Neutral	0.91	0.98	0.95	303	0.92	0.98	0.95	375
Sad	0.95	0.92	0.93	300	0.92	0.89	0.90	393
Happy	0.94	0.89	0.91	300	0.88	0.94	0.91	393
Angry	0.91	0.92	0.91	300	0.89	0.94	0.91	390
Disgust	0.87	0.87	0.87	300	0.88	0.82	0.85	300
Fear	0.93	0.94	0.94	300	0.93	0.86	0.89	300

As detailed in Table 2, in the combined dataset, 'disgust' records the lowest F1 score at 0.85, while 'neutral' achieves the highest at 0.95. Mirroring the human trend accuracy, the model performs lowest for the 'disgust' emotion, as indicated in [22]. This model reports an overall accuracy of 91% with an F1 score of 90.89% with 7 emotions.

From the confusion matrix in Fig. 4, it is seen that the model demonstrates strong classification accuracy for all classes, particularly for surprise, neutral, sad, happy and angry which represents the model's overall robustness. However, some confusions are observed between similar emotions, such as 'disgust' and classified as 'angry' in 25 samples. It indicates the human trend of classifying similar emotions.

The loss curves demonstrated in Fig. 5 for both (SUBESCO and combined) datasets flatten after 10 epochs, implying the model's convergence with no overfitting. The validation loss curves (green for SUBESCO and purple for combined) follow the trend: they increase initially before dropping sharply in the first few epochs. These early fluctuations are attributed to the model's fine-tuning or variance in the validation set, eventually stabilising.

A comparative analysis is provided in Fig. 6 of the model's accuracy against the other models across various emotions. It is seen that most of the studies have

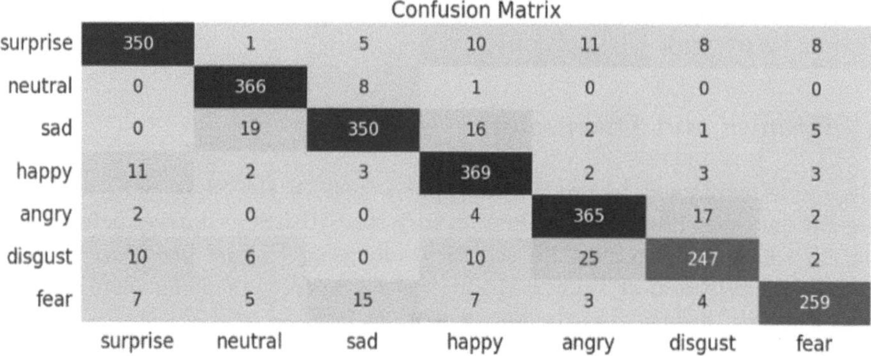

Fig. 4. Confusion matrix.

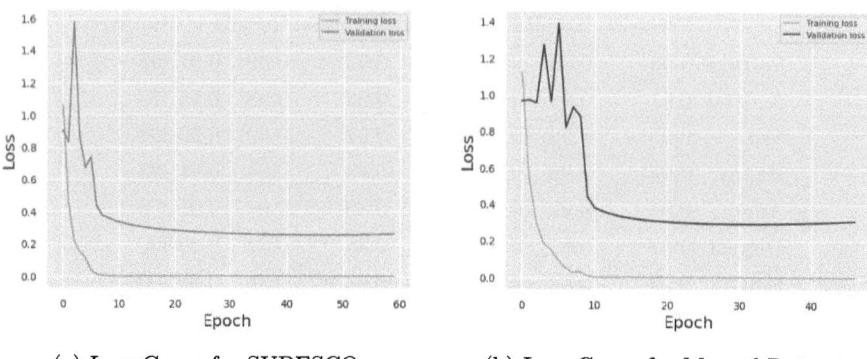

(a) Loss Curve for SUBESCO   (b) Loss Curve for Merged Dataset

Fig. 5. Loss Curves.

been conducted with the emotion classified into seven classes. However, downscaling the classes labelled in the original dataset enables models to achieve better accuracy, but it becomes less useful in real-life scenarios. In [5], Chakraborty et al. trained their model using SUBESCO+BanglaSER, and 92% accuracy was achieved, but with class labels, positive, neutral and negative, which reduces the error rate significantly and the classification becomes generic. The model implemented in this study achieved 91% accuracy with the highest number of emotion classes and outperformed the others while using the combined dataset.

Table 3 highlights the model's achievement over other models on the combined dataset for seven emotions, with an accuracy of 91% positioning it among the highest-performing models. This demonstrates that this model has achieved the highest accuracy considering the highest number of emotions. It ensures a more robust solution in the Bangla speech emotion recognition as it has a good balance with the inclusion of both SUBESCO and BanglaSER.

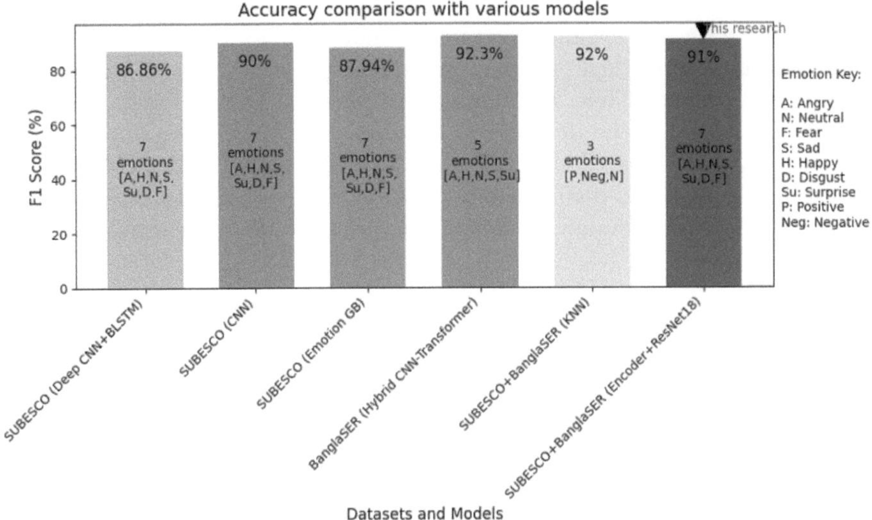

Fig. 6. Model Comparison Graph.

Table 3. Comparison table

Dataset	Number of Emotions	Accuracy
SUBESCO [21]	7	86.86%
SUBESCO [4]	7	90%
BanglaSER [20]	5	92.3%
SUBESCO [10]	7	87.94%
SUBESCO+BanglaSER [7]	3	92%
SUBESCO+BanglaSER	7	91%

5   Conclusion and Future Work

The applied Encoder-ResNet architecture composed of CNN and Transformer layers showed notable performance covering seven distinct emotions. By leveraging MFCC feature extraction using the SUBESCO and BanglaSER datasets, across seven emotions, the model achieved 92% accuracy on SUBESCO and 91% accuracy on the combined datasets. Addressing a critical research gap, the results demonstrate the system's strong ability to recognise Bangla speech sentiment. The model provides a comprehensive classification of seven emotions, advancing state-of-the-art methods and enhancing functional deployment.

Despite these promising outcomes, several limitations exist. The scarcity of available datasets and the complexities of emotion detection, even in humans, often yield lower accuracy. Besides, both of the datasets were generated in a very controlled studio environment with trained voice actors, which may not represent the variance occurring in the real world emotional speech. Hence, similar datasets with exact similar features do not provide proper scope for effective cross-validation, which leaves room to test the robustness of the model in an extensive context. Thus, to improve the real-world applicability, the future work should focus on the diversity of datasets, including variations in accents and dialects, as well as test on different datasets created under different conditions. Additionally, to distinguish between closely related emotions, advanced feature engineering techniques incorporating multi-modality can overcome the challenges.

Disclosure of Interests. The authors have no competing interests to declare that are relevant to the content of this article.

References

1. Al-Nafjan, A., Alharthi, K., Kurdi, H.: Lightweight building of an electroencephalogram-based emotion detection system. Brain Sci. **10**(11), 781 (2020). https://doi.org/10.3390/brainsci10110781
2. Athavipach, C., Pan-ngum, S., Israsena, P.: A wearable in-ear EEG device for emotion monitoring. Sensors **19**(18), 4014 (2019). https://doi.org/10.3390/s19184014
3. Ayvaz, U., Gürüler, H., Khan, F., Ahmed, N., Whangbo, T., Abdusalomov, A.B.: Automatic speaker recognition using mel-frequency cepstral coefficients through machine learning. Comput. Mater. Continua **71**(3), 5511–5521 (2022). https://doi.org/10.32604/cmc.2022.023278
4. Aziz, S., Arif, N.H., Ahbab, S., Ahmed, S., Ahmed, T., Kabir, M.H.: Improved speech emotion recognition in Bengali language using deep learning. In: 2023 International Conference on Computer and Information Technology (ICCIT) (2023). https://doi.org/10.1109/iccit60459.2023.10441053
5. Billah, M.M., Sarker, M.L., Akhand, M.A.H., Kamal, M.A.S.: Emotion recognition with intensity level from Bangla speech using feature transformation and cascaded deep learning model. Int. J. Advanced Comput. Sci. Appl. **15**(4) (2024). https://doi.org/10.14569/ijacsa.2024.0150460
6. Bitouk, D., Verma, R., Nenkova, A.: Class-level spectral features for emotion recognition. Speech Commun. **52**(7–8), 613–625 (2010). https://doi.org/10.1016/j.specom.2010.02.010
7. Chakraborty Shruti, A., Hossain Rifat, R., Kamal, M., Alam, M.G.R.: A comparative study on Bengali speech sentiment analysis based on audio data. In: 2023 IEEE International Conference on Big Data and Smart Computing (BigComp) (2023). https://doi.org/10.1109/bigcomp57234.2023.00043
8. Das, R.K., Islam, N., Ahmed, M.R., Islam, S., Shatabda, S., Islam, A.M.: Banglaser: a speech emotion recognition dataset for the Bangla language. Data Brief **42**, 108091 (2022). https://doi.org/10.1016/j.dib.2022.108091
9. Davis, S., Mermelstein, P.: Comparison of parametric representations for monosyllabic word recognition in continuously spoken sentences. IEEE Trans. Acoust. Speech Sig. Process. **28**(4), 357–366 (1980). https://doi.org/10.1109/tassp.1980.1163420

10. Deb, P.: Multitask audio analysis for emotion, gender, and speaker recognition in Bangla speech comparing features and models. In: 2023 International Conference on Advanced Computing Technologies and Applications (ICACTA) (2023). https://doi.org/10.1109/icacta58201.2023.10393734
11. Devnath, J., Hossain, M.S., Rahman, M., Saha, H., Habib, A., Sultan, M.N.: Emotion recognition from isolated Bengali speech. J. Theor. Appl. Inf. Technol. **31**(10) (2020). https://www.jatit.org/volumes/Vol98No10/1Vol98No10.pdf
12. Dhar, P., Guha, S.: A system to predict emotion from Bengali speech. Int. J. Math. Sci. Comput. **7**(1), 26–35 (2021). https://doi.org/10.5815/ijmsc.2021.01.04
13. Gregori Ayon, R.D., Rabbi, M.S., Habiba, U., Hasana, M.: Bangla speech emotion detection using machine learning ensemble methods. Adv. Sci. Technol. Eng. Syst. J. **7**(6), 70–76 (2022). https://doi.org/10.25046/aj070608
14. Hassan, M.M., Raihan, M., Hassan, M.M., Bairagi, A.K.: Bser: alearning framework for Bangla speech emotion recognition. In: 2024 6th International Conference on Electrical Engineering and Information and Communication Technology (ICEE-ICT) (2024). https://doi.org/10.1109/iceeict62016.2024.10534493
15. Hauser, S.C., McIntyre, S., Israr, A., Olausson, H., Gerling, G.J.: Uncovering human-to-human physical interactions that underlie emotional and affective touch communication. In: 2019 IEEE World Haptics Conference (WHC) (2019). https://doi.org/10.1109/whc.2019.8816169
16. He, K., Zhang, X., Ren, S., Sun, J.: Deep residual learning for image recognition. In: Proceedings of the IEEE Conference on Computer Vision and Pattern Recognition (CVPR), pp. 770–778. IEEE (2016). https://doi.org/10.1109/CVPR.2016.90
17. Islam, M.R., et al.: A machine learning approach for emotion classification in Bengali speech. Int. J. Adv. Comput. Sci. Appl. **14**(10) (2023). https://doi.org/10.14569/ijacsa.2023.0141093
18. Pal, S., Mukhopadhyay, S., Suryadevara, N.: Development and progress in sensors and technologies for human emotion recognition. Sensors **21**(16), 5554 (2021). https://doi.org/10.3390/s21165554
19. Saad, F., Mahmud, H., Kabir, M.R., Shaheen, M.A., Farastu, P., Hasan, M.K.: A case study on the independence of speech emotion recognition in Bangla and English languages using language-independent prosodic features. arXiv preprint arXiv:2111.10776 (2021). https://doi.org/10.48550/arxiv.2111.10776
20. Shuvo, S.H.A., Khan, R.: Bangla speech-based emotion detection using a hybrid CNN-transformer approach. In: 2023 8th International Conference on Communication, Image and Signal Processing (CCISP) (2023). https://doi.org/10.1109/ccisp59915.2023.10355685
21. Sultana, S., Iqbal, M.Z., Selim, M.R., Rashid, M.M., Rahman, M.S.: Bangla speech emotion recognition and cross-lingual study using deep CNN and BLSTM networks. IEEE Access **10**, 564–578 (2022). https://doi.org/10.1109/access.2021.3136251
22. Sultana, S., Rahman, M.S., Selim, M.R., Iqbal, M.Z.: SUST Bangla emotional speech corpus (SUBESCO): an audio-only emotional speech corpus for Bangla. PLoS ONE **16**(4), e0250173 (2021). https://doi.org/10.1371/journal.pone.0250173
23. Vaswani, A., et al.: Attention is all you need. In: Guyon, I., et al. (eds.) Advances in Neural Information Processing Systems (NeurIPS), vol. 30. Curran Associates, Inc. (2017). https://proceedings.neurips.cc/paper/2017/hash/3f5ee243547dee91fbd053c1c4a845aa-Abstract.html

Enhancing Functional Language Processing: A Structured and Efficient Interpretation Approach

Mohan Manoj Kumar Bonthu[✉]

New England College, Henniker, NH, USA
`mohanmanojbonthu123@gmail.com`

Abstract. This paper introduces an optimized approach to processing functional programming languages by eliminating unnecessary computational overhead through structured interpretation. By utilizing a stronglytyped programming environment, the need for complex data structures, specialized type systems, or universal categorization methods is eliminated, resulting in a streamlined and efficient execution model. The proposed framework leverages structured encoding techniques and higherorder function representations to construct efficient evaluators, compilers, and transformation methods for typed programming languages. This approach also accommodates staged execution, enabling faster processing while preserving strict type safety. The methodology demonstrates how the construction of embedded programming languages can be simplified while simultaneously enhancing efficiency and adaptability. This method offers a highly scalable solution for structured programming without compromising expressiveness.

Keywords: Functional programming · Typed languages · Structured interpretation · Optimized execution · Higher-order functions

1 Introduction

In domains where symbolic, numeric, and high-efficiency computing intersect, a persistent challenge exists in striking a balance between low-level optimization and high-level abstraction. This is particularly evident even in fundamental computational tasks such as linear algebra. Numerous variables often influence the implementation of widely used methods like Gaussian Elimination (GE), which serves as the central illustration throughout this study. These variations may include the choice of matrix storage format, the necessity of deriving auxiliary results such as rank or determinant, or the strategy for pivot selection.

The evolving nature of contemporary hardware further complicates matters, frequently demanding manual tuning that cannot be handled by compilers due to the requirement for application-specific insights. A prior investigation [3] analyzing industrial-grade implementations of GE in Maple uncovered 35 distinct versions of the algorithm reflecting six orthogonal factors, in addition to 45 variations of closely associated procedures. While handcrafted code tuned for specific requirements is one approach, this

H. Kannan et al. (Eds.): AIKP 2025, CCIS 2804, pp. 212–222, 2026.
https://doi.org/10.1007/978-3-032-14706-6_17

often leads to code duplication and maintenance challenges. Alternatively, one may opt for an all-encompassing, abstract version [14], but such abstraction comes at the expense of performance, especially in computationally intensive environments [3].

A more attractive paradigm emerges from generative programming [7, 23, 28, 32] which supports the automated creation of tailored code by leveraging high-level specifications [15, 35]. However, generative approaches are not without complications. For instance, string-based code generators frequently lack structural guarantees, making debugging difficult when output fails to compile. Other challenges include variable hygiene [19] and ensuring the type safety of emitted code. While techniques like Lisp macros, hygienic macros in Scheme, camlp4 in OCaml [27], C++ template metaprogramming, and Template Haskell [8] mitigate some of these issues, MetaOCaml [2, 21] remains one of the few environments that comprehensively ensures type soundness during code synthesis [29, 31].

Nevertheless, deeper concerns persist. Questions arise about the performance of generated output: does it require further optimization passes such as constant folding, elimination of dead code, or common subexpression identification? Can the code generator remain readable, extensible, and maintainable while encoding domain-specific insights—such as avoiding full pivoting or floating-point division when dealing with integer matrices over Q.

MetaOCaml adopts a purely generative stance: generated constructs are treated opaquely and are not subjected to introspection or further transformations (intensional analysis). This model provides stronger theoretical guarantees [30] and avoids the semantic pitfalls encountered when manipulating code representations directly [29]. Nonetheless, integrating optimization logic or formal verification tools directly into the code generation pipeline—as proposed in telescoping languages or auto-tuning frameworks [4, 16, 26, 33]—remains an ambitious but currently impractical direction due to complexity and reliability concerns.

Consequently, effective use of MetaOCaml requires precision in the generator itself, as illustrated in [29]. Tackling more advanced constructs such as nested loops, conditionals, and dynamically scoped variable bindings necessitates sophisticated techniques like abstract interpretation [18]. Additionally, issues such as managing symbolic names, clarity in continuation-passing style (CPS) constructs, and modularity in code generators pose significant design challenges. CPS, although powerful, often sacrifices code clarity, making it less appealing in practice despite its utility in managing name generation and scope.

The current study showcases developments addressing these challenges using GE as a reference point. The contributions are as follows:

- Enhancement of a let-insertion and memoization monad from [11, 18] to support the generation of conditionals and iterative constructs, recognizing let-insertion itself as a form of control effect.
- Design and integration of a—doM—-style syntax, inspired by Haskell's—do— notation, to enhance the clarity and readability of monadic generator code.
- Application of functors, including higher-order variants, to encapsulate algorithmic variations as modular aspects, enabling composability even when aspects involve state or require presence in multiple generator paths.

– Utilization of type sharing constraints in functor signatures to encode domainspecific rules and ensure semantic correctness of the generated output.

The remainder of this manuscript is structured as follows: Section 3 introduces the MetaOCaml framework for code generation, highlighting the significance of name scoping and CPS techniques. It also presents the monadic structure and the complications in producing control-flow constructs. Section 3 details the use of OCaml's parametric modules to isolate individual algorithmic features, thereby enabling independent customization. Related efforts are summarized in Sect. 4. The paper concludes with future directions and a discussion of implications. Representative code excerpts can be found in the appendices, with complete sources accessible at [5].

2   Construction of Binding Constructs, Continuation Passing Transformation, and Monadic Encapsulation

The synthesis of programmatic constructs is achieved via fundamental generators augmented with composition combinators. MetaOCaml, exemplifying a multiphase metaprogramming language [29], offers all necessary mechanisms for this task: the ability to formulate code values, combine them, and eventually execute the synthesized programs. Figure presents the most elementary generator,—one—, along with other more intricate code constructors.

MetaOCaml utilizes quoting via .<...>. for constructing future-stage computations, while anti-quoting through .~ allows for immediate evaluation within those staged contexts. For instance, in the simplest_code example, the generator function gen is evaluated, involving applications of plus, all of which operate on quoted expressions such as .<x>. and .<y>..

These code values are handled opaquely at generation time. The function—gen— yields a code fragment, which is seamlessly spliced into the surrounding quotation. Since MetaOCaml allows the introspection of code values, one can observe the fully expanded result, which lacks any visible trace of intermediate helper functions such as—gen—or—plus—, demonstrating full inlining and staging evaluation.

An optimization using let-binding during generation time allows pre- computation of repeated expressions. However, to realize let-bindings in the generated output code, a distinct strategy is required. The conventional—letgen—pattern, used like

—let ce = letgen (plus y one) in plus ce (plus x ce)—aims to emit output resembling— .¡let t = y + 1 in t + (x + t)¿.—. Yet, since—letgen—must synthesize a complete expression, not merely a fragment awaiting its continuation (the body), this form becomes infeasible directly.

```
1        let one = .<1>. and plus x y = .<.~x + .~y>.
2        let simplest_code = let gen x y = plus x (plus y one) in 3      .<fun x y -> .~(gen
.<x>. .<y>.)>.
4 \evalresult{.<fun x_1 -> fun y_2 -> (x_1 + (y_2 + 1))>.}
5

6        let simplest_param_code plus one = let gen x y = plus x ( plus y one) in
7        .<fun x y -> .~(gen .<x>. .<y>.)>.
8

9        let param_code1 plus one =
10       let gen x y = plus (plus y one) (plus x (plus y one))
              in
11       .<fun x y -> .~(gen .<x>. .<y>.)>.
12

13       let param_code1' plus one =
14       let gen x y = let ce = (plus y one) in plus ce (plus x ce) in
15       .<fun x y -> .~(gen .<x>. .<y>.)>.
16       param_code1' plus one
17       \evalresult{.<fun x_1 -> fun y_2 -> ((y_2 + 1) + (x_1 + ( y_2 + 1)))>.}
```

Listing 1.1: Illustration of code generation through combinators. The $\Longrightarrow$ symbol denotes evaluation output

This constraint is overcome by adopting a continuation-passing style (CPS), as first recognized in partial evaluation contexts [1] and later employed for staged meta-programming [11, 18]. The generator param code2 plus one now produces the desired inlined let-code at the output stage.

```
1  let letgen exp k = .<let t = .~exp in .~(k .<t>.)>.
2  let param_code2 plus one =
3  let gen x y k = letgen (plus y one) (fun ce -> k (plus ce (plus x ce)))
4  and k0 x = x
5  in .<fun x y -> .~(gen .<x>. .<y>. k0)>.
6  param_code2 plus one
```

Listing 1.2: Continuation-based code generation using letgen.

When comparing generation-time let-binding:
—let ce = (plus y one) in plus ce (plus x ce)—to the CPS-based let-binding within the generated output:
—letgen (plus y one) (fun ce -¿ k (plus ce (plus x ce)))—
The structural divergence between direct and continuation-passing styles becomes evident.

In the direct style, the expression—init—returns a value, while in CPS,—init—is restructured to take a continuation as an argument, invoking it once evaluation completes. Although minor in simple examples, the nesting overhead and continuation threading in

CPS scale unfavorably in larger constructs, deterring manual adoption of CPS, especially by numerical or non-functional programmers.

To mitigate CPS verbosity, Haskell's—do—notation [25] offers a convenient syntax for expressing monadic computations in a linear and imperative-like manner. The CPS transformation aligns naturally with monadic encapsulation [22], and this monadic style not only structures side-effects such as state and control but also permits composability with further computational layers—such as nondeterminism, exceptions, or logging [20].

A monad [22] represents a type of computation that yields a result and may encapsulate auxiliary behavior or side effects. A valid monad supports two essential operations:—return—to lift a pure value and—bind—to sequence computations. These operators must obey associativity and identity laws, ensuring compositional semantics.

```
1   type ('v,'s,'w) monad = 's -> ('s -> 'v -> 'w) -> 'w
2   let ret (a :'v) : ('v,'s,'w) monad = fun s k -> k s a
3   let bind a f = fun s k -> a s (fun s' b -> f b s' k)
4   let fetch s k = k s s
5   and store v s k = k (v::s) ()
6
7   let k0 s v = v
8   let runM m = m [] k0
9
10  let l1 f = fun x -> doM { t <-- x; f t }
11  let l2 f = fun x y -> doM { tx <-- x; ty <-- y; f tx ty }
12
13  let retN a = fun s k -> .<let t = .~a in .~(k s .<t>.)>.
14
15      let ifL test th el = ret .< if .~test then .~th else .~el
              >.
16      let ifM test th el = fun s k ->
17      k s .< if .~(test s k0) then .~(th s k0) else .~(el s k0) >.
```

Listing 1.3: Definition and implementation of the abstract monad

This monad models two primary side effects: global state manipulation and control alterations. The former is realized via a polymorphic list (emulating an extensible union), while the latter reflects deviations from normal control flow—such as early returns or code injections—within staged code.

Among the monadic constructs,—retN a—introduces let-binding into the output code. Unlike conventional monadic values, its behavior resembles that of control abstractions (e.g., abort), as it does not directly yield control to its continuation.

To evaluate a monadic expression and obtain the resulting code artifact, one invokes runM, which supplies an empty initial state and a trivial identity continuation. Revisiting the previous param_code2 generator, its monadic version param_code3 integrates naturally within this structure.

While superficially similar to the CPS-based representation, the introduction of a syntactic abstraction through the—doM—macro [5], facilitated by camlp4, enhances readability and masks the continuation threading.

Additional constructs, such as branching via—ifL—, further demonstrate monadic encapsulation of control. However,—ifL—operates on pre-computed code fragments. For monadic values, a lifted variant like—ifM—is required, ensuring proper sequencing of effects—particularly relevant when let-insertions must occur after conditional guards, as in bounds-checking scenarios. For instance, using—ifM'—before verifying an array index can cause undefined behavior, whereas—ifM—preserves safety by delaying access until after condition evaluation.

This design exemplifies how staged code generation intrinsically involves effect sequencing, and reinforces the necessity of tailored control structures—such as monadic conditionals, case splits, and loop constructs—for reliable code synthesis in multi-stage programming.

3 Modularity Through Aspects and Functors

Although monadic constructs suffice for representing fine-grained program synthesis, broader structural decomposition necessitates higher-level abstraction facilities. Any such modularization strategy is permissible, provided it remains isolated from the synthesized target program.

Despite the evolution of terminology within the Object-Oriented Design discipline, the foundational tenets of modular construction, articulated initially by Parnas [24] and Dijkstra [9], continue to underscore the importance of encapsulation and the demarcation of functionality. In the context of matrix decomposition via Gaussian Elimination (GE), identifying implementation variances and isolating responsibilities becomes essential for designing reusable and adaptable code generators. A comprehensive analysis by [3] outlines the principal dimensions along which such variability occurs:

1. **Algebraic Set**: The underlying numeric type of matrix elements varies widely— ranging from common number systems like Z, Q, Zp, and floatingpoint representations, to more general constructions like polynomial rings over fields. Out of approximately 85 examined implementations, 20 unique algebraic domains were cataloged.
2. **Storage Model**: Implementations differ in how matrices are stored whether via nested arrays, flat vectors, associative maps, or compressed sparse formats—and also in the indexing convention adopted (e.g., zero-based vs one-based). Some schemes offer optimizations tailored for fast-row interchanges.
3. **Return Artifacts**: Outputs range from simply the transformed matrix to combinations including rank, determinant, and permutation matrices.

    Systems like Maple's LinearAlgebra:-LUDecomposition expose a power set of return values, yielding $2^6 + 2^5 + 2^2 = 100$ configurations.
4. **Exact Arithmetic**: Whether or not the elimination procedure allows division without remainder affects both correctness and domain applicability.
5. **Pivot Strategy**: Selection strategies may include no pivoting, partial pivoting along columns, or full pivoting schemes.
6. **Selective Elimination**: Whether the transformation involves the complete matrix or only a subset of its columns. The current implementation omits this variant.

Beyond these parameters, two recurring properties exhibit cross-cutting influence across other configuration choices:

1. **Magnitude Heuristics**: In cases where a metric of size is definable over elements, it may guide pivot selection to promote numerical or algebraic stability.
2. **Canonical Forms and Equality**: Certain arithmetic domains require normalization of operations and may necessitate specialized mechanisms to detect structural zero.

These features are distinguished due to their non-localized impact—such as when pivoting logic is conditional on the availability of a size function in the element domain.

A minimal generalization strategy involves abstracting over the element domain. The algebraic system must support operations like additive identity and inverse, multiplicative identity, multiplication, subtraction (unary and binary), and exact division. In addition, optional normalization and comparison metrics may be included. These operations are grouped within OCaml *module* specifications, enabling extensibility and polymorphism through parameterized structures known as *functors*. The domain interface, termed—DOMAIN—, formalizes this contract.

Values are typically lifted twice: initially from base values—v—to their code representations—'a vc—, and then to monadic computations—('a vc, 's, 'w) monad—. For instance, the integer implementation—IntegerDomain—adheres to the—DOMAIN—interface, allowing the compiler to statically verify completeness and correctness—thus ensuring issues such as missing functions or mismatched types are caught at compile-time. Domains lacking general division operations can still conform by providing appropriately restricted definitions.

Similarly, matrix representations are abstracted as containers, each parameterized over a specific domain module. The—CONTAINER2D—interface prescribes functions for dimension retrieval (—dim1—, —dim2—), cell access (—get—, —set—), structural duplication (—copy—), and row/column manipulations. These standard interfaces enable optimization opportunities without altering user-visible behavior.

While parameterizing over matrix storage is relatively simple, specifying the output form introduces greater complexity. Rather than employing large sum types with multiple constructors—an approach criticized in [3]—this system introduces a module interface with an abstract result type—res—. Each instantiation defines—res— differently, such as a triplet—contr * Det.outdet * int—capturing the U-factor, determinant, and matrix rank.

To support the flexible tracking of intermediate states—like the determinant, rank, or permutation history—auxiliary variables may need to be declared, updated, and converted into final results. These tracking elements are incorporated into the broader monadic state. The tracking of the determinant, in particular, necessitates mechanisms for initialization (—decl—), incremental updates based on permutations or pivots, and transformation into the final result format—outdet—. When determinant tracking is unnecessary, a trivial instantiation with—outdet = unit—emits no associated code. In contrast, for integral matrices, some form of monitoring is indispensable, even if unused in the final output.

State sharing across independent functors—such as for determinant or rank—is handled through open records and polymorphic variants, providing a clean and functional composition mechanism. These components can interact without explicit coupling, thereby preserving modularity.

The central code-generation functor, —Gen—, accepts modules for the domain, matrix container, pivoting policy (e.g., full, partial, or none), update strategy (fractionless or unrestricted division), and result specification. Some parameters—like—PIVOT—are functors themselves, accepting domain and container modules as input. Constraints ensure all components share a consistent domain type, thereby avoiding incompatibilities. While modules are stateless by design, state-dependent behaviors (e.g., determinant updates) are mediated through the monadic state to maintain purity and compositionality.

In addition to type consistency constraints, semantic constraints are enforced via module interfaces. For example, an update strategy that assumes unrestricted division is only permissible when the domain genuinely supports it. Attempting to apply such a strategy to the integer domain results in a compilation error, thus preventing incorrect usage early in the generator's lifecycle.

A concrete instantiation of—Gen—such as—GenFA1.gen—produces code that may be inspected or executed directly. When all features (e.g., full pivoting, determinant tracking, and rank monitoring) are enabled, the output is a triple—int array * int * int—. Conversely, when these features are omitted, the generated code contains no extraneous artifacts—no redundant variables or unnecessary conditionals—demonstrating the efficacy of modular aspect composition. Additional code samples and benchmarking data are available at [5], offering further insight into performance and configurability.

4 Related and Future Work

The monadic structure utilized throughout this study aligns conceptually with those introduced in [11, 18], though with significant functional distinctions. While prior efforts have incorporated only—retN—and recursive constructs to facilitate compile-time repetition, the current approach omits recursive monadic fixpoints, emphasizing instead monadic constructs to dynamically produce conditional statements and iterative logic.

Frameworks like—Blitz++—[32] and the broader use of C++ template metaprogramming similarly focus on minimizing abstraction penalties. By leveraging traits and conceptual programming, certain problem-specific logic can be embedded directly. Nonetheless, such performance gains are contingent upon complete method inlining by the compiler—an assurance that remains non-trivial. Moreover, static error feedback (such as type mismatches or concept misapplication) is typically only surfaced during compilation of the resulting code, complicating the process of tracing those issues back to their origin within the code generator.

The ATLAS project [35] also contributes meaningfully to this domain, albeit with a more rudimentary form of code composition. As noted by its developers, the increasing complexity of generator logic tends to rise with the system's adaptability, potentially deterring external participation. The methodology presented here addresses that challenge by constructing flexible, modular code synthesis mechanisms that facilitate external contributions.

Similarly, the SPIRAL project [26] represents a comprehensive initiative in this space, yet it hinges heavily on semantic code examination using transformation rules that, while intuitively valid, lack formal proof of completeness or confluence. Both ATLAS and SPIRAL attain hardware-specific performance enhancements through heuristic-based exploration—capabilities that remain beyond the scope of this work.

The polymorphic formulation of Gaussian Elimination presented herein draws inspiration from the highly abstracted patterns established in Axiom [14] and Aldor [34]. Although Aldor's compiler frequently eliminates unnecessary abstraction overhead, it does so without definitive guarantees—unlike the predictable abstraction handling demonstrated by the present methodology.

Earlier explorations such as [13] investigated the tailored optimization of mathematical computations. While these techniques reduce runtime cost by inlining components expressed as higher-order constructs, they fall short of enabling dynamic type refinement or efficiently managing stateful interactions among modular components.

Further, [12] documented preliminary ventures in both manual and automated multistage computation using an annotated Scheme-based subset—lacking both static types and imperative paradigms. The efficiency of the produced programs in that context depended on a subsequent optimization phase.

Current research endeavors are focusing on encapsulating staging logic within a minimal number of parameterized modules (functors), aiming to isolate the complexity of code generation. This could allow the core generator (represented by—Gen—) to remain free of annotations, supporting seamless interoperability between traditional OCaml environments and multi-stage compilation contexts. The annotation-free version may also serve as a reference point for performance evaluations and regression validation. Automating the generation of extensions from such modular OCaml structures presents a compelling avenue for future inquiry.

To the best of the authors' knowledge, the fusion of functor-based modularization and staged metaprogramming has not been previously explored in code generation frameworks.

Future research includes examining the interplay between delimited control structures and generator constructs such as—ifM—. Enhancing syntactic expressiveness with constructs like—whileM—and—ifM—could produce syntax even closer to conventional direct-style code, potentially improving readability. Expanding the current monadic structure into a monad transformer is another promising direction.

Additional dimensions remain to be addressed: variations in input data formats (e.g., augmented matrices), diagnostic support for illegal operations (such as computing the determinant of a non-square matrix), cache and memory layout optimizations, iteration unrolling strategies [6], notifications for undecidable conditions (e.g., probabilistically non-zero values), among others. More complex members within the LU decomposition family encapsulate even broader design considerations.

5 Conclusion

This study presented a method for generating numerically intensive code that is richly parameterized across multiple abstraction dimensions yet introduces no additional runtime overhead. By integrating immutable module-based abstractions with a monadic framework supporting compositional state, the proposed architecture enables the seamless combination of functional concerns without introducing risks related to data sharing or unintended references. The primary limitations on composability arise from type system rules and explicitly defined semantic boundaries, such as those governing algebraic structures where division is not universally applicable (e.g., within ring theory).

An intriguing comparison can be drawn to aspect-oriented programming frameworks such as AspectJ [17], where aspect logic is generally loosely typed and integrated into existing codebases retrospectively. In contrast, the present methodology constructs functionality from foundational elements, embedding aspectual logic intrinsically during code synthesis. This positions the current approach closer to statically verified aspect integration, in contrast with the dynamic aspect weaving more commonly found in prior literature.

References

1. Bondorf, A.: Improving binding times without explicit CPS-conversion. In: 1992 ACM Conference on Lisp and Functional Programming, pp. 1–10. San Francisco, California (1992)
2. Pfenning, F., Smaragdakis, Y. (eds.): GPCE 2003. LNCS, vol. 2830. Springer, Heidelberg (2003). https://doi.org/10.1007/b13639
3. Carette, J.: Gaussian Elimination: a case study in efficient genericity with MetaOCaml (2005), submitted
4. Chen, Z., Dongarra, J., Luszczek, P., Rothe, K.: Lapack for clusters project: An example of self adapting numerical software. Hawaii International Conference on System Sciences HICSS-37 (2004). http://www.netlib.org/utk/people/JackDongarra/PAPERS/lfc-hicss.pdf
5. Source code. http://www.cas.mcmaster.ca/~carette/metamonads/
6. Cohen, A., Donadio, S., Garzara'n, M.J., Herrmann, C., Padua, D.: In search for a program generator to implement generic transformations for high-performance computing. http://polaris.cs.uiuc.edu/~garzaran/doc/ocaml04.pdf, metaOCaml Workshop, October 2004
7. Czarnecki, K., Eisenecker, U.W.: Generative programming: methods, tools, and applications. ACM Press/Addison-Wesley Publishing Co. (2000)
8. Czarnecki, K., O'Donnell, J.T., Striegnitz, J., Taha, W.: DSL implementation in MetaOCaml, Template Haskell, and C++. In: Lengauer, C., Batory, D.S., Consel, C., Odersky, M. (eds.) Domain-Specific Program Generation. Lecture Notes in Computer Science, vol. 3016, pp. 51–72. Springer (2003)
9. Dijkstra, E.W.: On the role of scientific thought. http://www.cs.utexas.edu/users/EWD/ewd04xx/EWD447.PDF, published as [10]
10. Dijkstra, E.W.: On the role of scientific thought. In: Selected Writings on Computing: A Personal Perspective, pp. 60–66. Springer-Verlag (1982)
11. Eckhardt, J.L., Kaiabachev, R., Swadi, K.N., Taha, W., Kiselyov, O.: Practical aspects of multi-stage programming (Feb 2004). http://www.cs.rice.edu/~taha/publications/preprints/2004-02-16.pdf, rice University Techical Report TR05-451, http://www.cs.rice.edu/~taha/publications/preprints/2004-02-16.pdf
12. Glu¨ck, R., Jørgensen, J.: An automatic program generator for multi-level specialization. Lisp Symbolic Comput. **10**(2), 113–158 (1997)
13. Glu¨ck, R., Nakashige, R., Zo¨chling, R.: Binding-time analysis applied to mathematical algorithms. In: System Modelling and Optimization (1995). http://repository.readscheme.org/ftp/papers/topps/D-244.pdf
14. Jenks, R.D., Sutor, R.S.: AXIOM: The Scientific Computation System. Springer Verlag (1992)
15. John, V.W., Reynders, I., Cummings, J.C.: The POOMA framework. Comput. Phys **12**(5), 453–459 (1998). https://doi.org/10.1063/1.168723
16. Kennedy, K., et al.: Telescoping languages: A strategy for automatic generation of scientific problem-solving systems from annotated libraries. J. Parallel Distrib. Comput. **61**(12), 1803–1826 (2001)

17. Kiczales, G., et al.: Aspect-oriented programming. In: Ak¸sit, M., Matsuoka, S. (eds.) Proceedings European Conference on Object-Oriented Programming, vol. 1241, pp. 220–242. Springer-Verlag, Berlin, Heidelberg, and New York (1997). http://citeseer.csail.mit.edu/kiczales97aspectoriented.html
18. Kiselyov, O., Swadi, K.N., Taha, W.: A methodology for generating verified combinatorial circuits. In: EMSOFT '04: Proceedings of the fourth ACM international conference on Embedded software. pp. 249–258. ACM Press, New York, NY, USA (2004). http://doi.acm.org/10.1145/1017753.1017794
19. Kohlbecker, E.E., Friedman, D.P., Felleisen, M., Duba, B.F.: Hygienic macro expansion. In: LISP and Functional Programming, pp. 151–161 (1986)
20. Liang, S., Hudak, P., Jones, M.: Monad transformers and modular interpreters. In: POPL '95: Conference Record of the Annual ACM Symposium on Principles of Programming Languages, pp. 333–343. ACM Press, New York (1995)
21. MetaOCaml. http://www.metaocaml.org
22. Moggi, E.: Notions of computation and monads. Information and Computation **93**(1), 55–92 (1991). http://www.disi.unige.it/person/MoggiE/ftp/ic91.ps.gz
23. Musser, D.R., Stepanov, A.A.: Algorithm-oriented generic libraries. Software Pract. Exper. **24**(7), 623–642 (1994). http://citeseer.lcs.mit.edu/musser94algorithmoriented.html
24. Parnas, D.L.: On the criteria to be used in decomposing systems into modules. Commun. ACM **15**(12), 1053–1058 (1972)
25. Peyton Jones, S., et al.: The revised haskell 98 report. Cambridge University Press (2003). http://titles.cambridge.org/catalogue.asp?isbn=0521826144, also on http://haskell.org/
26. Pu¨schel, M., et al.: SPIRAL: Code generation for DSP transforms. In: Proceedings of the IEEE, special issue on "Program Generation, Optimization, and Adaptation" **93**(2) (2005)
27. de Rauglaudre, D.: Camlp4 reference manual (2002). http://caml.inria.fr/camlp4/ manual/
28. Siek, J., Lee, L.Q., Lumsdaine, A.: The boost graph library: user guide and reference manual. Addison-Wesley (2002)
29. Taha, W.: Multi-Stage Programming: its theory and applications. Ph.D. thesis, Oregon Graduate Institute of Science and Technology (1999)
30. Taha, W.: A sound reduction semantics for untyped CBN multi-stage computation. Or, the theory of MetaML is non-trival. In: PEPM. pp. 34–43 (2000)
31. Taha, W., Sheard, T.: Multi-stage programming with explicit annotations. In: Proceedings of the Symposium on Partial Evaluation and Semantic-Based Program Manipulation (PEPM), pp. 203–217. ACM Press, Amsterdam (1997)
32. Veldhuizen, T.L.: Arrays in Blitz++. In: Proceedings of the 2nd International Scientific Computing in Object-Oriented Parallel Environments (ISCOPE'98). Lecture Notes in Computer Science, Springer-Verlag (1998)
33. Veldhuizen, T.L.: Active Libraries and Universal Languages. Ph.D. thesis, Indiana University Computer Science (2004). http://osl.iu.edu/~tveldhui/papers/2004/dissertation.pdf
34. Watt, S.M.: Aldor. In: Grabmeier, J., Kaltofen, E., Weispfennig, V. (eds.) Computer Algebra Handbook: Foundations, Applications, Systems. Springer Verlag (2003)
35. Whaley, R.C., Petitet, A., Dongarra, J.J.: Automated empirical optimization of software and the ATLAS project. Parallel Comput. **27**(1–2), 3–35 (2001)

Graph-Augmented Transformer for Enhanced Structure-Aware Arabic Abstractive Summarization

Wadeea R. Naji[1,3]([✉]), Suresha[1], Fahd A. Ghanem[1], Mohammed A. S. Al-Mohamadi[2], Ahmed R. A. Shamsan[2], and Channabasava Chola[1]

[1] Department of Studies in Computer Science, University of Mysore, Mysuru 570006, India
wadeearashad@gmail.com
[2] Department of Studies in Computer Science, Kuvempu University, Shimoga 577451, India
[3] Department of Computer Science and Information Technology, Ibb University, Ibb, Yemen

Abstract. Arabic abstractive summarization poses a set of unique challenges as opposed to other languages; Arabic has rich morphology and complex syntax accompanied with scarce high quality annotated resources. Sequential transformer models tend to neglect long range syntactic and discourse relations, hurting overall coherence and coherence with facts. In this paper we propose a novel GA-Transformer: Graph-Augmented Transformer, which explicitly incorporates structural information into summarization. The model creates a graph using dependency parses and coreference chains, presents it utilizing Graph Neural Network (GNN), and effectively integrates structural explicit representations with transformer-based serial encoders through cross-modal attention. This hybrid structure allows the model to utilize local word dependencies as well as global discourse relations when generating summaries. Experiments on AlArabiyaNews and ArXivSumm datasets demonstrate our method achieves the best ROUGE, BLEU, BERTScore results, along with substantial improvement of human-evaluated fluency, coherence and factual accuracy. Ablation studies validate the complementary properties of dependency and coreference graphs in minimizing redundancy, improving coherence and maintaining entity transitions. These results attest to the advantage of integrating explicit linguistic properties in the Transformer-based models for Arabic abstractive summarization.

Keywords: Arabic abstractive summarization · Graph-Augmented Transformer · Graph Neural Networks · Dependency parsing · Coreference resolution · Structure-aware NLP · Transformer-GNN fusion

1 Introduction

With the fast spread of Arabic digital content in news, legal and scientific domains have led to a desperate necessity for summarization systems that are able to summarize large pieces of text into coherent and factually correct summaries [1, 2]. Extractive summarization extracts the sentences as they appear in the original documents, but abstractive summary generates new sentences and can provide a better fluency, paraphrasing, fusion of content [3–5].

H. Kannan et al. (Eds.): AIKP 2025, CCIS 2804, pp. 223–236, 2026.
https://doi.org/10.1007/978-3-032-14706-6_18

Despite substantial progress in English summarization, Arabic remains underexplored due to its rich morphology, complex syntactic structures, and limited availability of high-quality annotated data [6, 7]. Popular Transformer-based models such as BERT [8], T5 [9], and Arabic variants like AraT5 [10] and MARBERT [11] process text as linear sequences. This sequential processing may overlook critical syntactic and discourse relationships. Recent evidence shows that incorporating explicit structural features, such as dependency trees and coreference chains, can improve coherence and factual accuracy, especially in morphologically rich, low-resource languages [12, 13]. Graph-based representations naturally encode such structures, enabling reasoning over long-range dependencies. However, most graph-enhanced models are designed for English, with minimal exploration in Arabic.

In this work, we present the Graph-Augmented Transformer (GA-Transformer), a hybrid architecture that integrates syntactic and discourse-level graph representations with Transformer self-attention. The model constructs a heterogeneous document graph from dependency parses and coreference links, encodes it using a Graph Neural Network (GNN), and fuses the structural features with sequential Transformer outputs through cross-modal attention. This design enables the model to jointly leverage local grammatical dependencies and global discourse relationships during summary generation. This paper is structured as follows: Sect. 2 presents related work on Arabic text summarization. Section 3 describes in detail the proposed methodology. Section 4 presents the results and discussion. Finally, Sect. 5 concludes the study with suggestions for future work.

2 Related Work

Transformers have revolutionized abstractive summarization by enabling large-scale pre-training and flexible sequence-to-sequence generation. Models such as BERT [8], T5 [9], and multilingual variants like mBART [14] and mT5 [15] achieve strong performance across languages by learning from massive multilingual corpora. In the Arabic context, specialized models such as AraT5 [10] and MARBERT [11] have been developed to address issues of diglossia, morphological complexity, and orthographic variation. While these architectures have improved Arabic text generation quality, they rely exclusively on sequential representations and often overlook syntactic and discourse-level relationships that are crucial for factual accuracy and coherence.

To address such limitations, recent work in summarization has explored the integration of explicit linguistic structures into neural models. The GNNs have been used to encode dependency trees in syntax [16, 17, 18], as well as coreference. chains [19], and discourse relations [12]. An example of this is that dependency-conscious architecture can improve is factual accuracy in the English summarization, whereas Wang et al. [21] proposed a heterogeneous graph encoder, which combines syntactic and semantic edges, produces significant one's advances on such benchmarks as CNN/DailyMail and XSum. Graph-based methods have been investigated in terms of Arabic NLP. sentiment analysis and extractive summarization. Alzahrani et al. [22] employed dependency graphs to enhance the performance of sentiment classification, and Alselwi. and Taşcı [23] used extractive summarization based on graphs with the help of PageRank and. word embeddings to reduce Arabic text redundancy. Nevertheless, these studies either concentrate on other NLP activities or include structural information in isolation elements as opposed to being in a single end-to-end abstractive structure. Lately hybrid Transformer-GNNs have started appearing. Onan and Alhumyani [24] introduced KETGS, that is a combination of entity and discourse graphs. A Transformer based extractive summarizer and Chen et al. [25] created DIGSum, which uses dynamic interaction graph representations to be able to capture dialogue. summarization structure. Along with these promising developments, there is a knowledge void: there is a gap in literature. and end abstractive summarization structures of Arabic which combine the two. dependency and coreference structures. The proposed GA-Transformer fills this. gap by incorporating syntactic as well as discourse-level graphs into a Transformer GNN architecture, where the model of local grammatical dependencies may be modeled. and global entity coherence.

3 Methodology

The suggested GA-Transformer model is an abstractive summarization of the Arabic language in structure framework integrating sequential modeling and making syntactic and explicit. discourse-level features. There are five components in the architecture: input processing and graph building, sequential encoding through a Transformer, structural a Transformer decoder to summary, encoding with a GNN, cross-modal fusion generation. Figure 1 shows the general flow of work.

3.1 Problem Formulation

Let $D = \{t_1, t_2, ..., t_n\}$ be the input document, where t_i is a token from the Arabic vocabulary $\mathcal{V}$. The goal is to generate a summary $S = \{s_1, s_2, ..., s_m\}$, such that S is abstractive, coherent, and factually consistent.

We formalize this as a sequence-to-sequence mapping enhanced by a heterogeneous document graph G = (V, E), where V is the set of nodes (tokens) and E representing syntactic dependency and coreference relations. This graph serves as a structural scaffold that complements the transformer's sequential encoding, enabling the model to incorporate both grammatical structure and discourse-level coherence.

3.2 Datasets

We test the GA-Transformer using two Arabic datasets:AlArabiyaNews: 50,000 news stories (average length 450 words) of which there is a match summaries of 50–70 words. The data will be separated into 80% training, 10% test splitting, 10 percentage validation.

- arXivSumm: 8,500 scientific abstracts in Arabic, translated to characterize them with.

    technical words and morphological compound. The data is split into 70% training, 15 percent validation and 15 percent testing subsets. The pre-processing is followed by tokenization with Farasa and syntactic and coreference. annotations on CAMeL Tools [26].

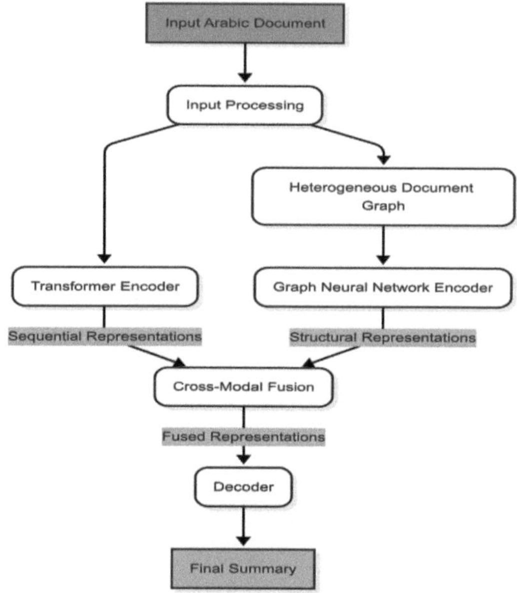

Fig. 1. Overview of the GA-Transformer architecture for Arabic abstractive summarization.

3.3 Graph Construction

The graph construction pipeline, shown in Fig. 2, transforms the input text into a structured graph representation. This step ensures that the model possesses explicit knowledge of grammatical structure and entity references before the summarization process begins.

1- **Named Entity Recognition (NER)** detects entities such as people, places, and organizations.
2- **Coreference resolution** links different mentions of the same entity (e.g., "the present" and "he").
3- **Dependency Parsing** identifies grammatical relationships between words (e.g., subject-verb-object links).

The output is a heterogeneous graph where:

- **Nodes** are tokens. Represented by initial embeddings

$$h_i^{(0)} = W_e t_i + W_p p_i$$

where W_e is the word embedding matrix, W_p is the positional embedding matrix, and p_i is the position of token t_i. The node set $V = \{v_1, ..., v_n\}$ corresponds to tokens with initial features $\mathbf{h}_i^{(0)}$.

- Edges capture either:

  - **Syntactic dependencies**: Direct edges (i, j, r) identified with relation r.

– **Coreference links**: Undirected edges that connect repeated mentions of the same entity.

Thus, $E = E_{\text{dep}} \cup E_{\text{coref}}$, forming a heterogeneous.graph that captures grammatical structure, and entity cohesion.

Fig. 2. Overview of the graph construction pipeline.

3.4 Graph Neural Network Encoder

After constructing the graph, an edge-type-conditioned Gated.Graph Neural Network (GGNN) [27] is used for encoding. The idea is to allow each token the ability to exchange contextual information with its syntactic, and coreferential neighbors. This helps enrich its representation with both local grammatical, and global discourse-level context. For each propagation step k:

$$m_i^{(k)} = \sum_{j \in \mathcal{N}(i)} W_{r_{ji}} h_j^{(k-1)}$$

here $\mathcal{N}(i)$ is the set of neighbors of node i. The term $W_{r_{ji}}$ is a relation-specific transformation matrix.

The node state is updated through a Gated Recurrent Unit (GRU) as follows:

$$h_i^{(k)} = \text{GRU}(m_i^{(k)}, h_i^{(k-1)})$$

After $K = 4$ propagation steps, the final graph-enhanced node representations are given by:

$$H_{\text{graph}} = [h_1^{(K)}, ..., h_n^{(K)}]$$

3.5 Transformer Encoder

In a parallel process, the input sequence is passed through a transformer encoder to learn semantic relationships.without relying on predefined structural links. This is important, because the sequential context captured by the transformer adds a broader semantic understanding.that complements the structural information learned by the graph encoder. The multi-head self-attention is calculated as:

$$\text{Attention}(Q, K, V) = \text{softmax}\left(\frac{QK^T}{\sqrt{d_k}}\right)V$$

where Q, K, and V denote the query, key, and value matrices.

Each attention head models the contextual dependencies among all tokens, capturing their semantic similarities. After twelve layers, the final sequential representations are obtained as:

$$H_{\text{seq}} = \text{TransformerEncoder}(D)$$

3.6 Cross-Modal Fusion

The cross-modal fusion layer,.shown in Fig. 3, combines the sequential features (H_{seq}) with the structural features (H_{graph}^T). In this layer, each token's semantic context.interacts with its structural counterpart, resulting in a richer joint representation.

Formally,

$$A_{\text{fuse}} = \text{softmax}\left(\frac{H_{\text{seq}} H_{\text{graph}}^T}{\sqrt{d}}\right) \qquad H_{\text{fused}} = A_{\text{fuse}} H_{\text{graph}}$$

The final encoder output is defined as:

$$\mathbf{H}_{\text{enc}} = \text{LayerNorm}(\mathbf{H}_{\text{seq}} + \mathbf{H}_{\text{fused}})$$

3.7 Decoder and Summary Generation

The decoder functions as an autoregressive Transformer that generates the summary of one token at a time. Each new token is predicted based on the previously generated tokens and the fused encoder representation. Formally, this process is expressed as:

$$s_t = \text{DecoderBlock}(s_{<t}, H_{\text{enc}})$$

The probability of generating token s_t is given by:

$$P(s_t|s_{<t}, D) = \text{softmax}(W_o s_t)$$

and the model is trained to maximize the objective

$$\mathcal{L} = \sum_{t=1}^{m} \log P(s_t|s_{<t}, D)$$

This allows the model to combine implicit sequential patterns learned by the transformer with explicit linguistic structure provided by the GNN.

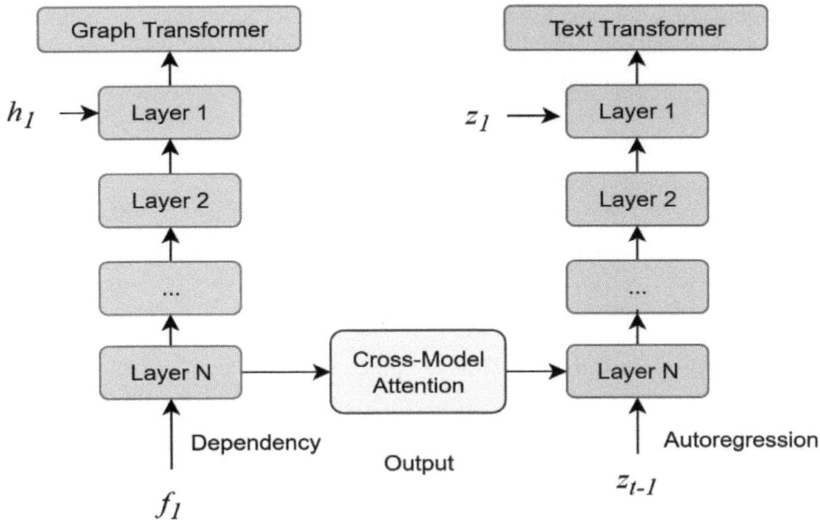

Fig. 3. Cross-modal fusion mechanism integrating structural and sequential representations.

3.8 Model Training and Inference

The model is trained using the AdamW optimizer [28] with a learning rate of 3×10^{-5}, linear warm-up over the first 10% of training steps, and weight decay.

During inference, beam search (beam width = 5) is used to generate candidate summaries.

The final summary S is obtained as:

$$S = \operatorname*{argmax}_{S} \prod_{t=1}^{m} P(s_t | s_{<t}, D; \mathrm{H}_{\mathrm{enc}})$$

4 Results

4.1 Comparative Performance Analysis

We first report the performance of the proposed GA-Transformer and the baseline models on standard automatic evaluation metrics, including ROUGE-1 (R-1), ROUGE-2 (R-2), ROUGE-L (R-L), BLEU-4, and BERTScore. These metrics collectively capture different aspects of summary quality: ROUGE evaluates lexical and semantic overlap with the reference summaries, BLEU measures phrase-level precision, and BERTScore estimates semantic similarity based on contextual embeddings.

Table 1 presents the results on the AlArabiyaNews and ArXivSumm test sets. The GA-Transformer achieves the highest scores across all metrics on both datasets. On AlArabiyaNews, GA-Transformer improves R-1 by **+4.2** points over AraT5-base, while on ArXivSumm the gain is even larger (**+5.3** points), reflecting the advantage of structural augmentation in handling information-dense text. Gains in R-2 and R-L indicate better coverage of key content, while BLEU-4 and BERTScore improvements suggest enhanced fluency and semantic fidelity. Figure 4 further illustrates these improvements, showing consistent advantages across metrics and domains.

Table 1. Automatic evaluation results for GA-Transformer and baseline models.

Model	R-1	R-2	R-L	BLEU-4	BERTScore
mT5-base	42.1	18.3	39.6	28.5	78.2
AraT5-base	43.7	19.6	41.2	30.1	79.8
MARBERT-Sum	44.3	20.1	41.8	31.0	80.4
GA-Transformer	**47.9**	**23.1**	**45.3**	**34.6**	**83.7**

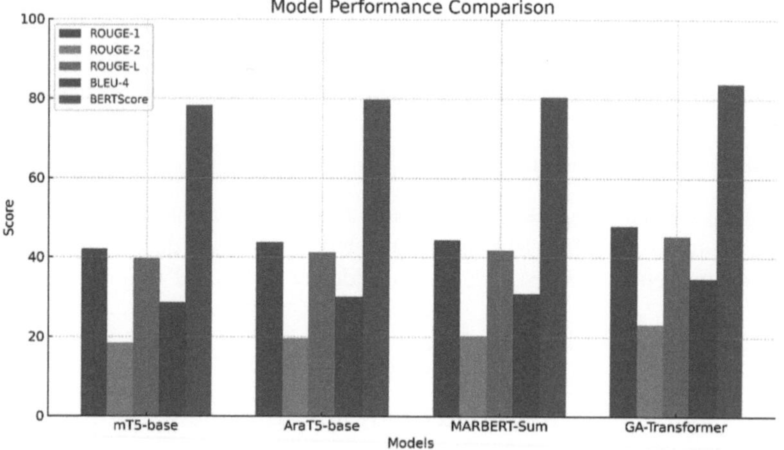

Fig. 4. Comparative performance of GA-Transformer and baseline models.

4.2 Human Evaluation

To complement automatic metrics, we conduct a human evaluation to assess the perceived quality of summaries. Three native Arabic speakers rate the outputs of each model on a 1–5 Likert scale for four criteria: fluency (grammatical correctness and readability), relevance (inclusion of important content), coherence (logical flow between sentences), and factual consistency (faithfulness to the source text). Each annotator assessed 100 randomly selected summaries from the AlArabiyaNews test set, and scores are averaged across annotators.

Table 2 presents the results. The GA-Transformer achieved the highest average ratings across all criteria, with particularly strong gains in factual consistency (**+0.8** points over AraT5-base), confirming that incorporating coreference and dependency structure improves accuracy and reduces hallucination. Improvements in coherence and fluency further demonstrate the benefits of cross-modal fusion between sequential and structural features (Fig. 5).

Table 2. Human evaluation scores for GA-Transformer and baselines.

Model	Fluency	Relevance	Coherence	Factual Consistency
mT5-base	3.8	3.6	3.5	3.2
AraT5-base	4.0	3.9	3.8	3.6
MARBERT-Sum	4.1	4.0	3.9	3.7
GA-Transformer	**4.6**	**4.5**	**4.5**	**4.4**

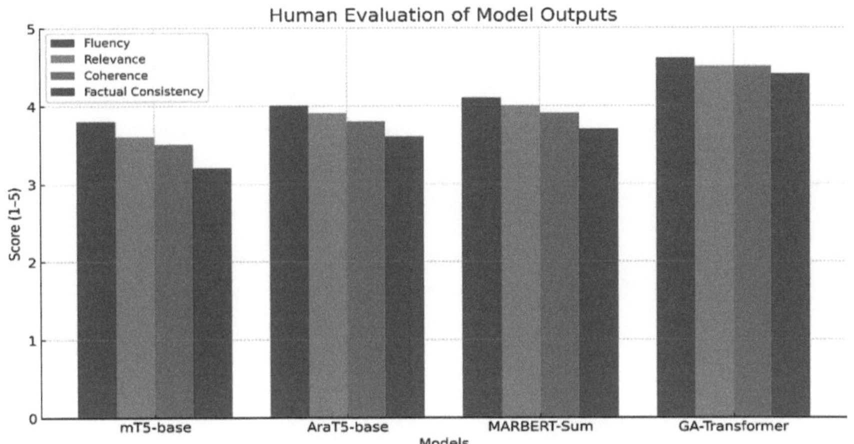

Fig. 5. Human evaluation results for proposed models.

4.3 Ablation Studies

We did an ablation experiment, in which the ablation or modification was gradually eliminated or modified. individual modules. In particular, we have compared the influence of eliminating (1) the dependency. graph, (2) the coreference graph and (3) cross-modal attention mechanism. This is done by quantifying how much the structural information and the fusion strategy play in. enhancing the quality of summarization. Training conditions are the same in all the models. for a fair comparison. Table 3 represents the automatic assessment of R-1, R-2, R-L, BLEU-4, and BERTScore of the full GA-Transformer and the ablated variants.

Table 3. Ablation study results for GA-Transformer components.

Model Variant	R-1	R-2	R-L	BLEU-4	BERTScore
Full GA-Transformer	47.9	23.1	45.3	34.6	83.7
–Coreference edges	46.2	22.3	43.7	33.4	80.7
–Dependency edges	45.8	22.1	43.3	33.1	80

(*continued*)

Table 3. (continued)

Model Variant	R-1	R-2	R-L	BLEU-4	BERTScore
– Graph encoder (seq-only)	44.5	21.5	42.1	32.1	77.8
–Cross-modal fusion	46.7	22.5	44.2	33.7	81.6

Either deleting the dependency or coreference graph leads to the outcome as illustrated in Fig. 6. a significant decline in performance, and R-2 and BERTScore decreases reveal. reduced capacity to get semantic relations and structural context. The largest When the cross-modal attention module is taken away, decline is observed as that indicates its importance. crucial in creating multiple graphs based and textual representations on enhancing summary quality.

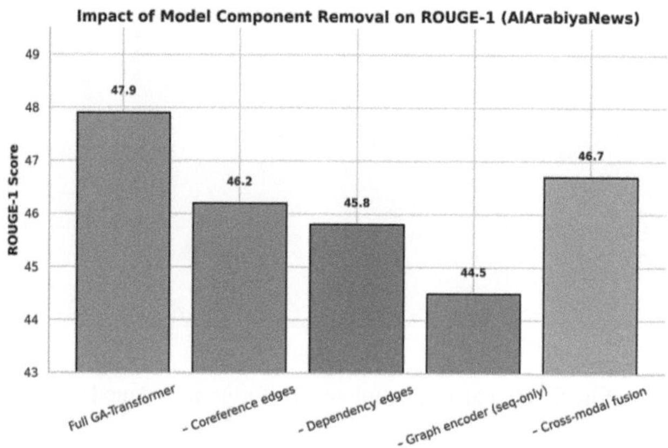

Fig. 6. Impact of model component removal on R-1 (AlArabiyaNews dataset).

Computational Performance

All experiments were run on NVIDIA A100 GPU with the same conditions. Only a moderate (~18%) rise in is presented in the proposed GA-Transformer construction and encoding time in the graph and GNN cost, and speed of inference remains nearly unchanged. These results attest to the fact that the model provides significant returns. in consistency and practical consistency appropriate in factual coherence and computational efficiency of massive Arabic summarization.

4.4 Qualitative Results and Case Study

To complement automatic metrics, we examined outputs from the AlArabiyaNews test set. The GA-Transformer consistently maintained entity consistency and long-range dependencies, yielding coherent summaries that preserved key events and factual details. These improvements stemmed from integrating dependency and coreference graphs for structural awareness. The main weaknesses were occasional omission of fine-grained details (e.g., numbers, dates) and rare reordering of events in complex narratives. Table 4 presents qualitative examples comparing AraT4-base and GA-Transformer outputs.

Table 4. Qualitative examples comparing AraT5-base and GA-Transformer summaries.

Source Text	Model	Generated Summary	Observation
"أعلنت الشركة عن إطلاق منتج جديد .وقد تم تطويره على مدى عامين من قبل فريق بحثي كبير." "The company announced a new product. It was developed over two years by a large research team."	AraT5-base	"أطلقت الشركة منتجًا جديدًا." "The company launched a new product."	Lacks cross-sentence integration; misses development details.
	GA-Transformer	"أطلقت الشركة منتجًا جديدًا طوّره فريق بحثي على مدى عامين." "...developed by a research team over two years."	**Coreference edges** resolve "it" and **dependency parsing** attaches time phrase correctly.
"زار الرئيس المدينة لافتتاح مشروع ضخم .وكان المشروع قد بدأ قبل خمس سنوات." "The president visited the city to inaugurate a major project. The project started five years ago."	AraT5-base	"زار الرئيس المدينة لافتتاح مشروع ضخم." "The president visited the city to inaugurate a major project."	Omits temporal detail; extractive only.
	GA-Transformer	"زار الرئيس المدينة لافتتاح مشروع ضخم بدأ قبل خمس سنوات." "...to inaugurate a major project that started five years ago."	**Dependency parsing** links temporal clauses to correct entity; **cross-modal fusion** preserves timeline.
"حصلت الجامعة على جائزة مرموقة في مجال البحث العلمي .وقد تم ترشيحها من قبل لجنة دولية مستقلة." "The university received a prestigious award in scientific research. It was nominated by an independent international committee."	AraT5-base	"حصلت الجامعة على جائزة مرموقة." "The university received a prestigious award."	Loses nominating entity detail.
	GA-Transformer	"حصلت الجامعة على جائزة مرموقة رشحتها لجنة دولية مستقلة." "...awarded by an independent international committee."	**Coreference resolution** integrates nominating entity; improves factual completeness.
"اكتشف الفريق طريقة جديدة لتحلية المياه .وتتميز هذه الطريقة بانخفاض التكلفة وسهولة التطبيق." "The team discovered a new method for desalinating water. This method is low-cost and easy to implement.'	AraT5-base	"لتحلية جديدة طريقة الفريق اكتشف المياه." "The team discovered a new method for desalinating water."	Omits unique benefits; extractive summary.
	GA-Transformer	"اكتشف الفريق طريقة جديدة لتحلية المياه منخفضة التكلفة وسهلة التطبيق." "...a low-cost and easy-to-implement method for desalinating water."	**GNN encoder** links descriptive attributes to correct entity, ensuring detail retention.

Examples in Table 4 compare AraT5-base and GA-Transformer outputs for Arabic abstractive summarization. Each case includes the source text, generated summaries, and observations explicitly linking GA-Transformer's improvements to specific components of the proposed architecture (coreference edges, dependency parsing, cross-modal fusion, and GNN encoder), demonstrating how structural information enhances informativeness, coherence, and factual completeness.

4.5 Discussion

The GA-Transformer's improvements confirm the value of explicitly modeling syntactic dependencies and discourse-level coreference in Arabic abstractive summarization. These structural elements counter well-known. Weaknesses of strictly sequential models, especially the disposition to lose non-factual information and lack coherence in the synthesis of information across multiple sentences. Dependency edges are useful in maintaining grammatical correctness, even though coreference edges provide stability of tracking entities in the text, that give summaries more informative (as well as more faithful to the) original context. Empirical evidence indicates that structure augmentation is particularly advantageous to documents that are multifaceted, rich in information, which is demonstrated by more vivid. Performance improvement on ArXivSumm as compared to AlArabiyaNews. Although implementing GNN entails extra preprocessing and training time by 18 percent, the great improvements in factual consistency and discourse coherence justifies this computational cost. The cross-modal fusion mechanism is the most effective model that involves the harmonization of dynamically sequential and graph-based signals, enabling the system to adapt to it flexibly differentiating between syntactic complexity and discourse patterns in different domains. Notably, the suggested GA-Transformer is inherently language-agnostic, as it only needs just regular NLP pre-processors - that is, tokenization, dependency parsing, and coreference resolution, that is, that it can easily be ported to other languages beyond Arabic. This renders the framework easily adjustable to other morphologically rich or low resource. languages whose explicit structural modeling includes those like Urdu, Hebrew or Amharic can address the lack of annotated data. The integration of syntactic and discourse graphs therefore offers a general mechanism for capturing long-range dependencies and maintaining entity consistency, independent of language family.

5 Conclusion

This work presents GA-Transformer, a graph-augmented transformer architecture for Arabic abstractive summarization that integrates syntactic-dependency and discourse-level coreference structures through a graph neural network and cross-modal fusion. Experiments on two datasets demonstrate consistent improvements over strong baselines in both automatic metrics and human evaluations, with notable large gains observed for complex and information-dense texts. Ablation studies further confirm that both structural components contribute significantly to factual accuracy, coherence, and grammatical quality.

Future work will extend the framework to dialectal Arabic, incorporate additional semantic information such as semantic-role labeling, and explore end-to-end differentiable graph construction to minimize preprocessing costs. We also plan to investigate domain-adaptation strategies and evaluate the scalability of the approach in multilingual settings to assess the broader applicability of structural augmentation in low-resource summarization.

References

1. El-Kassas, W.S., Salama, C.R., Rafea, A.A., Mohamed, H.K.: Automatic text summarization: a comprehensive survey. Expert Syst. Appl. **165** (2021)
2. Ibrahim Altmami, N., El Bachir Menai, M.: Automatic summarization of scientific articles: a survey. J. King Saud Univ. – Comput. Inform. Sci. https://doi.org/10.1016/j.jksuci.2020.04.020
3. Kamble, S., Mandage, S., Topale, S., Vagare, D., Babbar, P.: Survey on summarization techniques and existing work. Int. J. Appl. Eng. Res. **12**, 69–86 (2017)
4. Marathe, P.: Comprehensive survey on abstractive text summarization. Int. J. Eng. Res. **V9**, 832–834 (2020)
5. Shakil, H., Farooq, A., Kalita, J.: Abstractive text summarization: State of the art, challenges, and improvements. Neurocomputing **603** (2024)
6. Muaad, A.Y., Raza, S., Naseem, U., Davanagere, H.J.J.: Arabic text detection: a survey of recent progress challenges and opportunities. Appl. Intell. **53**, 29845–29862 (2023). https://doi.org/10.1007/s10489-023-04992-9
7. Al-Saleh, A.B., Menai, M.E.B.: Automatic Arabic text summarization: a survey. Artif. Intell. Rev. **45**, 203–234 (2016)
8. Hirst, G., Lin, J., Nogueira, R., Yates, A.: Pretrained transformers for text ranking: BERT and beyond. Synth. Lect. Hum. Lang. Technol. **14**, 1–325 (2021)
9. Raffel, C., Shazeer, N., Roberts, A., Lee, K., Narang, S., Matena, M., et al.: Exploring the limits of transfer learning with a unified text-to-text transformer. J. Mach. Learn. Res. **21**, 1–67 (2020)
10. El Moatez, B.N., Elmadany, A.R., Abdul-Mageed, M.: AraT5: text-to-text transformers for arabic language generation. Proc. Ann. Meet. Assoc. Comput.l Linguist. **1**, 628–647 (2022)
11. Abdul-Mageed, M., Elmadany, A.R., Nagoudi, E.M.B.: ARBERT & MARBERT: Deep bidirectional transformers for Arabic. ACL-IJCNLP 2021 - 59th Annual Meeting of the Association for Computational Linguistics and the 11th International Joint Conference on Natural Language Processing, Proceedings of the Conference, pp. 7088–7105 (2021)
12. Chen, J., Yang, D.: Structure-aware abstractive conversation summarization via discourse and action graphs. NAACL-HLT 2021 - 2021 Conference of the North American Chapter of the Association for Computational Linguistics: Human Language Technologies, Proceedings of the Conference. https://arxiv.org/pdf/2104.08400
13. Feng, X., Feng, X., Qin, B., Geng, X.: Dialogue discourse-aware graph model and data augmentation for meeting summarization. In: IJCAI International Joint Conference on Artificial Intelligence. https://arxiv.org/pdf/2012.03502
14. Liu, Y., Gu, J., Goyal, N., Li, X., Edunov, S., Ghazvininejad, M., et al.: Multilingual denoising pre-training for neural machine translation. Trans. Assoc. Comput. Linguist. **8**, 726–742 (2020)
15. Xue, L., Constant, N., Roberts, A., Kale, M., Al-Rfou, R., Siddhant, A., et al.: mT5: a massively multilingual pre-trained text-to-text transformer. In: NAACL-HLT 2021 - 2021 Conference of the North American Chapter of the Association for Computational Linguistics: Human Language Technologies, Proceedings of the Conference , vol. 76, pp. 483–498 (2021)
16. Yang, Y., Tong, Y., Ma, S.: ZD-P of the, 2016 undefined. A position encoding convolutional neural network based on dependency tree for relation classification. aclanthology.org, pp. 2475–85 (2016). https://aclanthology.org/D16-1007.pdf

17. Li, B., Fan, Y., Sataer, Y., Gao, Z., Sciences, Y.G.-A.: Improving semantic dependency parsing with higher-order information encoded by graph neural networks. mdpi.com (2022). https://www.mdpi.com/2076-3417/12/8/4089

18. Hou, X., Qi, P., Wang, G., Ying, R., Huang, J., … XH preprint arXiv, et al.: Graph ensemble learning over multiple dependency trees for aspect-level sentiment. https://arxiv.org/abs/2103.11794

19. Liu, R., Mao, R., Luu, A.T., Cambria, E.: A brief survey on recent advances in coreference resolution. Springer. https://link.springer.com/article//10.1007/s10462-023-10506-3

20. Chen, R., Li, Y., Jiang, Y., Sun, B., Wang, J., Electronics, Z.L.-, et al.: Fact-aware generative text summarization with dependency graphs. mdpi.com [Internet]. cited 2025 Aug 15. https://www.mdpi.com/2079-9292/13/16/3230

21. Wang, D., Liu, P., Zheng, Y., Qiu, X., Huang, X.: Heterogeneous graph neural networks for extractive document summarization. In: Proceedings of the Annual Meeting of the Association for Computational Linguistics. https://arxiv.org/pdf/2004.12393

22. Alzahrani, A., Alqarni, M., Aljamaan, H.: Dependency-guided sentiment analysis for arabic text using graph convolutional networks. IEEE Access **10**, 87321–87332 (2022)

23. Alselwi, G., Taşcı, T.: Extractive arabic text summarization using pagerank and word embedding. Arab. J. Sci. Eng. **49**, 13115–13130 (2024)

24. Onan, A., Mathematics, H.A.: Knowledge-Enhanced Transformer Graph Summarization (KETGS): Integrating Entity and Discourse Relations for Advanced Extractive Text Summarization (2024). https://www.mdpi.com/2227-7390/12/23/3638

25. Chen, Y., Zhang, Z., … DS-… C on E.: DIGSum: dynamic interaction graph representation for dialogue summarization. Spiedigitallibrary (2025)

26. Obeid, O., Zalmout, N., Khalifa, S., Taji, D., Oudah, M., Alhafni, B., et al.: CAMeL tools: an open-source python toolkit for Arabic natural language processing. https://aclanthology.org/2020.lrec-1.868/

27. Li, Y., Zemel, R., Brockschmidt, M., Tarlow, D.: Gated graph sequence neural networks. In: 4th International Conference on Learning Representations, ICLR 2016 - Conference Track Proceedings (2016). https://arxiv.org/pdf/1511.05493

28. Loshchilov, I., Hutter, F.: Decoupled weight decay regularization. In: 7th International Conference on Learning Representations, ICLR 2019 (2019)

AI-Driven Evaluation of Environmental, Social, and Governance Disclosures

Abejide Ade-Ibijola[1]([envelope]) [ORCID] and Aneetha Sukhari[2] [ORCID]

[1] Research Group on Data, Artificial Intelligence, and Innovations for Digital Transformation, Johannesburg Business School, University of Johannesburg, Johannesburg, South Africa
abejideai@uj.ac.za
[2] College of Accounting Sciences, University of South Africa, Pretoria, South Africa
sukhaar@unisa.ac.za

Abstract. In recent years, environmental, social, and governance (ESG) reporting has emerged as a crucial metric for measuring and reporting progress toward the targets set out by the United Nations' Sustainable Development Goals. Investors, stakeholders, and regulators increasingly demand accurate ESG evaluations to inform investment decisions, risk management, and compliance strategies. However, existing ESG scoring methodologies suffer from several limitations, including subjectivity, inconsistency, and high costs. To address these challenges, this study proposes an innovative AI-powered tool that utilizes unsupervised machine learning and NLP techniques to comprehensively score companies' ESG metrics with accuracy, transparency, and efficiency. The study focuses on developing a prototype software that extracts data from various sources, including reports, websites, and social media. The aim of the study is to apply the Turing Test to determine whether a human can achieve the same ESG score as the AI tool. The paper commences with a literature review on ESG reporting and AI-powered tools that assess ESG disclosures. Thereafter, the design science research is applied in the development of the AI tool. Using the Turing Test, an experiment is conducted to evaluate whether the results obtained by the AI tool are similar to those of humans. The results of the Turing Test showed that humans and AI achieved similar scores in evaluating ESG disclosures. The design and development of the AI tool contribute to the development of more effective ESG evaluation methodologies, promoting sustainable investment practices, responsible business conduct, and better decision-making among stakeholders.

Keywords: ESG disclosure · Artificial Intelligence applications · Turing Test

1 Introduction

Sustainability reporting is the process by which a company discloses information about its environmental, social, and governance (ESG) performance. ESG disclosures are a set of measurable criteria used by investors and various stakeholders to assess a company's sustainability and ethical impact. It provides insights into how the company is managing sustainability-related risks and opportunities. The International Financial Reporting Standards (IFRS) Foundation, an accounting standard-setting body, established the

H. Kannan et al. (Eds.): AIKP 2025, CCIS 2804, pp. 237–246, 2026.
https://doi.org/10.1007/978-3-032-14706-6_19

International Sustainability Standards Board (ISSB), which was previously known as the Sustainability Accounting Standards Board (SASB). The ISSB issued IFRS S1 Sustainability Disclosure Standards [1] to enhance investor-company dialogue, ensuring that investors receive decision-useful, globally comparable information. IFRS S1 prescribes how an entity prepares and reports its sustainability-related financial disclosures. It outlines general requirements for the content and presentation of those disclosures, ensuring that the information disclosed is useful to primary users in making informed decisions related to the company's resources. ESG disclosures is widely available; however, existing research predominantly relies on historical ESG datasets, which limits the adaptability of predictive machine learning models [2].

Recent studies show that ESG factors have a significant relationship with company performance. [3–5]. [3] used a machine learning algorithm to analyze the relationship between individual ESG variables and their effect on corporate performance, and the interaction between ESG variables and stock price dynamics. The study also used a computational methodology based on machine learning to analyze the relationship between ESG factors and stock returns. The study concluded that ESG investments lead to higher long-term returns for investors, thereby promoting the sustainable development of financial markets and generating benefits for the real economy and the environment. [5] explored the factors influencing the financial performance of mutual equity funds and found a positive correlation between ESG scores and financial performance. A machine learning approach was adopted to detect which components of the financial statements explain the ESG ratings in databases and found that the financial statements items represent a powerful tool to explain the ESG ratings. Similarly, [4] found that companies with higher ESG scores had a higher financial performance. These findings emphasize the importance of developing comprehensive AI-powered tools to evaluate ESG disclosures [6]. In this paper, we develop an AI model, which uses AI-powered ESG monitoring systems, combined with machine learning and NLP techniques. The software enables a more responsive and proactive approach for users of ESG information.

2   Literature Review

2.1   Legitimacy Theory

Legitimacy theory is a theoretical framework often used to explain ESG disclosures [7]. According to the legitimacy theory, companies seek to ensure that '*they follow the rules and regulations of the societies in which they operate. A company's survival is dependent upon the extent to which it is perceived as legitimate*' [8]. This highlights the importance of standardizing ESG reporting metrics, which are comparable across companies, industries, and countries, thereby facilitating meaningful comparisons. Prior research found that larger companies and those that are more visible to the public tend to share more ESG information [9]. Companies in environmentally sensitive industries like mining or energy also share more ESG information [10, 11]. Companies with larger investors or foreign ownership tend to provide better quality ESG information, which can reduce capital costs and enhance firm value [12, 13]. Sustainability committees, female diversity, and independent boards are all positively linked to better ESG disclosures [14]. However, some disclosures may be symbolic which raises concerns about greenwashing and misleading stakeholders [15]. In the next section, AI-powered tools used to measure ESG are discussed.

2.2 Previous Tools Developed to Measure ESG

Prior studies have developed tools to evaluate ESG disclosures, using NLP and machine learning techniques [3–5, 16–20].

[16] developed an NLP tool to evaluate ESG disclosures. Firstly, the authors identified news headlines that mentioned a given company and classified the headlines as "ESG-relevant" or "ESG-irrelevant". Thereafter, the headlines were split into categories, i.e., environmental, social, and governance. The study used a combination of machine learning and deep learning approaches and found that the AI tool correctly processed 96.7% of the headlines in detecting environmental-related headlines along with their correct sentiment. The study also found that the distribution among the ESG categories is highly imbalanced, with significantly fewer articles related to governance, concluding that the tool is only suitable for the analysis of ESG featured in the news and performs well in environmental disclosures and struggles with social and governance disclosures. [20] developed an NLP tool, which analysed expert-annotated ESG datasets. The tool evaluated the ESG scores as the number of ESG words divided by the number of sentences in the annual report. The study concluded that pre-trained models outperformed the base model by 93% for social and environmental disclosures and 89% for governance and social disclosures.

[17] developed an automatic workflow that collects ESG data from different types of unstructured data sources, such as PDF documents, image documents, flat text, table structures, and web pages. The method used was a hybrid and adaptive AI tool that combined large language models, Human-In-The-Loop AI techniques, continuous learning, and knowledge representation methods. The platform enabled the automation of business processes that require the understanding of complex documents and unstructured data sources, allowing for the extraction of relevant ESG data with high accuracy. The authors utilized deep learning algorithms by leveraging human feedback, which allowed the model to improve itself over time.

[18] developed an ESG tracker system that uses real-time tracking to analyse ESG disclosures. Online reports, news articles, and social media posts tend to be static and do not reflect changes in the company in real-time but rather the accumulation of changes over a fixed period of time. The authors developed a tool by training a set of models to understand the unique vocabulary of the ESG domain. The system provides a dashboard that enables users to search, select companies, and view relative attention values, sentiment analysis, and keyword acceleration for each company. The real-time tracker reduces the complexity and time in analysing sustainability reports.

3 Methodology

Information systems researchers often use design science research (DSR). By creating artifacts that solve real-world problems, the DSR model generates knowledge [21]. DSR results shed light on the freshly generated artifact and why it enhances or disrupts its context. The DSR process includes problem identification and motivation, problem solution objectives, artefact design and development, demonstration, and assessment. Each DSR phase in this paper is detailed below.

3.1 Problem Identification and Motivation

The first step in DSR is to identify the real-world problem and motivate the significance of solving the problem. The real-world problem that this study aims to solve is related towards the analysis of ESG disclosures which provides information for stakeholders to assess the targets set out by the United Nations's Sustainable Development Goals (SDGs). ESG information is unstructured data and emanates in fragmented components from different sources such as rating agencies, websites, social media, news reports, etc. [22]. Relying on ESG information generated from such sources is challenging because companies' sustainable assets increase over time, reports are long and tedious, requiring substantial time to analyse, and corporate reports generated by the company itself may be biased [18]. In addition, companies constantly adjust their language and wording, and may omit comparable information [18].

3.2 Definition of the Objectives for a Solution to the Problem

The second step in DSR is to outline the solution that addresses the real-world problem identified in Sect. 3.1. The real-world problem will be solved by the design and development of an AI-powered prototype application, which is an application that evaluates ESG information from various sources using machine learning and natural language processing techniques. The tool provides a standardised approach to measure ESG metrics for companies.

3.3 Design and Development of the Artefact

The AI-powered tool demonstrates the most comprehensive use of AI model orchestration. The scoring pipeline begins with a flexible data ingestion layer that accepts real-time inputs via a REST API and supports bulk uploads in CSV format. This layer ingests structured and unstructured data from sources like sustainability reports, regulatory filings, and news feeds. Next, the normalization engine transforms raw metrics into a standardized format aligned with the Sustainability Accounting Standards Board (SASB) framework. This process includes unit conversions, sector-specific adjustments, alignment with reporting periods, and imputation of missing data using peer benchmarks. Once the data is normalized, it is routed to the model most suited for the task, based on real-time performance metrics, historical accuracy in ESG subdomains, and the complexity of the input. The scoring engine then applies a weighted algorithm that assigns significance to various ESG factors: environmental (45%), social (30%), and governance (25%). This calculation produces a final score, along with confidence intervals and improvement recommendations, returned as a JSON response and downloadable PDF report.

```
POST /esg-score
{
"entity": "CorporationXYZ",
"data_sources": ["sustainability_report", "news_feed"],
"reporting_framework": "SASB",
"industry_code": "IF-EC"
}
```

Performance benchmarks indicate that DeepSeek Prover offers the highest accuracy for environmental and governance metrics, while Gemma 7B excels in response speed. The comparative performance is summarized below (Table 1):

Table 1. Comparison between DeepSeek Power and Gemma 7B

Model	Environmental	Social	Governance	Avg. Speed
DeepSeek Prover v2	93.2%	89.7%	91.5%	1.8 s
DeepSeek v3	90.1%	87.3%	88.9%	1.3 s
Gemma 7B-it	88.7%	85.2%	86.1%	0.9 s
OpenChat 7B	86.4%	82.8%	84.3%	0.7 s

To improve speed and scalability, the system employs Redis caching to store frequently accessed scores and uses parallel processing to analyse different sections of large reports simultaneously. Additionally, sentiment analysis of news sources augments the scoring process, and a confidence scoring system estimates the reliability of each metric. The authors used existing pre-trained models, namely Gemma 7B-it, Deep Seek prover v2, DeepSeek v3, and Open Chat 7B.

3.4 Demonstration of the Artefact

The following video https://shorturl.at/pTCcK displays the visual functionality of the AI-powered tool. The home screen is depicted below in Fig. 1. An example of a company was selected to demonstrate the application's functionality. The company website address, location, name of company and industry must be entered on the application and the application searches for the information from various sources to calculate the ESG score. The user would click on "Generate" to view the ESG scores.

Figure 2 displays the overall ESG score, the ESG radar chart, and the ESG bar chart. For further details, the user can click on "View reasoning," which would take the user to Fig. 3 below.

Figure 3 below provides a detailed analysis of each category (environmental, social, and governance) of the ESG score, and includes the reasoning for each score. The reasoning for the scores discusses aspects such as how well the company is disclosing the elements of ESG and areas for improvement.

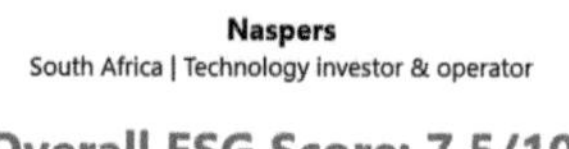

Fig. 1. Screenshot - Home screen of the AI-powered tool

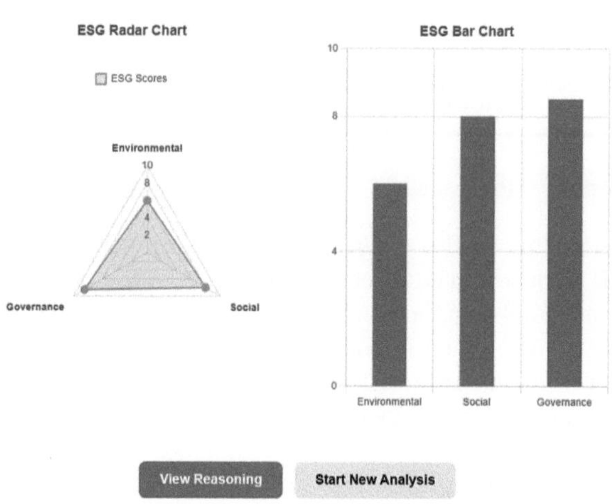

Fig. 2. Screenshot - Example of the overall ESG score

Additional Insights

Notable gap in Scope 3 emissions tracking despite net-zero pledge. Positive sentiment around African tech ecosystem development, but criticism regarding executive compensation (CEO pay ratio 120:1) and portfolio company labor practices occasionally surface in media analysis.

Category	Reasoning	Score
Environmental	Naspers operates primarily as a technology investor and operator, with limited direct environmental impact. The company has made commitments to carbon neutrality by 2035 and reports Scope 1 and 2 emissions. However, there is limited disclosure on Scope 3 emissions, which are significant given its investment portfolio. Environmental initiatives include renewable energy procurement and e-waste management programs, but these are not yet comprehensive across all subsidiaries.	6/10
Social	Strong diversity and inclusion policies, with women holding 33% of senior management positions. Significant investments in digital inclusion initiatives across emerging markets through Prosus Foundation. Employee satisfaction appears high based on Glassdoor reviews (4.0 rating), though recent layoffs at portfolio companies have caused some negative sentiment. Community development programs in education and skills training are robust in South Africa.	8/10
Governance	Excellent board independence (80% independent directors) and clear separation between Chairman and CEO roles. Comprehensive ESG reporting aligned with SASB standards. However, complex cross-holding structure with Prosus creates governance challenges. Recent shareholder approval for share repurchase program demonstrates responsiveness to investor concerns about discount to NAV. Strong anti-corruption policies with whistleblower mechanisms.	8.5/10

Fig. 3. Screenshot - Additional insights into each score

3.5   Results

3.5.1   Research Instrument

The Turing Test was designed in 1950 by Alan Turing to evaluate if a machine could imitate the mind of a human and concluded that the Turing Test is a valid method for assessing machine intelligence and that a machine can be designed to think [23, 24]. In this paper, we apply the Turing Test to evaluate the machine intelligence of the AI-powered tool, by obtaining scores for ESG information from five human experts and comparing the scores to the AI-powered tool.

3.5.2   Data Analysis

The sample comprised five companies listed on the Johannesburg Stock Exchange. Five experts evaluated publicly available information and provided a score for each company. The scores from the experts were compared to the scores generated by the AI-powered tool. The results are discussed in the next section.

3.5.3 Data Analysis

The results of the regression analysis are presented in Fig. 4 below. Each marker is the mean average of the AI scores for each company on the x-axis and the expert average on the y-axis. A strong positive relationship was observed between expert average scores and AI scores (R2 = 0.91). The fitted regression model indicates that AI scores increase at a slightly faster rate than expert scores. Compared to perfect agreement (y = x), the AI tended to underestimate lower expert scores and overestimate higher expert scores. A few low-AI points (including one near AI = 1.6) exhibit significant disagreement and contribute to a higher intercept.

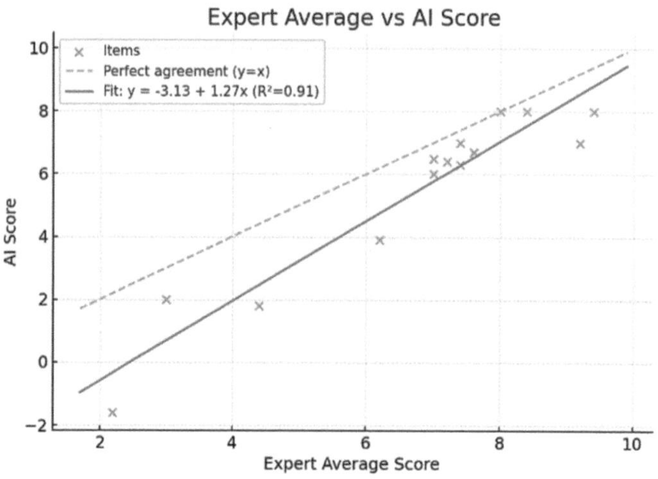

Fig. 4. Regression analysis – AI versus Human

4 Conclusion and Future Work

The objective of this paper was to develop software utilizing comprehensive machine learning and NLP techniques to evaluate ESG disclosures and to assess whether humans could obtain similar scores to AI. In order to achieve the test between the human and AI, the Turing Test was applied. Experts reviewed publicly available information. We then used a regression to compare the two sets of scores. The results from the regression analysis proved that the majority of the scores generated by AI were similar to the scores generated by humans. Prior work developed applications to evaluate ESG scores using machine learning and NLP techniques, however the tool developed in this paper differs by providing ESG scores for companies and provides detailed explanations about the reasoning for each score. This enables stakeholders to compare and contrast ESG scores across companies, sectors, and countries for informed decision-making purposes. The ESG tool can be useful for companies to analyse their ESG scores to identify aspects that could be improved to maintain their legitimacy. The study has its limitations such as potential bias in ESG source material and scalability to larger, more diverse datasets. Future research could explore the development of AI-powered tools to evaluate various aspects of non-financial reporting and apply the Turing Test to evaluate the effectiveness of the AI.

Acknowledgements. The authors would like to thank the GRIT Lab Africa young innovators that contributed to the AI artefact demonstrated in this project.

References

1. International Sustainability Standards Board: IFRS S1 General Requirements for Disclosure of Sustainability-related Financial Information (2022)
2. Seow, R.Y.C.: Transforming ESG analytics with machine learning: a systematic literature review using TCCM framework. Corp Soc Responsib Environ Manag. 1–32 (2025). https://doi.org/10.1002/csr.70089
3. Carlei, V., Cascioli, P., Ceccarelli, A., Furia, D.: Can machine learning explain alpha generated by ESG factors? Comput. Econ. **65**, 1457–1477 (2025). https://doi.org/10.1007/s10614-024-10602-8
4. D'Amato, V., D'Ecclesia, R., Levantesi, S.: Firms' profitability and ESG score: a machine learning approach. Appl. Stoch. Model. Bus. Ind. **40**, 243–261 (2024). https://doi.org/10.1002/asmb.2758
5. Momparler, A., Carmona, P., Climent, F.: Catalyzing sustainable investment: revealing ESG power in predicting fund performance with machine learning. Comput. Econ. **65**, 1617–1642 (2025). https://doi.org/10.1007/s10614-024-10618-0
6. Seow, R.Y.C.: Transforming ESG analytics with machine learning: a systematic literature review using TCCM framework. Corp Soc Responsib Environ Manag. 1–64 (2025). https://doi.org/10.1002/csr.70089
7. Deegan, C.: Financial accounting theory. McGraw-Hill Education (Australia), Australia (2014)
8. Suchman, M.: Managing legitimacy: strategic and Institutional Approaches. Acad Manag Rev. **20** (1995). https://doi.org/10.2991/icied-17.2018.3
9. Cormier, D., Magnan, M.: The revisited contribution of environmental reporting to investors' valuation of a firm's earnings: an international perspective. Ecol. Econ. **62**, 613–626 (2007). https://doi.org/10.1016/j.ecolecon.2006.07.030
10. Clarkson, P.M., Fang, X., Li, Y., Richardson, G.: The relevance of environmental disclosures: are such disclosures incrementally informative? J. Account. Public Policy **32**, 410–431 (2013). https://doi.org/10.1016/j.jaccpubpol.2013.06.008
11. Clarkson, P.M., Li, Y., Richardson, G.D., Vasvari, F.P.: Revisiting the relation between environmental performance and environmental disclosure: an empirical analysis. Account. Organ Soc. **33**, 303–327 (2008). https://doi.org/10.1016/j.aos.2007.05.003
12. Cheng, E.C.M., Courtenay, S.M.: Board composition, regulatory regime and voluntary disclosure. Int. J. Account. **41**, 262–289 (2006). https://doi.org/10.1016/j.intacc.2006.07.001
13. Dhaliwal, D., Li, O.Z., Tsang, A., Yang, Y.G.: Corporate social responsibility disclosure and the cost of equity capital: the roles of stakeholder orientation and financial transparency. J. Account. Public Policy **33**, 328–355 (2014). https://doi.org/10.1016/j.jaccpubpol.2014.04.006
14. Hussain, N., Rigoni, U., Orij, R.P.: Corporate governance and sustainability performance: analysis of triple bottom line performance. J. Bus. Ethics **149**, 411–432 (2018). https://doi.org/10.1007/s10551-016-3099-5

15. Mukherjee, A., Owen, R., Scott, J.M., Lyon, F.: Financing green innovation startups: a systematic literature review on early-stage SME funding. Ventur. Cap. **00**, 1–27 (2024). https://doi.org/10.1080/13691066.2024.2410730
16. Fischbach, J., et al P.: Automatic ESG assessment of companies by mining and evaluating media coverage data: NLP approach and tool. Proceedings - 2023 IEEE International Conference on Big Data, BigData 2023, pp. 2823–2830 (2023). https://doi.org/10.1109/BigData59044.2023.10386488
17. Visalli, F., et al.: ESG data collection with adaptive AI. Int Conf Enterp Inf Syst ICEIS - Proc. **1**, 468–475 (2023). https://doi.org/10.5220/0011844500003467
18. Momeni, E., Fraenkel, C., Kiss, P., Burgmann, A.: ESG tracker: unbiased and explainable ESG profile from real-time data. In: Proceedings of the Fifteenth International AAAI Conference onWeb and Social Media (2021)
19. Li, K.: Big data and machine learning in ESG research*. Asia-Pacific J Financ Stud. **54**, 6–21 (2025). https://doi.org/10.1111/ajfs.12503
20. Schimanski, T., Reding, A., Reding, N., Bingler, J., Kraus, M., Leippold, M.: Bridging the gap in ESG measurement: Using NLP to quantify environmental, social, and governance communication. Financ Res Lett. **61** (2024). https://doi.org/10.1016/j.frl.2024.104979
21. vom Brocke, J., Maedche, A.: The DSR grid: six core dimensions for effectively planning and communicating design science research projects. Electron. Mark. **29**(3), 379–385 (2019). https://doi.org/10.1007/s12525-019-00358-7
22. Telukdarie, A., Mahure, H., Sishi, M.: The digitization of ESG matrix. Procedia Comput Sci. **239**, 808–815 (2024). https://doi.org/10.1016/j.procs.2024.06.436
23. Turing, A.: Computing machinery and intelligence amplification. Mind. 25–44 (1950). https://doi.org/10.1109/9780470544297.ch3
24. Saygin, A.P., Cicekli, I., Akman, V.: Turing test: 50 years later. Minds Mach. **10**, 463–518 (2000). https://doi.org/10.1007/978-94-010-0105-2_2

Tourism Demand Forecasting for Single-Step and Multi-step Horizons Through Hierarchical Statistical Models and Reconciliation Techniques

Abhishek Rawat[1,2], Bharath Kumar Bolla[3(✉)], and Dinesh Reddy Bhumireddy[4]

[1] Decision Point Analytics, Gurugram, India
[2] Liverpool John Moores University, Liverpool, UK
[3] The Institute of Product Leadership, Bengaluru, India
`bolla111@gmail.com`
[4] Cardinal Health, Bengaluru, India

Abstract. Tourism demand forecasting presents unique challenges when data exhibit hierarchical structures across geographic levels, requiring forecasts that are accurate and coherent across aggregation levels. This study presents a comprehensive empirical evaluation of hierarchical forecasting approaches using Australian tourism data spanning 77 regions, seven states, and national totals from 1998 to 2016. We systematically compared three automated base forecasting methods (Auto-ARIMA, Auto-ETS, and Auto-CES) combined with four reconciliation strategies (Bottom-Up, Top-Down, and two MinTrace variants) across single-step and multi-step forecasting horizons. Our analysis reveals that the bottom-up approach consistently underperforms owing to error propagation from disaggregated levels, whereas reconciliation methods that enforce coherence constraints produce superior results. The combination of the Auto-ETS base forecaster with top-down reconciliation emerged as the optimal strategy, achieving the lowest error rates (RMSE: 160.13 for single-step, 299.41 for multi-step forecasts) while maintaining computational efficiency. Notably, the theoretically advanced MinTrace methods did not outperform the more straightforward top-down approach in this context. These findings challenge the assumption that complex reconciliation methods necessarily yield superior performance, demonstrating that well-captured aggregate-level patterns can be effectively disaggregated using top-down strategies. The results provide actionable guidance for tourism industry practitioners and extend their applicability to other domains with hierarchical data structures, including retail sales and energy demand forecasting.

Keywords: Hierarchical Forecasting · Tourism Demand Prediction · Optimal Reconciliation · Auto-ETS Models · Top-Down vs Bottom-Up · Hierarchical Time Series · Tourism Forecasting · Reconciliation Methods · Auto-ETS · Coherent Forecasts

H. Kannan et al. (Eds.): AIKP 2025, CCIS 2804, pp. 247–263, 2026.
https://doi.org/10.1007/978-3-032-14706-6_20

1 Introduction

Tourism has emerged as one of the largest and fastest-growing industries worldwide, contributing significantly to both global and national economies. Beyond generating employment opportunities in hospitality, transportation, and retail, the sector stimulates infrastructure development and fosters cultural exchange. In Australia, tourism plays a particularly prominent role, accounting for a notable share of the Gross Domestic Product (GDP). Each year, millions of international tourists visit the country, injecting billions of dollars into its economy. For instance, in 2018–2019, Australia welcomed over nine million visitors, generating approximately AUD 44.6 billion in revenue [1]. Such a large influx of tourists places immense pressure on resources, requiring stakeholders to manage accommodation, transportation, and local services efficiently and effectively. In this context, accurate forecasting of tourism demand is vital for ensuring smooth operations, sustainable growth, and enhanced visitor experiences [2].

Forecasting tourism demand is inherently complex because the data often display strong seasonality, long-term trends, and irregular fluctuations driven by external shocks [3]. As part of predictive analytics, demand forecasting applies both statistical and computational approaches to anticipate consumer behavior. Traditionally, forecasting methods have been categorized into two main approaches: qualitative methods, which rely on expert judgment, and quantitative methods, which rely on historical data and formal modeling [4]. While quantitative approaches have advanced considerably, their application to multilevel hierarchical systems, such as tourism, remains challenging [5].

Tourism demand data are inherently hierarchical. For example, observations can be recorded at the city level, aggregated into states, and combined to form a national forecast. This hierarchical organization introduces the concept of forecast coherence, which requires that lower-level forecasts sum to their respective higher-level aggregates. However, maintaining coherence is difficult when models are developed independently at each level [6].

Traditional reconciliation strategies illustrate these challenges. The Bottom-Up approach, which starts at the most granular level, often suffers from error propagation, where minor inaccuracies at the regional level accumulate and distort higher-level predictions [7]. Conversely, the Top-Down approach produces forecasts at the aggregate level and disaggregates them proportionally, ensuring coherence but potentially overlooking significant local variations [8]. These limitations have motivated the development of more advanced reconciliation methods that strike a balance between accuracy at the regional and aggregate levels.

Recent advances include the Minimum Trace (MinT) reconciliation framework, which adjusts base forecasts at all levels to satisfy aggregation constraints while minimizing the overall forecast variance [6]. Such approaches represent a significant improvement over purely Bottom-Up or Top-Down methods, providing forecasts that are both coherent and statistically efficient [9].

The novelty of the present study does not lie in proposing an entirely new forecasting algorithm but rather in offering a comprehensive comparative evaluation of existing techniques within the context of Australian tourism demand. Whereas earlier studies tended to evaluate either a single reconciliation method or a single base forecasting model, this study systematically compares three statistical base forecasters, Auto ARIMA, Auto

ETS, and Auto CES, across multiple reconciliation methods, including Bottom Up, Top Down, and MinT. By evaluating both single step (short horizon) and multi step (long horizon) forecasts, this study provides practical insights into how different strategies behave under varying conditions. Notably, the evaluation incorporates both computational efficiency and statistical accuracy, acknowledging that runtime is a crucial factor in real world decision making.

In summary, this study seeks to bridge the gap between theoretical advancements in hierarchical time-series forecasting [8] and their practical applications in the tourism sector. Specifically, this study aims to achieve the following three core objectives.

- To forecast Australian tourism demand at multiple hierarchical levels, including cities, states, and the national total.
- To compare different base forecasting models (Auto-ARIMA, Auto-ETS, Auto-CES) in combination with varying strategies of reconciliation (Bottom-Up, Top-Down, MinT).
- To evaluate various combinations based on statistical accuracy and computational efficiency in order to identify the most suitable framework for practical implementation.

2 Literature Review

The study of time series forecasting has developed over several decades, with continual efforts to refine its accuracy and robustness. Early forecasting research relied heavily on classical statistical techniques, such as exponential smoothing and autoregressive models, which laid the foundation for practical applications in multiple domains [6]. Over time, forecasting applications in tourism demand have begun to integrate more advanced tools, expanding from linear models to machine learning and hybrid approaches. This shift reflects the inherently dynamic and volatile nature of tourism data, which is influenced by seasonal cycles, long-term structural changes, and external shocks such as economic fluctuations or pandemics [10]. Although significant advancements have been made, no single forecasting method has consistently outperformed the others across all datasets and horizons [11]. This inconsistency has motivated further exploration of the structural characteristics of tourism data, particularly through the development of hierarchical forecasting frameworks.

2.1 Hierarchical Time Series and the Need for Coherency

A hierarchical time series (HTS) is composed of multiple time series organised within a structured, nested hierarchy [12]. For instance, in tourism, demand can be measured at the regional level, aggregated to states, and further combined into a national total, as shown in Fig. 1. The defining property of such data is that the forecasts at the disaggregated levels must sum to the forecasts at the more aggregated levels [6]. This requirement of coherency poses a unique modelling challenge, where forecasts need to be accurate at all levels while simultaneously respecting structural summing constraints. Without reconciliation, independently generated forecasts often violate this coherency, leading to results that may be misleading or practically unusable.

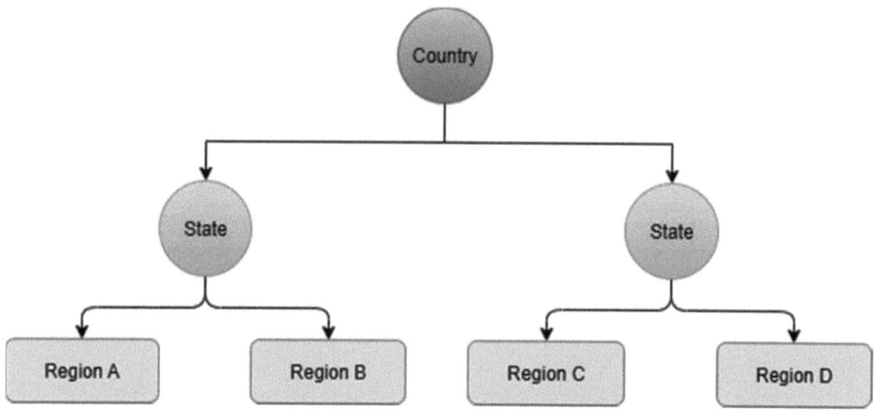

Fig. 1. Hierarchy of Tourism Demand Forecast

2.2 Traditional Reconciliation Methods

Several strategies have been proposed to maintain the coherence of HTS forecasting. The Bottom-Up approach is perhaps the most intuitive: forecasts are produced for each series at the lowest level of the hierarchy and then aggregated upwards to obtain forecasts for higher levels. This ensures that local information is not discarded. However, Bottom-Up forecasts are particularly sensitive to noise, as errors at lower levels accumulate and degrade the accuracy of higher-level predictions. Additionally, this method is computationally demanding for large hierarchies, making it less practical for real-world applications [13].

In contrast, the top-down approach begins with forecasts at the highest aggregation level, which are then disaggregated to lower levels according to historical or forecasted proportions. This guarantees coherence and typically produces stable aggregate forecasts. Nevertheless, this comes at the cost of losing granularity, as local variations and regional patterns are not explicitly modelled. For example, regional tourism surges due to local events may be masked when a purely top-level model is used [14].

A compromise between these two extremes is offered by the middle-out approach, where forecasts are generated at an intermediate level of aggregation. These are then disaggregated downwards using a top-down strategy and aggregated upwards using bottom-up strategies. The effectiveness of this method depends heavily on selecting an appropriate middle level, and there is no universally optimal choice for this [15].

2.3 Optimal Reconciliation and the MinT Framework

Recognizing the limitations of traditional reconciliation methods, Hyndman et al. [12] introduced the concept of Optimal Reconciliation. This framework treats base forecasts at all levels as potentially applicable but incoherent. The goal is to combine them mathematically to generate a new set of forecasts that are both coherent and optimally close to the original base forecasts. This is achieved by leveraging the summing matrix (S), which encodes the hierarchical structure, and the mapping matrix (G), which adjusts the base forecasts to ensure coherence. Thus, the reconciled forecasts can be expressed as

$$\tilde{y} = SG\hat{y}$$

where $\hat{y}$ are the base forecasts.

The key innovation lies in estimating the mapping matrix G. Wickramasuriya et al. [6] proposed the Minimum Trace (MinT) method, which finds the optimal G by minimizing the trace of the covariance matrix of reconciled forecast errors. This ensures that the reconciled forecasts respect the summing constraints while reducing the total forecast error variance. Variants of MinT include the use of Ordinary Least Squares (MinT-ols) and shrinkage estimators (MinT-shrink) to estimate the forecast error covariance matrix. These alternatives offer different trade-offs between accuracy and stability, making the framework adaptable to diverse data environments.

2.4 Integration of Machine Learning in Hierarchical Forecasting

Although statistical models, such as ARIMA, ETS, and CES, remain central to forecasting research [6], recent years have seen an increasing integration of machine learning (ML) and deep learning methods [16] into hierarchical forecasting [17]. ML approaches, including Support Vector Regression [18], ensemble learners such as XGBoost [19], and advanced neural architectures [20], offer the ability to capture nonlinear patterns and interactions that traditional models may miss. These models can be applied as base forecasters within the reconciliation framework or, in emerging research, as direct reconciliation mechanisms. Studies have demonstrated that hybrid models combining statistical forecasting with machine learning can improve performance, especially in cases of complex hierarchical structure [21]. Similarly, [18] explored the use of recurrent neural networks to capture long-term dependencies in tourism demand [22]. These advances suggest that ML-enhanced reconciliation may become a dominant research direction in the coming decades.

The literature reveals a clear trajectory: while traditional methods, such as Bottom-Up and Top-Down, remain foundational, the evolution toward optimal reconciliation techniques, such as MinT, has transformed the field by systematically addressing the coherency constraint. Furthermore, the growing inclusion of machine learning has expanded the methodological toolkit, enabling models to deal more effectively with the nonlinearity and volatility of tourism demand. The present study builds on this foundation by rigorously comparing classical statistical base forecasters within the optimal reconciliation framework, thereby establishing a strong empirical baseline for the future integration of advanced machine learning approaches.

3 Research Methodology

This study employs a structured methodological framework to examine and compare hierarchical forecasting techniques applied to Australian tourism demand (Fig. 2). The methodology progresses through four distinct but interconnected stages: data acquisition and preparation, exploratory analysis, model construction, and performance evaluation.

3.1 Data Acquisition and Preparation

The dataset utilized in this research consists of quarterly observations of Australian tourism flows from 1998 to 2016. Tourism activity is measured in thousands.

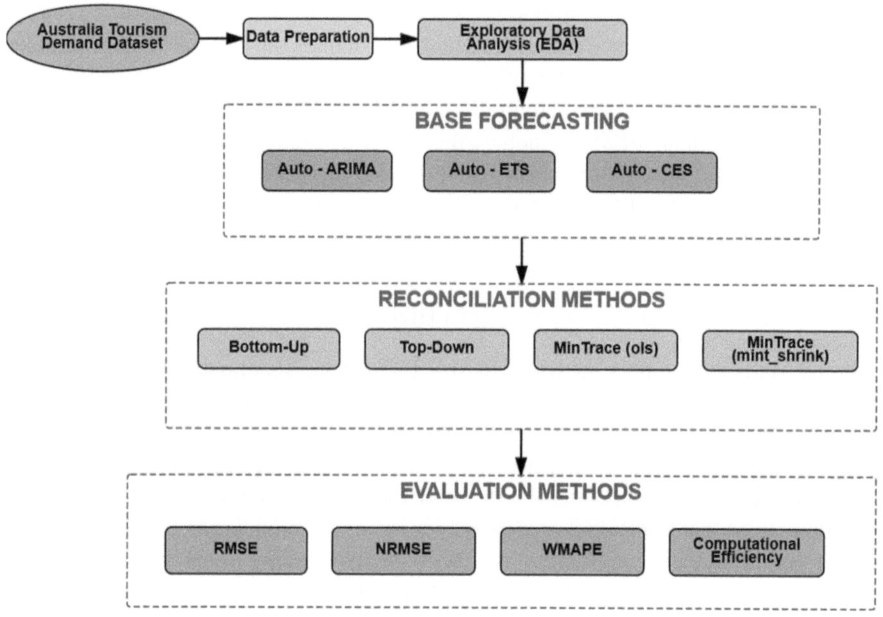

Fig. 2. Research methodology flowchart.

At the top of the hierarchy (Level 0) lies the national total of trips in Australia. This is disaggregated into seven states and territories (Level 1) and further disaggregated into 77 unique tourism regions (Level 2). This nested structure provides an ideal basis for implementing and testing hierarchical forecasting methods.

Before modelling, the raw dataset underwent a sequence of preparation steps to render it suitable for time series forecasting. The column representing quarterly periods was converted into a datetime object to ensure temporal ordering and compatibility with the statistical packages. The data were then transformed into the "long format" widely adopted by modern hierarchical forecasting libraries, where each row contains a unique identifier for the series (e.g., *State/Region*), a timestamp, and the observed value for trips.

A summation matrix S was constructed to enforce the hierarchical summation constraints mathematically. This matrix specifies how lower-level units combine to form higher-level units. For example, the 77 regional series roll up into their respective state totals, and the state series roll up into the national series. If y_t denotes the full vector of observations across all levels of the hierarchy at time **t**, then:

$$y_t = Sb_t$$

where b_t represents the vector of bottom-level (regional) series at time **t**. This relationship ensures coherence between the levels by design.

For performance assessment, the dataset was partitioned into two subsets: a training set consisting of data from 1998 to 2013 and a test set covering 2014 to 2016. The training set was used to estimate the forecasting models, whereas the test set was used to evaluate the predictive accuracy, providing an unbiased measure of the generalization capability.

3.2 Exploratory Data Analysis

Before model construction, an exploratory analysis was performed to examine the key characteristics of the dataset. Visual inspection and statistical summaries revealed that tourism demand is highly uneven across regions. Major metropolitan areas, such as Sydney and Melbourne, consistently recorded the highest number of trips, confirming their dominance as Australia's primary tourist hubs. At the state level, New South Wales, Queensland, and Victoria emerged as the leading contributors to the overall tourism volume.

Aggregated national-level data demonstrated two striking features: an underlying upward trend in tourism activity and a clear seasonal pattern. Seasonality was most pronounced at the end of each calendar year, coinciding with the Australian summer and Christmas holiday season, when domestic and international travel peaks. These patterns suggest that models must capture both long-term trends and recurring seasonal cycles to provide accurate forecasts of future conditions. Furthermore, short-term fluctuations, likely reflecting economic events or external shocks, were also evident. Such complexity underscores the importance of employing robust statistical methods that can adapt to multiple time horizons and to hierarchical dependencies.

3.3 Modelling Framework

The modelling strategy employed in this study follows the optimal reconciliation framework, which separates the forecasting task into two key stages: (1) generation of base forecasts and (2) reconciliation to achieve structural coherence.

Base Forecasting Models

Three automated statistical models were selected as base forecasters, each chosen for its proven track record in time series forecasting and ability to capture different data characteristics.

Auto-ARIMA (Auto-Regressive Integrated Moving Average): ARIMA models form one of the cornerstones of time series forecasting, designed to capture autocorrelation structures through autoregressive and moving average terms, whereas the integrated component accounts for non-stationarity. The automatic implementation (Auto-ARIMA) selects the most suitable model order *(p, d, q)* by minimizing information criteria such as the Akaike Information Criterion (AIC) [19]. The general ARIMA model is expressed as

$$\phi(B)(1 - B)^{d} y_t = \theta(B)\epsilon_t$$

where $\phi(B)$ and $\theta(B)$ are polynomials in the backshift operator **B**, **d** is the order of differencing, and ϵ_t is white noise.

Auto-ETS (Error, Trend, Seasonality): The ETS framework is a family of exponential smoothing models that explicitly represent the error, trend, and seasonal components [23]. The automated procedure searches across the additive and multiplicative specifications of these components, selecting the best-fitting configuration using information criteria. ETS models are particularly suited to series with strong seasonality and trends, as observed in Australian tourism data.

Auto-CES (Complex Exponential Smoothing): CES extends the exponential smoothing paradigm to accommodate more complex seasonal dynamics, including non-integer seasonal periods and interactions across multiple seasons. This makes it an appropriate choice for tourism data, where dual calendars (e.g., holiday seasons and school breaks) may influence demand patterns [24].

Reconciliation Methods

Once base forecasts were generated for all series in the hierarchy (77 regional, 7 state, and 1 national), four reconciliation methods were applied to produce the final set of coherent forecasts:

Bottom-Up (BU): Forecasts are first generated for the most granular regional series and then aggregated. Although this ensures no loss of local detail, it is prone to propagating noise from lower levels.

Top-Down (TD): Forecasts are generated only for the national series and then disaggregated into states and regions based on historical proportions. This produces stable aggregate forecasts but sacrifices regional specificity.

MinTrace (ols): A form of optimal reconciliation that adjusts forecasts across all levels by minimizing the total forecast error variance, with the covariance matrix estimated via Ordinary Least Squares [21].

MinTrace (shrinkage): A variant of MinTrace that uses shrinkage estimators for the covariance matrix, improving stability in cases where the number of series is large relative to the available observations.

The general form of the reconciled forecasts is as follows:

$$\tilde{\mathbf{y}} = \mathbf{S}\mathbf{G}\hat{\mathbf{y}}$$

where $\hat{\mathbf{y}}$ denotes the vector of base forecasts, $\mathbf{S}$ is the summing matrix, and $\mathbf{G}$ is the reconciliation matrix. Under the MinTrace approach, $\mathbf{G}$ is chosen such that:

$$\mathbf{G} = \left(\mathbf{S}^{\mathbf{T}}\mathbf{W}^{-1}\mathbf{S}\right)^{-1}\mathbf{S}^{\mathbf{T}}\mathbf{W}^{-1}$$

with $\mathbf{W}$ representing the covariance matrix of forecast errors.

Both single-step forecasting (one quarter ahead) and multi-step forecasting (twelve quarters or three years ahead) were performed to examine how performance varied across horizons.

3.4 Evaluation Framework

To assess performance, this study employed two dimensions: accuracy of forecasts and computational efficiency.

Accuracy Metrics
Three statistical metrics were used to quantify the predictive accuracy against the held-out test set:
Root Mean Square Error (RMSE)

$$\mathbf{RMSE} = \sqrt{\frac{1}{\mathbf{n}}\sum\nolimits_{\mathbf{i=1}}^{\mathbf{n}} (\mathbf{y_i} - \widehat{\mathbf{y_i}})^2} \tag{1}$$

The RMSE is one of the most widely used metrics in time series forecasting. It measures the standard deviation of the forecast errors and penalizes large deviations more heavily. However, while RMSE provides an absolute measure of forecast error, its interpretation is scale-dependent, meaning that the results are not directly comparable across time series of different magnitudes.

Normalised Root Mean Square Error (NRMSE)

$$NRMSE = \frac{RMSE}{y_{max} - y_{min}} \tag{2}$$

To address the limitation of scale dependence, the RMSE was normalized relative to the range of the observed values. The NRMSE makes it possible to compare forecast accuracy across series with different scales (e.g., comparing a small regional series with a large state-level or national series). This is especially important in a hierarchical setting, where series at different aggregation levels vary greatly in magnitude.

Weighted Mean Absolute Percentage Error (WMAPE)

$$WMAPE = \frac{\sum_{i=1}^{n} |y_i - \widehat{y_i}|}{\sum_{i=1}^{n} y_i} \times 100\% \tag{3}$$

MAPE is another commonly used metric that expresses forecast errors as percentages, making it an intuitive and easy-to-interpret measure of accuracy. However, the standard MAPE can be problematic in hierarchical forecasting because it gives equal weight to all series regardless of their size and becomes unstable when the actual values approach zero. To overcome these issues, we used the Weighted MAPE (WMAPE) [22], which scales errors according to the magnitude of the series. This ensures that large and economically significant series (such as national-level forecasts) have an appropriate influence on the overall error measure while still accounting for smaller regional contributions.

In summary, the NRMSE and WMAPE were chosen alongside the RMSE because they enable meaningful cross-series comparisons and appropriately balance the contributions of series at different levels of the hierarchy. These adjustments are crucial for evaluating hierarchical forecasting methods, in which the dataset inherently contains both large aggregate series and small disaggregate series with vastly different scales.

Computational Efficiency

In addition to accuracy, computational efficiency was recorded to evaluate the practical feasibility. The execution time required to fit each base forecasting model and apply the reconciliation methods was measured using Python's timing functions. This consideration is particularly significant for large-scale applications, where thousands of forecasts may need to be generated in real time, and operational decisions depend not only on accuracy but also on the ability to deliver results quickly.

4   Results and Discussions

The empirical results of this study provide a detailed comparison of hierarchical forecasting approaches to Australian tourism demand. Performance was assessed along two dimensions: forecast accuracy and computational efficiency, with both single-step (one quarter ahead) and multi-step (twelve quarters ahead) horizons considered. The findings are presented as follows.

4.1   Single-Step Forecast Performance

For one-step-ahead forecasting, the bottom-up approach consistently underperformed across all three base forecasters, namely, Auto-ARIMA, Auto-ETS, and Auto-CES. The forecasts from this method displayed overfitting behavior, producing volatile patterns that exaggerated the short-term fluctuations. This is attributed to the accumulation of noise from the 77 regional series, which undermines the reliability of aggregated results.

In contrast, the Top-Down and MinTrace reconciliation methods yielded superior results. Both the ordinary least squares (OLS) and shrinkage (mint_shrink) versions of MinTrace performed well, producing smoother forecasts that were aligned with the observed trend and seasonality. The Top-Down approach, in particular, stood out as the best-performing reconciliation strategy, especially when combined with the Auto-ETS base forecaster.

Table 1. Evaluation metrics for single-step forecasts

Base Forecaster I Reconciliation	RMSE	NRMSE	WMAPE (%)
AutoARIMA I Top-Down	231.77	0.009	9.30
AutoARIMA I MinTrace (ols)	252.71	0.010	9.57
AutoARIMA I MinTrace (shrink)	225.36	0.016	17.32
AutoETS I Top-Down	160.13	0.007	6.66
AutoETS I MinTrace (ols)	201.46	0.008	7.76

(continued)

Table 1. (continued)

Base Forecaster I Reconciliation	RMSE	NRMSE	WMAPE (%)
AutoETS I MinTrace (shrink)	162.75	0.007	6.91
AutoCES I Top-Down	170.17	0.007	6.91
AutoCES I MinTrace (ols)	218.53	0.009	8.71
AutoCES I MinTrace (shrink)	174.28	0.007	7.24

Table 1 highlights that Auto-ETS with Top-Down reconciliation provided the most accurate single-step forecasts, achieving the lowest RMSE (160.13), NRMSE (0.007), and WMAPE (6.66%). This indicates that strong aggregate forecasts from ETS, systematically disaggregated downwards, are particularly effective in capturing the structural dynamics of Australian tourism demand.

Computational Efficiency of Base Forecasters (Single-Step)

Table 2. Execution time for single-step base forecasts

Forecasting Method	Time (seconds)
Auto-ARIMA	25.99
Auto-ETS	31.56
Auto-CES	32.13

Auto-ARIMA emerged as the most efficient base forecaster, completing runs in less than 26 s, whereas Auto-ETS and Auto-CES required slightly longer (Table 2).

Computational Efficiency of Reconciliation Methods (Single-Step)

In addition to the base forecasters, the reconciliation methods were evaluated for computational cost (Table 3).

Table 3. Execution time for single-step reconciliation methods

Reconciliation Method	Time (seconds)
Bottom-Up	0.08
Top-Down	0.19
MinTrace (ols)	0.33
MinTrace (shrink)	0.45

The reconciliation stage was computationally lightweight, with all methods completed in less than half a second. While MinTrace (shrinkage) took slightly longer than the other methods, the difference was negligible compared to the time required to generate the base forecasts. Thus, reconciliation efficiency does not pose a barrier to implementation, even in large-scale applications of the model.

4.2 Multi-step Forecast Performance

Extending the analysis to a twelve-quarter horizon produced results consistent with the single-step findings. The Bottom-Up method once again yielded the weakest forecasts, with errors compounding over time. Both Top-Down and MinTrace reconciliations generated significantly more reliable and coherent predictions (Table 4) than the other methods.

Table 4. Accuracy metrics for multi-step forecasts

Base Forecaster/Reconciliation	RMSE	NRMSE	WMAPE (%)
AutoARIMA I BottomUp	397.12	0.015	19.53
AutoARIMA I Top-Down	367.28	0.014	13.06
AutoARIMA I MinTrace (ols)	418.38	0.016	14.18
AutoARIMA I MinTrace (mint_shrink)	366.42	0.014	13.02
AutoETS I Bottom-Up	371.16	0.014	17.50
AutoETS I Top-Down	299.41	0.012	10.43
AutoETS I MinTrace (ols)	334.94	0.013	11.40
AutoETS I MinTrace (mint_shrink)	301.73	0.012	10.49
AutoCES I Top-Down	363.21	0.014	17.34
AutoCES I Bottom-Up	302.10	0.012	10.47
AutoCES I MinTrace (ols)	351.52	0.013	11.86
AutoCES I MinTrace (mint_shrink)	307.67	0.012	10.68

The Auto-ETS+ Top-Down combination once again delivered the best results, achieving the lowest RMSE, NRMSE, and WMAPE values. The robustness of this configuration across both short- and long-term horizons demonstrates its suitability for forecasting tourism demand at various levels.

Computational Efficiency of Base Forecasters (Multi-step)

Table 5. Execution time for multi-step base forecasts

Forecasting Method	Time (seconds)
Auto-ARIMA	25.99
Auto-ETS	32.80
Auto-CES	32.42

The execution times were nearly identical to those of the single-step case, confirming that the forecast horizon length had little impact on the computational cost. Auto-ARIMA again proved fastest, whereas Auto-ETS and Auto-CES required marginally more time (Table 5).

Computational Efficiency of Reconciliation Methods (Multi-step)

Table 6. Execution time for multi-step reconciliation methods

Reconciliation Method	Time (seconds)
Bottom-Up	0.15
Top-Down	0.22
MinTrace (ols)	0.36
MinTrace (shrink)	0.48

Even with a longer forecast horizon, reconciliation remained computationally negligible, requiring less than half a second in each case. MinTrace-shrinkage was the slowest, but the differences across the reconciliation methods were minimal (Table 6).

4.3 Overall Discussion

The results confirm several important conclusions. First, the choice of reconciliation strategy is decisive for forecast accuracy. The Bottom-Up approach consistently amplified noise and underperformed, whereas the Top-Down and MinTrace methods yielded far superior outcomes.

Second, across both horizons, the Auto-ETS base forecaster with top-down reconciliation consistently provided the most accurate forecasts. Although MinTrace offers theoretically optimal reconciliation by leveraging information from all levels, its performance was not superior in this context. The stability and accuracy of the ETS national-level forecast made the top-down strategy particularly effective.

Third, the computational efficiency analysis revealed that base forecasting accounted for nearly all execution time, with reconciliation methods adding less than half a second to the total execution time. Auto-ARIMA was the fastest base forecaster, although Auto-ETS required only slightly more time while delivering superior accuracy.

Taken together, these findings establish that for the hierarchical forecasting of Australian tourism demand, **the** Auto-ETS + Top-Down combination offers the best balance of accuracy, robustness, and computational practicality.

5 Conclusions

This study aimed to evaluate hierarchical forecasting strategies for tourism demand and identify approaches that deliver both accuracy and coherence across multiple levels of aggregation. Using a large-scale dataset of quarterly Australian tourism flows, spanning regions, states, and the national total, the study systematically compared combinations of three widely used base forecasters, that is, Auto-ARIMA, Auto-ETS, and Auto-CES, with four reconciliation strategies, namely, Bottom-Up, Top-Down, and the two MinTrace variants. The analysis was conducted across both single- and multi-step forecasting horizons, and performance was judged based on the dual criteria of statistical accuracy and computational efficiency.

The findings clearly demonstrate that the bottom-up approach is consistently inadequate for this type of data. Although it preserves local information, its vulnerability to error propagation leads to forecasts that are unstable and less accurate at the aggregate level. In contrast, reconciliation methods that systematically enforce coherence, namely Top-Down and MinTrace, produced far more reliable results. Among these, the Auto-ETS base forecaster combined with a top-down reconciliation method emerged as the most robust and accurate strategy across both horizons. This outcome suggests that when the aggregate-level series is well captured—as ETS achieved in modelling trend and seasonality—disaggregation through the top-down method provides a stable and effective mechanism for producing coherent forecasts at lower levels.

The contribution of this study lies not in proposing a new algorithm but in conducting a comprehensive empirical evaluation of fundamental hierarchical forecasting methods within a critical real-world domain. By benchmarking statistical base forecasters against multiple reconciliation strategies and assessing both accuracy and computational cost, this study advances the literature by offering a holistic comparison rather than isolated evaluations. This study fills a significant gap, as much of the prior research has either focused on a single technique or neglected the computational feasibility dimension. The results validate the practical relevance of the optimal reconciliation framework, while also challenging the assumption that more complex methods will consistently outperform simpler strategies.

The core innovation of this research is its demonstration that, for Australian tourism demand, using a relatively well-structured yet straightforward approach, namely, Auto-ETS with Top-Down reconciliation, outperforms theoretically more advanced methods. This highlights the importance of aligning forecasting strategies with the intrinsic characteristics of the data rather than defaulting to complexity. Moreover, by providing a methodologically rigorous and transparent comparison, this study offers concrete, actionable recommendations for practitioners in the tourism sector, enabling them to adopt coherent forecasting frameworks that extend beyond traditional aggregate projections.

Finally, the broader contribution of this study extends beyond tourism. The methodology and findings are readily transferable to other domains where hierarchical data are prevalent, such as retail sales[18, 25], supply chain management and energy demand forecasting. By demonstrating how coherence-enforcing strategies can enhance accuracy while maintaining efficiency, this study strengthens the bridge between theoretical advancements in hierarchical forecasting and their practical application in real-world decision-making.

6 Future Work

Although this study provides a robust evaluation of hierarchical forecasting strategies, several limitations offer opportunities for future research. First, the analysis relied exclusively on univariate statistical models, which means that forecasts were generated solely from historical tourism demand data. This approach does not account for the influence of exogenous drivers, such as macroeconomic indicators, travel costs, exchange rates, or marketing expenditure. Future studies could extend the framework by incorporating multivariate models, such as Vector Autoregressions (VAR) or dynamic regression with ARIMA errors, which have shown promise in capturing external influences on tourism demand [25].

Second, the scope of this study was limited to statistical forecasters. Although these models are well established and interpretable, they may struggle to fully capture the nonlinear dependencies and structural breaks present in large-scale tourism data. Recent advancements in machine and deep learning present an exciting avenue for extending hierarchical forecasting. Algorithms such as Random Forests and XGBoost have demonstrated superior performance in demand prediction tasks owing to their ability to model complex interactions. Similarly, neural architectures, such as Long Short-Term Memory (LSTM) networks, have proven effective in capturing long-term temporal dependencies. Integrating these models within an optimal reconciliation framework could significantly enhance both accuracy and robustness.

Finally, although this study assessed computational efficiency, it did so in the context of a single dataset. Future research could investigate scalability by applying hierarchical forecasting to larger and more diverse datasets, including international tourism flows and real-time demand signals from online platforms. Such extensions would not only strengthen the generalizability of the findings but also provide deeper insights into the trade-offs between accuracy, interpretability, and computational feasibility.

References

1. Song, H., Qiu, R.T.R., Park, J.: A review of research on tourism demand forecasting: Launching the Annals of Tourism Research Curated Collection on tourism demand forecasting. Ann. Tour. Res. **75**, 338–362 (2019). https://doi.org/10.1016/j.annals.2018.12.001
2. Hu, Y.-C., Wu, G., Jiang, P.: Tourism demand forecasting using nonadditive forecast combinations. J. Hosp. Tour. Res. **47**, 775–799 (2023). https://doi.org/10.1177/109634802110 47857
3. Önder, I., Gunter, U.: Forecasting tourism demand with google trends for a major european city destination. Tour. Anal. **21** (2016). https://doi.org/10.3727/108354216x14559233984773
4. Kolambe, M.: Forecasting the future: a comprehensive review of time series prediction techniques. J. Electric. Syst. **20**, 575–586 (2024). https://doi.org/10.52783/jes.1478
5. Baggio, R., Sainaghi, R.: Complex and chaotic tourism systems: towards a quantitative approach. Int. J. Contemp. Hosp. Manag. **23**, 840–861 (2011). https://doi.org/10.1108/095961 11111153501
6. Wickramasuriya, S.L., Athanasopoulos, G., Hyndman, R.J.: Optimal forecast reconciliation for hierarchical and grouped time series through trace minimization. J. Am. Stat. Assoc. **114**, 804–819 (2019). https://doi.org/10.1080/01621459.2018.1448825

7. Regularized Regression for Hierarchical Forecasting Without Unbiasedness Conditions | Proceedings of the 25th ACM SIGKDD International Conference on Knowledge Discovery & Data Mining, https://dl.acm.org/doi/10.1145/3292500.3330976. Accessed 15 Oct 2025

8. Athanasopoulos, G., Ahmed, R.A., Hyndman, R.J.: Hierarchical forecasts for Australian domestic tourism. Int. J. Forecast. **25**, 146–166 (2009). https://doi.org/10.1016/j.ijforecast.2008.07.004

9. Athanasopoulos, G., Hyndman, R.J., Kourentzes, N., Panagiotelis, A.: Forecast reconciliation: a review. Int. J. Forecast. **40**, 430–456 (2024). https://doi.org/10.1016/j.ijforecast.2023.10.010

10. Panigrahi, S., Behera, H.S.: A hybrid ETS–ANN model for time series forecasting. Eng. Appl. Artif. Intell. **66**, 49–59 (2017). https://doi.org/10.1016/j.engappai.2017.07.007

11. Agyapong, J., Ayamga, E.A., Ibrahim Anyars, S.: Forecasting the future: applying Bayesian model averaging for exchange rates drivers in Ghana. Appl. Econ. **57**, 3876–3900 (2025). https://doi.org/10.1080/00036846.2024.2339188

12. Hyndman, R.J., Ahmed, R.A., Athanasopoulos, G., Shang, H.L.: Optimal combination forecasts for hierarchical time series. Comput. Stat. Data Anal. **55**, 2579–2589 (2011). https://doi.org/10.1016/j.csda.2011.03.006

13. Mancuso, P., Piccialli, V., Sudoso, A.M.: A machine learning approach for forecasting hierarchical time series. Expert Syst. Appl. **182**, 115102 (2021). https://doi.org/10.1016/j.eswa.2021.115102

14. Hyndman, R.J., Lee, A.J., Wang, E.: Fast computation of reconciled forecasts for hierarchical and grouped time series. Comput. Stat. Data Anal. **97**, 16–32 (2016). https://doi.org/10.1016/j.csda.2015.11.007

15. Verschoor, J.: The impact of different levels of data aggregation on demand forecasting accuracy

16. Atha, S., Bolla, B.K.: Do Deep Learning models and news headlines outperform conventional prediction techniques on forex data? In: Rout, R.R., Ghosh, S.K., Jana, P.K., Tripathy, A.K., Sahoo, J.P., Li, K.-C. (eds.) Advances in Distributed Computing and Machine Learning, pp. 413–423. Springer Nature, Singapore (2022). https://doi.org/10.1007/978-981-19-1018-0_35

17. Patil, H., Bolla, B.K., Sabeesh, E., Bhumireddy, D.R.: Comparative study of predicting stock index using deep learning models. In: Pareek, P., Gupta, N., and Reis, M.J.C.S. (eds.) Cognitive Computing and Cyber Physical Systems, pp. 45–57. Springer Nature Switzerland, Cham (2024). https://doi.org/10.1007/978-3-031-48888-7_4

18. Karmy, J.P., Maldonado, S.: Hierarchical time series forecasting via Support Vector Regression in the European Travel Retail Industry. Expert Syst. Appl. **137**, 59–73 (2019). https://doi.org/10.1016/j.eswa.2019.06.060

19. Forecasting tourist arrivals using STL-XGBoost method - Minmin He, Xiyuan Qian, 2025. https://journals.sagepub.com/doi/abs/10.1177/13548166241313411. Accessed 15 Oct 2025

20. Munyao, J.N., Oluoch, L.A., Iftikhar, H., Rodrigues, P.C.: Recurrent neural networks for hierarchical time series forecasting: An application to the S&P 500 market value. Phys. A: Statist. Mech. Appl. **678**, 130869 (2025). https://doi.org/10.1016/j.physa.2025.130869

21. Hierarchical Forecasting at Scale, https://arxiv.org/html/2310.12809v2, last accessed 2025/10/15

22. Tourism Demand Forecasting Based on a Hybrid Temporal Neural Network Model for Sustainable Tourism. https://www.mdpi.com/2071-1050/17/5/2210. Accessed 15 Oct 2025

23. Sulandari, W., Suhartono, S., Seno Saleh, S., Rodrigues, P.: Exponential smoothing on modeling and forecasting multiple seasonal time series: an overview. Fluctuat. Noise Let. **20**, 2130003 (2021). https://doi.org/10.1142/S0219477521300032

24. Forecasting Time Series With Complex Seasonal Patterns Using Exponential Smoothing: Journal of the American Statistical Association: Vol 106, No 496. https://www.tandfonline.com/doi/abs/10.1198/jasa.2011.tm09771. Accessed 15 Oct 2025
25. The Impact of the Economic Crisis and the Pandemic on the Portuguese Tourism Industry: An Econometric Approach. https://www.mdpi.com/2071-1050/17/19/8896. Accessed 15 Oct 2025

Career Advisory with Artificial Intelligence

Abejide Ade-Ibijola$^{(\boxtimes)}$ (ID)

Research Group on Data, Artificial Intelligence, and Innovations for Digital Transformation, JBS Innovation Lab, Johannesburg Business School, University of Johannesburg, Johannesburg, South Africa
`abejideai@uj.ac.za, abejide@gritlabafrica.org`

Abstract. Finding a job is becoming more difficult in the current day. This is due to the advancements in artificial intelligence (AI) and trends in the jobs that can be automated, or tasks that are doable by machines. If AI has a say in job displacement, we could also use it in the prediction of future jobs. This is an important exercise for young Africans studying in higher education institutions. In this paper, we have proposed an AI-powered career advisory system that uses real-time job market data, skills mapping, and predictive analytics to offer personalised guidance to students about jobs that are going extinct, relevant skills that will be relevant, and future prospects. This work employs design science research methodology, integrating user selection with AI algorithms to dynamically recommend career paths. Our evaluation by students highlights a 72% approval of their trust in the system, a 64% likelihood of recommendation to other users, and improved alignment of user skills with future job opportunities. The system shows significant potential to improve the readiness of the workforce and bridge the gaps between education and employment. This AI-driven approach can redefine career advisory systems, allowing students to adapt to the evolving job market and mitigate the risks of unemployment.

Keywords: AI career advisory · career guidance · job recommendations · skill integration · AI in career counseling

1 Introduction

A career is more than just a job; it is an important aspect of our lives that shapes our identity, provides financial stability, and helps in the development of society [9,17,53]. A well-chosen career paves the way to financial security and independence by enabling us to make a decent living, meet our needs, and follow our dreams [23,44]. Our careers can determine who we are and how we think [7,20,27]. A fulfilling career is crucial for living a successful and meaningful life. It allows us to tap into our potential to make a meaningful impact in our lives as we continue to learn, develop new abilities, and take on new challenges [22,37,50].

H. Kannan et al. (Eds.): AIKP 2025, CCIS 2804, pp. 264–279, 2026.
https://doi.org/10.1007/978-3-032-14706-6_21

As traditional jobs become obsolete, there is a growing demand for workers with specialised skills such as data science and artificial intelligence. By 2030, it is estimated that 22% of current workforce activities could (or will) be automated [18,46]. Hard-labour jobs, such as those in brick-and-mortar establishments and other traditional roles like cashiers, are slowly fading or disappearing [1,13]. The World Economic Forum's 2023 report mentions that while 69 million jobs are expected to be created, 83 million will be extinct due to the shift in the division of labour between humans and machines [14].

Within the same time and context, most students/trained professionals find it difficult to choose the right career due to a lack of adequate guidance, limited access to advisory resources, or insufficient information about future job trends [19,42]. Traditional approaches often fail to consider skills, the changing nature of jobs, and new technological advancements such as AI [3,36]. Many will argue that qualifications are also not so strong as they used to be, in the advent of COVID-19 where assessments are written at home [21,38,39] and ChatGPT where essays are written with AI [8].

Due to the rapid advancement of technology, certain jobs are becoming obsolete at a concerning rate, with 45% of tasks that can be automated [2]. Artificial intelligence and automation are reshaping industries, replacing human workers with machines [33,41,49]. Soft skills such as emotional intelligence, digital literacy, and the ability to think critically remain critical as they have been listed as skills that machines cannot easily mimic [10,45]. This shift has significant consequences for the workforce, as many individuals may find themselves unprepared for the future jobs [32,35]. According to a 2020 report by the McKinsey Global Institute, automation could displace up to 800 million workers globally by 2030, with many needing to transition to new occupations [30,47].

Existing career guidance solutions, including traditional counseling and static recommendation systems, face a number of significant limitations. These solutions often fail to incorporate real-time data about emerging careers or the rapidly evolving skill demands that will be critical in the next five to 10 years [40]. This lack of adaptability can leave students unprepared for the dynamic job market (especially in the African context, where there might not be many experienced or technical career counselors), where industries and occupations are constantly transforming. Additionally, these systems may not adequately address the increasing importance of AI-related skills, which are becoming essential across various sectors [3]. By neglecting to highlight the potential of AI and its applications in various career paths, these solutions may limit students' opportunities and hinder their ability to thrive in the future workforce [36].

AI-powered systems can help students explore non-traditional career paths and identify opportunities that may not be apparent through traditional methods. Additionally, these systems can provide continuous support and guidance throughout a student's career journey, helping them adapt to changing circumstances and make informed decisions.

Figure 1 presents a block diagram of how the AI Career Advisor works. The users begin on the landing page then the faculty page to select a faculty. The app then fetches data from a CSV dataset to display available courses for the selected faculty. The application dynamically generates card representing potential jobs, extinct jobs, learning resources, and AI/technical skills. Clicking on a card opens a modal popup displaying detailed information about the selected item.

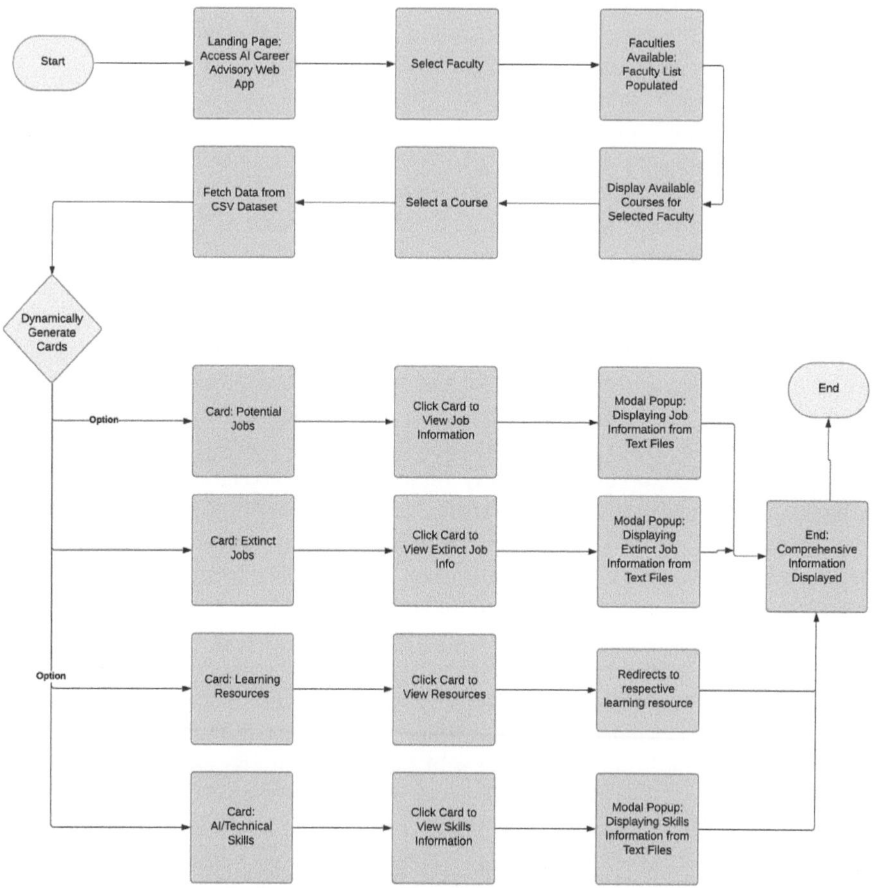

Fig. 1. How the system works.

The contribution of this paper are as follows. We have:

1. designed an AI-powered career advisory system using the design science research methodology,
2. tested and evaluated this system amongst students who need career advisory, and
3. conducted an evaluation of how this system supports students in career advisory.

The remainder of this paper is organised as follows: Sect. 2 reviews existing career advisory tools and highlights the gaps in their design and accessibility. Section 3 explains the design and methodology of the new system, including the use of the design science research methodology. Section 4 provides details on the implementation of the AI advisory system, covering key functionalities. Section 5 concludes the paper and outlines potential future work and recommendations to enhance the system further.

2   Literature Review and Related Works

The AI Advisory System presented in this paper uses AI to deliver relevant career guidance, as it offers a comprehensive approach to career planning, by dynamically integrating real-time job market analytics, educational data, and study choice. It not only recommends career paths aligned with a student's discipline and potential qualifications but also anticipates emerging trends in the job market, ensuring relevance and adaptability in a rapidly changing economic landscape.

Key features of this system include its ability to process large-scale data, identify patterns in industry growth, and predict skill demands. This offers students insights that extend beyond conventional advisory methods. Traditional systems often rely on static information, such as historical job placement records or generic aptitude assessments, which can be insufficient for addressing the dynamic nature of modern careers [51]. In contrast, this AI Advisory System employs advanced AI-driven algorithms and machine learning models to provide real-time, data-informed recommendations.

Furthermore, this system is designed to be highly accessible and scalable, making it suitable for a wide range of users, from high school students exploring initial career options to university graduates refining their career options. By bridging the gap between individual aspirations and the evolving job market, the system empowers students to make informed, strategic decisions about their career paths. This forward-thinking approach not only enhances the decision-making process but also contributes to addressing broader societal challenges, such as workforce alignment and skill shortages in emerging industries [6,24].

2.1   Career Advisory Tools

In this section we present a comparison of career advisory tools with the newly proposed AI Career Advisory App. This is presented in Table 1. An individual summary of these tools is as follows:

1. Holland Test: The Holland Test (RIASEC) is a career counseling tool that classifies people into six personality types: realistic, investigative, Artistic, Social, Enterprising, and Conventional. Developed by John Holland, it helps match individuals with careers and work environments that align with their personality traits, promoting job satisfaction and effectiveness [5,12,43].

2. O*NET Online: Provides detailed information on thousands of occupations, including job tasks, technology skills required, and salary information [28,29].
3. CliftonStrength: CliftonStrength focuses on identifying an individual's strengths rather than weaknesses, categorising them into 34 talent themes. Users can gain insights into career areas where they are likely to excel, based on these strengths. This tool requires a fee, but it is widely used by individuals looking to understand their unique strengths for personal and professional development [15,34].
4. LinkedIn Career Explorer: helps users find career paths by identifying transferable skills, suggesting skills to learn, and connecting them with job openings and industry contacts for a smoother career transition [11,31,48].
5. Myers-Briggs Type Indicator (MBTI): This tool assesses personality types based on preferences, helping individuals understand their strengths, interests, and potential career paths. It is widely used in career counseling, team building, and personal growth to enhance self-awareness and interpersonal skills [4,16,25,52].

Career advisory tools have limitations; they usually give broad recommendations and do not have the feel of a human counselor; their data can be outdated or incomplete [26,28]. Some career advisory tools are industry-specific and may be biased [29]. These tools often focus on the quantitative aspects and do not pay enough attention to soft skills and personal values, limiting the choices of occupations and do not take into consideration shifts in fields or personal circumstances [26]

2.2 Summary

This section gives insight to various existing career advisory tools, such as the Holland Test, O*NET Online, CliftonStrengths, LinkedIn Career Explorer, and the Myers-Briggs Type Indicator (MBTI), which offer personalised career guidance by assessing personality traits, skills, and interests. While these tools provide valuable insights, they have notable limitations, including broad recommendations that lack a personal touch, potential reliance on outdated or incomplete data and neglecting technical skills that could be in demand leading to a failure to adapt to shifts in fields. The next section covers the methodology, outlining the approach for exploring how AI-powered career advisory tools can overcome these challenges, offering more adaptive and data-driven career guidance.

3 Methodology

This study adopts a *Design Science Research Methodology (DSRM)* framework to develop and evaluate the effectiveness of an AI-based career advisory tool compared to traditional methods. The methodology follows a structured six-step process, ensuring a systematic approach to problem-solving and artifact evaluation.

Table 1. Comparison Between AI Career Prospects App and Other Career Advisory Tools

Career Advisory Tools	Difference with AI Career Advisory App
Holland Test	Holland Code provides a valuable framework for understanding career interests and personality types, while the AI career advisory app offers more personalized recommendations by considering factors such as qualification and skills. It can also provide insights into emerging job opportunities and potential career paths that align with the user's choice of study
O*NET Online	O*NET focuses on providing comprehensive occupational data and job descriptions, while AI Career Prospects uses AI to analyze the impact of automation on different careers and gives real-time insights into potential job extinction, alongside recommending emerging AI skills
CliftonStrength	CliftonStrengths is a tool for identifying individual strengths and talents. However, an AI career advisory app can take this a step further by analyzing potential strengths in the context of current and future job market trends. It can provide personalized recommendations for career paths that align with the user's strength, while also suggesting opportunities for skill development to enhance their career prospects
Linkedin Career Explorer	LinkedIn Career Explorer helps users find career paths by identifying transferable skills and suggesting skills to learn. In comparison, AI career advisory analyzes market trends, highlighting roles aligned with emerging technologies and suggesting targeted learning paths for future-ready skills
Myers-Briggs Type Indicator	MBTI assesses personality types to help individuals understand their strengths and career paths. AI career advisory app focuses on industry demand, automation, and required skills, offering a more adaptive and data-driven approach for personalized career guidance

3.1 Problem Identification and Motivation

The initial step involved defining the research problem and understanding its importance. Through a literature review and stakeholder interviews, gaps in traditional career advisory systems were identified. The analysis revealed issues such as insufficient personalisation in career recommendations, a lack of data-driven insights that reflect dynamic labor market trends, and challenges in addressing the influence of AI on future job markets. This phase highlighted the need for an AI-driven advisory system capable of providing adaptive, personalized, and data-backed guidance tailored to diverse users.

3.2   Objective of the Solution

The objective of the research was to design and implement an AI-based career advisory tool that enhances career guidance by addressing identified gaps. The system aims to provide personalized career recommendations, leverage data analytics to adapt to evolving job market trends, and ensure inclusivity across user demographics with diverse levels of technological literacy.

3.3   Design and Development

The system was created using a *User-Centered Design (UCD)* approach, ensuring iterative refinement based on user feedback. The development process began with user research, involving surveys, interviews, and focus groups with students, early-career professionals, and the unemployed. This research uncovered specific challenges, such as identifying new professions, matching personal skills to market demand, and navigating labor market instability.

Following this, a prototype was developed with features that included AI-driven recommendations, an intuitive interface, and support for both mobile and desktop platforms. The design underwent iterative refinement, where feedback from usability testing was used to make adjustments to the interface, improve recommendation accuracy, and enhance the overall user experience. This approach ensured the system catered to a wide range of users with varying levels of technological literacy.

3.4   Demonstration

The system was tested through A/B testing and ethnographic research to evaluate its performance and user acceptance. During the A/B testing phase, multiple versions of the system were tested with diverse users to identify the most effective design elements. For instance, comparisons were made between mobile-optimized and desktop versions to understand user preferences and optimize the experience for each platform. Additionally, the placement and wording of calls-to-action, such as buttons labeled "Explore Careers," were tested to assess their influence on user engagement and navigation.

Ethnographic research further enriched the evaluation process by offering insights into the social, cultural, and psychological factors influencing career decisions. Observations and interviews were conducted with individuals in both rural and urban settings, providing a deeper understanding of the behaviors, motivations, and challenges faced by users in their career decision-making journeys.

3.5   Evaluation

The effectiveness of the system was evaluated based on usability, effectiveness, and adoption. Usability testing ensured the system was easy to navigate, even for users with limited technological skills. Effectiveness was measured by assessing the accuracy and relevance of the career recommendations provided by the system. Adoption was gauged through user feedback, focusing on satisfaction levels and the likelihood of continued use. The insights gained from surveys, user testing, and focus groups guided the iterative improvement of the system.

3.6   Communication

Finally, the findings from this research were documented and shared through detailed reports and presentations to stakeholders. These communications emphasized the contributions of the system to enhancing career advisory practices and provided a foundation for future developments. The iterative and user-centered approach ensured that the developed system effectively addressed the identified problem and achieved its objectives.

3.7   Summary

The methodology outlines the use of the DSRM framework to design and evaluate an AI-based career advisory system. Key steps included identifying gaps in traditional tools, setting objectives for a personalized solution, and developing a user-centered prototype refined through feedback. Testing via A/B testing and ethnographic research assessed usability, engagement, and accuracy, guiding improvements. Findings highlighted the system's potential to enhance career advisory practices. The next section covers implementation, results, and evaluation.

4   Implementation, Evaluation, and Results

4.1   Implementation Details

AI Career Advisory Tool is designed to offer insight on career paths for the future taking into account the integration of artificial intelligence in the job market.

Components

- **HTML**: Structure and content of the webpages
- **CSS**: Styling of the webpages integrated with bootstrap for a responsive layout, ensuring optimal viewing on different devices
- **Javascript**: dynamic interactions and processing data
- **CSV files**: Storing information of over 100 courses from the University of Johannesburg
- **Text files**: Used to map the Jobs, Skills to their descriptions

Landing Page. Figure 2 shows the landing page for AI Career Advisory. The theme colours of GRIT Lab Africa was used for the styling (GRIT Lab Africa is a free training societal impact project that runs in several African countries).

Fig. 2. Landing page.

Faculties and Courses. Figure 3a shows a range of faculty offered at the University of Johannesburg. Each faculty has specific courses, narrowing the search to one specific faculty. Figure 3b shows all the available undergraduate courses in the Faculty of Science. The course are retrieved from a csv file based on which faculty was selected.

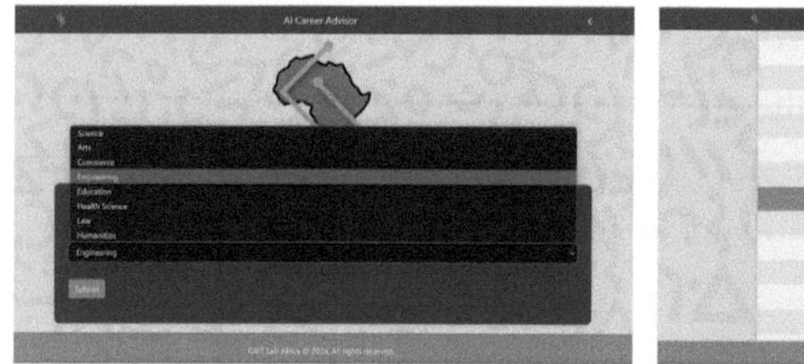

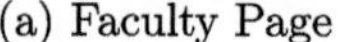

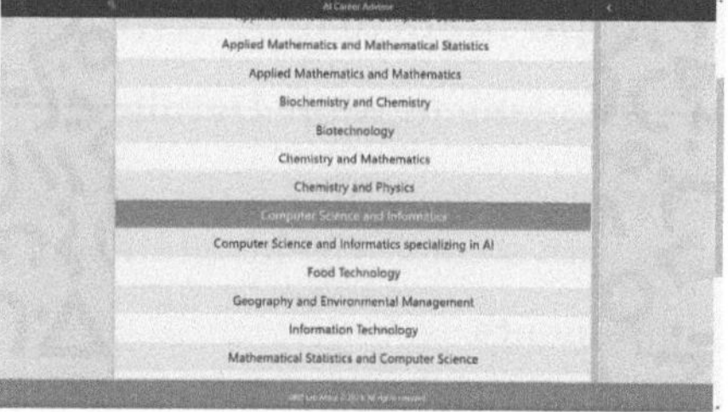

(a) Faculty Page   (b) Course Page (Science Faculty)

Fig. 3. Qualification Pages.

Prospects. The application fetches data from a row in the csv dataset based on the course selected. The data is then used to populate dynamically generated cards displaying potential jobs, extinct jobs, AI/technical skills, and learning resources as shown in Fig. 4a. Each card is clickable, triggering a modal popup to display additional information retrieved from text files as shown in Fig. 4b.

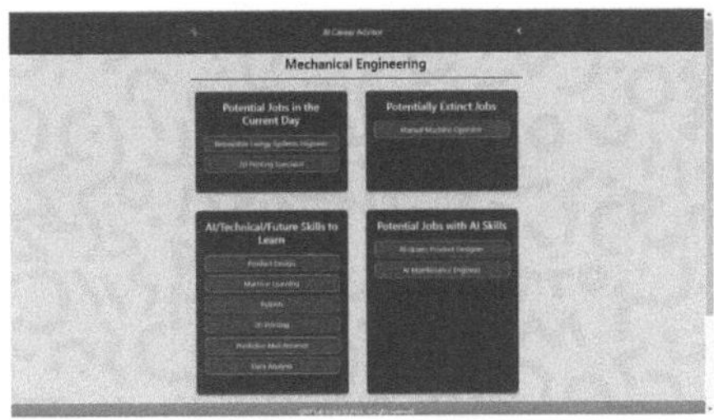

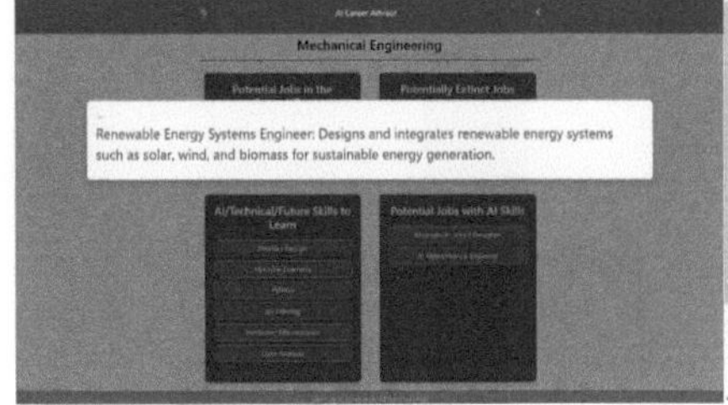

(a) Course prospects   (b) Career description

Fig. 4. Course and career information.

Qualitative survey data were statistically analysed to identify trends in user satisfaction, engagement, and trust in AI-based tools. The sample size of 25, though relatively small, was chosen to provide focused insights into user satisfaction and trust in AI-based tools. While smaller samples limit the inference and statistical power, they allow for an in-depth exploration of user behaviors and preferences, particularly in a homogeneous group such as targeted users of the AI advisory app. The results should be interpreted with caution, as they may be sensitive to outliers and may not fully represent broader populations. To mitigate these limitations, future research should incorporate larger sample sizes and diverse user groups to validate the findings. For this study, the focus remains on identifying preliminary trends and providing a foundation for further development and evaluation of the app.

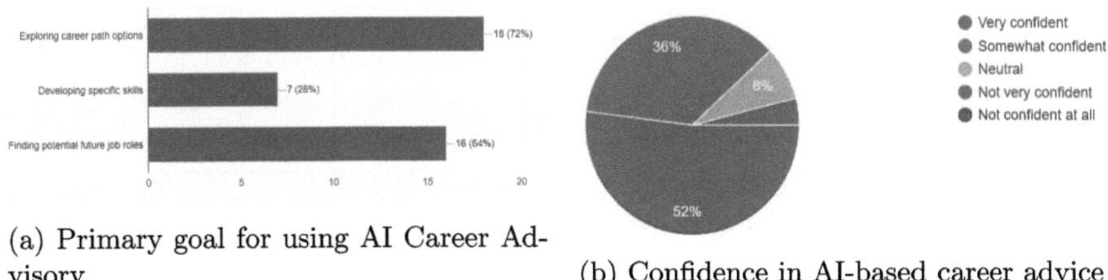

(a) Primary goal for using AI Career Advisory   (b) Confidence in AI-based career advice

Fig. 5. User Expectations and Confidence in AI Career Advisory.

4.2 Data Analysis

User Expectations and Confidence. The provided plots in Fig. 5 offer insights into users' expectations and confidence in AI driven career advisory tools. The bar graph shown in Fig. 5 shows that the majority of users (72%) aim to explore various career paths, while a significant portion (64%) seeks guidance on future job trends. For confidence in AI driven career advice, the pie chart

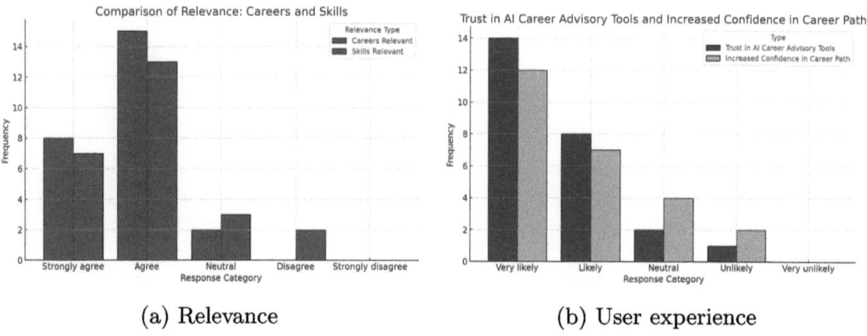

(a) Relevance   (b) User experience

Fig. 6. Data analysis on the relevance of job and skill recommendations (left) and users' experience with the app (right).

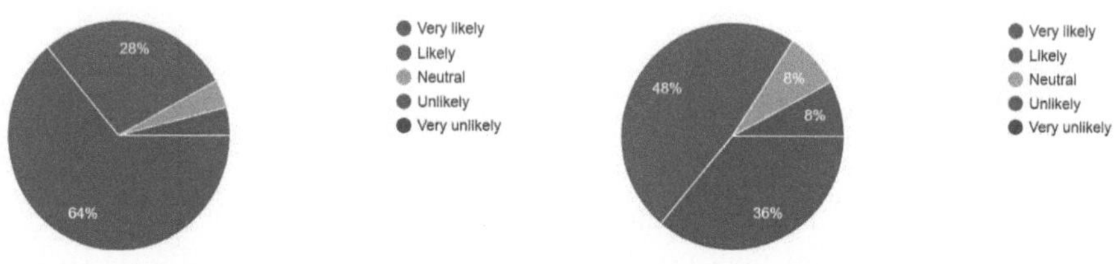

(a) Likelihood of recommending AI career advisory tool to others?

(b) Likelihood of using this tool to refine ones career goals in the future?

Fig. 7. AI Career Advisory Tool Feedback.

shown in Fig. 5b, the distribution is skewed towards positive sentiments. Over half of the respondents (52%) express very high confidence, while an additional 30% are somewhat confident. These results suggest that users are optimistic about the potential of AI with regards to providing valuable career insights, with a strong focus on exploration and future trends. However, a non-negligible portion remains cautious, highlighting the need for continued development and improve of AI-powered career advisory tools to build trust and confidence.

Relevance and User Experience. The plots in Fig. 6 offer insights into users' opinions on the relevance of job and skill recommendations, as well as their experience with the AI career advisory tool. The relevance pie chart in Fig. 6a shows that a significant majority of users agree or strongly agree that the career recommendations are relevant, while a smaller portion finds the skill recommendations relevant. This suggests that the tool may be more effective in providing career path suggestions than specific skill-based guidance. The bar chart in Fig. 6b illustrates a strong positive correlation between trust in AI career advisory tools and increased confidence in their career paths after using AI career advisory. This suggests that AI-powered tools can be effective in empowering individuals to make informed career decisions. However, a small portion of respondents expressed a neutral stance towards both trust and confidence, indicating that there is still room for improvement in AI tool development to ensure widespread user satisfaction.

Likelihood of Recommending and Future Use. The provided pie charts in Fig. 7 offer insights into users' willingness to recommend and utilize the AI career advisory tool. Regarding recommendations in Fig. 7a, a significant proportion (64%) indicate they are very likely or likely to recommend the tool to others. This positive sentiment is further supported by the high percentage (46%) of users who express very high or high likelihood of using the tool to refine their career goals in the future shown in Fig. 7b. These findings suggest that the AI career advisory tool is generally well-received and perceived as a valuable resource for career planning and decision-making.

4.3   Tool Evaluation

The AI-based career advisory tool was evaluated based on its accuracy and user experience. Qualitative data provided an in-depth view of user experience, highlighting specific feedback on the tool's strengths and areas for improvement. By analyzing user satisfaction and engagement, the study identified factors that contribute to higher trust in AI recommendations and increased confidence in career planning. This evaluation offered a robust understanding of how effectively AI can support and enhance career advisory practices.

5   Conclusion, Recommendation, and Future Works

5.1   Conclusion

In conclusion, the AI Career Advisory App is more personalised than regular approaches, focusing on real-time information about the job market and new AI skills it helps users to receive relevant recommendations on career choice and outlook on future employment. These surveys revealed that there is high confidence in the use of Artificial Intelligence advice and user is willing to repeat the experience. Such enhancements as with interactive questionnaires or augmented resources for occupations could improve the use of the app and can prove to be valuable as a career-planning tool in the existing and the future job market.

5.2   Recommendation

Collecting user feedback has highlighted several areas for improvement in the AI Career Advisory App. The addition of a questionnaire involving user interests and skills would enhance the accuracy of career path recommendations. Incorporating diverse learning resources, such as online courses from Coursera, Udacity, and edX, would provide users with more comprehensive learning opportunities. Additionally, the app could benefit from video content to supplement courses and increase user engagement.

5.3 Future Works

To further enhance the app, it is recommended to provide more detailed descriptions of career paths using bullet points to avoid wordiness. Expanding the range of career paths, including emerging and innovative roles in the tech field, would broaden the scope of opportunities. Improving response time, design, and overall responsiveness would significantly enhance the user experience. By implementing these recommendations, the app can become a powerful tool, providing tailored career guidance and inspiring users on their journey.

Acknowledgment. The author would like to acknowledge his mentees (beneficiaries of the GRIT Lab Africa non-profit training programme) that contributed to the operational aspects of the development of the tool described in this work.

References

1. Acemoglu, D., Restrepo, P.: Robots and jobs: evidence from us labor markets. J. Polit. Econ. **128**(6), 2188–2244 (2020)
2. Acemoglu, D., Restrepo, P.: Tasks, automation, and the rise in us wage inequality. Econometrica **90**(5), 1973–2016 (2022)
3. Alekseeva, L., Azar, J., Giné, M., Samila, S., Taska, B.: The demand for AI skills in the labor market. Labour Econ. **71**, 102002 (2021)
4. Mohammad Hossein Amirhosseini and Hassan Kazemian: Machine learning approach to personality type prediction based on the myers-briggs type indicator. Multimodal Technol. Interact. **4**(1), 9 (2020)
5. Ayriza, Y., Triyanto, A., Setiawati, F.A., Gunawan, N.E.: Exploring children's career interests and knowledge based on Holland's theory. Int. J. Instr. **13**(4), 643–662 (2020)
6. Bankins, S., Jooss, S., Restubog, S.L.D., Marrone, M., Ocampo, A.C., Shoss, M.: Navigating career stages in the age of artificial intelligence: a systematic interdisciplinary review and agenda for future research. J. Vocational Behav. 104011 (2024)
7. Batool, S.S., Ghayas, S.: Process of career identity formation among adolescents: components and factors. Heliyon **6**(9) (2020)
8. Bin-Nashwan, S.A., Sadallah, M., Bouteraa, M.: Use of ChatGPT in academia: academic integrity hangs in the balance. Technol. Soc. **75**, 102370 (2023)
9. Blustein, D.L.: The Importance of Work in an Age of Uncertainty: The Eroding Work Experience in America. Oxford University Press, Oxford (2019)
10. Czerwinski, M., Hernandez, J., McDuff, D.: Building an AI that feels: AI systems with emotional intelligence could learn faster and be more helpful. IEEE Spectr. **58**(5), 32–38 (2021)
11. Davis, J., Wolff, H.-G., Forret, M.L., Sullivan, S.E.: Networking via Linkedin: an examination of usage and career benefits. J. Vocat. Behav. **118**, 103396 (2020)
12. D'Silva, G., Jani, M., Jadhav, V., Bhoir, A., Amin, P.: Career counselling chatbot using cognitive science and artificial intelligence. In: Vasudevan, H., Michalas, A., Shekokar, N., Narvekar, M. (eds.) Advanced Computing Technologies and Applications. AIS, pp. 1–9. Springer, Singapore (2020). https://doi.org/10.1007/978-981-15-3242-9_1

13. Filippi, E., Banno, M., Trento, S.: Automation technologies and their impact on employment: a review, synthesis and future research agenda. Technol. Forecast. Soc. Chang. **191**, 122448 (2023)
14. World Economic Forum. The future of jobs report 2023 (2023)
15. Fraaza, A., Urban, E.: Cliftonstrengths for students: developing engaged and thriving students through strengths awareness and development (2019)
16. Furnham, A.: Myers-briggs type indicator (MBTI). In: Encyclopedia of Personality and Individual Differences, pp. 3059–3062 (2020)
17. Gati, I., Kulcsár, V.: Making better career decisions: from challenges to opportunities. J. Vocat. Behav. **126**, 103545 (2021)
18. Hasan, A.R.: Artificial intelligence (AI) in accounting & auditing: a literature review. Open J. Bus. Manag. **10**(1), 440–465 (2021)
19. Herath, G.A.C.A., Kumara, B.T.G.S., Ishanka, U.A.P., Rathnayaka, R.M.K.T.: Computer-assisted career guidance tools for students' career path planning: a review on enabling technologies and applications. J. Inf. Technol. Educ. Res. **23**, 6 (2024)
20. Ibarra, H.: Working Identity, Updated Edition, With a New Preface: Unconventional Strategies for Reinventing Your Career. Harvard Business Press (2023)
21. Ives, B., Cazan, A.-M.: Did the COVID-19 pandemic lead to an increase in academic misconduct in higher education? High. Educ. **86**(5), 977–994 (2023)
22. Jia-Jun, Z., Hua-Ming, S.: The impact of career growth on knowledge-based employee engagement: the mediating role of affective commitment and the moderating role of perceived organizational support. Front. Psychol. **13**, 805208 (2022)
23. Khalaf, M.E., Abubakr, N.H., Alenezi, H., Ziada, H.: The motivation and confidence in choosing dentistry as a career amongst dental students: a mixed-methods study. Eur. J. Dent. Educ. **26**(1), 66–75 (2022)
24. Kim, J., Ro, K.: A study on the data collection and convergence of career advisor system using AI. J. Digit. Converg. **17**(2), 177–185 (2019)
25. King, S.P., Mason, B.A.: Myers-Briggs type indicator. In: The Wiley Encyclopedia of Personality and Individual Differences: Measurement and Assessment, pp. 315–319 (2020)
26. Kulcsár, V., Dobrean, A., Gati, I.: Challenges and difficulties in career decision making: their causes, and their effects on the process and the decision. J. Vocat. Behav. **116**, 103346 (2020)
27. Lawrence, T.B., Phillips, N.: Constructing Organizational Life: How Social-Symbolic Work Shapes Selves, Organizations, and Institutions. Oxford University Press, Oxford (2019)
28. Lent, R.W., Brown, S.D.: Career decision making, fast and slow: toward an integrative model of intervention for sustainable career choice. J. Vocat. Behav. **120**, 103448 (2020)
29. Liu, J., Wang, T., Yao, F., Huang, J., He, R., Li, J.: Career cocoons: analyzing occupational mobility with graph embedding model. In: 2023 6th International Conference on Data Science and Information Technology (DSIT), pp. 115–123. IEEE (2023)
30. Manyika, J., et al.: The future of work after COVID-19 (2020)
31. Marin, I., Amel, H.: Web platform for job recommendation based on machine learning. In: ENASE, pp. 676–683 (2023)
32. Masriadi, P., Dasmadi, M., Ekaningrum, N.E., Hidayat, M.S., Yuliaty, F.: Exploring the future of work: impact of automation and artificial intelligence on employment. ENDLESS: Int. J. Future Stud. **6**(1), 125 (2023)

33. McLeay, F., Osburg, V.S., Yoganathan, V., Patterson, A.: Replaced by a robot: service implications in the age of the machine. J. Serv. Res. **24**(1), 104–121 (2021)
34. Miles, A.F.: Career Assessment Feedback Specificity and Students' Academic and Career Outcomes. Ph.D. thesis, The George Washington University (2024)
35. Mindell, D.A., Reynolds, E., et al.: The Work of the Future: Building Better Jobs in an Age of Intelligent Machines. MIT Press, Cambridge (2023)
36. Morandini, S., et al.: The impact of artificial intelligence on workers' skills: upskilling and reskilling in organisations. Inform. Sci. **26**, 39–68 (2023)
37. Nakuloadi, H., Rustina, E., Widodo, T.: Antecedents of career optimism, career success, and competence for career sustainability as a professional lecturer in Indonesia. Ekombis Rev.: Jurnal Ilmiah Ekonomi dan Bisnis **12**, 10 (2024)
38. Newton, P.M.: The validity of unproctored online exams is undermined by cheating. Proc. Natl. Acad. Sci. U.S.A. **120**(41), e2312978120 (2023)
39. Newton, P.M., Essex, K.: How common is cheating in online exams and did it increase during the COVID-19 pandemic? A systematic review. J. Acad. Ethics **22**(2), 323–343 (2024)
40. Savickas, M.: Career Counseling. American Psychological Association, Washington, DC (2019)
41. Semuels, A.: Millions of Americans have lost jobs in the pandemic–and robots and AI are replacing them faster than ever. Time Mag. **6**, 2020 (2020)
42. Sharif, N., Ahmad, N., Sarwar, S., et al.: Factors influencing career choices. IBT J. Bus. Stud. (JBS) **1**(1) (2019)
43. Sheldon, K.M., Holliday, G., Titova, L., Benson, C.: Comparing Holland and self-determination theory measures of career preference as predictors of career choice. J. Career Assess. **28**(1), 28–42 (2020)
44. Singh, V., Gupta, S.: Gen z's career expectations and job-seeking behaviours. Media Educ. Natl. Educ. Policy, 72
45. Subramani, K., Manoharan, G.: Humanizing the role of artificial intelligence in revolutionizing emotional intelligence. In: 2024 3rd International Conference on Computational Modelling, Simulation and Optimization (ICCMSO), pp. 237–242. IEEE (2024)
46. Taylor, A., Nelson, J., O'Donnell, S., Davies, E., Hillary, J.: The Skills Imperative 2035: What Does the Literature Tell Us about Essential Skills Most Needed for Work? Working Paper 1. ERIC (2022)
47. Tiwari, R.: The impact of AI and machine learning on job displacement and employment opportunities. Int. J. Eng. Technol. Manag. Res. **7**(1) (2023)
48. Urdaneta-Ponte, M.C., Oleagordia-Ruiz, I., Mendez-Zorrilla, A., Using Linkedin endorsements to reinforce an ontology and machine learning-based recommender system to improve professional skills. Electronics **11**(8), 1190 (2022)
49. Vorobeva, D., El Fassi, Y., Pinto, D.C., Hildebrand, D., Herter, M.M., Mattila, A.S.: Thinking skills don't protect service workers from replacement by artificial intelligence. J. Serv. Res. **25**(4), 601–613 (2022)
50. Westman, S., et al.: Artificial intelligence for career guidance – current requirements and prospects for the future. IAFOR J. Educ. **9**, 43–62 (2021)
51. Yanamala, K.K.R.: Strategic implications of AI integration in workforce planning and talent forecasting. J. Adv. Comput. Syst. **4**(1), 1–9 (2024)
52. Yanti, N.E., Surjono, H.D., Sunarto, S.: Development of web-based information media for career choice recommendations according to personality type of MBTI. In: International Conference on Online and Blended Learning 2019 (ICOBL 2019), pp. 186–189. Atlantis Press (2020)

53. Zwysen, W., Longhi, S.: Employment and earning differences in the early career of ethnic minority British graduates: the importance of university career, parental background and area characteristics. J. Ethn. Migr. Stud. **44**(1), 154–172 (2018)

Street-Cred: A Tool for Estimating the Credibility of Small Businesses Using AI-Generated Ranking of Key Growth Indicators

Abejide Ade-Ibijola[1]([✉]) [iD] and Opeoluwa Iwashokun[2] [iD]

[1] Research Group On Data, Artificial Intelligence, and Innovations for Digital Transformation, JBS Innovation Lab, Johannesburg Business School, University of Johannesburg, Johannesburg, South Africa
abejideai@uj.ac.za, abejide@gritlabafrica.org
[2] Data Science Across Disciplines Research Group, Faculty of Engineering and Built Environment, University of Johannesburg, Johannesburg, South Africa
iwashokuno@uj.ac.za

Abstract. The importance of credibility rating to the perceived growth of a business entity cannot be over-emphasized. A business's customer attraction and retention are largely influenced by its reputation. Therefore, enabling structures to maintain that a business stays afloat, focusing on the business's credibility is of great necessity. Small businesses are burgeoning and may be less concerned about setting aside funds to evaluate and reevaluate their growth in the industry. This paper solves the challenge of business visibility rating with Artificial Intelligence for small businesses with a growth mindset to scale based on an experimental simulation of an AI tool. We designed the tool to estimate a business' credibility using AI-generated key growth indicators to rank a business across industry standard. The gamified tool estimates the credibility rating of a given business based on a series of question-answering plays. The questions are weighted, scored, and comparable to inquiries made at governmental parastatals toward creating a record of credible small businesses. The tool evaluation by small business respondents gives an 68% above average satisfactory level. The respondents were fascinated by the use of a gamified tool to learn about measures of business credibility. Small businesses can engage this tool for self-evaluation as a reflection of their business growth. This provides better knowledge support and monitoring with less human interference from concerned government agencies or departments that are implored to train them.

Keywords: small businesses · key growth indicators · AI-generated ranking · experimental simulation · assistive tools

1 Introduction

A credibility rating provides a framework for aggregating attributes of various comparable business brands so they may be assessed relative to each other towards a ranking for reputation or order of hierarchy [1–3]. Largely influencing the business reputation

H. Kannan et al. (Eds.): AIKP 2025, CCIS 2804, pp. 280–286, 2026.
https://doi.org/10.1007/978-3-032-14706-6_22

risks, business credibility ratings offer intangible profit advantages promoting business growth by the stakeholder's perceived measure of trustworthiness and reliability [1, 4, 5]. Growth indicators considered for the credibility of businesses include financial solvency and customer satisfaction [1], such that a business brand or reputation is often associated with the quantifiable level of customers' perception.

Growth indicators for organisations can assess their performance, identify areas for improvement, and drive strategic conversations for sustainable growth and success [5]. It becomes of vital importance for monitoring performance and the measurement of the credibility of growing businesses. These are measurable and can be assisted by a tool. For example, there are existing digital trackers for customer experiences on product satisfaction levels on many websites. Growth indicators are not just numbers but a representation of the health of a business highlighting potential risks and possible areas of improvement to guide a business's strategic planning [4].

Credibility rating contributes to businesses' reputation and perceived quality by customers. It was observed that it is measured individually by businesses using various tools and digital add-on facilities at their disposal. This poses a challenge of ineffective measure of a brand's market share as self-measure of brand reputation leads to no improvement. Another possible challenge is the likely ignorance of start-ups and small businesses of the knowledge of measures of developing the brand reputation even as the business kicks off. Therefore this study considers seeks to consider "How can AI tool provide knowledge of credibility status to small businesses?" and "What is the measure of acceptance of such a tool to small businessses in South Africa?" as research questions. The use of AI in teaching and learning innovation may be extended to various trainings administered to small businesses creating a personal and engaging experience. The paper contributes to knowledge by providing:

1. an AI tool design for the credibility check and scoring of small businesses,
2. development of a learning process for small and medium-scale business organizations for driving sustainability and growth, and
3. overall perception of small businesses on credibility rating.

The remainder of the paper is divided into four additional sections. Section 2 contains the existing literature and theoretical underpinning. Section 3 describes the methodology for this research and Sect. 4 highlights the data results and evaluation from the tool design and a concluding summary is in Sect. 5.

2 Related Work

Existing literature covers various AI capabilities for increasing business values for small businesses on performances and process levels [6–8]. For example, the Internet and online-facing business capabilities enable small businesses to need and largely use AI technologies for digital marketing and brand development for scaling up business [6]. Existing literature demonstrates the concept of business trust from consumers or users as vital to credibility rating [9] while some works of literature are concerned with the reputation of the business in online markets as it affects the formation of customers' trust researchers [10]. The concept of online reputation is fluid and easily diminished by irate customers or increased by one-time delightful customers. The perception of one customer on one product may inform the bias in the perception of thousands of other customers who view the business product relative to other products [9, 11]. Businesses and customers would make an informed reputation and trust with standards presented as weighted questions with clear feedback compared to one-time online customer responses for perceiving a business.

2.1 Key Growth Indicators for Small Businesses

The key growth indicators point towards an overall current reputation for a business organization in focus. A business at the kick-off stage may be highly focused on profit maximization rather than expansion hence desirous of measures of immediate gains while reputation may be at risk [12]. Measuring these indicators involves assessing various growth factors that reflect not only their financial health but operational effectiveness, and market position. Business value creation deepens with the ability to understand, monitor, estimate and assess the value creation activity in theory and practice [13].

Appropriate set of indicators for measuring small business value aligns with brand recognition [14], productivity metrics in record details [13], social media channels [15], corporate social responsibilities [16], government policies and regulation impact [17], cash flows from operations indicative of revenue growth [13], retention, and acquisition of new customers/clients which determines lifetime value and growth of customer/client base [18]. We focus on these indicators for measuring how the business may be perceived by intending buyers or potential business clients, as given by the aforementioned literature. Although not directly measurable, it can have direct implication on the success or failure of the business.

2.2 Impact of Tools for Small Businesses

There are works of literature on the use of AI technologies for various business impact. The aspect of the use of AI tools for learning and education in business is not so popular compared to many business automation projects. AI tools have significantly impacted small businesses for growth and operational efficiency. It has provided substantial benefits to small businesses in the area of automating routine tasks, personalised customer relations, digital marketing and analytics, insight analytics for improving decision making, and enhancing personalised customer self-service or employee training. We have found none that directly influences learning and measuring of a business reputation and credibility.

3 Research Methodology

Our research work identified a small-business need for which a tool may assist. A gaming mobile application was developed to assist the need for training of small businesses focusing on the need for knowledge on credibility rating which is a silent but salient indicator of business growth. We used a quantitative analysis to measure the perception and acceptance of the mobile application in a small businesses network. The rest of the methods for the design and evaluation of the tool are discussed in this section.

3.1 Data Collection

An existing mobile app for teaching and learning of small businesses improvement knowledge was used in this research study. The mobile app designed by Machines with Minds provides basic knowledge skills to small businesses in a gamified quiz fashion. The mobile app was customised by pre-loading it with questions and answers of varying weights that amounts to a cumulative score for which a business credibility rating is measured. The mobile app can be seen in action at quick demonstration. The primary objective of the study was to investigate the impact of providing knowledge on business credibility measures to small businesses in South Africa using a mobile app. We further measured the usability of the mobile app as an appropriate channel for this knowledge acquisition. To get the necessary data for analysis, targeted small business respondents were urged to download to engage the app, then fill a google form available here.

3.2 Participants

The research participants were selected based on purposive sampling. We reached out to a network of small business owners who were encouraged to interact with the mobile app and provide their feedback. We received nine (9) respondents as at the time of our compilation. The purposive sampling method allowed us to reach out to business owners within our immediate network and other known network groups. These were contacted and provided the links for the forms and mobile app download through Whatsapp group forums and direct Whatsapp messages.

3.3 SMEs Knowledge Acquisition Through Gaming

We present the mobile app that was customised for use for this study. The welcome page has some instructions on how to engage with the tool. It requires no login and allows the user to engage in a series of questions with cumulative score which reflects the business being described in the solutions provided. See Fig. 1 for the mobile app description. The game can be played multiple times to improve a business credibility score which viz a viz teaches teh playing user how to translate this knowledge into business skills for which a small business enterprise's credibility score may be improved. The questions are based on the KPIs earlier identified in this study and the order of the questions is controlled by automation driven by the current score and weights of the previous question.

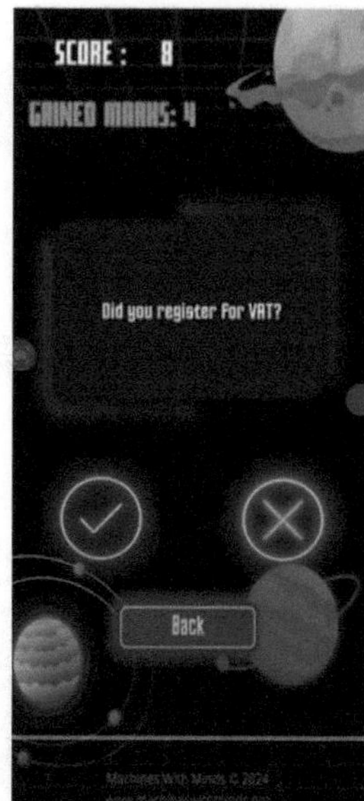

Fig. 1. Credibility Checker Mobile App Interface

4   Results and Discussion

We present the results of the evaluation of the mobile app. All participants owned a business and had engaged with the AI tool mobile app. A significant percentage of 43% of the respondents knew nothing or had only a faint idea of credibility measures in business before interacting with the app. Only 66.7% of the respondents trusted the mobile app measure of business credibility, however, they are acquired some knowledge from the quiz-like interesting game experience with the tool given by a total of 100% repondents in this regards. See Fig. 2.

5   Conclusion, Limitations, and Further Study

The study explored the possibilities of knowledge acquisition for SMEs using AI tool for teaching innovation. This is an untapped area for which many businesses can benefit from in an experience that is personalised and gamified. Our research study showed interesting potentials for its use and growth. We note that there are limitations of age barrier, busy business owners, and cultural biases to the use of games. The limitations are real but do not define all classes of startup owners. Hence we propose that this channel be explored and customised for various business training support to SMEs.

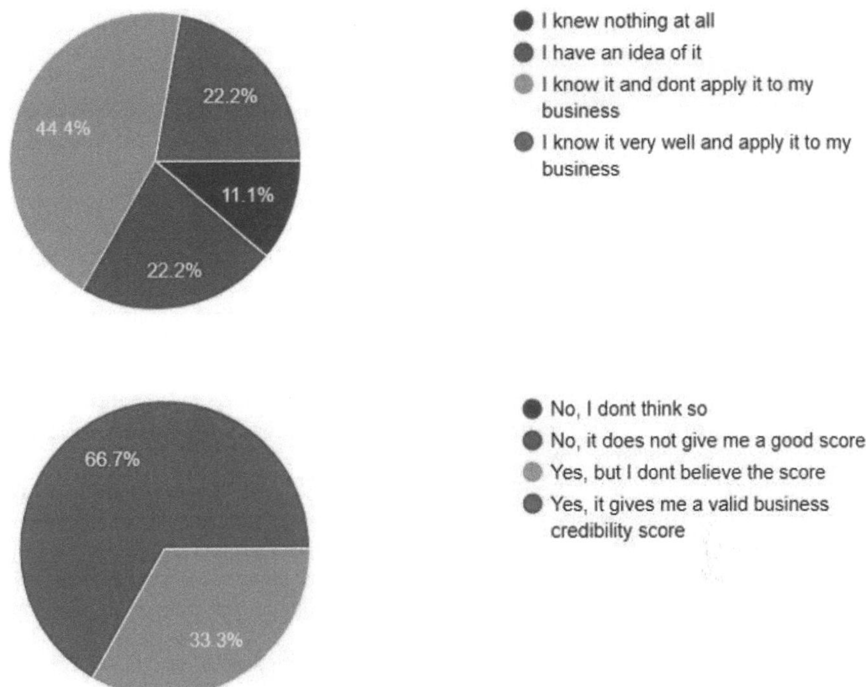

Fig. 2. Credibility Checker Mobile App Interface

Disclosure of Interests. The authors have no conflict of interest regarding the publication of this paper.

References

1. Lanz, L., Mello, S., Tomei, P., Marins, P.: Corporate reputation, ethical brand and trust in the brazilian industry. Sistemas Gestão **16**, 122–132 (2021)
2. FasterCapital. What is company credibility scores? (2024). https://fastercapital.com/content/What-is-Company-Credibility-Scores.html#The-Benefits-of-Knowing-Your-Company-s-Credibility-Score//. Accessed on 08 may 2024
3. Narkevičius, R.: Establishing and increasing the credibility of a start-up company in construction industry (2017). https://kth.diva-portal.org/smash/get/diva2:1197634/FULLTEXT01.pdf. Accessed on 08 may 2024
4. Anum, I., Khan, M., Azmat, S.: Brand credibility: navigating the pathway to customer satisfaction and loyalty. Pakistan J. Hum. Soc. Sci. **11**, 11 (2023)
5. Garcia-Sánchez, I.-M., Raimo, N., Uribe-Bohorquez, M.-V., Vitolla, F.: Corporate reputation and stakeholder engagement: do assurance quality and assurer attributes matter?. Int. J. Audit. **26**(3), 388–403 (2022). https://onlinelibrary.wiley.com/doi/abs/10.1111/ijau.12287
6. Coltey, E., Alonso, D., Vassigh, S., Chen, S.-C.: Towards an aidriven marketplace for small businesses during covid-19. SN Comput. Sci. **3**(2) (2022). https://doi.org/10.1007/s42979-022-01349-w

7. Wamba-Taguimdje, S.-L., Wamba, S.F., Kamdjoug, J.R.K., Wanko, C.E.T.: Influence of artificial intelligence (ai) on firm performance: the business value of ai-based transformation projects. Bus. Process. Manag. J. **26**(7), 1893–1924 (2020)

8. Perifanis, N.-A., Kitsios, F.: Investigating the influence of artificial intelligence on business value in the digital era of strategy: a literature review. Information **14**(2) (2023). https://www.mdpi.com/2078-2489/14/2/85

9. Guo, W., Luo, Q.: Investigating the impact of intelligent personal assistants on the purchase intentions of generation z consumers: the moderating role of brand credibility. J. Retail. Consumer Serv. **73**, 103353 (2023). https://www.sciencedirect.com/science/article/pii/S0969698923001005

10. Veh, A., Göbel, M., Vogel, R.: Corporate reputation in management research: a review of the literature and assessment of the concept. Bus. Res. **12**(2), 315–353 (2019). https://ideas.repec.org/a/spr/busres/v12y2019i2d10

11. Qureshi, K.A., Malick, R.A.S.: Explainable tweet credibility ranker: a comprehensive credibility solution. Comput. Electric. Eng. **112**, 109028 (2023). www.sciencedirect.com/science/article/pii/S0045790623004524

12. Gherghina, C., Botezatu, M.A., Hosszu, A., Simionescu, L.N.: Small and medium-sized enterprises (smes): the engine of economic growth through investments and innovation. Sustainability **12**(1) (2020). https://www.mdpi.com/2071-1050/12/1/347

13. Tamulevičiene, D., Androniceanu, A.: Selection of the indicators to measure an enterprise's value and its changes in the controlling system for medium-sized enterprises. Entrepren. Sustain. Issues **7**(3), 1440–1458 (2020)

14. Rizwan Ullah Khan, I.Q., Salamzadeh, Y., Yang, A.: The impact of customer relationship management and company reputation on customer loyalty: the mediating role of customer satisfaction. J. Relationship Market. **21**(1), 1–26 (2022). https://doi.org/10.1080/15332667.2020.1840904

15. Palalic, R., Ramadani, V., Mariam Gilani, S., Gërguri-Rashiti, S., Dana, L.P.: Social media and consumer buying behavior decision: what entrepreneurs should know? Manage. Dec. **59**(6), 1249–1270 (2021)

16. Islam, T., et al.: The impact of corporate social responsibility on customer loyalty: the mediating role of corporate reputation, customer satisfaction, and trust. Sustain. Product. Consump. **25**, 123–135 (2021)

17. Iriani, S.S., Nuswantara, D.A., Kartika, A.D., Purwohandoko, P.: The impact of government regulations on consumers behaviour during the covid19 pandemic: a case study in indonesia. J. Asian Finan. Econ. Bus. **8**(4), 939–948 (2021)

18. Kumar, V., Rajan, B.: Customer lifetime value: what, how, and why. In: The Routledge Companion to Strategic Marketing, pp. 422–448. Routledge (2020)

Author Index

MIX
Papier aus verantwortungsvollen Quellen
Paper from responsible sources
FSC® C105338
FSC
www.fsc.org